# THE AFTERMATH OF REVOLT

*India, 1857-1870*

# THE AFTERMATH
# OF REVOLT

## INDIA, 1857-1870

*BY THOMAS R. METCALF*

PRINCETON, NEW JERSEY
PRINCETON UNIVERSITY PRESS
1964

Publication of this book has been aided
by the Whitney Darrow Publication Reserve Fund
of Princeton University Press

Printed in the United States of America
by Princeton University Press, Princeton, New Jersey

*TO MY PARENTS*

PREFACE

THE Mutiny of 1857 has often been regarded as an isolated event, rising out of the level plain of mid-nineteenth century India. Touched off by a furor over greased cartridges and caste, the revolt flared suddenly in the heat of an Indian May, as though a match had been applied to dry tinder. But it died out almost as quickly. By 1860, so the traditional view has it, the embers were extinguished and the country had settled back into the dull routine of bureaucratic rule; the calm was not to be broken again, except for the fragile brilliance of Lytton's Viceroyalty, until the nationalist movement made its presence felt at the turn of the century. To be sure India faded quickly from British consciousness after the stirring events at Delhi and Lucknow, and the annual Indian debates in Parliament soon ceased to attract any attention outside a small circle of merchants and retired civil servants. But the events of 1857 nevertheless left a deep and abiding mark both on the fabric of Indian society and on the nature of British rule. The structure of the Raj and the relations of the British and Indian peoples alike emerged decisively altered from the ordeal of rebellion. Although not often apparent on the surface, the India of the Queen was markedly different from the India of the Company.

This book is a study of that revolt, and of the mark which it left on India. It makes no claim to be a comprehensive history of India from 1857 to 1870. Nor is it primarily an account of the events of 1857, for they have been exhaustively treated in many standard histories. It is rather an analysis of the significance of the Mutiny for the Indian Empire and the

Indian people in the years that followed. Social reform, education, land settlement policy, the position of the tenant and the moneylender, relations with the Indian states, the structure of the Government, and the growth of racial sentiment, are all examined in turn; and the influence of the Mutiny on each is assessed in detail. An attempt is made, moreover, to place the India of the 1860's in the broader context of Victorian liberalism. While the events of 1857 were forcing the British to re-examine their India policy, liberalism at home was undergoing a slow but profound transformation. By 1860 it was no longer the heady, intoxicating brew it had been during the 1830's, when a group of earnest young men, brash, self-confident, and aggressive, had set out to remodel England according to the principles of Bentham and Ricardo. The prosperous, complacent England of mid-century aroused little reforming enthusiasm. Following Trollope and Bagehot, most liberals now clung to the semi-reformed constitution, with its aristocratic bias, and carefully refrained from hastening the pace of change. Unlike Bentham, they rarely looked outside the confines of laissez faire, and they shrank above all from the task of enforcing social equality. When this conservative brand of liberalism was combined in India with the lessons of the Mutiny, the result was an Empire at once more stable and more fragile. It rested upon the solid support of the conservative and aristocratic classes and upon the principle of complete non-interference in the traditional structure of Indian society, and it evoked an allegiance above and beyond its value as a force for the regeneration of India. Yet, precisely because of this, the Empire after the Mutiny was less viable than before, for the British no longer sympathized with the demands of the educated class for a share of power. They were disabled from meeting the nationalist challenge in a friendly and responsive spirit.

To a large extent the main actors on the stage in this drama are British, not Indian. Even the educated Indians, though rapidly growing in number, play a relatively minor role. This is because the British were still in the 1860's the driving force in shaping the Indian polity. The post-Mutiny decade was, in fact, with the possible exception of Curzon's Viceroyalty, the last great creative era for the British in India. From the 1870's onward they were concerned almost exclusively with the simple day-to-day operation of the administrative machinery. With the rise of the nationalist movement after 1885 they were increasingly on the defensive, reacting to the pressure of Indian opinion. In 1860, on the other hand, fresh from their victories over the rebels of 1857, the British had India at their feet. They were able to dictate a settlement from a position of unquestioned mastery, and to enforce their will upon a subdued and chastened people. Almost inevitably, therefore, in an assessment of the impact of the Mutiny upon India, the activities of the British claim a disproportionate share of attention.

Some surprise may be occasioned by the omission of any reference to the abolition of the East India Company and the establishment of Crown government. Although one of the more important consequences of the Mutiny, this act had very little practical significance. The Company was wound up not because its activities had in any way precipitated the outbreak, or because it had acted indecisively in suppressing it. The Mutiny simply subjected the delays and inadequacies of "double government" to a glaring light of publicity, and thus provided a convenient excuse for putting an end to that venerable but anomalous corporation. The replacement of the Company by the Crown was nothing more than a change in the organ by which British policy was formulated, and it involved by itself no change in that policy.

It should perhaps be pointed out that the terms "mutiny" and "revolt" are used interchangeably throughout to refer to the events of 1857. They are to be taken simply as convenient descriptive labels and imply no particular theory of the

Mutiny. My own views as to the nature of the Mutiny are put forward in the second chapter. Similarly the word "India" refers either to the former British Indian Empire or to the sub-continent as a whole.

I have tried throughout to use the most widely accepted spellings of Indian words. Occasionally, in cases where current usage might lead to confusion in the minds of those not acquainted with India, older forms are retained. Oudh, for instance, is preferred to Avadh, and Benares to Varanasi. Diacritical marks are avoided, and terms which recur frequently (e.g., zamindar, ryot, taluqdar) are not italicized. Original spellings are of course preserved in the quotations.

This book owes much to many people. I should like to express my gratitude above all to the Ford Foundation, whose foreign area training fellowship program made possible a year of study in England and India. The faculty research funds of the Institute of International Studies of the University of California provided much needed travel and research assistance during the preparation of the manuscript. I wish to thank my Research Assistant, Mr. Claude G. Nelson, for preparing the various charts and tables in the book. I am indebted to the staffs of several libraries for their invaluable assistance. I should like to mention in particular Mr. Sourin Roy, the Acting Director of the National Archives of India and his staff, most notably Mr. V. C. Joshi; Mr. S. C. Sutton and the staff of the India Office Library; Mrs. B. English, the Director of the Harewood Estate Record Office, Leeds; and Mr. B. Kesavan at the National Library, Calcutta. I am also indebted to Mr. M. Maclagan of Trinity College, Oxford, for permission to consult the private papers of Earl Canning in his possession. I should like to acknowledge the help and encouragement I received in the initial stages of my work from Dr. Ronald Robinson of St. John's College, Cambridge. He first roused my interest in imperial affairs and put me on the track which led to this research subject. My work owes a great deal also to Professor David Owen at Harvard, who presided over the study in an earlier incarnation as a doctoral dissertation, and encouraged me to proceed further. The manuscript has benefitted from the reading and criticism of several people, among them Mr. Ralph Retzlaff at Berkeley and Dr. Percival Spear of Selwyn College, Cambridge. I alone am of course responsible for any errors or shortcomings.

T.R.M.

*Berkeley, California*
*December 1963*

# TABLE OF CONTENTS

# THE AFTERMATH OF REVOLT

*India, 1857-1870*

*Abbreviations in Notes*

| | |
|---|---|
| S.C. | Secret Consultations |
| F.C. | Foreign Consultations |
| P.P. | Parliamentary Papers |
| C.C. | Chief Commissioner |
| Sec. Govt. | Secretary to Government |
| S. of S. | Secretary of State |
| G.G. | Governor-General |
| For. Rev. | Foreign Revenue Proceedings |
| For. Gen. | Foreign General Proceedings |
| For. Pol. | Foreign Political Proceedings |
| For. Judl. | Foreign Judicial Proceedings |
| Home Judl. | Home Judicial Proceedings |
| Home Rev. | Home Revenue Proceedings |

# CHAPTER I

# INTRODUCTION: THE ERA OF REFORM

THE arrival of Lord William Bentinck in Calcutta in 1828 as Governor-General touched off an unprecedented era of reform and innovation in India. Now, for the first time, the British openly set their hand to the task of raising the moral and intellectual character of those over whom they found themselves. For thirty years, spurred on by the liberal and reforming enthusiasm of early Victorian England, they labored to transform Indian society upon a European model. In the hothouse atmosphere of the time, India seemed destined to be transformed overnight into a progressive modern society. Yet in 1857 the country was convulsed by a rebellion which shook the British Indian Empire to its foundations. The policy of reform, and the ultimate goals of British rule, had both to be reconsidered. To understand the significance of the events of 1857 it is necessary therefore first to examine the nature of early Victorian radicalism and its impact on India.

The India in which Bentinck landed had only recently come under full British control, and it exhibited a curious mixture of Mughal survivals, administrative innovations, and mercantile conservatism. Though stripped of its commercial character and subjected to the surveillance of a Board of Control in London, the old East India Company retained the powers of government. The directors of the Company controlled all India patronage, apart from the provincial gov-

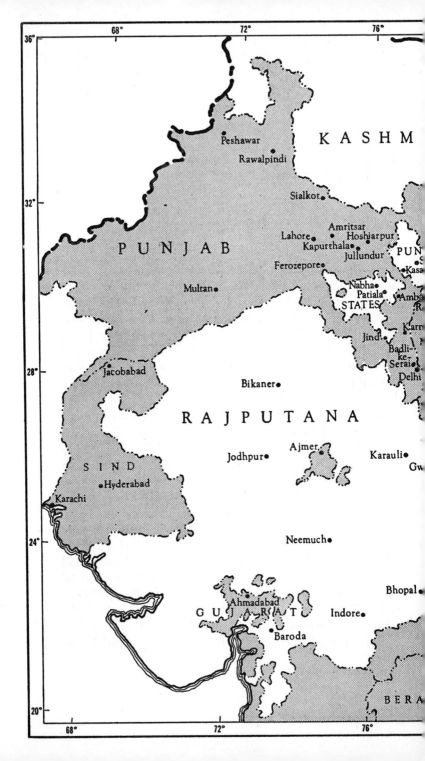

ernorships, and all dispatches to India originated in their offices on Leadenhall Street. As a mercantile body the Company was inherently, even obstinately, conservative. It had always opposed all measures likely to increase expenditure or interrupt the growth of trade; this suspicion of change persisted into the 1820's despite the loss of its trading character. The Company was determined to do nothing which might unsettle the minds of its Indian subjects. Missionaries were excluded from its territories so far as possible, and traditional customs were treated with the utmost respect. Even so barbarous a practice as *sati*, the burning of widows on their husbands' funeral pyres, was given implicit sanction. Nevertheless by 1828 the signs of change could be detected even on Leadenhall Street. Charles Grant, as a Director of the Company, had long been active on behalf of the missionary movement, while after 1819 one of the Company's highest permanent posts, that of Assistant Examiner of India Correspondence, was held by a utilitarian radical, James Mill. His office was the source of many of the ideas which were to reach fruition during the 1830's, after Mill himself had become Examiner and Bentinck had reached Calcutta.

In India the Government before Bentinck's arrival was moved by much the same sentiments as their official superiors. They carefully respected Indian customs and did their best to conciliate all elements of Indian society. The British hold over India was after all still uncertain, and they were not at all anxious to stir up unnecessary trouble. As Mountstuart Elphinstone remarked when the suppression of *sati* was first proposed, "If we succeed we save 100 or 1,000 victims from voluntary immolation. If we fail we involve sixty millions in all the horrors of war and revolution . . . and we shut out every hope of that slow but certain improvement that is now going on among the natives."[1] In India as in England these

---

[1] Elphinstone to Marriott, 9 September 1819, cited in Kenneth Ballhatchet, *Social Policy and Social Change in Western India 1817-1830* (London, 1957), pp. 279-80.

political considerations were reinforced by the prejudices of conservatism. Although misunderstanding and blundering had wrought a good deal of change in the traditional institutions of India, particularly in the realm of land tenure, the goal of British policy before 1830 was almost invariably that of preservation. From the earliest time onward, all the most prominent Indian officials had looked sympathetically upon the ancient civilization of India and its varied religious beliefs. Following in the footsteps of Edmund Burke, they saw in India a civilization little inferior to their own, which ran quite smoothly upon its own principles and in keeping with its own traditions. It had no need of reform. Indeed, if civilization were to become an article of trade between Britain and India, Sir Thomas Munro told a House of Commons Committee in 1813, "I am convinced that this country [Britain] will gain by the import cargo." Britain's function in India was simply the provision of sound efficient government.[2]

This conservative ideal was to a large extent impossible of realization, for British standards of order and efficiency could not be introduced without destroying the traditional mechanism of government.[3] But by far the greatest blow to the hopes of the conservatives came from the growth during the first quarter of the nineteenth century of a new reforming sentiment in Great Britain. This new outlook sprang from those social and economic changes which accompanied the Industrial Revolution. As the vast expansion of the Lancashire cotton industry reversed Britain's balance of trade with India, so too did the self-confidence of the new era erase the old sympathetic view of Indian civilization. After 1800 the individualist competitive society of industrial Britain was increas-

---

[2] George D. Bearce, *British Attitudes Toward India 1784-1858* (Oxford, 1961), ch. i; Eric Stokes, *The English Utilitarians and India* (Oxford, 1959), pp. 9-25; Munro Evidence of 12 April 1813, P.P. 1812-13, VII, 131. For biographical data see appendix.

[3] For an analysis of the decay of village institutions in the Northwest despite strenuous efforts to preserve them, see Percival Spear, *Twilight of the Mughuls* (Cambridge, 1951), pp. 109-12.

ingly looked upon as the acme of an advanced and progressive civilization. India, a barbarous and superstitious land, was consigned to the lowest rank on the scale of civilization. Its only hope lay in complete reformation.

At the heart of this reforming enthusiasm lay the doctrines of liberalism and evangelicalism. Though radically different in origin—the one a movement of religious revival, the other a doctrine of defiant secularism—evangelicalism and liberalism had much in common. Both were movements of individualism which sought to free the individual from his age-old bondage to noble and priest. Both had a remarkable faith in the power of ideas and institutions to mould men's character. For the evangelical, the experience of salvation was almost always one of sudden illumination—"being born again in Christ"—following the consciousness and repentance of sin; for the liberal, human nature could be totally and completely transformed, if not by sudden revelation in the evangelical manner, then by the workings of law, education, and free trade. In both its religious and its secular form, moreover, this confident optimism rested on the same assumption—that human nature was inherently the same in all races, and that inherited characteristics were readily alterable. Neither liberal nor evangelical ever doubted that reform could be anything other than successful. Hence the two groups struck out together against the stagnation and backwardness they found in traditional India, and together prescribed the remedies which would rouse it from its torpor.

The first and clearest expression of the liberal attitude to India is found in James Mill's *The History of British India*, first published in 1818. A man who prided himself on having never been to India, Mill described in great detail the "hideous state of society" he found there, and went on unhesitatingly to fix responsibility for it upon the tyrannical powers exercised by the Brahmin and princely classes. Between them, he insisted, the unchecked despotism of their rulers and a religious system "built upon the most enormous and tormenting superstition that ever harassed and degraded any portion of mankind" had made the Hindus, in mind and body, "the most enslaved portion of the human race."[4] But, he continued, since the source of India's ills was bad government, it was possible to raise the condition of the people simply by the provision of good government. All that was needed was a code of laws which would release individual energy by protecting its efforts, thus freeing the individual from the despotism of custom and the tyranny of the Brahmin. In fact, as a disciple of Jeremy Bentham, Mill insisted that "the most effectual step which can be taken by any government to diminish the vices of the people is to take away from the laws every imperfection."

Even education was by contrast relatively unimportant: "The most efficient part of education is that which is derived from the tone and temper of the society; and the tone and temper of the society depend altogether on the laws and the government. Again; ignorance is the natural concomitant of poverty; a people wretchedly poor are always ignorant. But poverty is the effect of bad laws, and bad government; and is never a characteristic of any people who are governed well. It is necessary, therefore, before education can operate to any great result, that the poverty of the people should be redressed; that their laws and government should operate beneficently."[5] Once the Indian legal system enshrined the principles of clearness, certainty, promptitude, and cheapness, with penalties graduated according to the nature of the offense, it would, he concluded, confer "unspeakable benefits" upon the Indian people; indeed a system of law was "the only great political blessing" they were then capable of receiving.[6]

John Stuart Mill inherited from his father both the family tie with India and the mantle of liberal leadership. He entered India House in 1823 on his father's recommendation and rose, as his father had done, to the position of Examiner. From

[4] James Mill, *The History of British India* (London, 1820), II, 166-67.

[5] *Ibid.*, v, 521, 541-43.

[6] *Ibid.*, pp. 474-75, 479.

there he was able, like his father, to exert considerable influence on the formation of India policy until his retirement
in 1858.[7] The younger Mill viewed Indian civilization from
much the same perspective as the elder, though his denuncia-
tions of its "barbarism" were far less vehement. It was still
for him a stagnant and unprogressive society whose only hope
lay in the infusion of the liberal virtues of individuality and
rationalism. But J. S. Mill had much less faith in the power
of law acting by itself. The educative task of government,
he felt, required not just the promulgation of a code of laws,
but a "parental despotism" which trained its subjects in
Western knowledge and self-government. Once a person has
learned to read and discuss intelligently, he said, he will be
"a reflecting, an observing, and therefore naturally a self-
governing, a moral, and a successful human being."[8]

This emphasis upon education reflects Mill's divergence
from the utilitarianism of Bentham and his father. Whereas
they saw man as an inherently selfish being, capable of being
acted upon only by the external sanctions of law, he insisted
that man could be taught to pursue the public good and to
develop social and sympathetic feelings. Once such feelings
had been cultivated, he said, internal moral sanctions would
replace those which acted solely upon his selfish interests.[9] This
broadening of the utilitarian program, so that it encompassed
not only legal reform but education and a concern for moral
character, destroyed its cohesiveness as a doctrine. No longer
did it possess that logical consistency, that clarity and simplicity of aim, which had won it the acclaim of the Philosophic
Radicals in the 1830's. But though J. S. Mill by his searching

[7] For discussion of Mill's work in India House see his *Autobiography* (London, 1955), pp. 68-69; Stokes, *Utilitarians and India*, pp. 49-50; and Bearce,
*British Attitudes*, pp. 277-80.

[8] John Stuart Mill, *Representative Government*, Everyman's Library (London, 1957), p. 199; John Stuart Mill, *Dissertations and Discussions* (Boston,
1864), II, 282.

[9] John Stuart Mill, *Utilitarianism*, Everyman's Library (London, 1957), ch.
iii, pp. 26-31.

criticism made radicalism a good deal more diffuse and eclectic, he in no way destroyed its reforming enthusiasm. If a somewhat more speculative thinker than his father, the younger Mill was equally a reformer; and he still cherished the vision of a time when India, by good government and education, would have climbed the ladder of civilization to its topmost rung. Father and son alike, the Mills always remained confident that human character could be indefinitely transformed and that all forms of restraint would in time become superfluous.

The ultimate objective of the British connection with India was, in the liberal view, the development of self-governing institutions, for only under representative government, "the ideally best polity" as J. S. Mill called it, could individual liberty ever truly flourish. From the start the liberals of the early Victorian era renounced all intention of establishing in India a permanent empire based upon commercial exploitation. Disciples of Adam Smith, they had long since abandoned the old mercantile view of empire; indeed they looked with considerable repugnance upon the activities of Clive and Hastings in Bengal. They asserted instead, with Burke, that the Indian Government was a trust confided to Great Britain by providence on behalf of the Indian people. A "government of leading strings," its sole justification was that of teaching the people to walk by themselves. And, as J. S. Mill pointed out in his essay on *Representative Government*, it could claim allegiance only so long as it was actively engaged in the performance of that duty.[10] When the inevitable day of separation came, it would be an occasion not for regret but for rejoicing. It would mark the consummation of Britain's imperial trusteeship and the culmination of its work in India. "Trained by us to happiness and independence, and endowed with our learning and political institutions," as Charles Trevelyan put

[10] Mill, *Representative Government*, pp. 199, 382.

it, "India will remain the proudest monument of British benevolence."[11]

More mundane considerations were of course blended with the idealism. There was, for instance, the greatly enhanced opportunity for trade once European civilization were diffused throughout India. It would be, as Macaulay pointed out, "on the most selfish view of the case, far better for us that the people of India were well governed and independent of us, than ill governed and subject to us; that they were ruled by their kings, but wearing our broadcloth, and working with our cutlery, than that they were performing their salaams to English collectors and English magistrates, but were too ignorant to value, or too poor to buy, English manufactures. To trade with civilized men is infinitely more profitable than to govern savages."[12] At the heart of the liberal view of empire, however, lay the conviction that Britain had been given dominion over India, not to subdue that nation, but to raise it in the scale of civilization. The triumphs to which it should look forward were "the pacific triumphs of reason over barbarism"; the empire it should construct was "the imperishable empire of our arts and our morals, our literature and our laws." The day on which Britain gave its independence to an India instructed in European knowledge and able to manage European institutions as its own would be "the proudest day in English history."[13]

Alone among the liberal reformers James Mill rejected the ideal of an independent India. The great concern of the people of India, he said, was that the business of government should be well and cheaply performed. It was of little or no consequence who were the people that performed it. To elevate the character of a people, he told a House of Commons Committee in 1831, the important thing was to protect them.

[11] Charles Trevelyan, *On the Education of the People of India* (London, 1838), p. 195.

[12] Speech of 10 July 1833, Hansard, xix, 535.

[13] *Ibid.*, p. 536.

"Elevation is the natural state of a man who has nothing to fear; and the best riches are the effects of man's own industry: effects which never fail when the protection is good."[14] This opinion reflects once again the elder Mill's upbringing in the stricter and more authoritarian doctrines of utilitarianism. For Mill, as for Bentham, happiness and not liberty was the end of government, and happiness was promoted solely by the protection of the individual in his person and property. So long as it provided good laws and efficient government, Britain could rest assured that it was discharging its duty to India. The encouragement of representative government was neither necessary nor desirable.

James Mill and his fellow Benthamites played an important role in the Indian reform movement. As Eric Stokes has pointed out in his study of the *English Utilitarians and India*, they gave it a coherent body of doctrine and directed attention to the practical problems of law and land revenue administration. But the movement was more than just an attempt to remodel India in the image of Jeremy Bentham. Even in the 1830's, at the height of utilitarian influence, few reformers were strict Benthamites. Most combined an interest in legal reform with evangelical Christianity and a general concern for education and moral improvement. The distinctive mark of the reform era was not utilitarianism, or indeed any exclusive doctrine; it was rather a certain cast of mind, distinguished by a belief in the malleability of human character and a limitless enthusiasm for the reformation of Indian society. This fusion of the various aspects of liberalism is perhaps most clearly marked in the young and ardent Charles Trevelyan. Metcalfe's assistant at Delhi in the late 1820's and a member of the Secretariat in Calcutta under Bentinck, Trevelyan threw himself with zest into all the schemes for reform which were pulsing through the Indian Government. As Macaulay remarked of him in 1834: "He is quite at the head of that active

[14] Evidence of 25 August 1831, P.P. 1831, v, 400.

party among the younger servants of the Company who take the side of improvement. . . . He has no small talk. His mind is full of schemes of moral and political improvement, and his zeal boils over in his talk. His topics, even in court-ship, are steam navigation, the education of the natives, the equalisation of the sugar duties, the substitution of the Roman for the Arabic alphabet in the Oriental languages."[15]

Apart from his work on the abolition of the internal transit duties, Trevelyan's most important contribution to the reform movement was his book *On the Education of the People of India*, published in 1838 after his return to England. Pleading for the extension of English education, he expressed in this book much of the hopeful and eclectic spirit of liberalism in an age when India seemed "on the eve of a great moral change." The core of his argument was the conviction that by educating the people of India in European knowledge, Britain could secure their "moral and intellectual emancipation" and set them upon the path of progress. Nor would the results of this process be purely secular. Once the Indian appetite for knowledge had been whetted, he said, the Hindu religion itself would soon collapse. "It is so entirely destitute of anything like evidence, and is identified with so many gross immoralities and physical absurdities, that it gives way at once before the light of European science."[16] The same optimism can be found in Macaulay. Writing to his father in 1836, he said that it was his firm belief that, if the plans for English education were followed up, there would not be a single idolator among the respectable class in Bengal thirty years hence. This would be effected, he said, without any efforts to proselytize, without the smallest interference with religious liberty, merely by the natural operation of knowledge and reflection.[17]

[15] Macaulay to his sister, Margaret, 7 December 1834, in G. O. Trevelyan, *The Life and Letters of Lord Macaulay* (London, 1876), I, 385.

[16] C. E. Trevelyan, *Education of the People of India*, pp. 203-05. See also Trevelyan to Bentinck, 9 April 1834, cited in Bearce, *British Attitudes*, p. 161.

[17] Macaulay to his father, Zachary Macaulay, 12 October 1836, in G. O. Trevelyan, *Life of Macaulay*, I, 455-56.

From religious reform Trevelyan went on to describe the economic and political transformation which English education would bring about. The encouragement of Indian political development was, he said, as much demanded by self-interest as by duty. The connection between two such distant countries as England and India could not, he insisted, in the nature of things be permanent, for it was ultimately impossible to prevent the Indian people from regaining their independence:

"But there are two ways of arriving at this point. One of these is through the medium of revolution; the other, through that of reform. In one, the forward movement is sudden and violent; in the other, it is gradual and peaceable. One must end in a complete alienation of mind and separation of interests between ourselves and the natives; the other in a permanent alliance, founded on mutual benefit and good-will. The only means at our disposal for preventing the one and securing the other class of results is, to set the natives on a process of European improvement. . . . They will then cease to desire and aim at independence on the old Indian footing. . . . The political education of a nation must be a work of time; and while it is in progress, we shall be as safe as it is possible for us to be. The natives shall not rise against us, because we shall stoop to raise them; there will be no reaction, because there will be no pressure: the national energy will be fully and harmlessly employed in acquiring and diffusing European knowledge, and in naturalising European institutions."

The separation, he concluded, would thus be peaceably and gradually effected. "We shall exchange profitable subjects for still more profitable allies." Tied to Britain by the bonds of commerce, an independent India would be "a solid foundation of strength and prosperity to our whole nation."[18]

This liberal ideology did not sweep all before it. Throughout the era of reform a sizable number of conservative officials

[18] Trevelyan, *Education of the People of India*, pp. 192-95.

could always be found, and in the 1840's, under Ellenborough and Hardinge, they controlled the government itself. Conservative sentiment was most prominent in Madras and Bombay, where many officers continued to adhere to the views of their distinguished predecessors, Sir Thomas Munro and Mountstuart Elphinstone. Sir John Malcolm, Elphinstone's successor as Governor of Bombay (1827-1830), during his tenure of office continually battled the "new era men" who believed in root and branch reformation of Indian society.[19] In 1832 before a House of Commons Committee, he heatedly denounced the "precipitate attempts" being made to improve the condition of the people. The vast difference in character and condition of the inhabitants of the various provinces of India, he said, "has been too often overlooked by those who were eager for the introduction of their favourite plans." He urged the Government instead to proceed cautiously and to adapt itself as much as possible to the usages and customs of those over whom it ruled.[20] Sir Charles Metcalfe in Calcutta was at the same time musing in a pessimistic vein on the decline and fall of empire. "Empires grow old, decay, and perish," he wrote Bentinck; "ours in India can hardly be called old, but seems destined to be short-lived. We appear to have passed the brilliancy and vigor of our youth, and it may be that we have reached a premature old age."[21] A member of Bentinck's Council, he was, as he himself realized, hopelessly out of place, a stranger in an alien world.

Perhaps the most outspoken and influential conservative of the early Victorian era was Lord Ellenborough. Governor-General for two and a half years (1842-1844) and President of the Board of Control on four separate occasions from 1828 to 1858, he left a stronger mark on the Indian scene than most

[19] Ballhatchet, *Social Policy*, p. 295.

[20] Evidence to House of Commons Committee, 17 April 1832, P.P. 1831-32, XIV, 36, 38.

[21] Minute of 11 October 1829, in J. W. Kaye, *Selections from the Papers of Lord Metcalfe* (London, 1855), pp. 162-63.

of his contemporaries. Ellenborough combined an aristocratic distaste for popular education with a conviction that the British Empire represented the highest possible form of government for India. Hence he rejected the liberal ideal of using education as a vehicle of Indian moral improvement. He denounced as dangerous to the security of the Empire all attempts to spread Christianity in India or to reform the customs and habits of the people. Ellenborough did not deny that Britain had "a great moral duty to perform" in India, but he looked upon this duty primarily in economic terms. Britain should use its power in such a way as to raise the level of material prosperity in the country. As Governor-General he regarded the expansion of public works as the major objective of his administration. Addressing the Court of Directors on the eve of his departure for India, he stated that his aim was to "emulate the magnificent beneficence of the Mahometan Emperors." He defined Britain's mission in India as being that of contributing "with due circumspection and regard for the feelings and even the prejudices of the natives, whatever useful knowledge we have ourselves inherited or acquired" towards developing the vast resources of the country.[22] The encouragement of public works, and such further measures as the abolition of internal transit duties, which Ellenborough vigorously pushed forward, won widespread acclaim, for liberal opinion had always looked forward to Indian economic development. But Ellenborough parted company with the liberals in his insistence that improvement must always take place within the framework of a strong British government. It was on this ground that he refused to encourage the spread of education, except for training in useful technical skills. As he pointed out to a House of Commons Committee in 1852, the desire to extend education among the natives was fraught

[22] Speech to Court of Directors, 3 November 1841, cited in A. H. Imlah, *Lord Ellenborough* (Cambridge, Mass., 1939), p. 176. See also Ellenborough to Bentinck, 1829 [n.d.], cited in D. C. Boulger, *Lord William Bentinck* (Oxford, 1892), p. 67.

with real danger, for "no intelligent people would submit to our government." He urged that the "great civil offices" upon which the continued existence of British power depended be kept in British hands.[23]

Despite this persistence of conservative sentiment into the 1830's, and its resurgence under Lord Ellenborough, the ideology of reform was never seriously challenged in the years before the Mutiny. The overwhelming majority of Indian officials were always swept up in that powerful current of liberalism which flowed through contemporary England. Indeed the East India Company's College at Haileybury, where all civil servants received their training, was one of the strongest centers of liberal orthodoxy. After two years' study of law with the Benthamite William Empson, and of political economy with such men as Malthus and James Stephen, the young civilian came away, as George Campbell recounted, "with a very sound belief in the greatest happiness of the greatest number."[24]

## Education

The nature of the era of reform can best be understood by examining its results in the four important fields of education, social reform, relations with the native Indian states, and land tenure. In education the liberals achieved their most lasting and conspicuous success. When the British arrived in India, they found a widespread but decaying system of indigenous education. Most villages had schools of some sort in which the local boys of clean caste (never girls or outcaste children) were instructed in the rudiments of reading, writing, and arithmetic. The number of boys who received some ele-

[23] Evidence to House of Commons Committee, 18 June 1852, P.P. 1852, x, 250. See also speech of 5 July 1833 in House of Lords, Hansard, xix, 191.

[24] George Campbell, *Memoirs of My Indian Career* (London, 1893), i, 10. Malthus was Professor of Political Economy, 1806-1836. Stephen followed the Rev. Mr. Richard Jones as Professor, 1855-1857. Empson was Professor of Law, 1824-1852. See M. Monier-Williams, *Memorials of Old Haileybury College* (London, 1894), pp. 170-99.

mentary education was often surprisingly high, but their schooling was usually very informal, the standard of attainment exceedingly low, and the schoolmasters ill-paid and ill-educated. The schools were financed almost exclusively by contributions from wealthy landowners and by fees collected from the students.[25] Above these local vernacular schools were the colleges in which the classical literatures of Sanskrit, Persian, and Arabic were taught to the members of the higher castes. Endowed by local rajas and zamindars as an act of piety, the Sanskrit schools, with their instruction in grammar and Vedic literature, played an important role in keeping alive the traditions of ancient Indian culture. In the nineteenth century as before they were largely a Brahmin preserve. In the district of Burdwan, for instance, William Adam discovered in 1838 that out of 1,358 students in 190 Sanskrit schools all but 62 were Brahmins.[26] During the late eighteenth and early nineteenth centuries Persian education was also in a flourishing condition, among Hindus as well as Muslims, for Persian had been the language of cultural intercourse under the Mughals and it remained the official language of British India until 1835. In South Bihar, William Adam found 279 Persian schools with 1,424 scholars; of these 865 were Hindus, largely of the Kayasth caste.[27]

Under British rule both the vernacular village schools and the colleges for the study of classical literature underwent a slow process of decay. In the villages years of anarchy and maladministration often left the inhabitants so impoverished that they were forced to close their schools for want of funds, while the new British Government, preoccupied with its commercial and political activities, completely ignored those schools which remained. So far as the Government did aid education,

[25] For a description of these village schools see the report of A. D. Campbell, Collector of Bellary, 17 August 1823, P.P. 1831-32, IX, 502; and Minute of Sir Thomas Munro of 10 March 1826, *ibid.*, p. 506.

[26] William Adam, *Third Report on the State of Education in Bengal* (Calcutta, 1838), pp. 52, 60.

[27] *Ibid.*, p. 72.

it confined its efforts to the support of classical Sanskrit and
Arabic learning. Until 1813 almost all of the Company's very
limited expenditure on education was devoted to the maintenance of the Calcutta Madrassah, founded by Warren Hastings, and the Sanskrit College in Benares established by
Jonathan Duncan. When increased funds were made available
under the Charter Act of 1813, Oriental learning continued
to be the sole beneficiary. The General Committee of Public
Instruction, belatedly established in 1823, was dominated by
Oriental scholars, among them the great Sanskritist H. H.
Wilson; and they insisted that the Government follow in the
footsteps of its Hindu and Muslim predecessors. Though not
opposed to the dissemination of Western knowledge, they
wished to see it introduced through the classical languages
so as to do the least violence to the country's traditions; and
of course as Orientalists they were convinced that there was
much of value in India's traditional learning.[28]

During the 1820's the pressure of reforming sentiment began
to make itself felt in Indian education. In 1824 the activities
of the Committee of Public Instruction in Bengal were subjected to severe criticism by James Mill. Speaking through
the Court of Directors, he asserted that "the great end should
not have been to teach Hindoo learning, but useful learning."
By teaching merely Hindu and Mohammedan literature, he
said, "you bound yourself to teach a great deal of what was
frivolous, not a little of what was purely mischievous, and
a small remainder, indeed, in which utility was in any way
concerned."[29] This enthusiasm for Western learning was not
confined to English liberals. By the 1820's there was a rapidly
growing demand for English education among the urban
middle class of Bengal. The overwhelming success of English

[28] See Annual Report of General Committee of Public Instruction, December 1831, quoted in B. K. Boman-Behram, *Educational Controversies in
India* (Bombay, 1943), pp. 127-30.
[29] Revenue Dispatch of 18 February 1824, *Selections from Educational
Records* (Calcutta, 1920), I, 92.

arms had convinced the more thoughtful among them that the improvement of their country could take place only through the study of Western science and literature, while the practical-minded were drawn to the new education by the material rewards it held out in the sphere of Government employment. In December 1823, while James Mill was drafting his dispatch, Ram Mohan Roy, the greatest prophet of the new era, addressed to the Governor-General, Lord Amherst, a similar protest against the Orientalist policy of the Indian Government. What India required, he said, was not the revival of Sanskrit learning, but the promotion of "a more liberal and enlightened system of instruction, embracing mathematics, natural philosophy, chemistry and anatomy, with other useful sciences."[30] Western education, far from being forced upon the Indian people by a small band of English reformers, was eagerly sought by all those who had come in contact with British ideas and British power.

The reforming party finally triumphed over the Orientalists, however, only in 1835, after their ranks had been augmented by the arrival in Calcutta of Lord William Bentinck and Thomas Macaulay. Although a late-comer to the Indian scene, taking up his seat on the Council in 1834, Macaulay gave a powerful stimulus to the cause of English education through his famous Minute on Education of February 1835. In this document he marshalled all the eloquence at his command to demolish the arguments of the Orientalist party. The question now before us, he said, is whether "when we can teach European science, we shall teach systems which, by universal confession, whenever they differ from those of Europe, differ for the worse; and whether, when we can patronise sound Philosophy and true History, we shall countenance, at the public expense, medical doctrines, which would disgrace an English farrier,— Astronomy, which would move laughter in girls at an English boarding school,—History, abounding with

[30] Letter to Lord Amherst of 11 December 1823, *ibid.*, p. 101.

kings thirty feet high, and reigns thirty thousand years long,—
and Geography, made up of seas of treacle and seas of but-
ter."[31] Like Macaulay and the young Trevelyan, Bentinck
was appalled at the poverty and degradation he found about
him, and convinced that the spread of knowledge would provide "a universal cure." In 1834 he had even called general
education "my panacea for the regeneration of India."[32] He
was thus easily moved by Macaulay's persuasive (if somewhat
exaggerated) rhetoric; and on 7 March 1835, barely a month
after Macaulay had penned his Minute, he put an end to the
protracted controversy over the relative merits of Western and
Oriental education by ruling that the "great object" of the
British Government in India was henceforth to be the "promotion of European literature and science."[33]

The Government decided at the same time to use the
English language as the medium of instruction in the schools.
This was not a necessary corollary of the decision to concentrate upon the provision of Western education. James Mill,
for instance, believed that general enlightenment could be
brought about more quickly and efficiently by the translation
of European books into the local vernacular languages.[34] But
Bentinck, Macaulay, and Trevelyan all agreed that the ver-
naculars were too poorly developed to serve as the vehicle of a
liberal education, and they pointed out furthermore that it
was impossible for the Government with its limited means to
attempt to educate the mass of the people. Their aim was, as
Macaulay put it, to create a class who could act as "inter-
preters between us and the millions whom we govern; a class
of persons Indian in blood and colour, but English in taste,
in opinions, in morals, and in intellect." Upon them could then

[31] Minute of 2 February 1835, *ibid.*, pp. 110-11.

[32] Bentinck letter of 1 June 1834, cited in T. G. Spear, "Lord Bentinck,"
*Journal of Indian History*, XIX (1940), 109.

[33] Resolution of the Government of India, 7 March 1835, *Selections from
Educational Records*, I, 130-31.

[34] Evidence to House of Commons Committee, 21 February 1832, P.P.
1831-32, IX, 56.

be laid the responsibility of developing a vernacular literature and disseminating knowledge to those below them.[35]

For the next twenty years (1835-1854) Indian education was directed primarily toward this goal. By 1845 English high schools had been established by the Government in the major district towns of Bengal and the North-Western Provinces; in Bombay City, Poona, Surat, and Thana in the Bombay Presidency; and in the city of Madras. In addition the Government maintained the old Oriental colleges in Calcutta and Benares, some ninety-five vernacular primary schools in Bombay, and a few scattered vernacular schools elsewhere.[36] From the start this system of education was subjected to severe criticism. The Christian mission societies, who conducted almost as many schools as the Government, objected strongly to its secular character, while in Bombay, where vernacular education had received substantial support since Elphinstone's time, the local authorities protested against what they considered the excessive emphasis placed upon the English language as the medium of instruction. Unless vernacular education was given greater encouragement, they said, the fruits of education would be restricted to "a number of scribes and inferior agents for public and private offices, and a few enlightened individuals,—isolated, by their very superiority, from their fellow countrymen."[37] Indeed by 1850 it was becoming apparent to officials throughout India that knowledge of English was prized only as a means of gaining government employment. Few educated Indians showed any interest in enriching the vernacular literatures or teaching those beneath them. The "downward filtration" or "percolation" theory of education was an acknowledged failure.

In 1854 the Government attempted to meet these criticisms

[35] Minute of 2 February 1835, *Selections from Educational Records*, I, 116.
[36] P.P. 1847-48, XLVIII, 174-75.
[37] Minute by Colonel Jervis of the Bombay Board of Education, 24 February 1847, *Selections from Educational Records*, II, 12. This position was endorsed by the Governor of Bombay in a letter to the Board of Education, 5 April 1848, *ibid.*, pp. 19-20.

by the introduction of a more comprehensive system of education, incorporating both missionary and vernacular schools.
The new policy was outlined in an Educational Dispatch of
19 July 1854 drawn up by Sir Charles Wood, President of the
Board of Control. Although noticeably less antagonistic to
Oriental learning than Macaulay had been twenty years before, Wood still insisted that Western learning was far superior
to Oriental, and that it must remain the basis of Indian
education. From there he went on to propose the establishment
of an articulated educational system extending from indigenous
primary schools through local vernacular and English high
schools to universities located in the Presidency towns. He
urged the Government in particular to direct its attention to
the dissemination of "useful and practical knowledge suited
to every station in life" among the great mass of the people.[38]
But as the cost of such a scheme was far beyond the limited
resources of the Government, Wood turned to private agency.
All schools which offered a good secular education, even those
operated by religious groups, were made eligible for grants-
in-aid on the English pattern. They had only to submit to
Government inspection and maintain adequate local management.[39] In accordance with these rules, grants were at once
awarded to the overwhelming majority of mission schools and
to those vernacular primary schools which had been set up
in Bombay and the North-Western Provinces by the local
authorities. The establishment of universities on the London
model at Bombay, Calcutta, and Madras followed in 1857.
The dispatch of 1854, although adhering to the basic principles
laid down in Bentinck's time, thus opened a new era in Indian
education. Its implications for the India of the 1860's will be
examined in a subsequent chapter.

## Religious and Social Reform

To the enthusiastic reformer the introduction of Western
education was only the first step in the regeneration of India.

[38] P.P. 1854, XLVII, 162.        [39] *Ibid.*, p. 163.

Real progress, in his view, required not just the diffusion of Western learning but the subversion of the Hindu religious system, for Brahminism, idolatry, and caste were the forces holding the Indian mind most firmly in subjection. Charles Trevelyan spoke for most liberal reformers when he asserted that "nothing short of the conversion of the natives to Christianity would effect any real moral change."[40] But there was widespread disagreement among them as to the role the Government should play in toppling the structure of idolatry. The missionaries asserted that since God had laid upon Britain the solemn duty of evangelizing India, the Government should not hesitate to throw its weight into the struggle. They demanded above all open Government patronage of Christian education and vigorous warfare upon the abuses associated with the Hindu religion. Few reformers outside the Church were willing to take up such an extreme position. Trevelyan, for instance, insisted that the Government ought to convey only secular education in its schools. Although he admitted that all education not based on Christian instruction was imperfect, the time had not yet arrived, he told a House of Lords Committee in 1853, "to attempt this very forward and advanced step, which at this stage of our progress would only lead to a violent reaction." He added, in a prophetic vein, "We ought never to lose sight of the possible effect upon our native army of any measures that may be urged upon us which would be likely to excite the religious feelings of the Mahomedans and Hindoos."[41]

In any case Trevelyan, like most of the early reformers, was convinced that the spread of Western education would by itself open the way for the light of the Gospel. Once the young Indian had been taught to weigh evidence, and had adopted Western standards of morality, Trevelyan pointed out, he invariably abandoned his ancestral faith; and as no

[40] Evidence to House of Lords Committee, 23 June 1853, P.P. 1852-53, xxxII, 184.
[41] Evidence to House of Lords Committee, 28 June 1853, *ibid.*, pp. 203-04.

man, least of all the Hindu, could long exist without the com-
forts of religion, he would soon go on to Christianity of his
own accord. The conversion of India would thus be accomplished without resort to the coercive power of the state. The
Government, in Trevelyan's view, should confine itself to the
maintenance of religious neutrality and the suppression of
such outward manifestations of the Hindu system as were
repugnant to common morality and decency.[42]

When the Government took up the cause of reform, under
Bentinck and his successors, it was Trevelyan's, not the missionary, point of view, that was adopted. An outright attack
upon the structure of Hinduism was regarded as far too
dangerous an undertaking. The Government schools were
organized upon a strictly secular basis, and the traditional
policy of religious neutrality was re-affirmed. But within these
limits there still remained ample scope for reform. The first
abuse to come under attack was the practice of *sati*, which
few Englishmen were ever able to view without feelings of
horror. Though spearheaded by the missionary party, the
campaign for its suppression evoked widespread sympathy
among all classes of the population, and found support even
in India among such men as Ram Mohan Roy. Decisive action
had, however, in this as in so many other areas, to await
the coming of Lord William Bentinck, who in December
1829, little more than a year after taking office, prohibited the
practice of *sati* in the Bengal Presidency. He was, he said,
moved solely by a desire to benefit the Hindus. "I know
nothing so important to the improvement of their future condition as the establishment of a purer morality, whatever their
belief. . . . The first step to this better understanding will be
dissociation of religious belief and practice from blood and
murder." Explicitly disowning any intention of converting
them to Christianity, he insisted that "I write and feel as a
legislator for the Hindus and as I believe many enlightened

[42] Evidence of 23 June 1853, *ibid.*, pp. 183-85.

Hindus think and feel."[43] The Government under Bentinck thus ranged itself, if not with the Christian missionaries, then with the advanced party of Indian reformers. Together they set out, despite the opposition of the more orthodox, to remodel India according to the dictates of Western secular morality.

The Government continued for the next twenty-five years to base its actions upon Bentinck's conviction that "the paramount dictates of justice and humanity" demanded the eradication of those practices "revolting to the feelings of human nature" which were not enjoined by the Hindu religion as an imperative duty.[44] By far the most vigorous of the later reformers was Lord Dalhousie, Governor-General from 1848 to 1856. A man fired by the vision of a reformed and Westernized India, he did not hesitate to declare war on the revolting practices tolerated by the Indian public. He openly proclaimed the opposition of the Government to female infanticide and human sacrifice, and did his best to eradicate the practice of *sati* in the princely states.[45] His most important steps in the direction of reform, however, were Act XXI of 1850, giving Christian converts the right to inherit their ancestral property, and Act XV of 1856, permitting Hindu widows to remarry. The necessity for the first arose from the fact that under both Hindu and Muslim law an apostate forfeited all right to inherit property. This naturally raised a substantial barrier to the spread of Christianity and was regarded by many Englishmen as a serious injustice. The missionaries had long clamored for the enactment of some legislative remedy, but the Government hesitated because they considered themselves bound to uphold the provisions of Hindu and Muslim law. Dalhousie by contrast insisted that the Government alone possessed the right to regulate succes-

[43] Minute of 8 November 1829, quoted in D. C. Boulger, *Lord William Bentinck*, p. 111.

[44] Regulation Prohibiting Sati, 4 December 1829, *ibid.*, p. 90.

[45] W. Lee-Warner, *The Life of the Marquis of Dalhousie* (London, 1904), II, 210-11.

sion to property, and that it could not tolerate the infliction
of civil injury upon anyone by reason of his religious belief.[46]
The Act as passed made no mention of Christianity. It simply
embodied the principle that changes of religion should not
entail civil disability. But the act benefitted converts to Christianity exclusively, and came under heavy fire from the Hindu
community on the ground that as the convert would be unable
to perform the religious duties required of the inheritor of
property, the spiritual welfare of the deceased owner would
suffer.

The Hindu Widow Remarriage Act was in many ways a
logical sequel to the abolition of *sati*. If a widow was to be
prevented from throwing herself into the flames, it was only
natural that she should be given the opportunity of remarrying
and leading a normal life. Indeed a small band of Hindu
reformers, led by the redoubtable Ishwarchandra Vidyasagar,
were enthusiastic advocates of the measure from the beginning.
Long a supporter of female education, Vidyasagar labored
valiantly to rally Hindu opinion behind the measure, and to
convince the Government that it could be enacted without
danger. The majority of orthodox Hindus, however, clung
to the traditional view that widows should remain unmarried.
The proposed legislation encountered widespread and bitter
hostility. But the Government, as in the case of *sati*, joined
forces with the reforming party. Appalled by the "evil and
cruel" character of enforced chastity, Dalhousie refused to bow
to the clamor of orthodox opinion. The Act was put on the
statute book in 1856 in the early days of Canning's administration.

While these reforms were under consideration, evangelical
enthusiasm was rapidly gaining strength among the British in
India. By mid-century adherents of "vital" Christianity could
be found throughout the services, often in influential posts.

[46] Minute of 9 April 1850, quoted in J. W. Kaye, *Christianity in India*
(London, 1859), p. 464; letter of 16 April 1850, in J. G. A. Baird, ed.,
*Private Letters of the Marquess of Dalhousie* (London, 1910), p. 118.

The densest concentrations were perhaps in the army, where many officers felt it was their duty to convert their regiments, and in the Punjab, which attracted many of the more ardent spirits in the Government after its annexation in 1849. With British power seemingly firmly established, there existed, as Trevelyan noted with some alarm in 1853, a disposition "to go from the extreme of excessive timidity to that of over-confidence."[47] Perhaps the clearest indicator of the changed atmosphere was the enhanced value placed upon missionary education. Recommending the award of grants-in-aid to mission schools, Dalhousie noted that he had hitherto carefully followed the traditional policy of the Indian Government in all religious matters; but, he said, "for these days we carry the principle of neutrality too far; . . . even in a political point of view, we err in ignoring so completely as we do the agency of ministers of our own true faith in extending education among the people."[48] This proposal was not without its critics even at the time. J. P. Grant, on the Governor-General's Council, asserted that such grants would be construed by the people of India as Government encouragement of missionary activity, and as such would be extremely hazardous.[49] But official sentiment was overwhelmingly in favor of aiding the mission schools, for they provided a cheap way of expanding education, and the measure was accordingly sanctioned in the dispatch of July 1854. To avoid implicating the Government too deeply in Christian proselytism, grants were awarded only in support of the secular education conveyed in such schools, and schools run by Indians (of which there were at that time almost none) were also made eligible.

Neutrality thus remained the avowed basis of British policy throughout the quarter century from 1828 to 1856. On no occasion did the Government give official countenance to the

---

[47] Evidence to House of Lords Committee, 23 June 1853, P.P. 1852-53, XXXII, 189.

[48] Minute of 6 June 1854, P.P. 1857-58, XLII, 416.

[49] Minute of 12 October 1854, *ibid.*, p. 419.

evangelical party or to proselytizing endeavor, however much evangelical enthusiasm might lie barely concealed beneath the surface. Legislation was always justified in terms of "good sense, reason, and morality," and rarely ventured far outside the bounds of official neutrality.[50] Nevertheless, under the guidance of men like Bentinck and Dalhousie, the Government was openly transformed into an instrument of aggressive social change. If obliged to leave untouched the basic structure of Hinduism, they sought its destruction through the spread of Western education and the enforcement of a "purer morality." They found their Indian allies among that small band of reformers who had been touched by the spirit of the West.

## The Reformers and the Princely States

Despite their success in moulding the policy of the Indian Government, the reformers found their influence set at nought across the borders of the numerous princely states. There, profoundly shocked and disgusted, they could only watch while the Indian princes, following the old traditions of personal rule, dispensed justice as whim dictated and succumbed to the temptations of arbitrary power. Even more disturbing than the fact of princely misgovernment, in the reformers' view, was the encouragement such misgovernment received from Britain. Under the system of subsidiary alliances developed by Wellesley and Hastings, Britain as the paramount power took responsibility for the defence and external relations of the various princely states but scrupulously refrained from interfering with their internal administration. Although this policy succeeded admirably in its original objective—that of securing the peace and tranquillity of India at the lowest possible cost—it enabled the prince, protected as he was by British military power, to defy the wishes of his subjects with impunity. Deprived even of the right of insurrection, Mill

[50] See Speech of Robert Lowe to House of Commons, 21 July 1853, Hansard, cxxix, 559.

protested, the people were now "worse off than before we interfered at all." Hence the reformers found themselves converted, despite their pacifist and anti-imperial sentiments, into apostles of annexation. Mill himself was among the first to demand boldly that Britain put an end to princely rule. Not to enhance Britain's imperial glory, he told a House of Commons Committee in 1832, but to secure the happiness of the people, these states should be taken over. "Unless you take the collection of the revenue into your hands, and appoint your own collectors, with your own people to supervise those collectors, you may be perfectly sure the people will be plundered. In like manner, there will be no justice unless you administer it."[51]

The first steps toward annexation were taken by Lord William Bentinck. He placed Mysore under British administration, he annexed the state of Coorg in order to secure to its inhabitants "the blessings of a just and equitable government," and he warned the dissolute King of Oudh that continued neglect of his duties would lead to the forfeiture of his kingdom.[52] But not until the time of Lord Dalhousie was annexation enunciated as a conscious goal of British policy. Previous accessions of territory were almost always the result of political or military necessity. Dalhousie, however, convinced that British rule was immensely superior to Indian and that princely states were an anachronism in an era of progress, decided that Britain could no longer shirk its duties to the people of India. As he wrote in August 1848 at the start of his administration: "I cannot conceive it possible for any one to dispute the policy of taking advantage of every just opportunity which presents itself for consolidating the territories which already belong to us, by taking possession of States that may lapse in the midst of them; for thus getting rid of those petty intervening principalities, which may be made a means of

[51] Evidence to House of Commons Committee, 16 February 1832, P.P. 1831-32, XIV, 6-7.
[52] Minute of 30 July 1831, *ibid.*, pp. 400-05; William Lee-Warner, *The Native States of India* (London, 1910), pp. 142-45.

annoyance, but which can never, I venture to think, be a
source of strength, for adding to the resources of the public
treasury, and for extending the uniform application of our
system of government to those whose best interests, we sin-
cerely believe, will be promoted thereby."[53]

The device which Dalhousie used to gain possession of seven
states in seven years was the doctrine of lapse. As the paramount power, Britain held the right to regulate succession to
the thrones of India. Recognition was given as a matter of
course to heirs in the direct line of succession, but when a
prince died without heirs, the Government had the right to
take over his state. Ordinarily a prince was able to avert
this fate by adopting on his deathbed a son who succeeded to
the throne as if he were the legal heir. Dalhousie's innovation
lay in consistently refusing to sanction such adoptions. On all
occasions, he said, "where heirs natural shall fail, the territory
should be made to lapse, and adoption should not be permitted, excepting in those cases in which some strong political
reason may render it necessary to depart from this general
rule."[54] Dalhousie specifically limited the application of this
rule to dependent states created by the British Government
or owing their existence to it. But in fact he wielded the doctrine of lapse so extensively as to arouse suspicion even among
the most ancient Hindu princes. He was restrained only by
the Home Government from taking over the small semi-
independent Rajput state of Kerauli; and of the seven states
he did annex, three—Satara, Jhansi, and Nagpur—were
Maratha principalities of the first rank.

Dalhousie's policy met with little criticism at home. Sir
John Hobhouse and Sir Charles Wood, who presided at the
Board of Control during the greater part of Dalhousie's ad-
ministration, gave him their full support; the Court of Direc-
tors approved all his annexations except that of Kerauli; and
John Stuart Mill, at the time employed in the Political

[53] Minute of 30 August 1848, P.P. 1849, xxxix, 227.
[54] *Ibid.*

Department of India House, drafted many of the dispatches conveying the Court's approval.[55] The younger Mill, like his father, saw in the Indian states simply impediments in the way of progress. In India, on the other hand, Dalhousie found himself confronted with a host of critics. Most of them were men who adhered to the conservative views of Malcolm and Elphinstone, and many, such as Sir George Clerk, twice Governor of Bombay, held responsible positions in the Indian Government. Perhaps the most outspoken opponents of annexation were the Residents at the threatened princely courts. Bartle Frere at Satara, Henry Lawrence at Lahore, and C. G. Mansel at Nagpur led the opposition to the extinction of their states; and they found their allies in Calcutta among those, like Colonel John Low, whose previous service had been spent at the courts of Indian princes. Long service in the "political" line in fact almost invariably instilled in an officer a sympathy with the princely class and a measure of respect for the traditional institutions of India. He saw, as the reformers rarely did, how attached the people often were to their ancient dynasties; and he was willing to judge them by Indian rather than European standards. Furthermore the conservative of the 1850's, like his predecessor in Elphinstone's time, was keenly aware of the political value of a circle of contented "Hindoo allies" and the danger of antagonizing the influential and ambitious classes by placing them under the restraints of British rule.[56]

Dalhousie's final annexation was that of Oudh in 1856, not as a lapse, but on the ground of persistent misgovernment.

[55] See Lee-Warner, *Life of Dalhousie*, II, 150-54 and 161-62. For a list of the dispatches Mill drafted see I.O.L., Home Miscellaneous, vol. 832.

[56] See J. Martineau, *The Life and Correspondence of Sir Bartle Frere* (London, 1895), I, 64-65; H. Edwardes and H. Merivale, *The Life of Sir Henry Lawrence* (London, 1872) II, 125; Minute by C. G. Mansel of 14 December 1853, P.P. 1854, XLVIII, 337; and Minute by Low of 10 February 1854, *ibid.*, pp. 355-60. Low was a member of the Governor-General's Council, 1853-1858, and had long been Resident at Lucknow. Clerk was Governor of Bombay, 1847-1848 and 1860-1862.

A product of the collapse of Mughal power in India, the state of Oudh comprised some of the richest territory in the central Ganges valley. The early Nawabs were strong and capable rulers, whose alliance the British, then confined to Bengal, had eagerly sought. Throughout the last quarter of the eighteenth century Oudh was maintained by the British as a buffer against hostile incursions from the Northwest, and several battalions of British troops were stationed in Lucknow for the use of the Nawab. In 1801 Lord Wellesley forced the Nawab to cede half his territory to Great Britain and to sign a new treaty under which he bound himself to establish in the remainder a system of administration "conducive to the prosperity of his subjects."[57] This treaty, which brought Oudh into Wellesley's network of subsidiary alliances, formed the basis of British relations with that state until its annexation. Oudh continued to be relatively well governed by Indian standards until the death of Saadat Ali in 1814. From that time onward, however, the condition of the country rapidly deteriorated. Under Saadat Ali's weak and irresolute successors, the collection of the land revenue was farmed out to local contractors, the minor officers of Government were freed of virtually all restraint, and corruption permeated the entire administration. In the outlying districts the local landholders contended for mastery with the alien revenue farmers, while at Lucknow the successive sovereigns of the country, increasingly under the influence of courtiers and dancing girls, devoted themselves almost exclusively to their own amusement. By the time of Wajid Ali Shah (1847-1856), the process had gone so far that the Resident, W. H. Sleeman, wrote despairingly to the Governor-General: "Oude must at present be considered to be without any regular government. . . . The only orders given by him [the King] are through his eunuchs and singers, or rather by them in his name; and no order given by the Minister can be carried into effect

[57] The ceded territories included Rohilkhand, the Ganges-Jumna Doab below Agra, and the districts of Azamgarh, Gorakhpur, and Basti on the east.

beyond the capital, where the large landholders are masters, and the troops rendered useless, for want of pay. The corps of cavalry and infantry at the capital are almost all under the command of the singers and eunuchs."[58]

From the beginning of their connection with Oudh the British had regarded its government with disapproval, and they looked on with horror as the country sank into a state of anarchy for which they considered themselves at least partially responsible. But as the Nawabs of Oudh paid their debts regularly, and were almost embarrassingly loyal, there were few opportunities for intervention. Repeated remonstrances and protests had no effect. Bentinck in 1831, and Hardinge in 1847, alike visited Lucknow to warn the King (as the Nawab was now styled) that failure to reform the administration would result in the forfeiture of his authority; but neither visit produced any perceptible change. Dalhousie concluded therefore that the time had come when more extreme measures were required if Britain was ever to carry out its duty of securing to the people of Oudh an efficient system of government. In this opinion he was supported by the overwhelming majority of Indian officers, including three successive Residents at the court of Lucknow, Colonels Low and Sleeman and James Outram.

Although conservatives, dedicated to the maintenance of Indian states, the three Residents reluctantly agreed that in Oudh Britain could no longer uphold an "effete and incapable dynasty" at the cost of five million people whose welfare and happiness it was pledged to promote.[59] Their recommendations for reform, however, fell short of annexation. Sleeman, for instance, suggested that Britain take over the government of Oudh in perpetuity, but leave the titular sovereignty of the country to the King, and keep its revenues separate from

[58] Letter of 24 October 1849, cited in P.P. 1856, xlv, 506.

[59] Outram to Sec. Govt. India, 15 March 1855, P.P. 1856, xlv, 392; Sleeman Report of 10 December 1851, *ibid.*, pp. 358-59; Low Minute of 28 March 1855, *ibid.*, p. 493.

those of British India.[60] Dalhousie himself, although willing
to appropriate any surplus Oudh revenue for the Imperial
Exchequer, was remarkably solicitous for the welfare of the
King. Since the rulers of Oudh had been uniformly faithful
to the British cause for over half a century, he recommended
that they be permitted to retain their royal title provided they
made over the civil and military administration of their
dominions to the East India Company. He was confident he
could induce the King to sign a treaty of this sort by threaten-
ing to withdraw the British Resident and troops, thus abandoning the King to the mercies of his subjects.[61] This proposal
was severely criticized by the members of Dalhousie's Council,
and by the Home Government, on the ground that it left
the door open to possible civil war in Oudh if the King
refused to sign.[62] Hence Dalhousie's plan was dropped, and
Oudh was annexed outright in February 1856.

## Land Revenue Settlement

Once a province had been brought under British administration, the Government found itself faced with the problem
of arranging a settlement of the land revenue. This was a
question of crucial importance, for the land revenue was the
heart of the administrative system, and the one subject which
brought the British Government into intimate contact with
the Indian peasantry. The state in India traditionally derived
the bulk of its income from the taxation of land; under the
later Mughals it regularly absorbed half or more of the gross
produce of the soil, although much of this was often inter-

[60] Sleeman to Sir James Hogg, 28 October 1852, in W. H. Sleeman,
*A Journey Through the Kingdom of Oude in 1849-50* (London, 1858), II,
376-83. See also Henry Lawrence, "The Kingdom of Oude" (1845), in
*Essays on the Indian Army and Oude* (Serampore, 1859), p. 341.

[61] Minute of 18 June 1855, P.P. 1856, XLV, 534.

[62] Dispatch of 21 November 1855, Political Dispatch No. 33 of 1855.
This dispatch was drafted by J. S. Mill. For Mill's view that the annexation
of Oudh was the "criminally tardy discharge of an imperative duty" see
his "A Few Words on Non-Intervention" (1859), in *Dissertations and Discussions*, III, 255.

cepted by various intermediaries. In order to collect this
revenue, the Government had to settle the responsibility
for its payment on some person, and in so doing to define
the rights in the land of the various classes of society. This
process, known as the land revenue settlement, had a profound effect on the distribution of power within Indian society.
Whichever class obtained the settlement, and the rights and
privileges it entailed, was in effect master of the land, able to
reduce all others to virtual dependence upon its generosity.
As the rulers of India, the British thus held in their hands
an instrument of great power in shaping the structure of
rural society. They could insure the dominance of any favored
class simply by making them responsible for the payment
of the land revenue.

When the liberal reformers arrived on the scene, they found
two contrasting land systems already in operation, in Bengal
and southern India. The Permanent Settlement of Bengal,
concluded in 1793 by Lord Cornwallis, awarded proprietary
rights in the soil to a class of aristocratic zamindars. Originally
tax collectors for the Mughal Empire, the zamindars had succeeded during the eighteenth century in strengthening their
hold upon the land so that by the time the British arrived
they possessed many of the attributes of an established aristocracy. Their tenure had become hereditary, they dispensed
justice among the local villagers, and they retained most of
the revenue they collected. But even then they were not proprietors in an English sense, for their new position had never
received the sanction of a legal title, and the concept of
unfettered private ownership was in any case alien to the
Indian social order. In settling with the zamindars, Cornwallis
was moved both by practical and by theoretical considerations.
As John Shore had pointed out in 1789, there was at the time
little real alternative to a zamindari settlement, for the Government possessed neither the intimate knowledge of rural
society nor the well-developed administrative machinery re-

quired to deal directly with the cultivators of the soil.[63] As a
Whig aristocrat, moreover, Cornwallis was naturally drawn
to a system of property relations in which a substantial landed
gentry played the dominant role. The stabilizing influence
of such a class was, he felt, an essential condition of order
and prosperity in civil society. He went on to make the settlement permanent because he believed that only an unalterable
assessment could give them a real sense of security and incentive to improve their lands.[64] The zamindars thus emerged
from the settlement operations in a far stronger position than
they had ever before enjoyed. If deprived of their bands of
armed retainers, and subjected to a harsh law of sale for
arrears, they gained an uncontested title to their estates and
the support of the courts in bending the peasantry to their will.

Meanwhile in Madras Sir Thomas Munro was developing
a system of settlement under which the Government dealt
directly with the individual peasant cultivator. First instituted
in the Baramahal during the 1790's, this ryotwari system had
to make its way against the established orthodoxy of the
Bengal pattern of zamindari settlement, which both Shore
and Wellesley tried to force upon the Madras Government,
and which eventually prevailed only after Munro had won
the support of the House of Commons in 1812. The ryotwari
system reflected in its origins both the simpler social structure
of Madras, where land was generally held by individual
cultivators rather than zamindars, and the romantic paternalism of its founder. For Munro, as for the Romantic poets at
home, the peasant embodied the pastoral virtues of an uncor-
rupted society, whose traditional simple way of life it was the
duty of the Government to preserve. This conservative ideal
was not of course fully carried out, for the village headman,

[63] Minute of 18 June 1789, in W. K. Firminger, *The Fifth Report from
the Select Committee of the House of Commons on the Affairs of the East
India Company* (Calcutta, 1917-1918), II, 37-39.

[64] Dispatch to Court of Directors, 2 August 1789, in C. Ross, *Correspondence of Charles, First Marquis Cornwallis* (London, 1859), I, 545-46; Minute
of 18 September 1789, *ibid.*, pp. 553-54.

through whom the native governments had collected the revenue, was pushed aside, and private property rights were introduced. But the ryotwari system in Madras did much less violence to the indigenous pattern of landholding than the settlements carried out in the north and, apart from the excessively high revenue assessments, worked with a minimum of social friction. Not surprisingly, the same ryotwari ideals lay behind the initial settlement of the Bombay Deccan under Mountstuart Elphinstone and Sir John Malcolm. Although they did their best to preserve some of the privileges of the old aristocracy, and where possible settled the land with this class, they were no less conservative than Munro. Their conservatism simply embraced the upper classes, the Peshwa's lieutenants and *jaghirdars*, as well as the peasantry.[65]

In the North-Western Provinces[66] the indigenous pattern of landholding was quite different from that in Bombay and the South, and the early settlements, although conservative in intent, therefore took on a different shape. The basic unit of rural society in northern India was the co-parcenary joint village, in which the land was the possession of a unified group of cultivators bound together by ties of common ancestry. The community as a group, under the direction of a *muqaddam* or headman, managed the affairs of the village and paid the land revenue to whoever was entitled to receive it. Each member of the community usually held certain fields which he cultivated, and from which he drew his own subsistence; but he had no claim to them as of right as he would under ryotwari tenure. Above these village communities were a class of revenue-collecting intermediaries known as taluq-

[65] See Evidence of Sir John Malcolm to House of Commons Committee, 17 April 1832, P.P. 1831-32, XIV, 35, 37; and Ballhatchet, *Social Policy*, pp. 36, 75.

[66] These provinces comprised the districts ceded by the Nawab of Oudh in 1801, those conquered from the Marathas in 1803, and the districts of Bundelkhand and Benares. At first called the Ceded and Conquered Provinces, they were known as the North-Western Provinces from 1836 to 1902. For clarity's sake the latter term is used throughout this work.

dars. Men of diverse origin, they had, like the Bengal
zamindars, vastly enhanced their power during the eighteenth
century and were often able to defy or even dispossess the
local rajas. They were not, however, throughout most of the
North-Western Provinces as numerous or as well entrenched
as the Bengal zamindars.

During the early years of British rule the Government
settled with the large taluqdars and revenue farmers wherever
they could be found. Their reasons for doing this were primarily political. The North-Western Provinces were still a
frontier area, exposed to attack from potentially hostile
Maratha and Sikh neighbors, and the new territories had as
yet barely been reduced to order; hence it was important to
obtain the support of those who could aid in repelling invasion
and maintaining tranquillity. In 1822, however, the British
reversed themselves. With the conquest of the Marathas in
1818 the conciliation of the taluqdars ceased to be a matter of
urgent political necessity, while Holt Mackensie in his famous
Minute of July 1819 brought forcibly to the notice of the Government the claim of the corporate village community to be
recognized as the proprietor of the soil.[67] Under Regulation
VII of 1822, therefore, the former policy of taluqdari settlement was abandoned and a detailed field-by-field survey instituted as a preliminary to the introduction of a new settlement
with the village communities. In 1833, little progress having
been made, the cumbrous and unwieldy survey machinery
was overhauled, and the settlement entrusted to R. M. Bird of
the Sadr Board of Revenue at Allahabad. It was finally completed under the guidance of James Thomason, Lieutenant-
Governor from 1843 to 1853.

The settlements carried out under these regulations reflect
in part the conservative and paternalist sentiments characteristic of the age of Munro and Elphinstone. Bird and Thomason
did their best to preserve the existing village institutions,

---

[67] Minute of 1 July 1819, *Selections from the Revenue Records of the
North-Western Provinces* (Calcutta, 1866), I, 9-192.

especially the custom of joint responsibility for the payment of the revenue, and to prevent land sold for arrears from passing outside the village brotherhood.[68] But they were also men caught up in the reforming zeal of early Victorian England. As a result the concept of village settlement was transformed in their hands into an instrument of aggressive social change. The ruthless way in which the taluqdars were set aside, in particular, owed much to the theories of Benthamite utilitarianism. Even though these men rarely claimed proprietary rights, they had a recognized position in the traditional social order, which a conservative settlement officer could hardly have overlooked. For Bird, Thomason, and those trained under them, however, the taluqdars were nothing more than "useless drones on the soil" whose exclusion from settlement would benefit both the state and the cultivator. At the base of this hostility lay Ricardo's theory of rent. According to Ricardo, rent was the differential advantage enjoyed by all soils of a higher quality than the poorest taken under cultivation. As population and the need for food expanded, it was necessary to have recourse to soils of poorer and poorer quality. The cultivation of such soil required a greater amount of capital and labor, and raised the price of produce, which had to be sufficient to cover the cost of production on the least economical unit. All those who possessed superior soil thus gained a substantial profit simply by virtue of owning such land. This surplus Ricardo called rent and it was a peculiarly suitable subject for taxation, for it was a windfall profit in no way affecting prices or production. It could, in fact, as James Mill delighted to point out, be taken away altogether by the Government without the least harm to agricultural incentive.[69]

In India this rent theory, and the Benthamite egalitarianism

[68] See Minute by J. Thomason on "Joint and Separate Responsibility in Co-Parcenary Mehals" of 25 September 1848, P.P. 1852-53, LXXV, 147-50. By the law of pre-emption the other village co-parceners were given the first opportunity of buying the land of a defaulting member.

[69] Evidence of James Mill to House of Commons Committee, 11 August 1831, P.P. 1831, V, 334; and 18 August 1831, *ibid.*, p. 367.

in which it was embedded, had revolutionary implications for rural society. It involved above all the repudiation of revenue-collecting intermediaries and the universal introduction of ryotwari settlement. Taluqdars and zamindars, contributing nothing to agricultural improvement, simply lived off the rent fund which rightly belonged to the Government. The improvement of India, as James Mill reiterated time and again, could take place only through the ryots by giving a proper protection to their property and to themselves in the exercise of their industry.[70] Few were willing to go the whole distance with Mill. But, as Stokes pointed out in his study of the *English Utilitarians and India,* such men as Mackensie and Bird in the northwest, and R. K. Pringle in Bombay, were deeply influenced by the Ricardian dogma; and many who were not strict utilitarians had imbibed their hostility to the aristocratic class. Even when the complex Ricardian rent theory was abandoned as the criterion of revenue assessment the taluqdars fared no better. There was simply no place for them in the individualist competitive society which the early reformers had set out to construct. This self-confident levelling policy did not go completely unchallenged. T. C. Robertson, Lieutenant-Governor, 1840-1843, and an officer trained in Bengal, denounced Bird's settlement as a "fearful experiment," calculated so to "flatten the whole surface of society as eventually to leave little of distinguishable eminence between the ruling power and the cultivators of the soil."[71] But his protest made no mark on the prevailing policy. His successor, James Thomason, looked on with equanimity as the taluqdars were dispossessed, and in 1851 even proposed that their pensions be reduced from 22½ to 10 per cent of the Government revenue on the death of the original grantee.[72]

[70] Evidence to House of Commons Committee, 2 August 1831, *ibid.,* p. 292; and 4 August 1831, *ibid.,* p. 309. See also *History of British India,* v, 416.

[71] Minute of 15 April 1842, P.P. 1852-53, LXXV, 125.

[72] Minute on "Talookdaree Allowances" of 24 October 1851, *ibid.,* pp. 290-91.

When the Punjab was annexed in 1849, its settlement was entrusted to men trained under Bird and Thomason. Most prominent among them was John Lawrence, a member of the unique Punjab Board of Administration from its inception in 1849 and the first Chief Commissioner of the province in 1853. As a young man he had played a part in the settlement of several districts in the North-Western Provinces, and he set out to introduce into the Punjab the same village system. As he saw it, justice demanded that the Sikh *sirdars* and *jaghirdars*, like the taluqdars of the northwest, be stripped of the lands and privileges they had wrested from the cultivators of the soil. "Politically these people will never support us," he said, "and to the country they are a perfect incubus."[73] He had, however, to contend with the opposition of his brother Henry, the former Resident at the court of Lahore and President of the Punjab Board. A man of strong conservative sentiments whose official career had largely been spent in the company of Indian princes, Henry Lawrence found his sympathies inevitably enlisted on the side of the aristocratic classes, whether ruling princes or landed zamindars. Therefore, once his attempt to preserve an independent Sikh state in the Punjab had collapsed, he did his best to break the fall of the old ruling class by dealing lightly with their offenses and securing them in possession of their estates at the lowest possible assessments. As he told his brother in January 1853, "I think we are doubly bound to treat them kindly, *because they are down*, and because they and their hangers-on have still some influence as affecting the public peace and contentment."[74] But Henry's efforts met with limited success. John regarded the claims of these men as exorbitant and saw no compensating gain for the loss of revenue such a policy would entail. In this opinion he was supported by the Governor-

[73] John Lawrence to F. Currie, 17 October 1846, Bosworth Smith, *Life of Lord Lawrence* (London, 7th ed., 1901), I, 201.

[74] H. Lawrence to J. Lawrence, 20 January 1853, Edwardes and Merivale, *Life of Henry Lawrence*, II, 195. See also letter to D. Simpson, 2 June 1850, *ibid.*, p. 172.

General Lord Dalhousie, who could no more tolerate a decaying aristocracy than a collection of semi-independent princes. Both alike were an affront to his sense of duty and good government. Finally therefore, after the acrimonious conflict of the two Lawrence brothers had almost paralyzed the Punjab administration, Dalhousie wound up the Punjab Board, sent Henry off to Rajputana, and gave John sole charge of the province. As a disillusioned Henry Lawrence, en route to his new post, wrote to his old patron, Lord Hardinge, "In short, without any decided intention of bringing all men and all things to one dead level, which to me appeared as unpolitic and cruel, the tendency of things seemed to me to be that way."[75]

In Oudh the reformers claimed their last great triumph. The Oudh land system was much like that of the adjacent North-Western Provinces, except that the perpetuation there for an additional fifty years of a weak native government had vastly strengthened the position of the taluqdar class. By 1856 many of them were able to defy the Nawab's officers with impunity, and they retained much of the revenue intended for the Exchequer in Lucknow. Like the taluqdars of the North-Western Provinces they were men of diverse origin. Many were the heads of local Rajput lineages, kinsmen of the village co-parceners; some had usurped power in the disturbed conditions of the later Nawabi; and others had risen by gaining the favor of the sovereign. Among the latter perhaps the most prominent was Man Singh of Shahganj, whose uncle, a trooper in the Oudh cavalry, had attracted the attention of Saadat Ali, and whose father Darshan Singh had amassed the family estates as a *chakledar* or revenue agent for the Nawab.[76] Upon annexation two-thirds of the land in Oudh was in the possession of taluqdars.

By the time Oudh was annexed Lord Dalhousie had become

[75] H. Lawrence to Hardinge, 6 March 1853, *ibid.*, p. 199.

[76] For the history of this family see *Gazetteer of the Province of Oudh* (Lucknow, 1877), III, 38-42.

so convinced of the value of village settlement that he ordered
it introduced without so much as a cursory investigation of
the actual nature of land tenure in the province. "The desire
and intention of the Government," he told Sir James Outram,
the Chief Commissioner, "is to deal with the actual occupants
of the soil, that is, with village Zemindars, or with the proprietary coparcenaries . . . and not to suffer the interposition
of middle-men, as Talookdars, Farmers of the revenue, and
such like."[77] Had the conservative Outram remained in
Lucknow, the harshness of these instructions might well have
been tempered by a sympathetic treatment of the taluqdars'
claims. But Outram went home on leave in May 1856, and
the province was entrusted to Coverly Jackson, a hot-tempered
young civilian from the Sadr Board of Revenue at Agra. He
proceeded ruthlessly to set aside the taluqdars in a search
for proprietary village communities. Long-dormant rights
were revived and recognized, large estates broken up, and
defaulting taluqdars stripped of their possessions. Many
taluqdars were so firmly entrenched that they could not be
dispossessed—they retained in the end over half their former
holdings—but the hostility shown toward them aroused a
deep and abiding resentment. In March 1857 Sir Henry Lawrence took over from the quarrelsome Jackson, and set out
to heal the wounds left by his predecessor. The taluqdars (and
for that matter the subordinate officials of the Government)
were for the first time treated with courtesy and consideration. But it was too late. Before Sir Henry had been three
months in Oudh the province was engulfed in rebellion.

[77] Sec. Govt. India to Outram, 4 February 1856, P.P. 1856, xlv, 606.

 CHAPTER II

# THE MUTINY AND ITS CAUSES

THE events of 1857 have long been the subject of bitter controversy, and have provoked more empassioned literature than any other single event in Indian history. The British officials of the time, caught up in the revolt and searching for some coherent explanation, put forward a bewildering array of conflicting opinions. At home survivors, soldiers, pamphleteers, and politicians, each fed the Englishman's voracious appetite for knowledge of the great crisis in the east with his own pet theory. The passage of time produced no greater measure of unanimity. Between the retired civil servant, for whom the Mutiny was only a momentary ripple on the placid waters of the British Raj, and the young Indian nationalist, who saw in it the first war of independence, there was very little in common. Even today lively dispute persists, and the centenary celebrations in 1957 touched off a new flood of polemical argument.

Yet the basic facts remain above controversy. Behind the outbreak lay the accumulating grievances of the Sepoy Army of Bengal. The Bengal Army, which alone was involved in the Mutiny, comprised in 1857 some 150,000 men, of whom 23,000 were Europeans. The latter, below strength to begin with as a result of withdrawals for the Crimean and Persian wars, were concentrated in the Punjab and Bengal. Between Agra and Barrackpore near Calcutta there were no European regiments at all, save one stationed at Dinapur in Bihar. An overwhelming proportion of the sepoys were Brahmins and other high-caste Hindus, and nearly one-third came from Oudh. They formed a coherent homogeneous group within the army, and provided both a focus for sedition and a network through which news and rumors could spread to the furthest cantonment.

By 1857 the Bengal Army was no longer the vigorous fighting force it had been in the days of Wellesley and Lake. Discipline had grown lax, the best British officers had abandoned their regiments for more attractive civil employment, and the sepoys, after many victories in which British troops had played only a small role, had become puffed up with a sense of their own importance. Many even believed that British rule in India was dependent upon their support and would collapse without it. To this slow deterioration of morale were added specific grievances with regard to pay, pension rights, and terms of service. The expansion of the Empire across the Indus drew the sepoy into unfamiliar territory, and then deprived him after annexation of the opportunity to draw extra pay for foreign service. The annexation of Oudh was particularly onerous because it cost him those special privileges he had formerly enjoyed in his homeland as the servant of the Company. There was, beyond this, general dissatisfaction at the limited prospects of promotion, at the enervating system of seniority, and at the contemptuous arrogance of junior European officers.[1]

But professional discontent was only the beginning. By 1857 the sepoys were convinced that the English were out to take away their caste and convert them forcibly to Christianity. Although most Englishmen considered this fear a product of the superstitious mind of the sepoy, there was just enough evidence to make the story credible, and the British, socially isolated from the Indian people, were incapable of arresting its growth. To the sepoy the pervasive evangelical atmosphere

[1] J. W. Kaye, *A History of the Sepoy War in India* (London, 1875), I, 342-52.

in which his superiors lived spoke louder than all the proclamations of Government neutrality. He saw not only Christian
missionaries circulating through the country but such men
as Colonel Wheler, Commander of the 34th N.I. at Barrackpore, openly preaching the Gospel to all classes, including
sepoys, and making no attempt to hide his zeal for their conversion.

Following several indirect attacks upon caste, in January
1857 came the stipulations regarding greased cartridges. The
cartridges for the new Enfield rifle, which was then being
introduced in India, were rumored to be greased with a com-
bination of beef and pork fat, the touch of which would
contaminate both Hindu and Muslim. The news spread like
wildfire among the sepoys, and seemed to confirm all their
previous fears and suspicions. On investigation the rumors
turned out to be well-founded, and the Government hastened
to withdraw the objectionable grease. But the damage had
already been done. Even though the men were allowed to
grease their own cartridges, no one could now convince the
sepoy that his caste was not in danger. Henry Lawrence, report-
ing a conversation he had had with a jemadar of the Oudh
artillery, said that he "was startled by the dogged persistence
of the man . . . in the belief that for ten years past the Government has been engaged in measures for the forcible or rather
fraudulent conversion of all the natives." When reminded of
the extent of British power, the man replied that: "he knew
we had plenty of money, but that Europeans were expensive,
and that therefore we wished to take Hindoos to sea to conquer
the world for us. . . . 'You want us all to eat what you like
that we may be stronger and go anywhere.' He gave us
credit for nothing . . . and *hates* us thoroughly."[2]

The actual outbreak took place at Meerut on 10 May. At
that station eighty-five sepoys who had refused the cartridges
were placed in irons and sentenced to ten years' imprisonment.

[2] Lawrence to Canning, 9 May 1857, Canning Papers.

The next day their comrades rose up in protest, released the prisoners, fired the station, and set off for Delhi, forty miles away. By an act of criminal folly the mutineers were not pursued, despite the presence in Meerut of a large European garrison. They were therefore able to seize the undefended city without difficulty, and set up the Mughal Emperor Bahadur Shah, a bewildered old man of 82, as their leader. In Delhi the mutineers possessed a fortress of formidable strength, in Bahadur Shah a symbol of the imperial past. The King was as surprised as the British at the outbreak of revolt, and took up the leadership with some reluctance.[3] Yet so great was the prestige of the old empire that even his nominal adherence gave the revolt the sanction of legitimate authority and greatly enhanced its appeal. The fall of Delhi was quickly followed by risings at all the major stations in the North-Western Provinces and in Oudh. Without British troops to sustain them, the civil officers were obliged to flee for their lives, and the country lapsed into anarchy. Within a month the British held only the fort at Agra, some flimsy entrenchments at Kanpur, and the Residency at Lucknow. As Canning wrote on 19 June: "In Rohilcund and the Doab from Delhi to Cawnpore and Allahabad the country is not only in rebellion against us, but is utterly lawless. Every man's hand is against his neighbors; and nothing but our presence there in force and the patient hunting out and exemplary punishment of every mutineer and rebel will restore complete order."[4]

Both the Punjab and Bengal remained loyal. The Punjabi had little sympathy with the Hindustani sepoy, who had so recently conquered him, and no affection for the Mughal Empire, whose repressive policy he still remembered. In the Punjab, moreover, the British had a strong European force and vigorous civil officers; together they disarmed and rendered harmless the wavering sepoy regiments. The Punjab and Bengal

[3] See Percival Spear, *Twilight of the Mughuls* (Cambridge, 1951), pp. 202-04.

[4] Canning to Vernon Smith, 19 June 1857, Canning Papers.

became bastions of strength from which the British rallied their forces for the struggle in the disaffected areas.

From the beginning Canning set himself two main objectives: the expulsion of the rebels from Delhi, and collection of British troops in Calcutta "to be pushed up the country."[5] General Anson, the Commander in Chief, collected supplies, ammunition, and transport at Ambala, and set off for Delhi on 25 May. With Anson's death from cholera two days later, the command of the field force fell upon General Sir Henry Barnard. On 8 June the British defeated the rebel army at Badli-ke-Serai, and the same day established themselves on the ridge overlooking Delhi. The force, however, was too small to invest the city, and at times was barely able to maintain itself upon the ridge. Throughout the summer, while awaiting reinforcement from the Punjab, the British fought off persistent rebel attacks. In August, with the arrival of Nicholson's movable column, the tide slowly began to turn. A month later Delhi was stormed and taken after six days of desperate street fighting. The King was captured and sent as a state prisoner to Rangoon.

Meanwhile, on the other side of India, all available troops were being sent up the Ganges to secure the crucial stations of Benares and Allahabad. From there, if all went well, the Government hoped to relieve the beleaguered Henry Lawrence at Lucknow and the ill-fated garrison of Kanpur. These operations proceeded very slowly, however, for there were a great many demands upon a limited number of men, and they could be sent upcountry only by bullock cart at the rate of 100 men a day. Among the first to reach Benares was Colonel James Neill of the Madras Fusiliers, a stern, self-righteous man, anxious to stamp out all traces of mutiny. After disarming the sepoys at Benares, he moved on to Allahabad, where the fort was secured and the city reoccupied on 11 June. There, resolved to restore order by inspiring fear, Neill unleashed a reign of terror unlike any seen in India since the days of Nadir Shah.

[5] Canning to Vernon Smith, 19 May 1857, Canning Papers.

English soldiers ravaged the countryside and stalked the streets of Allahabad, indiscriminately killing everyone they came across. Altogether apart from its ultimate effect in rousing racial antagonism, this vindictive slaughter prevented Neill from leaving Allahabad before the first of July, for he was unable to procure supplies or transport. Consequently the force which eventually set out for Kanpur under the command of General Havelock arrived too late to save the garrison. After sheltering for three weeks in a hastily thrown up entrenchment, the English residents of Kanpur surrendered on 27 June to their adversary, Nana Saheb. Guaranteed a safe passage down the river, they were instead murdered while attempting to board the boats. The survivors, women and children, were in their turn massacred just before Havelock reached the town.

There remained the relief of Lucknow. Heavily fortified, the Residency buildings stood up remarkably well under continual bombardment; and the inhabitants, despite the loss of Sir Henry Lawrence on 4 July, maintained a valiant resistance throughout the summer. Havelock crossed the Ganges on 25 July, but rebel troops contested every inch of ground, and the British force, badly depleted, was forced in mid-August to fall back upon Kanpur in order to secure its line of communications. Finally, on 25 September Havelock and James Outram, taking command as the new Chief Commissioner of Oudh, succeeded at great cost in reaching the Residency. But Lucknow was not relieved, it was only reinforced. Outram's force was too small to fight its way back to Kanpur cumbered with the women, children, and sick of the garrison. So they remained shut up with the original defenders until further reinforcements could be obtained.

By October troops from England were beginning to arrive in substantial numbers at Calcutta. They had been preceded in August by Lord Elgin's China force, Peel's Naval Brigade, and a new Commander in Chief, Sir Colin Campbell. With ample supplies and a large force of Europeans at last available, Campbell on 27 October set off on the winter campaign which

was to mark the effective end of the revolt. His first objective
was Lucknow. Relieved for the second and last time on 17
November, the garrison was now evacuated and the city
abandoned; only Sir James Outram, with a small force, remained behind in the nearby Alambagh as an earnest of the
British resolution to return. Campbell next dealt with the
Gwalior rebels under Tantia Topi, who, after months of
inactivity, had finally bestirred themselves and were threaten-
ing his base at Kanpur. Their defeat was followed by the
reconquest of the Doab and the reopening of communications
between Delhi and Allahabad in January.

From there Canning directed the Commander in Chief to
turn back to Oudh. As a rallying point for the sepoys and the
home of a dynasty only recently extinguished, Lucknow was
too important to be left any longer in rebel hands. Consequently Campbell retraced his steps to Kanpur, and after
coordinating his movements with those of the Nepalese force
under Jung Bahadur approaching Oudh from the east, marched
upon Lucknow in March 1858. A siege of little over a week
sufficed to bring the city to heel, and the victorious British
force entered to engage in an orgy of destruction and plunder.
The bulk of the rebels, however, escaped from the city, scatter-
ing across the plains of Oudh and into the jungles of the Terai.
The back of the opposition had been broken, but outside Lucknow British authority in Oudh was still non-existent. Leaving
the pacification of that province until autumn, Campbell at
once turned to the easier, but no less urgent, task of restoring
order in Rohilkhand, subject for almost a year to the Rohilla
leader, Khan Bahadur Khan. Four columns entered Rohilkhand during April, converged upon Bareilly, and there defeated the forces of Khan Bahadur Khan on 5 May. A month
later the last rebel leader was vanquished, and order restored.

The spring of 1858 also saw the suppression of the Mutiny
in Central India, the only area outside the Ganges plain
where it had gained substantial support. During 1857 up-
risings took place in Indore, Gwalior, Jhansi, Saugor, and

in parts of Rajasthan. Despite the mutiny of their troops, the reigning princes of this largely feudal area remained loyal; but the dispossessed Rani of Jhansi provided the rebel cause with its one truly outstanding leader. Although not implicated in the initial outbreak in Jhansi on 6 June, when the sepoy garrison rose and murdered the European residents of the town, she at once resumed the administration of her state, and, as British hostility to her became more pronounced, was eventually drawn to the rebel side.[6] In December 1857 Sir Hugh Rose arrived in Indore to take command of a new Field Force. The following month he set off to restore order in Central India. After securing Saugor District, Rose arrived before the walls of Jhansi on 21 March. The defenders kept the British at bay for two weeks, but with the defeat of Tantia's relieving force on 1 April the way was open for a successful assault on the citadel. The Rani escaped to join Tantia at his stronghold of Kalpi. In May they were once again forced to withdraw and the campaign seemed over. But by a brilliant stroke of genius the rebels doubled back to Gwalior, won over Sindia's troops, and seized the great rock fortress. Though taken by surprise, Sir Hugh Rose at once set out in pursuit. The Rani was killed in battle on 17 June and the fortress recovered three days later. Tantia fled, and with a small band of followers managed to elude the ubiquitous British forces for another nine months.

While Colin Campbell was campaigning in Rohilkhand, and Hugh Rose in Central India, the situation in Oudh had grown steadily worse. On 5 June the new Chief Commissioner, Robert Montgomery, reported: "We hold Lucknow District and the line of road to Cawnpore. Most of our other posts have been abandoned. . . . Throughout the coun-

[6] The Rani's responsibility for the Jhansi massacre has long been a subject of controversy. It is now generally agreed that she was personally innocent, but the British at the time did not think so, and refused to treat with her except as a rebel. She consequently had no option but to join the rebel camp. See Surendra Nath Sen, *Eighteen Fifty-Seven* (Delhi, 1957), pp. 273-80.

try of Oudh the rebels are complete masters and harass all followers of the British."[7] The coercion of the Begam's forces and the rebellious taluqdars therefore comprised the final item on Campbell's agenda. Faizabad was taken by Hope Grant in July, but the rains then brought large-scale military operations to a halt. During the summer, by the award of extremely favorable terms, many taluqdars were induced to submit, but the complete subjugation of the country had to await the autumn campaign, which opened in October. By the end of December the remnants of the rebel forces had all been pushed across the border into Nepal. There they took refuge in the Himalayan jungles with the Begam, Nana Saheb, and other fugitive leaders. On 5 January 1859 Montgomery reported that "the utmost tranquility prevails throughout Oude."[8] The Mutiny was over.

Although by 1859 the Mutiny had run its course, the controversy which it provoked had just begun. Was it a spontaneous outburst of sepoy discontent or an organized and premeditated revolt? Was it a mutiny limited to the army or a popular rebellion? Did the rebels intend to establish an independent Indian state once they had driven the British out? Why did the revolt ultimately fail despite the initial advantages of surprise and numbers?

The collapse of the Mutiny can perhaps be accounted for most easily. In the final analysis it failed because the British were willing and able to pour almost unlimited supplies of men and money into the country. In the mid-nineteenth century they possessed such material power and such confidence in their imperial mission that the issue was never in doubt. No matter how great the sacrifice, no Englishman, even in the darkest days of 1857, ever considered abandoning India.[9]

[7] S.C. 30 July 1858, No. 63.

[8] Robert Montgomery to Canning, 5 January 1859, Canning Papers.

[9] At one point, however, John Lawrence did recommend that Peshawar be given to Dost Mohammed of Afghanistan, in order to free additional troops for the assault on Delhi. The proposal was indignantly rejected by H. B. Edwardes, Commissioner of Peshawar, and ultimately proved unnecessary.

But the rebels never made effective use of those advantages which they did possess, especially in the early stages of the revolt. Had the sepoys risen as a body and marched not only upon Delhi but upon Calcutta, they might well have swept the British into the Bay of Bengal, so overwhelming was their superiority. Instead, however, the various risings were uncoordinated and isolated, and the sepoys, once free of British authority, rarely knew what to do next. Weak British garrisons were left unmolested; elementary precautions, such as the demolition of bridges, were overlooked; and large bodies of troops, most notably the Gwalior Contingent, were allowed to remain inactive for long periods of time. The rebel leaders were so wrapped up in their own individual grievances that the British were able to defeat them one at a time. As Sir John Lawrence commented, "In many instances the mutineers seemed to act as if a curse rested on their cause. Had a single leader of ability arisen among them, nay had they followed any other course than that they did pursue in many instances, we must have been lost beyond redemption."[10] The sepoys fought valiantly and often courageously. But without leadership, and without the self-confidence and determination which sustained the British, their cause was hopeless.

The sudden and unexpected way in which the Mutiny burst upon the country has always excited the suspicion that it must have been planned in advance. Many Englishmen, taken completely by surprise, could in fact find no explanation for this baffling outbreak other than deliberate conspiracy. Just whose hand lay behind the conspiracy was, however, never too clear. Some looked to the King of Delhi; others blamed the King of Oudh, the Nana Saheb, or disaffected Brahmins. James Outram was convinced that the revolt was "the fruit of Mussulman intrigue, in the hopes of gaining empire at the expiration of the century during which it had

[10] Minute of 21 April 1858, in *Punjab Government Records* (Lahore, 1911), VII, Part 2, 391.

been held by the conquerors from the west." With this object
in view, he said, "they persuaded the wretched sepoys, the
most credulous and childish . . . race of Hindoos, that we
were about to ruin their caste prior to the forcible introduction of the Christian faith."[11] This theory has always had a
superficial attractiveness and finds support among Indian
nationalists even today, for it gives the revolt a central purpose and a cohesive unity. Yet there is little evidence of
premeditated conspiracy. The famous and mysterious chapattis, which were circulated through the villages of northern
India just before the outbreak, might support such a thesis
were it not for the fact that no one has ever been able satisfactorily to explain their true meaning. The chapattis apparently meant different things to different people, and to
many signified nothing at all. Nor is there any evidence to
indicate that the rebel leaders were ever in treasonable communication with any foreign power, or, for that matter, with
each other before May 1857. The King of Delhi was certainly
caught by surprise, while the Nana Saheb, although he might
have anticipated the outbreak and been ready to take advantage of it, can scarcely be charged with organizing and foment-
ing it. The whole history of the Mutiny in fact renders
unlikely the existence of any widespread conspiracy.[12]

The extent of support which the uprising gained outside the
army has been a subject of particularly heated debate. British
historians, anxious to minimize Indian grievances and to preserve the good faith of their own country, for many years insisted that the Mutiny was nothing more than a sepoy rising;
hence the name. They concentrated on the greased cartridges,

[11] Outram to Dalhousie, 7 January 1858, in Lee-Warner, *Life of Dalhousie*,
II, 370. See also Canning to Vernon Smith, 5 June 1857, Canning Papers. In
this context the Nana Saheb's travels to Lucknow and Delhi in the spring of
1857 took on, for many people, a particularly sinister appearance. See Kaye,
*Sepoy War*, I, 573-80.

[12] See Sayyid Ahmad Khan, *An Essay on the Causes of the Indian Revolt*
(Calcutta, 1860), pp. 3-4; and R. C. Majumdar, *The Sepoy Mutiny and the
Revolt of 1857* (Calcutta, 1957), Bk. IV, ch. i.

the activities of the rebellious sepoys, and the British campaigns of 1857-1858. The civil unrest which accompanied the Mutiny was made light of, or ignored altogether. T. Rice Holmes, for instance, ascribed the disturbances outside the army to the "selfish desires" of discontented potentates and landholders, and to the "inborn love of mischief" of those classes who always chafed under the restraints of law and order. Once a general mutiny had broken forth, he said, "no power on earth could have prevented quasi-rebellious disturbances from following it. Just as the lawless and tyrannical barons of the twelfth century took advantage of the weakness of Stephen to plunder and oppress their weaker neighbors . . . ; just as a general mutiny on the part of the London police would be followed by a violent outbrust of crime on the part of the London thieves and roughs; so would the talookdars, the dispossessed landholders, the Goojurs and the budmashes of India have welcomed the first symptom of governmental weakness as a signal for gratifying their selfish instincts." Although willing to acknowledge the existence of defects in the government, the British historian was, in the last analysis, committed to the defence of the Raj. It represented progress and civilization; its achievements were for him, as for all Englishmen, a source of pride. Whatever its shortcomings, they could not be "grave enough to provoke deliberate rebellion." Far from being the outcome of shameful misgovernment, the Indian uprising was rather the result of "that resolute assertion of the majesty of the law which is the first duty of every Government."[13]

At the same time, with the rise of nationalism, historians in India began to look upon the Mutiny as part of their country's struggle for freedom. The revolt took on the character of a war of independence; the rebel leaders became heroes fighting for a free India. Its central focus was no longer the sepoy or the greased cartridge, but a people groaning under

[13] T. Rice Holmes, *A History of the Indian Mutiny* (London, 1891), pp. 537-39.

foreign oppression. This view was first put forward, in impassioned (and often wildly inaccurate) language, by the revolutionary poet V. D. Savarkar in 1909; subsequent nationalist writers, though somewhat more restrained in their presentation, have usually trod much the same path.[14] Most of these men, however, were not trained historians, and their purpose in writing history was to stimulate patriotic sentiment. Consequently they ascribed to the rebel leaders of 1857 the same feelings they themselves possessed, and their work always taught a moral lesson: that the Indian people should emulate the heroic deeds of their fathers and throw off the British yoke. Although the coming of independence removed its political justification, this view of the Mutiny has retained its appeal and is fast taking root as the orthodox interpretation. An official publication of the Government of India in 1957 described the Mutiny as "the first expression of India's urge for freedom" and claimed that it was "inspired by a popular impulse to break the shackles of slavery."[15] In Lucknow a towering monument has been raised to the "martyrs" of 1857, while on all the signs in the Residency museum the word "rebel" has been carefully lined out and the word "Indian" printed in below. The national interpretation of the Mutiny has gained further support from the Marxist school of historians, who regard it as a typical "national-liberation uprising" of the peasantry. For this point of view they have the authority of Karl Marx himself, who as a correspondent of the *New York Daily Tribune* wrote a series of articles during 1857-1858 in which he commented upon the Mutiny, the imperial exploitation which provoked it, and the causes of its

[14] V. D. Savarkar, *The Indian War of Independence* (London, 1909). See also Asoka Mehta, *1857 The Great Rebellion* (Bombay, 1946), pp. 39-42 and passim.

[15] *1857 A Pictorial Presentation* (Publications Division, Delhi, 1957), p. xv. See also S. A. A. Rizvi, ed., *Freedom Struggle in Uttar Pradesh* (Lucknow, 1957), i, xiii-xiv; and S. B. Chaudhuri, *Civil Rebellion in the Indian Mutinies 1857-1859* (Calcutta, 1957), pp. 284, 299, and passim.

failure.[16] Marx undertook little theoretical analysis, but his modern disciples have made good the deficiency. The peasantry, they maintain, were the spearhead of a popular revolutionary movement, whose supreme achievement was the rebel court at Delhi, "a soldier-peasant democracy . . . within the framework of a constitutional monarchy." The revolt failed because the conservative forces, sensing the popular character of the rising, deserted to the British side. With this "feudal treachery" to sustain them, the imperialists were easily able to suppress the national uprising.[17]

Despite the tenacious hold of the nationalist thesis, leading Indian historians have in recent years been turning away from it. S. N. Sen, in his centenary study of the Mutiny, denied that the rebel leaders were in any way imbued with nationalist sentiment or that the revolt marked the start of the freedom struggle. As he put it: "The English Government had imperceptibly effected a social revolution. . . . The Mutiny leaders would have set the clock back, they would have done away with the new reforms, with the new order, and gone back to the good old days when a commoner could not expect equal justice with the noble, when the tenants were at the mercy of the talukdars, and when theft was punished with mutilation. In short, they wanted a counter-revolution."[18]

In his *Discovery of India* the late Prime Minister, Jawaharlal Nehru, took much the same stand. The revolt, he said, was led by feudal chiefs, fighting to maintain their traditional privileges. "Nationalism of the modern type was yet to come; India had still to go through much sorrow and travail before she learnt the lesson which would give her real freedom."[19]

[16] These articles have been collected and published as K. Marx and F. Engels, *The First Indian War of Independence 1857-1859* (Moscow, n.d.).

[17] P. C. Joshi, "1857 in Our History," in P. C. Joshi, ed., *Rebellion 1857: A Symposium* (Delhi, 1957), pp. 192-204. One writer even claimed that the rebellion ended as a peasant war against the landlord class as well as the foreign imperialists. Talmuz Khaldun, "The Great Rebellion," *ibid.*, p. 52.

[18] S. N. Sen, *Eighteen Fifty-Seven*, pp. 412-13.

[19] Jawaharlal Nehru, *The Discovery of India* (London, 1956), p. 325.

Recoiling even further from the nationalist position, R. C. Majumdar asserted that the rebel leaders were motivated by purely selfish considerations, and that, apart from the desire for plunder, there was little popular enthusiasm for the uprising. The peasantry, he said, welcomed the return of their English masters.

The British, on their side, have receded a long way from the views of Rice Holmes. The First World War shattered the old comfortable assumption of British superiority and opened the way to a more sympathetic understanding of Indian culture. In the 1920's, bereft of his Victorian self-confidence, the British Mutiny historian at last discovered "the other side of the medal."

Now that the Empire has disappeared altogether, and the services of the historian are no longer required in its defence, the British and the Indian view of the Mutiny at the scholarly level have almost coalesced. There is widespread agreement that it was something more than a sepoy mutiny, but something less than a national revolt. Throughout the North-Western Provinces, Oudh, and western Bihar the uprising undoubtedly commanded extensive popular support. In many areas, most notably in Oudh, the peasantry flocked to the rebel standard; elsewhere they remained at best sullen and passive while the rebel forces rooted out all trace of British authority. Yet the revolt took on this popular character only in Upper India, and even there it was more a turbulent agrarian upheaval, gathering together a wide variety of discontents, than an organized movement inspired by any conscious national sentiment. The rebel leaders likewise came exclusively from Upper India—the Bengalis were openly hostile—and used the revolt largely as a vent for their own personal grievances. They fought together against the British and together advocated the restoration of traditional ways and time-honored customs. To a remarkable extent they even submerged racial and religious differences in a joint Hindu-Muslim effort to shake off British rule. The revolt can so far be called a war of independence. But in their vision of the future the rebel leaders were hopelessly at odds. They could never agree on what to set in the place of the British Raj. No one conceived of India as an independent state on the European model, and the call for a return to the past only concealed deep and abiding conflicts among them. Some would revive the Mughal Empire; others, the followers of Nana Saheb, dreamed of a new and powerful Maratha state; still others, from the Rani of Jhansi to the "King of Fourteen Villages" in Mathura District, celebrated their own independence and prepared to fight against all comers.[20] United in defeat, the rebel leaders would have fallen at each other's throats in victory.

There can be no doubt that sepoy discontent was an essential ingredient of the rebellion. Without it the popular outburst would never have taken place. But once the sepoys had risen, the Mutiny derived its real strength from the adherence of the civil population. The sepoy uprising was in fact little more than the spark which touched off a smouldering mass of combustible material. People were attracted to the rebel cause for a wide variety of reasons. The most easily recruited were the conservative elements in Indian society, for they had suffered most by the introduction of British rule. The suppression of *sati*, the promotion of Western education, the introduction of telegraphs and railways, the sanction afforded widow remarriage and Christian mission activity—all profoundly alarmed the orthodox, for they seemed calculated to destroy the traditional Indian social system, and in particular to undermine the position of the professional religious classes. The Brahmin pandit and the Muslim maulvi alike looked to the future with fear. Among the large landholders, outside Bengal, discontent was no less widespread. Neither the Oudh

[20] On the "King of Fourteen Villages," and his pretensions to sovereignty, see Mark Thornhill, *The Personal Adventures and Experiences of a Magistrate During the Rise, Progress, and Suppression of the Indian Mutiny* (London, 1884), pp. 102-07.

taluqdar who had suffered at the hands of a Benthamite settlement officer, nor the holder of rent-free land who saw his title confiscated by a zealous Inam Commissioner, regarded the British Government with much affection. And the fate of these men sent shivers of apprehension through the remaining members of the landed aristocracy. The princes looked with equal suspicion upon the new era of reform and innovation. Dalhousie's annexations seemed to portend their virtual extinction as a class, while each court extinguished further contracted the area of Indian employment and let loose upon the country another group of embittered men, ready to snatch at any opportunity of improving their condition. The Brahmin challenged by a new educational system, the aristocrat deprived of his ancestral lands, the prince shorn of his state, the courtly retainer thrown out of employment—all readily joined in a common effort to overthrow the British Raj. The Mutiny was in many ways a last-ditch defence of the old order by those who had most to lose in the new.

The plight of these men touched a responsive chord among the common people of North India. Deeply conservative, they cherished their traditional ways and distrusted English innovations. In the fall of their superiors they saw their own humiliation. With the sepoys, they suspected the British Government of designs upon their caste and religion. Beyond this the agricultural classes had grievances of their own. They neither understood nor benefitted from the vaunted British legal system. Although it was designed for his protection, its extreme complexity only repelled the simple villager. To him the courts were instruments of oppression in the hands of the rich and the crafty.[21] The police were no better. Generally free of all restraint, they used their official power primarily as a means of personal gratification. Their abuse of power was so notorious that one British officer called them "a

[21] See the comments of Charles Raikes, Judge of the Sadr Court at Agra, in his *Notes on the Revolt in the North-Western Provinces of India* (London, 1858), pp. 6-7.

scourge to the people" and charged that "their oppressions and exactions form one of the chief grounds of dissatisfaction with our government."[22] Among the proprietary classes the British revenue system was the source of exceptionally bitter resentment. Despite continual reduction, assessments were still too often fixed "at an amount which the zamindars were not long able to pay" and rigidly collected according to fixed principles. The Collector of Budaon, William Edwards, maintained that "the assessments were far too heavy in nearly every district under settlement, and could not have been imposed, had not the attachment of an agricultural people to their hereditary lands been so great that they preferred agreeing to pay any amount of revenue rather than desert or be ousted from them."[23]

The effects of over-assessment were aggravated by a ready resort to the sale of land for arrears. In 1853 alone 110,000 acres in the North-Western Provinces went under the hammer. The landholder who escaped a sale for arrears often found himself bound to the local bania, or moneylender, who alone could provide him with the funds he required; and the moneylender, with the assistance of the court, was able to reduce his creditor to the position of a bond-servant or, by a forced sale, to take over his property altogether.[24] In this way land was rapidly passing from the hands of its traditional zamindari proprietors through the Government courts into the hands of a new class of auction purchasers and moneylenders. Outsiders in the village, these men rarely had its respect; indeed their reputation for pitiless extortion earned them almost universal contempt. The law, as Thornhill, the Magistrate of Mathura pointed out, "by assisting the extortions of the Bunniahs, casts on our Government the odium of much of their rapacity."[25] Moreover, the former proprietors

[22] William Edwards, *Facts and Reflections Connected with the Indian Rebellion* (Liverpool, 1859), p. 24.

[23] *Ibid.*, p. 19; and Thornhill, *Personal Adventures*, p. 33.

[24] On the power and status of the moneylender, see *infra.*, pp. 204-07.

[25] Thornhill, *Personal Adventures*, p. 332.

usually remained on the land as tenants at will, "smarting under a sense of degradation, and maintaining their hereditary hold as strong as ever over the sympathies and affections of the agricultural body."[26]

As a result, when the Mutiny broke out, the bulk of the people in the North-Western Provinces gave their support to the rebel cause. On 29 May the Lieutenant-Governor, J. R. Colvin, reported to Canning that "the country is in utter disorder," and the state of the districts bore out his opinion. Nowhere were British officers able to maintain law and order, or even to preserve their own lives, except in flight. The villagers invariably gave food and shelter to these fugitives, but such acts of kindness by no means implied any affection for the Government they represented. At best the country people simply ceased to yield obedience, and, arming for their own defence, acted as if British rule had disappeared forever. Often, however, they were actively hostile, joining, occasionally even anticipating, the sepoys in open revolt. In Saharanpur, in Mathura, throughout the Doab and Rohilkhand, and even into the Shahabad District of Bihar, the Mutiny assumed a distinct popular character. In Budaon, Edwards recorded, "the mass of the population rose in a body, and the entire district became a scene of anarchy and confusion"; Aligarh and Etah, according to Colvin, were "in a blaze of riot and ravage"; while further down the Doab, the Allahabad Commissioner reported, "the revolt at once assumed the character of a Mahomedan religious war," in which the zamindars "with scarcely an exception joined their brethren, with the object of exterminating the English and upsetting the Government." The mass of the Hindustani race, as George Campbell put it, had in this crisis wavered in their allegiance and become "more or less tinged by rebellion."[27]

[26] William Edwards, *Reminiscences of a Bengal Civilian* (London, 1866), p. 152; and Edwards, *Facts and Reflections*, p. 18.

[27] Edwards, *Reminiscences*, p. 154. Colvin to Canning, 29 May 1857, in Canning Papers; E. C. Bayley, Commissioner Allahabad Division to Sec. Govt. N.W.P. 15 November 1858 in *Narratives of Mutiny in the North-*

Once free of British rule, the people first pillaged the Government offices and treasury, and then turned to the banias. Everywhere immense delight was taken in the plunder of this class and the destruction of all records of debt. During his flight from Saharanpur the Magistrate, Dundas Robertson, observed that the villagers "were not content to burn or destroy the bunyahs' houses and property and throw their contents into the flames—this would have been too rapid a termination of their delights—but the account books were carried out of the town with them, and torn up in the surrounding gardens and highways."[28] In Mathura District Devi Singh, the "King of Fourteen Villages," after spending the morning transacting business, devoted the rest of the day to plundering the banias, which he did very deliberately, one each day, all the townspeople assisting.[29] Meanwhile those who had been sold out by the British were engaged in recovering their property. With the encouragement, and often the active assistance, of the villagers, they forcibly expelled the auction purchasers and once again took possession of their ancestral estates. Despite the action of the courts, the village community still regarded the hereditary proprietor as the rightful owner, and gladly saw him reinstated. The rebellion in the countryside therefore, although involving extensive transfer of property, was not a *jacquerie* directed against the propertied classes, but a repudiation of the British system and a return to the *status quo ante*. The only classes who suffered

---

*West Provinces* (Allahabad, 1859), p. 61; F. Thompson, Magistrate of Allahabad to Bayley, 9 November 1858, *ibid.*, p. 83; Kaye, *Sepoy War*, II, 259-60 and III, 245-50; Campbell, letter to *Times* of December 1857, cited in *Memoirs of My Indian Career*, II, 398-99.

[28] H. Dundas Robertson, *District Duties during the Revolt in the North-West Provinces of India* (London, 1859), p. 134.

[29] Thornhill, *Personal Adventures*, p. 106. Thornhill claimed that the people displayed toward the Government records the same animosity they did toward the account books of banias, for "they regarded them as the machinery by which we enforced our severe taxation and maintained that disciplined order which had become so distasteful to them." *Ibid.*, p. 87.

were those who owed their position to the British Government.

Even those among the villagers who had no property to regain welcomed the coming of the Mutiny, for it gave them an opportunity to prosecute feuds and animosities long held in check by the strong arm of the British Government. The Muslims of Rohilkhand saw in it a chance to regain their lost supremacy; the Rajputs set out to renew the martial exploits of their forefathers; while "every man with a grievance to redress or an enemy to injure" put the unexpected period of anarchy to good use.[30] Soon, however, anarchy began to lose its attractions. On 21 June Colvin reported that "the first burst of debtors against creditors—of old against new proprietors over, the population is anxious to be quiet again."[31] Gorged with plunder, they sat back to await the outcome of the struggle. They still had no particular love for the English and were "indifferent by whom the law is re-established."[32] But when British troops did appear, the peasantry thoroughly sick of anarchy, "settled down to their peaceful avocations as if nothing had ever taken place."[33]

Notwithstanding the general disaffection in the North-Western Provinces, some classes of the population remained loyal. Many of the larger zamindars and ruling princes, such as the Nawab of Rampur, perceptive enough to see who would eventually be victorious, rendered assistance to the British, or took upon themselves the duty of maintaining order while British rule was in abeyance. The mercantile classes, the urban traders and bankers, and in general all who had profited by British rule, remained faithful to their foreign masters. Often indeed they had no choice, for, as in the case of the banias and auction purchasers, they were the objects of popular venge-

[30] G. F. Harvey, Commissioner of Agra to Sec. Govt. N.W.P., 21 December 1858, in *Narratives of Mutiny in the North-West Provinces*, p. 337.

[31] Colvin to Canning, 21 June 1857, Canning Papers.

[32] J. W. Sherer, Collector of Fatehpur, to Outram, 17 September 1857; enclosure to Outram to Canning, 18 September 1857, in Canning Papers.

[33] Robertson, *District Duties*, p. 161.

ance. But such men were few in numbers, and except in isolated cases clearly unable to stay the tide of disaffection.

In Oudh the revolt was far more embittered, and the people far more hostile, for they fought for the independence of their country and the restoration of their King. Their country, as they saw it, had been forcibly annexed, and their King unjustly deposed, by a faithless foreign government. During its brief period of power, moreover, the British Government had done little to endear itself to its new subjects. Under the tactless and unimaginative rule of Coverly Jackson, they had needlessly aggravated all the influential classes and stirred up resentment throughout the province. The royal family were incensed by the appropriation of the Chhattar Manzil palace; court officials found their pensions cut off or withheld for over a year; and some 40,000 soldiers of the King's army were turned loose upon the country with no means of employment. At the same time the land revenue settlement had alienated many of the taluqdars by stripping them of their ancestral villages, and displeased all by subjecting them to a rigid and inexorable assessment. Even the appearance in March 1857 of the sympathetic Sir Henry Lawrence could not undo the damage. Oudh was ripe for revolt. Lawrence himself saw only too clearly the extent of disaffection around him. As he wrote to Canning on 18 April 1857:

"The city is said to contain six or seven hundred thousand souls and does certainly contain many thousands (20,000 I was told yesterday) of disbanded soldiers and of hungry and starving dependents of the late Government. There *must* be intrigue and disaffection in such a mass. I hear of no incivility but I observe angry looks. . . . Much discontent has been caused by the demolition of buildings and still more by threats of further similar measures. . . .

"The revenue measures have been unsatisfactory. . . . Reductions have recently been made to the amount of 15, 20, 30, and 35 per cent, showing how heavy was last year's assessment. The talookdars have been also, I fear, hardly

dealt with. At least in Fyzabad Division they have lost half
their villages. Several Talookdars have lost all. . . ."[34]

Immediately after the initial sepoy rising at Lucknow on
30 May, the out-stations broke into revolt, and the civil government of the province promptly collapsed. Eleven days after
the mutiny at Lucknow there was not a single representative
of the British Government to be found at any of the stations
in Oudh. The taluqdars at once took possession of the villages
they had lost during the 1856 settlement, and in so doing
encountered surprisingly little resistance on the part of their
former tenants. Indeed the village zamindars hastened to
tender their allegiance. One District Officer, given shelter by
the taluqdar Hanumant Singh, saw his courtyard crowded
with these men less than a week after the dissolution of government in the district. Later, from the safety of Allahabad
he reported disconsolately that "They [the taluqdars] have
most of them quietly resumed the villages they had at the
time of annexation. The villagers except in rare instances don't
seem to have made a struggle even against it. They certainly
gave us no assistance."[35] As in the North-Western Provinces,
so in Oudh, the first act of rebellion was a return to the
traditional pattern of landholding. But in the North-Western
Provinces the hereditary landholder simply pushed a despised
auction purchaser off his property, while in Oudh villagers
who had been awarded settlement rights over their land
willingly handed it back and reverted to the status of tenant.
Bound to his taluqdar by ties of kinship and feudal loyalty,
the villager readily acknowledged his claim and rallied around
his standard. Together they set out to fight their common
enemy.

The bulk of the taluqdars did not at once go into active
opposition. On 27 June Henry Lawrence wrote that, although

[34] Lawrence to Canning, 18 April 1857, Canning Papers. See also Martin
Gubbins, *An Account of the Mutinies in Oudh* (London, 1858), pp. 76-78.

[35] Barrow to Sec. Govt. India, 28 June 1857, S.C. 25 September 1857, No.
509.

"our talookdars are feeding the mutineers and helping themselves to the villages they lost at the settlement," they "are not openly joining the mutineers."[36] Many in fact distinguished themselves by sheltering fugitive Englishmen and sending them safely out of the disturbed area. When the Mutiny broke at Faizabad, Raja Man Singh took into his fort at Shahganj, fifteen miles away, the women, children, and civil officers of the garrison. He then provided them with boats and sent them down the Gogra to Dinapur. The fugitives from the neighboring station of Sultanpur found shelter with Rustam Shah of Deyrah, while those from Salone, the third district in Faizabad Division, were hospitably received by Hanumant Singh of Dharupur and two weeks later conducted in safety to Allahabad. None of these taluqdars had any reason to be grateful to the British. Man Singh had been stripped of all but six villages and was actually in confinement until a few days before the outbreak at Faizabad. Rustam Shah, a Rajput taluqdar long resident in the district, had lost many ancestral villages. Hanumant Singh had similarly suffered at the hands of the new rulers, being deprived of over half his former holdings; yet, true to the traditions of Rajput chivalry, he gave protection even to the man who had taken away his property, the Deputy Commissioner, Captain L. Barrow. The same story was re-enacted in Bahraich. Charles Wingfield, the Commissioner, and the entire garrison, consisting of some nineteen Europeans, took refuge with the neighboring Raja of Balrampur, who eventually escorted them all to Gorakhpur.

As in the North-Western Provinces, however, these individual acts of kindness by no means signified any loyalty to the British Raj. When Barrow asked Hanumant Singh for his aid in suppressing the rebellion, the taluqdar replied: "Sahib, your countrymen came into this country and drove out our king. . . . At one blow you took from me land which

[36] Lawrence to Sec. Govt. India, 27 June 1857, S.C. 25 September 1857, No. 639.

from time immemorial had been in my family. I submitted. Suddenly misfortune came upon you. The people of the land rose against you. You came to me whom you had despoiled. I have saved you. But now,—now I march at the head of my retainers to Lakhnao to try and drive you from the country."[37]

The failure of Havelock's efforts to reach Lucknow in August finally prompted the more prominent taluqdars to send their forces into action against the Residency. Until that time many of them, most notably Man Singh, carefully kept open their lines of communication with the British. Finally, however, convinced the British cause was hopeless, they drifted into the rebel camp. By the end of the year all the principal taluqdars, with the exception of Balrampur, were openly hostile. Most, at one time or another, took an active part in the siege of the Residency; Man Singh was among those who contested the advance of Havelock and Outram in September. Even the taluqdars of Bahraich Division, who had not suffered in the 1856 settlement, sided with the rebels and sent their quota of troops to Lucknow. The Rajas of Bhinga and Churda, in Gonda District, lost no villages; the Raja of Gonda lost 30 villages out of 400, but had his assessment reduced by Rs. 10,000; while the Raja of Nanpara and Ushraf Baksh Khan were restored to their estates by the British. Yet all these men were bitterly hostile and conducted a last-ditch resistance in Bahraich until December 1858. This ingratitude greatly exasperated the British. They had expected that these men at least would remain loyal, for they had no legitimate grievances.

But in fact taluqdar hostility had deeper roots than mere resentment at the loss of villages. Feudal, perhaps even national, sentiments played a part. One taluqdar, Beni Madho of Shankarpur, refused to submit even when promised restoration of his estates on the ground that he owed allegiance, not to the British Government, but to the King of Oudh; after the

37 G. B. Malleson, *History of the Indian Mutiny* (London, 1896), I, 407.

destruction of his fort he fled with the Begam into Nepal. The taluqdars were also actuated by other, more selfish, motives. Above all they were reluctant to lose the arbitrary power they had hitherto exercised over those about them. Before annexation, secure in his mud fort, protected by a matted wall of live bamboo and a mile-wide strip of jungle, the taluqdar had defied the weak central government with impunity. The Bahraich taluqdars, cut off from Lucknow by the river Gogra, were the most untrammeled of all, and kept up a semi-independent status. When the British insisted that such men behave like ordinary subjects, they took the first opportunity of asserting their independence. They rebelled, as Charles Wingfield put it, "because they hated our rule no doubt, but they hated it merely because it reduced them to a level with the meanest before the law . . . because it compelled them to disband their armies, pay their revenue regularly, and not oppress their ryots."[38]

Throughout the siege of Lucknow, and well into 1858, the British had almost no friends in Oudh. Upon his arrival in Lucknow, Outram tried to win over some of the taluqdars and to gain the confidence of the people. Shopkeepers were assured that they would be treated with kindness and receive their own prices for their goods. But, he sadly recorded, "not a seer of provisions could be obtained nor did a man attempt to open a communication with us, with the exception of Man Singh."[39] Man Singh, shrewdly playing one side off against the other, remained elusive all winter. He tendered his allegiance only after the final fall of Lucknow, when British victory was certain. With a few exceptions the other taluqdars were less tractable. Most of them remained in arms until the summer of 1858, and many came in only when the British army took the field in October. A rebel force even

[38] Commissioner Gorakhpur to Sec. Govt. India, 6 February 1858, in Canning Papers Miscellaneous, No. 273. See also Minute of 17 May 1858 in File 1037, Oudh General Proceedings 1858-1859, U.P. Records, Allahabad.

[39] C. C. Oudh to Sec. Govt. India, 21 November 1857, S.C. 29 January 1858, No. 341.

besieged Man Singh in his fort of Shahganj for six weeks until he was relieved by Hope Grant at the end of July. Popular antagonism likewise began to melt only with the appearance in Oudh of substantial British forces. In May Barrow noted that "the tone of feeling towards us is changing," and the Government detected an undercurrent of passive loyalty among the landholders. But not until the countryside was finally swept clear of marauding rebels did the village zamindars "flock in, tender their allegiance, and pay their revenue."[40] By then of course there was no alternative, and the people quickly settled down to their normal activities.

## Contemporary Opinion

At the time of the Mutiny neither British nor Indian opinion was as rigid and inflexible as it later became. Englishmen could be found who regarded the uprising as a national revolt, provoked by the foolhardy and ill-considered measures of the Indian Government, while educated Indians often insisted that it was merely an affair of the sepoys, in which the common people took no part. If the debate was acrimonious—for the events were close at hand and men's emotions deeply involved—it was at least free and far-ranging. Everyone from London to Lucknow had his own theory of the Mutiny and his own set of recommendations for future reform.

In England the debate over the causes of the Mutiny was largely carried on within the framework of domestic political controversy. Its central focus was Parliament, roused for the first time in decades from its customary lethargy with regard to Indian affairs. The Conservatives took the initiative, for they saw in the Mutiny a handy stick with which to beat the incumbent Palmerston Government. No sooner had news of the fall of Delhi reached England than Ellenborough in the Lords and Disraeli in the Commons rose to put forward their

[40] Memo by Capt. Barrow, 22 May 1858 in Rizvi, *Freedom Struggle in Uttar Pradesh*, II, 422; Memo by Montgomery, 12 June 1858, S.C. 25 June 1858, No. 71; Montgomery to Canning, 19 November 1858, Canning Papers.

view of the crisis and to challenge the Government's handling of affairs. As Disraeli described it in a three-hour speech to the House of Commons on 27 July, the country was confronted not with a military mutiny but with a national revolt. The mutinous sepoys, he said, were "not so much the avengers of professional grievances as the exponents of general discontent." This discontent was the direct result of abandoning those principles on which British rule in India was founded. In the old days the Government had respected traditional laws and customs and upheld "the principle of Nationality." Now, however, driven by an excessive zeal for change, it had succeeded only in alienating all the influential classes in the country. The princes were antagonized by the "destruction of Native authority," the landholders by the "disturbance of the settlement of property," and the orthodox Hindu by the "tampering with religion" of a proselytizing Government. The greased cartridges were the pretext, not the cause, of the revolt. "The decline and fall of Empires are not affairs of greased cartridges. Such results are occasioned by adequate causes."[41] For Disraeli, as for most Conservatives, the "adequate causes" of the 1857 uprising were the reforms of the past twenty-five years, and the evangelical zeal which accompanied them. In the future, he said, the Government should return to the path of conciliation; the policy of reform had condemned itself.

The members of the Government refused to accept such a view of the Mutiny, with its implied criticism of policies for which they had been responsible. Vernon Smith, President of the Board of Control, rose immediately after Disraeli had finished speaking to vindicate the Government. He insisted that the revolt was exclusively military in character and had been anticipated by no one; hence the Government could not be accused of want of foresight. The policy of reform he defended on two grounds: that it simply reflected the irresistible pressure of public opinion in Britain, bent upon the moral

[41] Hansard, CXLVII, 442-75.

and religious improvement of India; and that much as it might have antagonized some classes, reform had immeasurably benefitted the mass of the people.[42] Though the army and a few aggrieved princes might be hostile, he said, the people "have not gone against us, but have for the most part been in our favour." To this argument the Government and its defenders invariably reverted, for, as Sir Charles Wood pointed out, the absence of popular disaffection was "the best testimony to the good government of India." No one could then charge Britain's reforming legislation with any responsibility for the outbreak.[43]

As the extent of the revolt became apparent, the reformers were placed increasingly on the defensive. The course of events in Oudh was particularly hard to reconcile with their theory that "what has occurred has been merely a military mutiny." They could not deny that the people of Oudh were up in arms. But they rejected Disraeli's contention that the annexation of the province was to blame, and attributed the revolt instead to accidental circumstances. The sepoys had largely been recruited in Oudh, they said, many had found their way there after the Mutiny had broken out, and these disaffected men readily obtained support and sympathy from their families. The hostility of the taluqdars the Government willingly acknowledged. As Ross Mangles, Chairman of the East India Directors, put it, "we made them our enemies by endeavouring to do justice to the great body of the agricultural population. It redounded in fact to the honour of the Government of India that those spoilers were our enemies."[44]

[42] *Ibid.*, pp. 484-90.

[43] Speech of 18 February 1858, Hansard, CXLVIII, 148. See also John Russell, speech of 27 July 1857, Hansard, CXLVII, 522.

[44] Disraeli speech of 3 December 1857, Hansard, CXLVIII, 119; Mangles speech of 18 March 1858, *ibid.*, CXLIX, 371; Wood speech of 1 August 1859, *ibid.*, CLV, 780. Canning explained the uprising in Bihar on the same ground; that it "like Oude, is sepoy country," and that "the districts in which disturbance is now rife are the homes of vast numbers of mutineers." Canning to Stanley, 10 July 1858, Canning Papers.

The same debate echoed outside the walls of Parliament. The English press, catering to the new public interest in India, joined the fray with enthusiasm. The *Quarterly Review* agreed with Disraeli that the Mutiny was "in reality a struggle between races, a revolt of the best classes of Hindostanees against a foreign invader of their sacred land"; and they urged the Government henceforth to eschew annexation, proselytism, and destruction of the native aristocracy.[45] The *Edinburgh Review*, on the other hand, insisted that "this singular movement" not only began as a military mutiny but "retained that character throughout its progress." The people remained quiet because they recognized and appreciated the blessings of British rule.[46] With few exceptions the periodical press, reflecting the self-confidence of mid-Victorian England, refused to connect the policy of Indian improvement with the revolt. They simply could not conceive of anyone consciously rejecting the benefits of British rule. Indeed they were at a loss to account for the uprising at all except on the ground that the Indian people were ignorant and credulous, like savages or children, "easily persuaded of the most monstrous absurdities."[47]

Englishmen in India were generally more perceptive, and less influenced by domestic political pressures. Yet even there those who had drunk at the fountain of reform looked at the Mutiny from a different perspective than those who cherished traditional ways. Dalhousie's disciples, the men of the "Punjab school," were the foremost exponents in India of the military theory of the Mutiny. Their own reputations, after all, were at stake. Sir John Lawrence, for instance, asserted confidently that "this Mutiny had its origin in the Army itself; that it is not attributable to any external or antecedent conspiracy whatever, although it was afterwards taken ad-

[45] *Quarterly Review*, CIII (1858), 255-56 and 274-75.

[46] *Edinburgh Review*, CVII (1858), 542-48.

[47] Economist, 19 September 1857, xv, 1037; and 15 August 1857, pp. 896-97.

vantage of by disaffected persons to compass their own ends; and that its proximate cause was the cartridge affair and nothing else."[48] Once the soldiers had risen, he admitted, the people in many areas were coerced into rebellion, and the predatory tribes came out of hiding. But active opposition was confined to a sepoy army conscious of its power and its grievances. Christian proselytism, he said, had nothing to do with it. The sepoys were excited, not by missionary preaching, but by a suspicion that the Government planned by "a bit of legerdemain" to deprive them of their caste. "Provided missionaries talked to them without acrimony, I believe they never would have objected to their talking for ever on religion."[49]

Lawrence's opinion was shared by many Punjab District Officers, and by William Muir, among others, in the North-Western Provinces.[50] Alike they sought the causes of the outbreak, not in the reforms of the preceding decade, but in the credulous and superstitious mind of the sepoy, so easily swayed by shadows and fancies. The revolt was really nothing more than an irrational panic on the subject of caste.

The conservative members of the Indian Civil Service, such as Sir Bartle Frere in Bombay, joined Ellenborough and Disraeli in their attack on the policy of indiscriminate reform. Never an admirer of Dalhousie or of his reforming enthusiasm, Frere readily concluded that the cartridges were only "the occasion for the outbreak of a feeling caused by a

[48] Sec. C. C. Punjab to Sec. Govt. India, 29 April 1858, *Punjab Government Records*, VII, Part 2, 395.

[49] Lawrence to Trevelyan, 16 December 1857, in R. Bosworth Smith, *Life of Lord Lawrence*, II, 187.

[50] See Lt. Col. S. A. Abbott, Deputy Commissioner Hoshiarpur to Commissioner Trans Sutlej States, 7 October 1857, *Punjab Government Records*, VIII, Part I, 200; F. Williams, Commissioner Meerut to Sec. Govt. N.W.P., 15 November 1858, F.C. 30 December 1859 (Supplement), No. 663; W. Muir to C. Beadon, 19 August 1857 and 17 September 1857, Sir William Muir, *Records of the Intelligence Department of the Government of the North-West Provinces of India during the Mutiny of 1857* (Edinburgh, 1902), II, 130 and 258.

long period of mismanagement."[51] Many District Officers in the North-Western Provinces drew the same conclusion from their experiences during the revolt. William Edwards and W. J. Probyn, Collectors of the adjoining districts of Budaon and Farrukhabad, are perhaps typical. Forced to abandon their posts at the outbreak of the revolt, the two men joined forces and eventually found asylum with an Oudh taluqdar, Hurdeo Baksh; at the end of August they made their way by boat to the safety of Kanpur. Their lengthy flight and enforced residence with Hurdeo Baksh gave them ample opportunity to observe the state of the country. They came away convinced that the mass of the agricultural population welcomed the end of British rule, and that the source of this feeling was to be found in a hated system of law, property relations, and revenue administration. To avert future outbursts these men recommended that the Government simplify the procedure of its courts, halt the sale of land for debt, and in general "better adapt our system of government to native sentiment." Above all, they said, the old families—both displaced village proprietors and landed gentry—should be confirmed in possession of their holdings. As J. W. Sherer, Collector of Fatehpur, remarked in September 1857, "The much vaunted settlement of the North West has been tried in the balance and found wanting." Recognition of the small holder, though intended as an act of justice and a benefit, was in fact a "fatal gift," productive of nothing but disaster. During the Mutiny rural society "righted itself," proprietor and tenant each resuming their traditional position by mutual agreement, and the futility of British intervention was made abundantly clear. Henceforth, they concluded, the Government should support the landed aristocracy, the natural leaders of the people, and make their interests identical with its own. None of these officers suggested that the British Government abdicate its responsibility for the welfare of the people or abandon the path of progress. But in the future, they said,

[51] Frere to Elphinstone, 7 June 1857, in Martineau, *Life of Frere*, I, 175.

the Government should exercise greater caution, and take care not to proceed too far in advance of popular sentiment.[52] The Mutiny in effect created a new breed of conservative among the District Officers of the Northwest, reinforcing the traditional conservatism of the Bombay and Madras civil servants.

Those who remained at the headquarters of Government, even in such beleaguered posts as Agra and Lucknow, usually advanced far less extreme views of the revolt than those forced to flee for their lives through the countryside. Martin Gubbins and Charles Raikes, for instance, claimed that the bulk of the people were "well affected to our rule" throughout, or at least quiet and contented when the Mutiny broke out.[53] William Muir, in the Intelligence Department at Agra, likewise denied that there was "any controversy between the *people* and the Government, except insofar as . . . the present weakness of the Government has encouraged the wild and pillaging part of the population to rise against its authority." Sepoys, "professional robbers," and "low Mahomedan rabble" were alone up in arms.[54] Yet their recommendations for the future are often scarcely distinguishable, except in emphasis, from those of their colleagues in the districts. Raikes suggested that the taluqdars henceforth be treated with liberality; Muir proposed a ban on the sale of land for debt; while Gubbins advocated a complete reformation of judicial procedure and district administration in the North-Western Provinces. Most Englishmen in fact, while arguing that the Mutiny was exclusively military in character, acted as if it were the result of popular dissatisfaction with the British administrative system. Often

[52] Sherer to Outram, 17 September 1857 and Probyn to Outram, 17 September 1857, enclosures to Outram to Canning, 18 September 1857, in Canning Papers; Edwards, *Facts and Reflections*, pp. 13 and 19-20. See also the accounts of M. Thornhill, Magistrate of Mathura, in his *Personal Adventures*, pp. 114-16 and 330-32; and of Dundas Robertson of Saharanpur in his *District Duties*, pp. 114 and 187-90.

[53] Gubbins, *The Mutinies in Oudh*, p. 79; Raikes, *Notes on the Revolt*, p. 8.

[54] Letter of 2 June 1857 in *Records of the Intelligence Department*, I, 35.

the reformer was as disillusioned as the conservative, and at times he drew back from measures he had previously advocated. Robert Montgomery and Charles Wingfield, for instance, were both trained in the North-Western Provinces under Bird and Thomason, both held strong views on peasant proprietorship before the Mutiny, yet in 1858 they were responsible for the restoration to power of the Oudh taluqdars. Even for the most enthusiastic radical the Mutiny was a sobering and chastening experience. As Raikes commented, "Our intentions towards India have generally been well inspired, and our principles right in the abstract," but changes had been introduced, particularly in Oudh, too rudely, too suddenly, and with too little consideration for the feelings of the people. "The fatal error of attempting to force the policy of Europe on the people of Asia . . . must be corrected for the future, as it has been atoned for in the past."[55] At home Sir Charles Wood responded in much the same fashion. Despite his defence of Dalhousie's Government, and his insistence that the Mutiny was merely military, he showed little enthusiasm for further doses of reform. As Secretary of State for India he continually implored the Indian Government to move with caution and to consult the feelings of the people in all matters affecting their customs or traditions. On the floor of the Commons and in the India Council he fended off evangelical demands for a "Christian policy" and stood up for those newly white-washed allies, the taluqdars of Oudh. In all of this Wood spoke for the overwhelming body of British opinion. No one denied that Britain still held India in trust, and that upon it was laid the duty of advancing the cause of civilization in the East. But few were now prepared to advance that cause at quite the same speed or with quite the same enthusiasm as before.

The Indian people were far less articulate than their British rulers. Education had penetrated only a little way into Indian

[55] Raikes, *Notes on the Revolt*, pp. 170-71.

society, and many of those who did know something about the events of 1857 were too frightened to speak out. Few wished to endanger their position by openly criticizing the Government which stood over them sword in hand. Still, both Bengal and the Muslim centers of Upper India possessed sizable communities of educated, and outspoken, young men. By 1857 a generation of young Bengalis had been subjected to the new Western education, and were fast growing to maturity. They could boast of an English language newspaper, the *Hindoo Patriot,* and a modern political organization, The British Indian Association. Highly cultured and politically alert, these men looked upon themselves as the future leaders of their country and they never hesitated to make known their grievances. Some, like Dwarkanath and Debendranath Tagore, were scions of aristocratic Bengali families. Others of more humble parentage raised themselves to positions of considerable eminence by their own efforts. Digambar Mitra, for instance, began his career as an English schoolmaster in Murshidabad, acted briefly as Estate Manager for a local zamindar, and then went into silk and indigo manufacture, where he amassed a considerable fortune. In 1851 he purchased a zamindari estate and launched himself into politics as Assistant Secretary of the British Indian Association. From there he went on to membership of the Bengal Legislative Council and the award of a C.S.I. and Rajaship from the British Government.[56]

Despite their disparate origins, the educated Bengalis of the mid-nineteenth century shared a common education and common political aspirations. Most considered themselves disciples of Ram Mohan Roy, although they did not always subscribe to his religious opinions, and many were products of the Hindu College during its great era of intellectual ferment under Derozio. The British Indian Association, founded in 1851, provided them with an effective political forum. Al-

---

[56] See Bholanauth Chunder, *Raja Digambar Mitra His Life and Career* (Calcutta, 1893).

though later an organ of purely zamindari opinion, in its early days the association comprised all the leading Bengali politicians, and pressed upon the Government a wide variety of reforms. Most notably it recommended the constitution of a Legislative Council, enjoying the same powers as those of the Colonies, and containing three native members from each Presidency, "so as in some respects to represent the sentiments of the people."[57]

When the Mutiny broke out, the educated Bengali community hastened to express its continued loyalty to the British Government. Addresses flooded into Government House from the British Indian Association, the Mohammedan Association, and other Calcutta organizations. Each offered its assistance in suppressing the uprising and vigorously denied any imputation of disloyalty. The bulk of the people, they insisted, were faithful, and viewed the "disgraceful and mutinous conduct of the native soldiery" with the deepest abhorrence and sorrow.[58] One Bengali writer even brought out a book in 1859 whose title clearly indicates its purpose: "The Mutinies and the People, or, Statements of Native Fidelity Exhibited During the Outbreak of 1857-1858." The insurrection, he said, was "purely military"; the people "by their active and spontaneous assistance" actually saved the Empire from destruction.[59] Much of this effusive outpouring of loyalty was a reaction to the racist sentiments of the Calcutta Europeans, who saw a hidden rebel in every Indian and treasonable intent in every conversation. But beneath the polemics lay a clear perception of the benefits British rule had brought to Bengal. The zamindar knew that his property and his low assessment were secure only so long as the British remained, while the educated classes, who looked forward to the regeneration of their coun-

[57] Petition of B.I.A. to Parliament, 7 April 1852, P.P. 1852-53, xxxiii, 267.
[58] B.I.A. to G.G., 23 May 1857, and Mohammedan Association to G.G., 28 May 1857, in S. K. Majumdar, ed., *Indian Speeches and Documents on British Rule 1821-1918* (Calcutta, 1937), pp. 56-58 and 64-69.
[59] The author was S. C. Mukhopadhyaya.

try on Western lines, were little likely to sympathize with those whose objective was the restoration of the past. Indeed they had everything to lose by a resurgence of orthodoxy and fanaticism. As the *Hindoo Patriot* pointed out:

"They [the educated Indians] have a splendid future before them, but which can be realized only by the existence of British rule. They are already the only class among the fixed population of the country which possesses any active political influence. They are in point of intelligence the foremost among their countrymen. In three more generations they will have the best part of the property of the country in their hands. For all political purposes they will be the people. . . . Realization of these prospects, however, entirely depends upon the continued existence of British rule. Most enlightened self-interest, accordingly, prompts the 'educated natives' to be loyal."[60]

Nor was the Bengali at all temperamentally inclined to military adventure. "Their pursuits and their triumphs are entirely civil. . . . They are aware that the British rule is the best suited to their quiet and intellectual tastes; that under it they might achieve the greatest amount of prosperity compatible with their position as a conquered race."[61]

Apart from proclaiming their loyalty, few Bengalis attempted any serious analysis of the causes or nature of the Mutiny. The *Hindoo Patriot* alone gave attention to the question. Established in 1853 by Grish Chunder Ghose, the paper was taken over by Harish Chandra Mukherjee in 1856 and for the next five years was the major vehicle of educated Bengali opinion. During the 1860's, after it fell under the control of Kristo Das Pal, the *Hindoo Patriot* followed the British Indian Association into the zamindari camp. Harish recognized that "the British Government, whatever its other faults, has given the country an amount of substantial benefit

---

[60] *Hindoo Patriot*, 11 June 1857, v, 188.
[61] *Ibid.*, 4 June 1857, p. 180.

which the lowest intellect can appreciate." But this loyalty, he said, was rational and calculating, based solely upon self-interest, with no sentimental affection for the British Raj. "So long as we are treated by Englishmen as an inferior race . . . much of warmth and ardour cannot be expected to enter into the composition of our loyalty." Few Indians therefore could suppress "a wish to see the British Government humiliated to a certain extent."[62] In the North-Western Provinces and Oudh, he continued, the revolt gained far more than covert sympathy. There what began as a sepoy mutiny ended as a "general rebellion." The revolt, according to Harish, originated in the army, and arose out of the conflict of a progressive civilization with "Asiatic stationaryism." Its leaders were men eager to wipe out the advances of the past century and gain power for themselves.[63] The uprising was so far the inevitable result of British rule in India and deserved little sympathy. But by pursuing a "high-handed course of aggression" the British Government did much to give the insurrection popular appeal.

Like Disraeli, whose opinions they cited with approval, the *Hindoo Patriot* drew up a long list of acts which had kindled popular hostility. Two, however, were most influential: the annexation of Oudh, and the settlement of the North-Western Provinces. More than anything else, they said, the annexation of Oudh shook the confidence of the Indian people in the good faith of the British Government and "prepared the country for revolt." This "flagrant political crime," moreover, gave the rebellion in Oudh the character of a legitimate war of independence. The people were fighting for their hereditary sovereign and their hereditary laws.[64] Similarly the wholesale agrarian revolution in the North-Western Provinces generated widespread discontent, even among its supposed beneficiaries, for the people clung to their old system of landholding. Tradi-

[62] *Ibid.*, 21 May 1857, p. 165.
[63] *Ibid.*, 9 July 1857, p. 221.
[64] *Ibid.*, 20 May 1858, VI, 156.

tional feudal loyalties were stronger than "democratical theories of landed possession." Consequently the North-Western Provinces burst into rebellion, and the old settlement collapsed, as soon as the sepoys had risen. Bengal was saved because it possessed a people "trained under the instincts of feudal allegiance," and a body of landlords committed to the defense of order. "Had it not been for the Permanent Settlement the whole of the Bengal Presidency would have been now lost to England."[65]

The *Hindoo Patriot* thus looked upon the Mutiny in much the same way as the conservatives in Britain. Indeed in one respect they went somewhat further than Disraeli. Not only did they indict with Disraeli the "spirit of territorial aggrandizement" and the "degradation of all classes to a democratic level," they pointed as well to the growth of racial antagonism and the continued exclusion of Indians from posts of responsibility. This too, they said, spread distrust and disaffection. But they did not subscribe to the entire conservative philosophy, nor did they follow Disraeli in all his recommendations. The editors of the *Hindoo Patriot* in fact, like so many educated Bengalis, were torn between their loyalty to "Hindoo civilization" and their self-appointed role as "the chosen instruments of European civilization in Asia." They detested that arrogance which led the British so often to treat the Indians as if they were untutored savages. India, they said, possessed an ancient culture, a noble philosophy, and a religion in no way inferior to Christianity. It had no need of missionaries or of crusading zealots bent upon the total reconstruction of society. The Indian people lived happily under their own institutions, and were if anything more passionately attached to traditional ways than the English. This sudden outburst of rebellion, they insisted, should have at least one salutary result: to teach the English "in their future intercourse with and legislation for the Natives . . . that they

[65] *Ibid.*, 22 April 1858, p. 124.

have a civilized people to deal with."[66] Yet at the same time, as men committed to the Westernization of India, the educated community wished to see education and social reform pushed forward with renewed vigor. They urged Britain on no account to abandon the cause of reform for fear of offending the sepoy and the orthodox. Pointing out that Britain "is said to have a mission in India," the *Hindoo Patriot* contended that "if the Indian nations will not fall in with the world in its way, they must be compelled to do it. . . . The rationale of all that England does and has yet done in the East is that she will not—and standing in the vanguard of civilization she ought not—allow progress to be barred by the refractoriness of any of her sons. . . . She must bring on all in the way providence directs all should go."[67] English education above all must not be hindered. Nothing else, they said, could so effectively undermine "the fabric of Hindoo idolatry" or eradicate "the social abuses and moral outrages" connected with religion.

This reforming enthusiasm, however, extended only to social reform and education. When it came to land policy, the *Hindoo Patriot* was more conservative than most Englishmen. They claimed that zamindari settlement was the only system of land tenure suited to India, and that an aristocratic, or as they called it a "feudal," society represented the highest form of social organization. The Permanent Settlement, they stated, "has done more than armies and schools to convert the people of Bengal, high and low, into loyal, prosperous, and intelligent British subjects." It was the "most powerful bond" between Britain and India and the source of Bengal's pre-eminence. The *Hindoo Patriot* accordingly suggested that, in resettling the North-Western Provinces after the Mutiny, the Government should put the old proprietors back into possession. The time had come to repudiate "mistaken theories of peasant proprietorship" and place the society of Upper

[66] *Ibid.*, 18 November 1858, p. 364.
[67] *Ibid.*, 8 October 1857, v, 357.

India upon its rightful feudal base.[68] The interests of the cultivators were not ignored. The *Hindoo Patriot* simply held, in
true Tory fashion, that the people prospered best under their
"natural" aristocratic leaders. The same sentiments permeated
the Bengali attitude toward education and government service.
The *Hindoo Patriot* advocated, for instance, the restriction of
civil service posts to men "of high family connections and
honourable lineage," and the retention of the old filtration
theory of education. The Government, they asserted, should
impart only a high order of education in English to the upper
classes. These men, "the upper ten thousand," would in turn
enlighten the multitude beneath them.[69] Ultimately, then, the
educated Bengali was the product of two distinct cultural
stimuli—his Western education and his aristocratic environment; and he bowed down before two idols—the English
School and the Permanent Settlement. If given ample scope,
they could regenerate India as they had regenerated Bengal.

In Upper India the educated community, largely Muslim,
clustered about the cities of Delhi and Lucknow. Few had any
sympathy with the British Government or had made any
effort to acquire an English education. Consequently, when
the Mutiny broke out many went over to the rebel side. Even
those who preferred the security of British rule often had no
option but to join the rebellion or flee for their lives. As
Muinuddin Hasan Khan, an Inspector of Police in Delhi, later
described it, "If I had remained a passive spectator of this rebellion my life would certainly have been taken, while if I
had left the city and joined the English, the honour of my
family would have been destroyed and the rebels would have
wrecked their vengeance upon them."[70] So he stayed to serve
as *kotwal* under the rebel Government, only to flee when the
British returned. Muinuddin attributed the revolt primarily

[68] *Ibid.*, 13 August 1857, p. 260; and 25 February 1858, VI, 60.
[69] *Ibid.*, 1 April 1858, p. 101; and 2 December 1858, p. 381.
[70] C. T. Metcalfe, *Two Native Narratives of the Mutiny in Delhi* (London,
1898), p. 56.

to the annexation of Oudh, an act of "gross injustice" which provoked "a universal desire for resistance." From then on, he said, the sepoys, the retainers of the king, and the landholders were determined to drive away the foreign "trespassers."[71] Another resident of Delhi, Munshi Mohanlal, who remained loyal, pointed out how the continued annexations, the peasant settlement of Oudh, and the imposition of law and order, had alienated large segments of the population. But, he continued, even those who had made their fortunes under British rule often "showed hidden delight at British reverses," for no amount of wealth could heal the wounds caused by the "distant and contemptible manner" in which they had been treated. To this, and to ignorance of the real strength of Great Britain, Mohanlal ascribed the wide popular appeal of the rebellion.[72]

The rebel leaders themselves compiled a long list of grievances to justify their action. In a Proclamation of 25 August 1857 the Delhi court asserted that all classes of the population "are being ruined under the tyranny and oppression of the infidel and treacherous English." The zamindars have felt the pressures of an exorbitant revenue demand, have seen their lands sold from under them, and have been dragged into court, and there disgraced, by mean and petty suitors. Merchants likewise have been subjected to numerous fines and taxes, while the British gathered up all the lucrative trade of the country, including that in indigo, opium, and cloth. Under an independent Government, they said, all these exactions would cease and the "dignity and honour" of the zamindars would be respected. Moreover, Indians would once again be eligible for those posts of responsibility and emolument from which they had been excluded by the British.[73] To many

[71] *Ibid.*, pp. 37-38.
[72] Memorandum on Causes of Mutiny of 8 November 1857 in Home Miscellaneous No. 725, Kaye Mutiny Papers, India Office Library.
[73] Cited in Charles Ball, *The History of the Indian Mutiny* (London, n.d.), II, 630-32. See also F.C. 8 October 1858, No. 197.

rebels, however, these sources of disaffection paled into insignificance beside their fear for their religion. With Khan Bahadur Khan, they were firmly convinced that "if these English continue in Hindoostan, they will kill everyone in the country and will utterly overthrow our religions."[74] This supposed attack upon Indian religion was, as they saw it, the basic cause of the Mutiny and the ultimate justification of their rebellion.

Among those Muslims who remained loyal, the most conspicuous, and outspoken, was Sayyid Ahmad Khan. Brought up at the Mughal court in Delhi, where his father was a close friend of the Emperor, Sayyid Ahmad received a traditional Urdu education. In 1837, to the surprise of his family, he joined the British service. Twenty years later, when the Mutiny broke out, he was *sadr amin* of Bijnour, a district eighty miles from Delhi in Rohilkhand. When the mutineers first appeared in Bijnour, Sayyid Ahmad arranged for the safe evacuation of the European residents, and for a time took charge of the district on behalf of the British Government. Eventually he was displaced by the rebel Nawab Mahmud Khan and forced to flee to Meerut. In recognition of his services during the uprising he was awarded a pension of Rs. 200 a month for life.[75]

In 1858, sensing the value of a study of the Mutiny from the Indian point of view, Sayyid Ahmad wrote an essay in Urdu which was translated and published by the Government of India in 1860. This essay, "On the Causes of the Indian Revolt," was the most significant single Indian contribution to the debate on the Mutiny. Like the British conservatives, and the *Hindoo Patriot*, Sayyid Ahmad believed that the Mutiny was a widespread rebellion, built upon a mass of popular disaffection. By 1857, he said, "the people wished for a change in the Government, and rejoiced heartily at the idea

[74] S.C. 30 April 1858, No. 22.
[75] G. F. I. Graham, *The Life and Work of Syed Ahmed Khan* (Edinburgh, 1885), Chs. i and iii.

of British rule being superseded by another." The greased cartridges only supplied the spark which touched off a vast explosion.[76] In his search for the causes of this disaffection, Sayyid Ahmad set aside several of the more popular explanations, including Muslim conspiracy, nationalist sentiment, and the annexation of Oudh. Much as annexation might have given rise to general dissatisfaction, he said, the princes, who were most aggrieved, did not revolt. He nevertheless cited a wide variety of social and economic grievances. Most important of all was the universal conviction that the British Government was bent upon converting the people to Christianity and forcing them to adopt European ways. No doubt, he said, this fear was based upon a misunderstanding of the true intentions of the Government. But it was no less firmly rooted, and the Government, by its reform legislation and its aid to missionaries, only heightened popular suspicion. Next to interference with religion, resumption of rent-free land stirred up the greatest amount of discontent. Indeed, he maintained, these two "were the original and principal causes of the dissatisfaction of the people of India."[77] From there Sayyid Ahmad went on to criticize the enforced sale of land, the severity of the revenue assessment, and the degradation of the Oudh taluqdars. By these measures, he said, many landholders were suddenly reduced from affluence to penury, while the remainder gradually grew poorer and poorer, until all alike were ripe for rebellion. The people were further impoverished by their exclusion from high Government employment, the abolition of rewards and *jaghirs*, and the displacement of Indian handicrafts by British manufactured goods. To make matters worse, he said, the Indian people, high and low, were treated with the utmost insolence and contempt by the officers of Government. "Even natives of the highest rank never come into the presence of officials, but with an inward fear and

[76] Sayyid Ahmad Khan, *Causes of the Revolt*, pp. 3 and 35.
[77] *Ibid.*, p. 25.

trembling."[78] Surely, Sayyid Ahmad concluded, a Government
which so insulted its subjects could hardly expect to secure
their loyalty and affection in a time of crisis.

To ward off rebellion Sayyid Ahmad proposed simply that
Indians be admitted to the Legislative Council. Had there
been Indians on the Legislative Council in 1857, he insisted,
there would have been no uprising. "Their non-admission
formed the main originating cause of this rebellion, to which
all other causes were secondary."[79] As the people had no voice
in their Government, he explained, the legislators had no way
of knowing how their proposals would be received, or whether
they were suited to the habits and customs of the people.
They blundered heedlessly on until the discontent was so
great that a "slight commotion produced a terrible outbreak."[80]
Even worse, he said, since the people had had no share in
framing legislation, they remained ignorant of its true intent.
Hence the motives of Government were often misunderstood,
and the people, with no one to set them right, fell into the
error of believing that their religion was in danger. Sayyid
Ahmad doubtless exaggerated the value of Indian representation as a check upon ill-considered legislation. The presence
of a few Indians on the Legislative Council would not by itself have dulled Dalhousie's reforming enthusiasm, or made
British legislation more palatable to the Indian people. Yet
his proposal ultimately implied that the people were entitled
to share in their own government, and that legislation should
always be adapted to their "peculiar habits and customs." To
do otherwise, he said, was to invite rebellion.

Sayyid Ahmad's essay touched off a lively debate in official
circles. Richard Temple, a disciple of Dalhousie and John
Lawrence, could not believe that the Indian people were so
impoverished, or so disaffected, as Sayyid Ahmad had alleged.
He undertook a point-by-point refutation of all the Sayyid's
charges. Some he dismissed outright as based upon appear-

[78] *Ibid.*, p. 42.     [79] *Ibid.*, p. 11.     [80] *Ibid.*, p. 12.

ances rather than facts. In particular, he said, the native gentry, overlooking "the gradual elevation of the mass," mistook the decadence of certain families for the impoverishment of the country. He was likewise unable to comprehend how the lack of Indians on the Legislative Council could have had anything to do with the rebellion.[81] Sir Bartle Frere and Sir James Outram, on the other hand, found altogether too much truth in this "most painfully interesting paper." As Frere pointed out, the essay clearly showed how "acts of our Government, well meant and well planned, sometimes do more harm than good, simply owing to our disregard for native opinion and our neglect of the maxim that our measures in India should not only be good in themselves but that they should commend themselves to the approval of the natives. We, as a rule, neither take care enough to know what the natives think of our measures, nor to explain the true grounds and objects of our measures to those affected by them."[82] After the Mutiny the British set out to remedy this shortcoming.

[81] Memorandum by Richard Temple of March 1860 printed as an appendix to Sayyid Ahmad's *Causes of the Revolt*, pp. 55-70.

[82] Notes by Frere and Outram of 28 March 1860 in Canning Papers Miscellaneous, No. 558.

# CHAPTER III

# EDUCATION AND SOCIAL REFORM

IN THE years immediately after the Mutiny few questions generated more heated controversy in England and among the British in India than the extent to which the policy of social reform had contributed to the uprising. Indeed accusations and recriminations on this subject almost dominated discussion of the Mutiny in England. But the debate was largely concerned with the events of the past. Much as conservatives might argue that "the religious and social innovations of the English" had stirred up massive popular discontent and much as supporters of the Government might insist that neither Dalhousie's reforms nor the spread of Christianity had anything to do with the events of 1857, on future policy there was a surprisingly wide measure of agreement between them. Apart from a few staunch evangelicals, no one wished to see the Government resume its frontal attack upon "immoral" customs or press forward the evangelization of India. The overwhelming majority of officials agreed that in a time of popular upheaval local prejudices had to be conciliated and Hindu customs left to reform themselves.

J. W. Kaye, Secretary at the India Office, voiced the predominant sentiment when he wrote in 1859 that greater caution "is rather to be counselled than less" during the next few years. "The prime object (for we can do nothing without it) of all our efforts . . . is the tranquillization of the public mind. . . . Until we have restored the national confidence in the non-aggressive spirit of the British Government, all that we do will be regarded with suspicion, and, perhaps, repelled with aversion."[1] Sir Charles Wood concurred whole-heartedly. As he told the House of Commons in August 1859: "We must be very careful not to give to the Natives of India any reason to believe that we are about to attack their religious feelings and prejudices. . . . No doubt in the recent case there was no just cause for suspicion; but they entertained that belief. We have seen the consequences, and if we hope to retain India in peace and tranquillity we must take care so to govern it as not only to consult the interests, but the feelings of the Native population."[2]

Almost all of Dalhousie's reform measures were subjected to severe criticism during and after the Mutiny. The Widow Remarriage Act was the target of especially strong fire, for it had, in Disraeli's words, seriously "disquieted the religious feelings of the Hindus."[3] Official inquiries carried out in 1858 bore out this contention. The local governments reported unanimously that the act had excited strong hostility and remained practically a dead letter. The higher classes of Hindus, one District Officer remarked, "regard it with ex-treme aversion and deprecate Government interference in what they declare to be directly a matter of religion."[4] In all India only 16 widows had been married under the provisions of the act, and of these 15 lived in or near Calcutta, where alone the principle of the act had gained any sympathy, and even there the widow, her husband, and their families were in every case outcasted by the community.[5] Still, inasmuch as the act was simply declaratory and forced no one to remarry, it was left on the statute book. Most British officials hoped that eventually, with the progress of education, it would grow in popularity.

[1] John William Kaye, *Christianity in India* (London, 1859), pp. 488-89.

[2] Speech of 1 August 1859, Hansard, CLV, 781.

[3] Speech of 27 July 1857, Hansard, CXLVII, 464.

[4] Magistrate of Muzaffarnagar to Commissioner of Meerut, 20 April 1858, Home Public, 4 March 1859, No. 25.

[5] Note by Cecil Beadon, Sec. Govt. India, of 28 January 1859, *ibid.*, No. 30.

Aid to missionary education brought the Government much more openly into conflict with Indian religion, and aroused considerably more opposition in England. Ellenborough was convinced that grants to mission schools, even when restricted to purposes of secular education, had alarmed the people and undermined "the neutrality to which we have at all times pledged ourselves to adhere." At the present moment, he maintained, "no measure could be adopted more calculated to tranquillize the minds of the Natives, and to restore to us their confidence, than that of withholding the aid of the Government from schools with which missionaries are connected."[6] Ellenborough's successor at the India Office, Lord Stanley, agreed that "while professing religious neutrality we have departed widely from it in fact." He admitted that grants to missionary schools were indirectly subsidies to religious bodies which enabled them more effectively to carry on their proselytizing work, and he urged that in the future such grants be carefully scrutinized and limited by stringent conditions.[7] Unlike Ellenborough, however, he did not recommend the complete abolition of the grant-in-aid system. Although the idea appealed to him, Stanley realized that public opinion at home would not tolerate such a drastic step. The Government simply could not withdraw altogether from a position it had so recently and so publicly assumed.

But grants were curtailed and new applications for aid rejected for some years after the Mutiny. The need for government economy after the heavy expenditure of 1857-1858 was partly responsible, and was indeed usually the ostensible reason for the reduction in aid; but the Government's determination to avoid further ties with the missionary movement reinforced this decision. One incident indicative of this new attitude is the treatment of the Church Missionary Society's application

[6] Letter to Chairman of East India Company, 28 April 1858, Ellenborough Papers.

[7] Stanley to Canning, 8 September 1858 and 21 January 1859, Canning Papers.

for a grant to educate the backward Santhal tribe of Bihar. Although sanctioned by the Government of India in 1856 under the grant-in-aid rules, the application was turned down by the Court of Directors in July 1857 on the ground that "the scheme identifies the Government in measures prosecuted by missionaries, and so exposes the arrangement to the risk of perverted misconstruction." Citing the importance of maintaining a "cautious line of proceeding" in educational matters, the Court instructed the Government of India to avoid "any steps which might have the appearance of uniting the Government with such a society in measures having the aim of converting any class of the population to Christianity."[8] When the scheme was revived and promoted by the Commissioner of the Santhal Parganas, George Yule, one of the few evangelical officers in Bengal, his proselytizing enthusiasm won him no support from the Government. But the Bengal authorities soon discovered that no other agency could compare with the C.M.S. for zeal and efficiency in this kind of work among an isolated tribal people; and so the grant was finally sanctioned in 1861, with the proviso that the C.M.S. contribute half the cost out of its own funds.[9] Thus the Government did not abandon the policy of aiding mission schools, despite occasional misgivings, nor did it repudiate any of the reform legislation enacted before the Mutiny. The events of 1857 did not so much uproot those reforms already established as blight whatever hopes existed for bold new measures of social advance.

This renewed emphasis on caution and conciliation was the product not only of imperial politics in an unsettled India but also of declining enthusiasm for reform at home. By mid-century both Benthamism and evangelicalism had lost much of their earlier crusading zeal. Although their ideas in a

[8] Sec. Govt. India to Sec. Govt. Bengal, 28 November 1856, P.P. 1859, xxiv, Part 1, 83. Dispatch of 22 July 1857 to G.G. in Council, Public Dispatch No. 97 of 1857, *ibid.*, pp. 3-4.
[9] Home Education, 5 November 1861, Nos. 3-10.

diluted form now leavened all of British society, their adherents were less numerous and their direct influence much
less marked than before. Radical reform was not just dangerous, it had ceased to be fashionable. In the Government mission, claims were greeted with distinct skepticism. Lord Derby,
in a speech of 3 December 1857, alluded to "what I own seems
to be the somewhat hopeless task of Christianizing India" and
urged the Government to show that it "stands aloof" from
any interference "by force or authority with their religion or
superstitions, however debased and revolting they may be to
our feelings."[10] Successive Secretaries of State found the missionary party to be little more than a troublesome band of
agitators and in their private correspondence continually expressed their irritation at the outbursts of evangelical enthusiasm to which they were subjected. As Sir Charles Wood
wrote to Lord Elphinstone in Bombay: "I cannot be much
impressed at an intensity of religious bigotry in India. It is
all the fashion here; and we have constantly explosions of
intemperate religious discord, not much more reasonable,
considering the circumstances of the two countries, than those
of your Hindoos at Ahmednuggur. But I can easily conceive
how infinitely the difficulty of governing the country must
be increased by such a spirit."[11] F. J. Halliday, Lieutenant-
Governor of Bengal, had equally little patience with "the
blundering stupidity of the Exeter Hall orators, of whom
indeed after most carefully reading their claptrap, it is always,
to me, most difficult to divine the meaning and object."[12]

At the same time, during the 1860's, popular enthusiasm
for missionary work was declining steadily. The various mission societies managed quickly to make good the very substantial losses they had suffered during the uprising. The
stations which had been destroyed were rebuilt, new missionaries were recruited to replace those slain, and special

[10] Speech of 3 December 1857, Hansard, CXLVIII, 53.
[11] Wood to Elphinstone, 3 December 1859, Wood Papers.
[12] Halliday to Canning, 23 February 1858, Canning Papers.

funds were raised in England. The Church Missionary Society collected £50,000 and the Society for the Propagation of the Gospel £19,000 for the restoration of property and the extension of mission activities in the North-Western Provinces, Oudh, and Punjab. But the initial burst of enthusiasm was not followed by any sustained effort, and the new stations soon languished for want of support. Even in the Punjab, where they received encouragement from the local officials, the new missions were not adequately manned and their effectiveness was extremely limited.[13] The C.M.S., as the largest Anglican body in India, felt the pinch most sharply. During the post-Mutiny decade they obtained almost no new recruits for the Indian mission field. While the number of missionaries on the rolls in India rose from 54 to 107 during the 1850's, it stood at only 109 in 1871. The total membership and average annual income of the society were equally stagnant. Henry Venn admitted in 1865 that while "the extent and influence of Evangelical Truth in the Church had very largely increased," missionary zeal had distinctly "retrograded." Missionary meetings, he said, were less well attended, and the "warm sympathy" of earlier years had almost completely evaporated.[14] Other societies experienced the same setback. The London Missionary Society, for instance, with an average of 150 missionaries in the field over the period 1847-1856, could muster only 140 in the subsequent decade.[15] Altogether the total number of missionaries in India from the five leading British societies declined from 262 to 234 during the decade 1861-1871.[16] This loss of popular support drastically curtailed the political power of the mission societies. Henceforth they were but one of several interest groups with

[13] Eugene Stock, *History of the Church Missionary Society* (London, 1899-1916), II, 276-77.

[14] *Ibid.*, pp. 336-37, 536.

[15] Richard Lovett, *The History of the London Missionary Society, 1795-1895* (London, 1899), II, 690.

[16] Stock, *Church Missionary Society*, II, 357.

which the India Office had to contend, and one which no
longer exerted a decisive influence on policy formation.

## The Evangelicals and a "Christian Policy"

Nevertheless, despite their dwindling influence, the missionaries still formed a powerful body of opinion, and their
views still struck a responsive chord in many Victorian Englishmen. The members of the Government, for instance, found
it expedient to avoid expressing their feelings too openly on
religious questions. Lord Stanley, during his tenure as Secretary of State, made no secret of his disdain for evangelical
"fanaticism," and on one occasion even referred to Christianity
as the "religion of Europe." This outspokenness, which
brought down upon him the wrath of the missionary party,
provoked a reprimand from Disraeli, who pointed out that
"it is as important to touch the feelings and sympathy of the
religious classes in England as to conciliate the natives of
India."[17] Disraeli was no more evangelical than Stanley, but
he realized the importance of keeping up at least an appearance of deference to evangelical opinion, so as not "to slight
the religious feelings of the country." Such talk did not, and
indeed was not meant to, influence the determination of
policy. Stanley's successor, Sir Charles Wood, clearly recognized this distinction. He repeatedly urged the Viceroy and
other officials in India to be "very cautious indeed in what
you say and publish," and to avoid provoking the "Saints" or
giving them a handle with which to attack the Government.
The missionaries, he reminded Canning in 1860, "can get up
a cry here which people unacquainted with India think very
fine and harmless. You know better."[18]

The continuing power of the missionary party, and the
extent of their popular appeal, can be seen most clearly in
their ardent campaign for a "Christian policy" in India in

[17] Disraeli to Stanley, 13 August 1858, cited in W. F. Moneypenny and
G. E. Buckle, *Life of Benjamin Disraeli* (New York, 1910-1920), IV, 168.
[18] Wood to Canning, 27 June 1860 and 10 August 1860, Wood Papers.

the years immediately after the Mutiny. Almost unanimously the missionaries and their evangelical allies in England looked upon the Mutiny as a blow sent by God to humble Britain for its remissness in evangelizing India. The British had long neglected their Christian duty in India and had sinned against God. The uprising was the logical outcome, a "visitation of Jehovah's displeasure" upon them. As the great Scottish missionary Alexander Duff put it: "God has, in a strange way, given us India in trust for the accomplishment of *His* grand evangelising designs concerning it. In the discharge of this solemn trust, we, as a people and a nation, have been shamefully criminally negligent. Hence it is . . . that the Lord has admonished us in the way of sore judgments. But having in some measure humbled ourselves before the Lord, He has delivered us, provided we realize the great object of our covenant—the subversion of Satan's empire."[19]

The "awful events" of 1857, in a word, simply convinced the missionaries that redoubled efforts must be made on behalf of Christian proselytism. "The great and pressing want of India" was neither education nor a just government, for these she already had; rather "India needs the Gospel, needs Christianity, in order to be re-righted and regenerated."[20] The missionaries denied that an open profession of Christianity by the Government involved any political danger. Indeed they insisted that a Christian policy was the best way of avoiding future outbursts of rebellion. The old neutrality policy, they maintained, had only aroused popular suspicion of British intentions, while the careful seclusion of the sepoys from missionary preaching had encouraged those delusions which led to the revolt. "Had the mutineers of the Bengal Army possessed some insight into the principles of the Christian religion, they would never have been misled in the manner

[19] Alexander Duff, *The Indian Rebellion* (London, 1858), p. 255.

[20] M. A. Sherring, *The Indian Church During the Great Rebellion* (London, 1859), p. 165. Sherring was an L.M.S. missionary in Benares and Mirzapur.

they were."[21] Christianity alone could create a loyal body of subjects, ready to stand by the Government in any emergency. The Indian Christian community, they proudly proclaimed, were not only loyal but willing to endure martyrdom for their faith.[22] This view of the causes of the Mutiny was accepted by no one outside the evangelical camp, for it was built upon a very selective use of evidence, but it did lend an air of plausibility to the missionary position and strengthened their conviction that Britain's moral duty demanded an active proselytizing policy.

The specific measures which the evangelicals pressed upon the Government varied from individual to individual, but there was wide agreement upon the following propositions: that the Government should disregard all distinctions of caste; should sever all connection with the rites and customs of the Hindu religion; should introduce the Bible as a class book in its schools; and should employ all legitimate means for the universal diffusion of Christianity throughout India.[23] In the years immediately after the Mutiny attention was directed primarily to securing Bible teaching in the Government schools; but the evangelical party never hesitated to bombard the Government with petitions and protests whenever they detected the slightest concession to Hindu customs or any sign of discrimination against the Christian community in India.

Not all Churchmen supported this campaign for a "Christian policy" in India. John Wilson, Duff's counterpart in Bombay, urged his fellow missionaries to work quietly for specific reforms rather than arouse antagonism by boldly challenging the Government. After all, he said, the Government had done

[21] C.M.S. Address to John Lawrence, 24 June 1859, cited in Stock, Church Missionary Society, II, 231-32.

[22] Sherring, The Indian Church During the Rebellion, pp. 12 and 339.

[23] See, for instance, speech of Archbishop of Canterbury in House of Lords, 23 July 1858, Hansard, CLI, 2011; C.M.S. Petition to the Queen, cited in Stock, Church Missionary Society, II, 242-43; and Duff, Indian Rebellion, pp. 304-05.

nothing to impede the spread of Christianity, nor had it prevented its officers from privately supporting missionary work.[24] Bishop Cotton in Calcutta took issue with the missionary demand for Bible teaching in the Government schools. He was convinced that with the Bible in the school library, and voluntary instruction after school hours permitted, "there remained no barrier imposed by the Government of India between the seeker after God and his teacher." He did admit that the Bible might have been introduced into the Government schools before the Mutiny, but he hastened to add that "an order for its introduction at the present time of suspicion and bad feeling would do more harm than good."[25] Often, moreover, practicing missionaries in India were aware of practical difficulties in the way of reform which escaped their more ardent colleagues at home. The scarcity of qualified Christian teachers, for example, was a major obstacle to Bible teaching in the Government schools, for no one wished to entrust the teaching of Scripture to "heathen schoolmasters."[26] Consequently there was a good deal less enthusiasm for the measure among missionaries in India than in England.

In the Government the missionary program met with widespread support only among the civil servants of the Punjab— but there it found some of its most dedicated adherents. Ever since its annexation the Punjab had attracted a high proportion of evangelical officials, and the events of the Mutiny only reinforced their convictions. They saw the hand of God in the seemingly miraculous escape of the province from rebellion, and this divine favor they attributed to the peculiarly

[24] George Smith, *Life of John Wilson* (London, 1878), p. 514.

[25] Sophia Anne Cotton, *Memoir of George Edward Lynch Cotton* (London, 1871), pp. 96 and 105. Cotton was severely criticized by many missionaries for his moderate opinions. They doubtless reflect in part at least his Broad Church upbringing (he had served under Arnold at Rugby and as Headmaster of Marlborough) and his semiofficial position as Bishop of Calcutta.

[26] Cotton, *Memoir*, p. 96. See also Halliday to Canning, 23 February 1858: "It is a rule with missionaries decreed from actual experience that it is better that the Bible should not be taught at all than taught by men who do not believe it." Canning Papers.

Christian character of the administration. After the Mutiny, therefore, the evangelicalism of the Punjab school continued unabated. Almost all the higher officials of the province, including its successive Lieutenant-Governors, John Lawrence, Robert Montgomery, and Donald Macleod, were adherents of "ardent" Christianity. By far the most outspoken, however, was Herbert B. Edwardes, Commissioner of Peshawar, 1853-1859.

Edwardes considered the Mutiny to be a "national chastisement," caused not by attempts to disseminate Christianity, but by "our keeping back Christianity from the people." In a speech delivered in Exeter Hall in 1860 he summoned the "Voice of God" to testify on behalf of his view of the Mutiny: "In these things we hear the Voice of God. It says, 'I gave India to England for the benefit of its 180 million peoples so that you might communicate the light of the Bible and the knowledge of the true God to these my Heathen creatures. You have neglected this charge . . . and I have chastened you. But I have condoned your offences. I have raised you up, when no other hand could save you. I once more consign this people to your charge . . . and say take warning from the past.' Let us take warning. A Christian policy is the only policy of hope."[27] In a Memorandum "On the Elimination of all Unchristian Principles from the Government of British India" in 1858 he spelled out his views of what a "Christian policy" should entail. At the head of the list was the introduction of Bible classes in the Government schools. "As there can be no safe system of education without Christianity for its base," he insisted, "it is our plain duty to make the Bible the basis of Native education." From there he went on to recommend that the Government no longer endow idolatry, recognize caste, observe Indian holidays, or administer Hindu and Mohammedan law. He concluded with a plea for the

[27] Speech of 1 May 1860 cited in Emma Edwardes, ed., *Memorials of the Life and Letters of Major General Sir Herbert B. Edwardes* (London, 1886), II, 267-68.

suppression of polygamy and child marriage. "Is this morality? Is it in any way consistent with Christianity? If not, let us reform it."[28]

Edwardes' memorandum provoked a good deal of soul-searching among his fellow officials in the Punjab. Although evangelicals themselves, few were prepared to go the whole way with him. Donald Macleod, at the time Financial Commissioner, agreed with Edwardes that India "has been entrusted to us by the Supreme Ruler" in order to spread the blessings of Christianity among the Indian people. "It becomes us," therefore, "to acknowledge and avow our conviction that the Christian religion is alone the true one, and to avail ourselves of every legitimate opportunity of encouraging and enabling our subjects to learn the truth and follow it." On this ground he advocated Bible teaching in the Government schools, so long as it was voluntary. But he drew back from Edwardes' other proposals as partaking "more of the Theocratic spirit of Judaism, than of the milder spirit of the Christian dispensation." He refused above all to countenance any measures which involved the persecution of the Hindus because of their faith or the use of the machinery of the state as an instrument of conversion. "Our whole duty as a Government is comprised in a practical avowal of our creed, combined with a most charitable forbearance towards the convictions of all."[29]

John Lawrence adopted much the same attitude. He believed the Government should offer the Bible in the schools because it was "fraught with the highest blessings" for the people. With Macleod he asserted that there would be no political danger in such a measure; what the Hindu really feared was forcible contamination and loss of caste, not "conversion of the heart" through education.[30] But he too recoiled from anything resembling compulsion or persecution. He refused in

[28] The Memorandum is printed in full in Edwardes, *Memorials*, II, 88-105.
[29] Minute of 26 February 1858, F.C. 7 January 1859, No. 123.
[30] Minute of 3 July 1858, *ibid*.

particular to sanction the abolition of religious endowments or the abrogation of Hindu and Mohammedan law, for he considered such proposals antagonistic to the spirit of Christianity and a breach of faith with the people, whose laws and property had long been guaranteed to them. Beyond this Lawrence invoked the ideal of toleration. "Our equal and impartial forbearance towards all creeds differing from our own," he said, "has always constituted one of our first claims to the confidence of the people" and has been "one of the pillars of our strength." Similarly with regard to the observance of Indian holidays, he appealed to the maxim of "doing to our native *employés* as we should wish others to do to us." Lawrence was also aware of the danger involved in radical measures of social reform, and pointed out that much of the legislation Edwardes recommended would arouse widespread discontent. Polygamy and child marriage, he said, although "socially very objectionable," could not be suppressed because the people clung to them and "would shed blood for their sake."[31] Lawrence's attitude, then, was markedly different from that of Edwardes and the missionaries. He saw that England's moral duty to India could be expressed through toleration and forbearance as well as through proselytism. He recognized that after the events of 1857 Britain simply could not afford to ignore Indian public opinion in pursuit of a "Christian policy." Yet for all this Lawrence was still very much an evangelical. He was moved by a deeply felt conviction that Britain had been placed in power over India in order to spread the knowledge of the true God; and his campaign for Bible classes in the Government schools was but a reflection of this driving Christian zeal.

Only one Punjab official seriously challenged the evangelical position, W. D. Arnold, Director of Public Instruction and the son of Thomas Arnold of Rugby. Arnold claimed that the evangelicals, for all their talk about moral duty, had miscon-

[31] Minute of 21 April 1858, *ibid.*, No. 121.

ceived Britain's true position in India. The British ruled India, he said, "only as trustees for the Hindu and Mohammedan community" and they had therefore no right to devote the resources of the country, or schools paid for out of Indian revenues, to the purposes of Christian proselytism.[32] To this the evangelical party promptly replied that "we are trustees to God, not to the Indians." Much as Arnold's concept of trusteeship might be appropriate to a constitutional government, Lawrence pointed out, in India Britain had gained power by the sword and by its own moral superiority. Hence "in doing the best we can for the people we are bound by our conscience and not by theirs."[33]

These theoretical arguments did not appeal to the Government of India. The Viceroy and his Council in Calcutta, and the Secretaries of State in London, concerned solely with restoring the confidence of the Indian people in the British Government, found Punjab proselytizing zeal both dangerous and distasteful. Sir Bartle Frere thought that even Lawrence's scheme for voluntary Bible classes would "convince the natives generally that we meant to use our temporal power for their conversion" and provoke a full-scale rebellion. The notion that "we know ourselves to be right, and that we cannot be wrong in using our power to enforce our conscientious convictions" he found altogether too reminiscent of the Inquisition.[34] Canning likewise looked with dismay at the whole Punjab agitation—at John Lawrence's campaign for Christian education no less than Edwardes' far-reaching proposals. On one occasion he even remarked to Frere that, "Really Sir John Lawrence ought to be shut up, and Edwardes have his head shaved. The latter is exactly what Mahomet would have been if born at Clapham instead of Mecca."[35] At home successive

[32] Minute of 26 May 1858, *ibid.*, No. 128.

[33] Minute of 3 July 1858, *ibid.*, No. 123.

[34] Frere to Stanley 19 December 1858 and to Goderich 4 January 1859 in Martineau, *Life of Frere*, I, 259-60.

[35] Canning to Frere, 1 November 1860, *ibid.*, p. 370.

Secretaries of State firmly opposed all schemes for Bible
teaching in the Government schools. Lord Stanley contended
that such a measure would be "of considerable hazard" in
the best of times, and was totally unacceptable in the disturbed
conditions of 1858-1859.[36] His successor, Sir Charles Wood,
went further. He claimed that Bible classes would not only
produce a "feeling against us bad in a political sense" but
would arouse such hostility toward missionaries that the
progress of Christianity itself would be checked.[37]

Meanwhile the evangelical officials in the Punjab had embarked on yet another crusade—that of opening the district
jails to missionary preachers. This question first arose in November 1858 when the American Mission at Sialkot requested
permission to preach to the prisoners in the local jail. The
District Officer, Edward Prinsep, gave them his hearty blessing; and he was supported by most of the higher officials in
the Punjab, who saw in jail preaching an excellent opportunity of spreading Christianity. To Macleod it was simply
another way of showing "our preference for that religion
which alone we believe to be true."[38] Lawrence, at the time
Lieutenant-Governor, felt that "their exclusion would not be
an act of neutrality but rather the creation of a disability,"
for "all natives when free being liable to hear the Gospel
preached, why should prisoners be exempted?"[39] However
when the papers reached the Viceroy in April 1859, the request was disallowed. Canning was shocked to discover that
responsible officials in the Punjab would seriously consider
such a measure, for it involved nothing less than "turning
the machinery of justice and civil government to religious purposes." He pointed out that "it is still firmly believed that we
have made men soldiers and have ordered them to bite

---

[36] Dispatch of 7 April 1859, Educational Dispatch No. 4 of 1859.

[37] Wood to Canning, 26 July 1859, Wood Papers.

[38] Macleod to Sec. Govt. Punjab, 21 February 1859, F.C. 27 May 1859,
No. 102.

[39] Sec. Govt. Punjab to Sec. Govt. India, 28 February 1859, *ibid.*, No. 96.

cartridges in order to convert them." Let us not now, he urged, "give a handle to the supposition that we sentence them to imprisonment in our jails for the same purpose under the pretence of administering justice."[40] Grant and Outram on his Council were furious at the thought of the Punjab Government willfully defying the principles of religious neutrality despite repeated orders on the subject. Outram even suggested that steps be taken to restrain the zeal of missionaries and government officials in the Punjab "within prudent bounds."[41] No disciplinary action was taken, but the incident shows how very much alone the Punjab officials were in their evangelicalism. Although the Punjab remained for many years a stronghold of evangelical Christianity (and of men whose Puritanical religion was matched only by their confident self-assurance), their influence upon the Government of India was negligible. Even so eminent a person as Sir John Lawrence could never budge the Government from its settled policy of conciliation in all questions affecting social customs or religious beliefs.

Although the Government took arms against the evangelicals, they did not on that account abandon the high ground of moral idealism. Despite its origin in political expediency, the new policy of conciliation and non-interference could be made palatable to the English conscience, for it enshrined the ideals of toleration and religious liberty. The Government was thus able to stay on the offensive throughout the contest with the evangelicals.[42] Indeed with the decline of reforming zeal the British increasingly viewed their mission in India in secular terms. They exalted the virtues of religious toleration and carefully disassociated themselves from comprehensive

[40] Minute of 27 April 1859, *ibid.*, No. 103.

[41] Minute by J. P. Grant of 30 April 1859, *ibid.*, No. 104; Minute by Outram of 1 May 1859, *ibid.*, No. 105.

[42] For a detailed criticism of the evangelical program from the standpoint of religious neutrality see J. W. Kaye, *Christianity in India*, pp. 489-96.

schemes of social reform. Religious neutrality had of course always been the avowed basis of British policy, but before the Mutiny it had been little more than an irritating impediment in the way of reform. Now toleration was itself raised to a moral ideal, and the Government confined itself to the role of arbiter and keeper of the peace. Indian religious belief, and the social customs bound up with it, were to be left strictly alone. This above all was the message of the Queen's Proclamation assuming the Government of India for the Crown. Although the Queen added to the draft proclamation drawn up by Lord Derby the phrase "firmly relying ourselves on the truth of Christianity and acknowledging the solace of religion," the document made no reference to reform or conversion. Rather it repudiated any "desire to impose our convictions on any of our subjects," and enjoined "all those who may be in authority under us" to abstain from interference with the religious belief or worship of the Indian people.[43]

The Mutiny did not of course completely destroy the vision of an India remodelled along Western Christian lines, free of superstition and idolatry. Few Englishmen could be brought to renounce an ideal which had become so deeply embedded in their whole concept of their mission in India. But they had now of necessity to rely for its realization on the slow growth of education and enlightenment within Indian society. As Kaye described it: "The State had already done as much as it behoved it to do, in vindication of its own religion, before the rebellion of 1857 burst over our heads. And I think it had done all that it prudently could do in the present state of the Hindoo mind, to divest, by authoritative interference, Hindooism of its most revolting attributes. More at some future period may be done, when we see that the harvest is ready; but at present it is wiser, I do not say to leave, but to

---

[43] Queen to Lord Derby, 15 August 1858 in *Letters of Queen Victoria*, III, 379. For the text of the Proclamation see C. Ilbert, *The Government of India* (Oxford, 1898), p. 572.

aid, the Hindoo mind to work out its own regeneration, than to force on from without the desired changes, which, to be effectual, must take growth from within."[44]

This laissez faire view of social change contrasts sharply with the heady exuberance of the pre-Mutiny reformers, and is of course in large measure a response to the harsh experiences of 1857. But it reflects as well the mid-century slackening of evangelical and Benthamite zeal. With less enthusiasm for wholesale reform, there was a greater willingness to wait for the slower processes of internal change to take effect. Although for men like Kaye and Wood the goal remained the same as it had been for the early reformers, they no longer expected to see it realized in their lifetime, nor did they look upon the Government as the instrument by which it would be brought to fruition. Kaye urged the British people, "whose mission I firmly believe it is, in God's good time, to evangelize the great Indian races" simply to be patient and to work quietly for the advancement of India. "Ignorant, unreflecting Christian zeal" or "any arrogant rushings-in," he pointed out, would only "retard the coming which they seek to accelerate."[45] In a similar vein Sir Charles Wood called for "the blessing of God on the missionary exertions which are being carried on" and expressed his faith in the inherent strength of Christianity "promoted in its true spirit by voluntary effort"; but he cautioned against any attempt to involve the Government.[46] Even the Court of Directors, in one of its last dispatches, entertained "the sanguine hope" that ultimately the healthy progress of society in India would be secured without compulsion, provided the administration were conducted with honesty and justice and the country remained open to missionary activity.[47] The vision of a regenerated India remained, after the Mutiny as before; but the "sanguine

---

[44] Kaye, *Christianity in India*, p. 497.

[45] *Ibid.*, pp. 500, 505-06.

[46] Wood to Canning, 10 September 1859, Wood Papers.

[47] Dispatch of 10 March 1858, Judicial Dispatch No. 8 of 1858.

hopes" of a laissez faire policy alone recalled the old reforming zeal.

## Legislation and the Hindu Social Order

Several measures of social reform did reach the statute book during the 1860's, but few involved any direct challenge to the structure of Hinduism. In some cases the new legislation merely continued the policy of separating the Government from Hindu religious practices. In 1833 the Government was requested by the Home authorities to sever all connection with the affairs of Indian religious institutions. During the subsequent decade the Government officials who had acted as managers of Hindu temples were replaced by local committees, and all pilgrim taxes were abolished, but the grants and allowances previously sanctioned for the maintenance of these temples were continued. They were regarded as endowment property which could not be resumed without breach of faith on the part of the Government. In 1858 the Bombay Missionary Conference demanded resumption of these grants on the ground that they constituted patronage of idolatry by the Government of India. They claimed that even if these endowments had been confirmed by treaty, there existed a higher obligation "imposed by God himself" which forbade their continuance. The Bombay Government refused to abrogate the grants. It insisted that they were held upon an indisputable title with which the Government had no right to interfere.[48] The Secretary of State upheld the Bombay Government. But on reading over the papers he discovered that the missionary allegations were not totally incorrect, for several of these endowments (though not the temples themselves) were under the superintendence of Government officers. The withdrawal of the Government from interference with the religious institutions of the country, he pointed out, was so far not com-

[48] Memorial of Bombay Missionary Conference, 22 February 1858, Home Public, 3 September 1858, No. 83. Minute by Lord Elphinstone, Governor of Bombay, *ibid.*, No. 84.

plete.[49] Accordingly an act was passed (No. XX of 1863), under which the entire superintendence of all Indian religious institutions and their endowments was transferred to trustees selected by the institutions themselves. Although prompted by a missionary petition, the act did not embody the missionary demands, for the endowments themselves remained intact. It simply extended and confirmed the principle of religious neutrality, and laid down firm rules to secure it.

An act passed in 1866, legalizing the remarriage of native converts to Christianity, likewise involved no attack upon Hindu customs. It merely permitted a Christian convert, deserted or repudiated by his spouse, to marry again without being guilty of bigamy. It was, as Maine pointed out when introducing the bill, "a law of liberty," freeing Christian converts from certain disabilities and working no hardship upon the Hindu.[50] In this respect it contrasts sharply with Dalhousie's legislation permitting the remarriage of Hindu widows, which was enacted in the teeth of a strong conviction in Hindu society that widows should remain unmarried. The debates on the 1866 act indicate indeed how far the pendulum had swung in the other direction. Maine charged that the Government had now become so solicitous of Hindu customs and feelings that it actually treated Christians with less consideration than other Indian communities. In legislating for Indian Christians, he said, "the very molehills of Hindu prejudice are exaggerated into mountains; and difficulties which in everyday Indian life crumble away at a touch are assumed to be of stupendous importance. . . . We do this because the converts are of our own faith, and because we are tender of our character for impartiality. But I do not know that we are entitled to be unjust even for the sake of seeming to be impartial. Surely the duty of the British Government to Christian converts is too plain for mistake. We will not force any man to be a Christian; . . . but if he chooses to

---

[49] Dispatch of 24 February 1859, Legislative Dispatch No. 2 of 1859.
[50] Speech of 4 November 1864 in Legislative Council, *Proceedings*, III, 163.

become a Christian, it would be shameful if we did not protect him in [the] rights of conscience."[51]

In fact, however, the Indian Christians were not badly treated, and although they were rarely accepted on terms of social equality, their loyalty won them in time something of a favored position. Despite a widespread belief to the contrary in England, no restrictions were placed upon the employment of Indian Christians by the Government. Extensive inquiries carried out in 1858 indicated that the apparent discrimination against them was due solely to their small numbers, their lack of education, and their reluctance to enter fields of employment outside mission work.[52]

In the decade after the Mutiny only one measure was enacted directly interfering with any Hindu social custom—the prohibition in 1865 of hook swinging at the Charak Puja festival. Two other measures were considered but never reached the statute book: the regulation of the practice of taking sick people to the riverside to die, and the suppression of polygamy. None of these customs were integral parts of the Hindu religion, nor were they at all widely practiced. Yet in each case the attempt at suppression aroused a good deal of controversy both in the official Indian world and among the educated classes of Bengal. They provide therefore perhaps the clearest illustration of the Government's reluctance to move in matters of social reform, and thus warrant some consideration.

Hook swinging was a practice by which a devotee would suspend himself from a raised pole by hooks pushed through the flesh of his back in order to demonstrate his religious devotion and his release from the feelings of pain. The practice was most prevalent in Bengal, where it was performed before the crowds gathered at the Charak Puja festival.[53] Its sup-

[51] Speech of 31 March 1866, *Proceedings*, v, 169.

[52] Home Public, 20 August 1858, No. 51-53.

[53] For a detailed description see J. A. Powell, "Hook-Swinging in India," *Folk-Lore* (1914), xxv, 147-97.

pression, as "a cruel and demoralizing public spectacle," was first considered in 1856, when the Court of Directors asked the Government of India to initiate inquiries on the subject. The question was revived in 1859 by the Secretary of State, Lord Stanley, who considered hook swinging an observance "flagrantly opposed to the dictates of common humanity" and urged the Bengal Government to see what could be done to discourage it.[54] The District Officers of Bengal, whose opinions were solicited on the question, generally deprecated any legislative interference. Several contended that hook swinging was an "innocent amusement" much like the exhibitions of fire eating or sword swallowing seen at an English fair. The performer, they said, suffered little pain (indeed he was often supported by ropes), and the performance as a whole had no demoralizing effect on the assembled crowd. The majority of the officers consulted agreed with the Secretary of State that the practice was cruel and degrading, but they preferred to rely upon education and "the progress of civilization" for its eradication. The Commissioner of Patna even suggested that some good might be done by "causing Hindoo youths in our Schools and Colleges to write Essays on the practice of hook swinging, and its effects on the spectators and society in general." Several officers also recommended that the Government try to enlist on its side "the sympathies of influential landed proprietors" and to use their influence in suppressing the practice. With only one or two exceptions, however, they all considered outright prohibition impolitic and mistimed.[55] The Lieutenant-Governor of Bengal, J. P. Grant, agreed. He was convinced the practice was already declining as the result of "some real mental progress amongst the gentry and educated class of Bengal," and he held out to the Government the prospect of "rapid and visible decay," without irritating

[54] Dispatch of 24 February 1859, Judicial Dispatch No. 2 of 1859.
[55] For the district reports see Home Public, 10 February 1860, No. 32.

or alarming anyone, once he had obtained the cooperation of "the leading men of the people."[56]

Matters remained at this point until 1864 when the Bengal Government, dissatisfied with the pace of progress, reopened the question. It now recommended outright prohibition, claiming that the Government had an obligation to throw its weight behind "the tendency of enlightened public opinion"; and it bulwarked its claim with an expression of support from the British Indian Association. Its secretary, Jotindra Mohan Tagore, boldly informed the Bengal Government that "there is scarcely a single educated native of Bengal who does not hate these revolting practices and anxiously wish for their cessation." Although he pointed out that it was of the utmost importance for the Government to avoid all semblance of interference with the customs associated with religion, he maintained that "the barbarities of the Churruck Poojah" were not an integral part of the Hindu religion and could be suppressed without alarming the people or damaging the Government's reputation for neutrality.[57] With this statement in hand the Government of India at last on 15 March 1865 issued a Resolution prohibiting the practice of hook swinging.

Decisive action came therefore only when the Government had convinced itself that legislation posed no threat to the Hindu religion and that it would be supported by all of the educated and influential classes in Indian society. Even such a relatively minor measure as the suppression of hook swinging had to be carefully weighed and its impact on Indian opinion closely assessed before it could be enacted. Often, indeed, the carrying out of reform was left to the leaders of Indian society, particularly to the zamindars, with little more than encouragement from the Government. The taluqdar association in Oudh, for instance, was entrusted by Lord Can-

[56] Minute of 31 December 1859, *ibid.*, No. 33.

[57] Sec. Govt. Bengal to Sec. B.I.A., 31 October 1864, Home Public, 24 March 1865, No. 137. Sec. B.I.A. to Sec. Govt. Bengal, 4 February 1865, *ibid.*, No. 138.

ning with responsibility for the suppression of female infanticide in that province, while the British Indian Association was asked to exert its influence on behalf of reform in Bengal, and was invariably consulted whenever legislation was proposed. Sir Charles Wood outlined the course he felt should be pursued in a letter to the Bengal Government in 1864 when they summarily ordered the removal of the burning ghats from the banks of the Hooghly: "The natives ought to have been consulted, measures taken to reconcile them to such a departure from their ancient habits, and to point out the advantage to themselves. They ought to be made willing co-operators with you in what you propose to do. I cannot think that issuing an order to discontinue a religious custom of many years standing could be prudent, and it may be very dangerous. . . . After our experience of the danger of shocking religions we should be very cautious."[58] This emphasis on cooperation clearly reflects the Government's own hesitancy and timidity in the unsettled days after the Mutiny but it was reinforced by the laissez faire sentiments of the mid-Victorian Englishman. In his view, reform, to be effective, had to arise from the transformation of society itself and express the aspirations of those whom it would affect.

Most educated Indians looked with favor on the eradication of those cruel practices and degrading rites associated with the Hindu faith. Their Western education and Anglicized way of life naturally inclined them to this course, and it was strengthened after the Mutiny by their abhorrence of the bigotry and ignorance in the rebel camp. Orthodox fanaticism, they realized, posed a direct challenge to the new learning on which they based their hopes for Bengal. But at the same time most Indian reformers were reluctant to see the British Government play too prominent a part in the promotion of reform. Much as they detested the "revolting practices" so common in popular Hinduism, they had no desire for rash interference on the part of the Government. Such action might

[58] Wood to Cecil Beadon, Lt.-Gov. Bengal, 26 April 1864, Wood Papers.

well give serious offence to the religious feelings of the bulk
of the people and could easily arouse suspicion among the
ill-informed. They preferred, with Prasanna Kumar Tagore,
to leave matters "in the hands of the schoolmaster, who is
already abroad and doing well."[59] Or, as the British Indian
Association summarized it in a letter to the Bengal Government: "Social and religious changes must be effected by the
natural progress of society; intellectual and moral development is the only right road to that progress; and the legal
authority of the Government should be the last resource of the
community to put down any social abuse or promote any
religious or moral reform."[60] This objection to reform imposed
by Government, particularly by an alien government, grew
stronger with the rise of nationalism and motivated, for instance, B. G. Tilak's opposition to the Age of Consent Bill
in 1891. Tilak objected not so much to the provisions of the
bill, which prohibited the consummation of marriage by young
children, as to the claim of a foreign government to impose
its will upon the domestic arrangements of Hindu families.[61]

Among the few Hindu reformers willing to see the Government take an active part in reform were the dedicated
Ishwarchandra Vidyasagar and the fiery Keshab Chandra
Sen. A crusader for the total abolition of all practices opposed
to logic or reason, Keshab advocated the removal of caste
distinctions, the emancipation of women, the prohibition of
child marriage, and the encouragement of widow remarriage.
A leading member of the Brahma Samaj, he stormed the
country during the 1860's preaching his doctrine of radical
reform; when forced out of the Samaj in 1866 by the more

[59] Minute of 25 September 1865, Home Public, December 1866, No. 12.
See also "Lord Stanley on the Religious Policy," in Nares Chandra Sen-
Gupta, ed., *Selections from the Writings of Hurrish Chunder Mookerji* (Cal-
cutta, 1910), pp. 332-35.

[60] Sec. B.I.A. to Sec. Govt. Bengal, 4 February 1865, Home Public, 24
March 1865, No. 138.

[61] See Charles H. Heimsath, "The Origin and Enactment of the Indian
Age of Consent Bill, 1891," *Journal of Asian Studies* (1962), XXI, 499-500.

conservative Debendranath Tagore, he formed his own competing (and highly successful) "Brahma Samaj of India."[62] Keshab had no qualms about government interference and repeatedly urged the Government to implement his program by legislative action. His proposals kindled a sympathetic response among the British in India, and even excited the admiration of the Christian missionaries, who had long denounced many of the same practices. But they were never taken up by the Government. His only mark on the statute book was Act III of 1872, which provided a form of civil marriage for those like the Brahma Samajists who were outside any recognized faith. Despite their sympathy with the ideals of the Brahma Samaj, the Government steadfastly refused after the Mutiny to move against an abuse simply because it was under fire by a small band of radical reformers. The vast dead weight of orthodox sentiment could no longer be pushed rudely to one side. Nor could the opposition of even the moderate reformers to Government intervention in Indian social life be complacently ignored. To this the fate of the proposals to suppress polygamy and exposure at the riverside bear witness.

Polygamy among Hindus was practically confined to the Kulin Brahmins of Bengal, but in that community it imposed considerable hardship upon the girls. The problem arose from the fact that the Kulins were one of the highest Brahmin castes and at the same time hypergamous; that is, the Kulin boy could take a wife from any one of several lower castes, while the Kulin girl could marry only within the immediate sub-caste group. Profiting from this high status and wide range of marriage opportunities, the Kulin man would often marry a large number of women whom he never intended to support and rarely saw after the marriage ceremony. The girl's parents would thus have the satisfaction of seeing their daughter married, for a substantial sum of money, to a high-

[62] J. N. Farquhar, *Modern Religious Movements in India* (New York, 1915), pp. 41-46.

caste Brahmin, but the girl herself was condemned to a life of virtual celibacy.[63]

The evils of this system were first brought to the notice of the Government in 1855 in a petition presented by the Maharaja of Burdwan, but the Mutiny intervened before any action could be taken. In 1863 further petitions urging the suppression of Kulinism were submitted by members of the Hindu community of Bengal. In response to this agitation the Bengal Government requested permission to introduce into its Legislative Council a bill for the prohibition of polygamy outside those limits clearly recognized by Hindu law—as when a wife was barren or sickly. The Government of India questioned whether popular feeling was prepared for legislation on this subject, and expressed its unwillingness to give that explicit sanction to other forms of polygamy which the proposed law would involve. A committee appointed to study the question was unable to recommend any legislation that would curb the abuses of Kulinism without also putting the Government in the position of sanctioning the general Hindu law of polygamy. The strongest opposition to legislative interference came, interestingly enough, from the Indian members of the committee. Three of the four—Ramnath Tagore, Digambar Mitra, and Jaykrishna Mukherji—held that the evils of polygamy had been much exaggerated, and were already on the decline. The whole question, they said, could "without injury to public morals, be left for settlement to the good sense and judgment of the people." Only the militant Ishwarchandra Vidyasagar maintained that the evils were not exaggerated and that legislation was necessary in order to bring about their complete suppression. Coupled with the difficulties of legislation, this division of opinion among the Indians themselves relieved the Government of any obligation it might have felt

[63] See J. H. Hutton, *Caste in India* (Oxford, 1961), pp. 53-54. In the case of Kulin women there was of course often no other way of getting them married at all.

to proceed further; and the question was dropped at this point.[64]

The practice of taking sick people to the river to die was widespread in the districts bordering the Ganges in Bengal, for immersion in the sacred stream at the moment of death was believed to assure salvation for the dying. In spite of its innocent appearance the Bengal Government considered this practice "barbarous and cruel," because a Hindu, once taken to the riverside, was looked upon with disgust as an outcast should he ever recover and return home; consequently, there was, as the Government put it, "a very powerful inducement to the commission of murder" on the part of relatives anxious to insure the death of a sick man. During the course of its regular surveillance of the vernacular press the Bengal Government in 1865 came across an article in the *Dacca Prakash* condemning the practice and urging its suppression. Delighted to find confirmation of its belief in a native newspaper, the Bengal authorities forwarded the article to the Government of India, commenting that "when the practice is thus denounced by the Hindoos themselves, it appears . . . that the time has come when the Government should interfere to put a stop to it."[65] The Government of India in its reply doubted whether much weight could be attached to one newspaper article "as representing the prevailing feeling on the subject among the real Hindoo community of Lower Bengal."[66] But the Bengal Government was nothing if not persistent. It cited numerous newspaper articles condemning the practice, and in 1866 urged that "such being the tone in which the question has been discussed . . . the Government may approach it without the least alarm and with the well founded assurance that whatever measures it may be thought expedient to adopt . . . would

---

[64] C. E. Buckland, *Bengal Under the Lieutenant-Governors* (Calcutta, 1902), I, 324-26.

[65] Sec. Govt. Bengal to Sec. Govt. India, 12 July 1865, Home Public, August 1865, No. 21.

[66] Sec. Govt. India to Sec. Govt. Bengal, 10 August 1865, *ibid.*, No. 23.

command the assent of many intelligent Hindoos and would soon be generally acquiesced in." The Government suggested that a notice to the Police be required before anyone could be taken to the river, and that all those responsible for the act be subject to two years' imprisonment if proper notice were not given.[67]

In the ensuing discussion little enthusiasm for the measure appeared either in the Central Government or among the educated Indian community. While admitting that the practice was "very repulsive," the Indians consulted unanimously deprecated government interference. The practice was one, they insisted, "which should be removed by education and enlightenment, and not by the hand of law." Legislative intervention would only "evoke the most serious discontent."[68] The Viceroy, John Lawrence, acknowledged that he too would like to see the practice discontinued, but he could not bring himself to believe that there was any real intent on the part of friends and relatives to accelerate the death of sick people; and he agreed with Grey and Maine on his Council that the proposed legislation "would evidence a reckless disregard of Native feelings and prejudices" ill-suited to an alien government. With them he preferred, in view of the obvious reluctance of the Indian community to see the Government take action in this matter, to rely for the eradication of the practice upon "the growing disbelief of the educated and influential classes in its efficacy."[69]

To rouse the Government to action in the political climate of the 1860's, then, a social evil had to be a great deal more obnoxious than exposure on a riverbank, and condemned by a wider circle than the *Dacca Prakash* and the Bengal Government. No amount of enthusiasm among a small band of

[67] Sec. Govt. Bengal to Sec. Govt. India, 31 August 1866, Home Public, December 1866, No. 11.

[68] Minute by Digambar Mitra of 25 October 1866, *ibid.*, No. 12.

[69] Notes by W. Grey of 26 October 1866, H. S. Maine of 30 October 1866, and J. Lawrence of 27 October 1866. See also Sec. Govt. India to Sec. Govt. Bengal, 14 November 1866, *ibid.*, No. 13.

Brahma Samajists could counterbalance the potential opposition of the large masses of conservative and orthodox opinion. Nor could it overcome the Government's determination to avoid controversial legislation. As the British refused after the Mutiny to listen to the demands of the evangelicals for a "Christian" policy, so too they refused to be dragged along in the wake of the advanced party of Indian reformers. Where once they had solicited the support of Indian opinion for a joint assault on "immoral customs," they now drew back from the proposals put forward by British and Indian alike.

## Education and the Mutiny

The impact of the Mutiny on the diffusion of education was much less pronounced than in the case of social reform. The English belief in the value of Western education remained unshaken throughout the trials of 1857, and the schools generally remained open except in those areas which had lapsed into anarchy. In the Punjab and Bengal, in fact, the schools were scarcely affected by the rebellion, and attendance quickly regained its former levels.[70] Even in the North-Western Provinces the schools survived in several districts. The Commissioner of Meerut reported that the village schools there had stayed open even after the British officers had fled. When asked to account for this "the people stated their intention to have maintained the schools, even if the rule of India had changed hands."[71] The schools were not, except in rare instances,[72] marked out as the objects of special vengeance by

[70] W. D. Arnold, "Report on Public Instruction in the Punjab 1857-58," For. Dept., Part A, 30 March 1860 (Supplement), No. 86. By May 1858 old attendance levels had been reached even in the Delhi Territory and expansion had recommenced.

[71] F. Williams, Commissioner of Meerut, to Sec. Govt. N.W.P., 15 November 1858, *Narratives of Mutiny in the Northwest Provinces*, p. 67. A. O. Hume, Collector of Etawah, reported that "not only have the schools remained open, in many instances all through these troubles, but in some cases the Zemindars have themselves paid the Masters . . . of course the number of pupils was, and still is, less than formerly." *Ibid.*, p. 389.

[72] C. B. Thornhill commented that in Agra "a special malignity appears

the rebels, although they suffered of course along with other British property. The Punjab authorities assured the Central Government that apart from a few isolated incidents in Rawalpindi District "there was no manifestation of fanaticism, prejudice, or mistrust on the part of the people against our educational institutions."[73]

Few Englishmen looked upon the expansion of Western education as one of the major causes of the revolt. Some evangelicals, such as Donald Macleod, asserted that the Government schools had spread disaffection by teaching atheistic and deistic ideas. Among the compilers of virulent proclamations, he said, "none have been more zealous or more bitter than the men reared in Government Colleges, deriving inspiration from the ideas which they have there imbibed."[74] Others, like Lord Ellenborough, who stood at the opposite end of the political spectrum, saw in the revolt confirmation of their belief that aid to missionary schools was the source of widespread discontent. Great is the danger, he pointed out, "not to our success in education alone, but to the peace of the Empire, by thus exciting as we practically do, the apprehension that the Government desires through education to convert the people."[75] Beyond this Ellenborough alleged that even the Government schools had aroused a good deal of unrest. As evidence he pointed to the education policy pursued in the province of Bihar. There the Government officers charged with introducing an expanded network of schools had encountered strong local opposition. The people were convinced,

---

to have been shewed [sic] in destroying all educational buildings. The normal school was the first burned and altho' as you know the College is Pukka, they piled up the furniture until the flames caught the great beam." Sec. Govt. N.W.P. to Sec. Govt. India, 29 July 1857, S.C. 25 September 1857, No. 104.

[73] Sec. C. C. Punjab to Sec. Govt. India, 14 August 1858, For. Dept., Part A, 30 March 1860 (Supplement), No. 27.

[74] Minute of 21 June 1858, F.C. 7 January 1859, No. 126.

[75] Letter of 28 April 1858 to the Chairman of the East India Company, Ellenborough Papers.

the Education Inspector, R. B. Chapman, reported in 1856, that the educational system was part of a "general scheme for the forcible conversion of the natives to Christianity." To counter this feeling he announced that schooling was compulsory and that the people should trust the Government not to command anything that was not good for them.[76] As Chapman well knew, this order was contrary to the definite instructions of the Central Government that education was to be offered on a voluntary basis; but he believed, as he explained later, that only a distinct order of Government could ever really evoke the cooperation of the Indian people in schemes for their improvement. "The idea of any Government, and especially of an *alien* Government, 'advising' and 'persuading' is either absolutely unintelligible to the Natives of such a Province as Behar (if not indeed of Asiatics generally), or suggestive only of some secret object which the Government dares not openly command."[77]

This belief in an "Asiatic mind" somehow not open to rational persuasion was by no means peculiar to Chapman; it was, as we shall see, quite common among the British in India at the time. On this occasion, however, Chapman's action only served to exacerbate popular ill will, and when Bihar later became a center of rebellion, it attracted considerable attention in England. It was superb grist for Ellenborough's mill. In April 1858 he addressed a resounding rebuke to Chapman through the Court of Directors:

"It is our intention that it shall be entirely optional with the natives whether they will avail themselves of the facilities of education which we afford to them, or not.

"It is the duty of all public servants to carry out with good faith the declared intentions of the Government under which they act.

[76] "General Report on Public Instruction in the Lower Provinces of Bengal for 1855-56," cited in P.P. 1859, xxiv, Part 1, 6-7.

[77] Chapman to Director of Public Instruction, 30 November 1858, Home Education, 4 March 1859, No. 7.

"A Government must not be supposed to say one thing and mean another. . . .

"The Government will adhere with good faith to its ancient policy of perfect neutrality in matters affecting the religion of the people of India."[78]

Ellenborough further recommended that where schools had been closed on account of the Mutiny "the aid of the Government should not again be afforded, unless there should be an unmistakeable desire on the part of the principal landholders and of the people, that the connection between the Government and the schools should be renewed."[79]

Education doubtless did play some part in stirring up discontent in Bihar. Even there, however, few schools were abandoned after the Mutiny, and the Secretary of State in 1859 could find no evidence for the continued existence of widespread hostility to education.[80] In any case, Bihar stood by itself. Neither Ellenborough nor anyone else could discover further instances in which the introduction of schools had aroused disaffection. For most Englishmen the Mutiny provided instead an opportunity to reaffirm the values of Western education. They insisted that the causes of the outbreak lay not in the spread of knowledge but in the persistence of ignorance. "The condition of popular ignorance," as F. J. Halliday put it, "is everywhere the condition of political danger. . . . The deeper and darker the ignorance, the more determined and persevering should be our endeavours to remove it."[81] They saw in the loyalty of the educated classes ample evidence of the truth of this contention. One District Officer even went so far as to say that "during the outbreak, as far as my experience goes, the most loyal, the most trustworthy were the young men who had received an advanced

[78] Educational Dispatch No. 52 of 13 April 1858, P.P. 1859, xxiv, Part 1, 8.
[79] Letter of 28 April 1858 to the Chairman of the East India Company. Ellenborough Papers.
[80] Educational Dispatch No. 4 of 7 April 1859, P.P. 1859, xxiv, Part 1, 45.
[81] Minute of 19 November 1858, Home Education, 13 January 1860, No. 2.

English education in the Government Institutions. . . . The only approach to the sense of duty which had animated Anglo-Saxons through this struggle was to be found among such educated men."[82] Or, as the Duke of Argyll told the House of Lords in 1859, "The people of India during the last few years [have] been obedient and loyal in proportion to their education and enlightenment."[83]

The educated classes had in fact no other alternative. In the Upper Provinces, where the revolt centered, many of them were Bengalis, as alien as the English, and often employed by the same bureaucratic machine. A Bengali Babu at Farruckhabad or Kanpur, Raikes noted, was in almost as great a peril as a Christian, so long as these cities were in rebel hands. "Not that the Baboo had personally any taste for martyrdom; for to tell the truth, he was the veriest coward under the sun, but simply because the Sepoy instinctively hated the English scholars, as part and parcel of the English community."[84] As a new class who had everything to lose by a resurgence of orthodoxy and fanaticism, the educated necessarily clung to the British standard. Their interests were still intimately bound up with the continuance of British rule, within which alone their hopes for their country could be worked out. This George Campbell had clearly perceived so far back as 1853:

"I do not apprehend by any means so immediately bad a result from the spread of education . . . as has been sometimes prophesied. Bengalese who learn English may become bad subjects and servants, and (if permitted to do so) may write any amount of treason; but I do not in the least apprehend their acting upon it. The classes most advanced in English education, and who talk like newspapers, are not yet those

[82] Commissioner of Meerut to Sec. Govt. N.W.P., 15 November 1858, *Narratives of Mutiny in the Northwest Provinces*, p. 67. See also C. Raikes, *Notes on the Revolt*, pp. 138-39.

[83] Speech of 15 April 1859, Hansard, CLIII, 1784.

[84] Raikes, *Notes on the Revolt*, p. 137.

from whom we have anything to fear; but on the contrary they are those who have gained *everything* by our rule, and whom neither interest nor inclination leads to deeds of daring involving any personal risk. For a long time to come if we incur any political danger, it will be from enemies of the original native stamp."[85]

In 1859 therefore, after reviewing the state of education in India, the Secretary of State urged the Government of India on no account to draw back from "the great duty" of raising the moral, intellectual, and physical condition of the Indian people by means of improved and extended facilities of education.[86] But the work proceeded slowly. At first the financial difficulties in which the Government found itself after the Mutiny stood in the way; throughout 1858 and 1859 the Home Government refused to sanction any increase in expenditure on education over the pre-Mutiny levels. Even after the immediate crisis was surmounted, however, the Government still kept the Education Department on a fairly tight financial rein. They believed that education was primarily a local matter, and that schools, so far as possible, should be self-supporting, financed by fees and by contributions from the wealthier classes. "The part which has to be played by Government is to organize, superintend, and direct the whole system, and to supplement the funds raised locally to such an extent" as might be necessary in each instance. Major reliance was to be placed, according to the principles laid down in the 1854 dispatch, not on Government schools, but on the provision of grants-in-aid to local bodies. In this way the Government's limited funds could go the greatest possible distance, and could help promote the development of a sense of self-reliance and individual initiative among the Indian people.[87]

---

[85] George Campbell, *India As It May Be* (London, 1853), p. 410.

[86] Educational Dispatch No. 4 of 7 April 1859, P.P. 1859, xxiv, Part I, 45.

[87] Financial Dept. Memo of 26 August 1863, Home Education, 21 December 1863, No. 3.

Although this Victorian ideal remained at the center of British educational policy for the remainder of the century, the grant-in-aid system proved to be something less than a panacea for Indian education. It was in fact only fitfully and half-heartedly carried into effect. For this the lack of public interest and the lessons of the Mutiny were jointly responsible. As the Government soon realized, there was little demand for vernacular primary education. The villagers, whom such education was designed to benefit, were able neither to pay for it nor to organize local schools. The State was thus obliged in 1859 to assume direct responsibility, and the provincial governments were authorized to levy a 1 per cent school cess on the land revenue. Yet even that act made little real difference, for none of the local governments, with the single exception of the North-Western Provinces, were prepared to devote much of their time or money to the promotion of vernacular education. The British official, like the well-to-do Indian, found English education far more attractive. This was partly because it provided more immediate and tangible benefits—not only the provision of clerks for government offices (so often alleged as the sole motive for the stress on English education) but the creation of a class of loyal subjects—and partly because there was always a strong and steady demand for instruction in the English language. The local governments continually reported that no school had any chance of success unless the English language was taught.[88] Indian education continued to be dominated after the Mutiny as before by secondary schools teaching in the English language.[89]

The Mutiny made its influence felt upon the educational

[88] In Madras, for instance, the Government introduced the English language in vernacular schools on the grounds that "it was necessary to render the schools popular, attendance at Talook schools at present depending in great measure on the amount of English taught and the stage at which it was introduced." Director of Public Instruction to Sec. Govt. Madras, 11 January 1859, Home Education, 3 June 1859, No. 2.

[89] See A. M. Monteith, "Notes on the State of Education in India 1865-66." See also Table 1.

## TABLE 1

EDUCATION IN INDIA, 1865-1866[a]

| | SCHOOLS | | STUDENTS | |
| | Public | Private | Public | Private |
|---|---|---|---|---|
| *Bengal* | | | | |
| Higher | 50 | 83 | 9,339 | 10,507 |
| Middle | 117 | 840 | 8,124 | 37,924 |
| Lower | 81 | 1,132 | 2,787 | 36,307 |
| Female | 3 | 192 | 153 | 5,070 |
| Total | 251 | 2,252 | 20,403 | 89,808 |
| *North-Western Provinces* | | | | |
| Higher | 5 | 4 | 1,545 | 1,214 |
| Middle | 265 | 78 | 20,206 | 10,232 |
| Lower | 3,097 | 5,161 | 95,535 | 59,720 |
| Female | 497 | 71 | 9,269 | 1,494 |
| Total | 3,864 | 5,320 | 126,609 | 72,660 |
| *Punjab* | | | | |
| Higher | 24 | 18 | 8,140 | 5,297 |
| Middle | 71 | 52 | 6,999 | 1,515 |
| Lower | 1,768 | 3 | 60,373 | 108 |
| Female | 333 | 696 | 6,834 | 12,727 |
| Total | 2,196 | 769 | 82,346 | 19,647 |
| *Madras* | | | | |
| Higher | 13 | 14 | 3,132 | 3,126 |
| Middle | 68 | 169 | 3,786 | 9,762 |
| Lower | 17 | 825 | 498 | 14,636 |
| Female | — | 139 | — | 3,315 |
| Total | 98 | 1,147 | 7,416 | 30,839 |
| *Bombay* | | | | |
| Higher | 9 | 2 | 1,741 | 665 |
| Middle | 165 | 20 | 23,794 | 2,358 |
| Lower | 1,121 | 69 | 67,124 | 4,174 |
| Female | 33 | — | — | — |
| Total | 1,328 | 91 | 92,659 | 7,197 |

(*continued*)

TABLE 1 (*continued*)

|  | SCHOOLS | | STUDENTS | |
|  | *Public* | *Private* | *Public* | *Private* |
|---|---|---|---|---|
| *Oudh* | | | | |
| Higher | 10 | 4 | 1,395 | 1,135 |
| Middle | 34 | 12 | 2,989 | 1,049 |
| Lower | 61 | 36 | 2,004 | 1,240 |
| Female | — | 11 | — | 270 |
| Total | 105 | 63 | 6,388 | 3,687 |
| *Central Provinces* | | | | |
| Higher | 1 | 1 | 270 | 223 |
| Middle | 105 | 11 | 10,033 | 940 |
| Lower | 546 | 680 | 18,984 | 13,774 |
| Female | 92 | — | 2,361 | — |
| Total | 744 | 692 | 31,648 | 14,937 |

ᵃ P.P. 1867-68, L, 37.

NOTE: (1) The higher class schools are those which educate up to the university entrance standard; the lower class schools are strictly elementary and vernacular.

(2) The private schools referred to include only those open to Government inspection; the number of other private schools is quite small.

system indirectly, by discouraging the Government from aiding missionary schools. When the grant-in-aid system was set up in 1854 almost its sole beneficiaries were the mission societies, for there were few other private bodies operating secondary schools in India. Sir Charles Wood and Lord Dalhousie, the authors of the grant-in-aid system, were fully aware of this fact; indeed the new system appealed to them precisely because it would enable them to take the fullest advantage of missionary activity in the field of education. Wood at the time spoke approvingly of "the diffusion of improved knowledge" which the mission societies had brought about in India, and praised their contribution "to the spread of that education which it is our object to promote."[90]

[90] Dispatch of 19 July 1854, P.P. 1854, XLVII, 163.

After the Mutiny, although Ellenborough's charges were
ignored and the grants to mission schools continued, the Government slowly disentangled itself from this intimate connection with missionary education. Applications for aid were
scrutinized with a cold and unsympathetic eye, grants were
doled out sparingly, and on occasion competing mission schools
were even driven out of business.[91] Many school inspectors,
moreover, were agnostics or Broad Churchmen, like W. D.
Arnold in the Punjab, and as such little inclined to go out
of their way to aid missionaries. They much preferred to see
the schools operated efficiently by the Government.[92] There
was no open repudiation of the missionary tie—indeed the
amount disbursed in grants rose slowly from year to year—but
the change in attitude was unmistakable. In 1863 the Church
Missionary Society even petitioned the Secretary of State to
protest against the treatment to which they had been subjected
since the Mutiny. They received a sympathetic hearing from
Sir Charles Wood, who admitted with some regret that the
grant-in-aid system had not made the progress which had
been expected, and he urged the local governments to remove
the impediments which stood in the way of its extension.[93] But
these protests made no mark on the prevailing indifference.
The Government was simply no longer interested in encouraging a system of education which they regarded as a
political liability. And with the continuing decay of evangelical
sentiment at home they were under less and less pressure to
keep up any kind of missionary orientation.

In the face of such official discouragement, the missionaries
began to question the value of their far-flung educational
activity. With the schools so fettered by regulations, they

[91] Syed Nurullah and J. P. Naik, *The History of Education in India* (Bombay, 1951), p. 242. Julius Richter, *A History of Missions in India* (New York,
1908), p. 313.

[92] Richter, *Missions in India*, p. 308.

[93] Dispatch of 23 January 1864, in *Selections from the Records of the Government of India* (1870), LXXVI, 175. Stock, *Church Missionary Society*, II,
531.

were, it was widely felt, rendered almost useless for their primary purpose, that of Christian teaching, and they were in any case producing very few converts. Even in the heart of the Christian district, in Tinnevelly, the C.M.S. won only 36 conversions through its high school in 27 years.[94] Some missionaries as a result urged their fellows to restrict their educational activities and devote more time to preaching in the bazaars. Others maintained that, although conversions were few in number, Christian education still played a vital role in the process of evangelism, for it spread knowledge of the Gospel among the highest classes of Hindus and favorably disposed them toward Christianity. "The general clearing away of ignorance, folly and superstition effected by education," Bishop Cotton pointed out, "are as likely to pave the way for Christ's spirit as the plan of hurrying from village to village, preaching for a day or two, and not reappearing [for a year]."[95] In the end the mission societies usually kept up schools already in operation but put less effort into expansion.

After the Mutiny, then, although the Government reaffirmed the value of education, and set out to widen the educational opportunities available to the Indian people, the amount of actual expansion was relatively limited. The theories of laissez faire and the determination to avoid outbursts of popular discontent between them tightly circumscribed the Government's freedom of action. The one forbade bold programs of State education, while the other ruled out a comprehensive scheme of grants-in-aid to mission schools. Beyond this lay the obstacle posed by a perennial shortage of funds and of trained personnel. The Government was never willing to give education the financial priority it required if real progress were to be made. Nor were they able to make the educational service an attractive alternative to the prestigious I.C.S., which continued to drain off the best and brightest of

[94] Stock, *Church Missionary Society*, II, 530.

[95] Journal entry of 16 March 1860, Cotton, *Memoir*, p. 140. See also C. F. Pascoe, *Two Hundred Years of the S.P.G.* (London, 1901), II, 617.

the young men who annually came out to India. The only possible solution under these circumstances, and that a partial one, lay in the provision of ample grants-in-aid to schools sponsored by the Indian community. Such schools developed slowly, however, and came into prominence only with the

TABLE 2

PUBLIC AND PRIVATE EDUCATIONAL INSTITUTIONS, 1851-1855[a]

|                      | Public (1855) | Missionary (1851) |
|----------------------|---------------|-------------------|
| Arts colleges        | 15            |                   |
| Secondary schools    | 169           | } 91              |
| Primary schools      | 1,202         | 1,099             |
| Professional schools | 13            |                   |
| Total                | 1,399         | 1,190             |

[a] Nurullah and Naik, *History of Education in India*, pp. 255 and 177-78.

PUBLIC AND PRIVATE EDUCATIONAL INSTITUTIONS, 1882[b]

|                      | Public | Private | |
|                      |        | Indian  | Missionary |
|----------------------|--------|---------|-----------|
| Arts colleges        | 38     | 5       | 18        |
| Secondary schools    | 1,363  | 1,341   | 757       |
| Primary schools      | 13,882 | 54,662  | 1,842     |
| Professional schools | 96     | 10      | 18        |
| Total                | 15,379 | 56,018  | 2,635     |

[b] Nurullah and Naik, pp. 255 and 260.

rise of political consciousness in the 1870's. Still, by 1882 the number of aided Indian secondary and primary schools exceeded those run by missionaries, and from that time forward they were looked upon as the major vehicle for the expansion of education in India.[96]

The Mutiny therefore had a significantly different impact upon the growth of Western education and upon the progress

[96] See list of schools in 1882 in Table 2.

of social reform. In the field of education the Mutiny was if anything a spur to redoubled activity. An educated Indian was a loyal subject. Social and religious reform, on the other hand, were no longer compatible with the requirements of political security. It was simply too dangerous to interfere directly with Indian customs and beliefs. The traditional order had a hitherto unsuspected vitality which could not be ignored. At the same time the educated Indian threw his weight into the balance against reform legislation. Almost invariably he preferred to reform his own society in his own way and at his own pace. Neither Indian nor Briton abandoned the goal of eventual social and religious regeneration. Both still looked forward to the growth of a purer morality and a reformed Hinduism, if not a Christian India. But the idea of enforcing it by legislation was of necessity given up, and greater reliance was placed upon the corrosive power of education. Once Western knowledge had permeated Indian society, "superstitious customs" and "idolatrous beliefs" would, it was assumed, disappear of their own accord. In this belief the British and their Indian allies were doomed to disappointment. With the rise of nationalism, political questions took precedence over those of social reform, and orthodox Hinduism even gained in strength, for it gave the Indian a sustenance he could not find in the alien culture of the West. Only after independence did the Government of India once again take up the question of social reform.

CHAPTER IV

# RESTORATION OF THE ARISTOCRACY

THE widespread popular uprising in Oudh during 1857 was a source of bitter disappointment to the British. They had confidently expected that the village occupants, so recently placed in possession of their estates, would come forward in support of the Government. Instead the peasantry rose up against the British and voluntarily subjected themselves to their former masters, the taluqdars. Several District Officers were even forced to undergo the humiliating experience of first begging protection from a taluqdar whom they had stripped of his possessions, and then watching village proprietors whom they had befriended tendering him their allegiance. The result was a growing disillusionment with the village system of land settlement. The British considered themselves betrayed by those in whom they had placed their trust. As Lord Canning commented in October 1858, looking back on the events in Oudh: "Our endeavour to better, as we thought, the village occupants in Oudh has not been appreciated by them. . . . It can hardly be doubted that if they had valued their restored rights, they would have shown some signs of a willingness to support a Government which had revived those rights. But they have done nothing of the kind. The Governor General is therefore of opinion that these village occupants deserve little consideration from us."[1] In a similar vein, Lord Ellenborough remarked of the 1856

[1] Sec. Govt. India to C. C. Oudh, 6 October 1858, F.C. 5 November 1858, No. 193.

The
NORTHWESTERN PROVINCES
and
OUDH

0      50      100      150
Miles

TEHRI
GARHWAL

GARHWAL

DEHRA
DUN

SAHARANPUR

ALMORA

MUZAFFARNAGAR  BIJNOUR

NAINI
TAL

MEERUT  MORADABAD  RAMPUR

BULANDSHAHR  BAREILLY  PILIBHIT

BUDAON

KHERI

ALIGARH

MATHURA  ETAH  SHAHJAHANPUR  SITAPUR  BAHRAICH

FARRUKHABAD  HARDOI  BANDA  GONDA

AGRA  MAINPURI  BARA

UNAO  BANKI  BASTI

ETAWAH  LUCKNOW  FAIZABAD  GORAKHPUR

KANPUR  RAE  SULTANPUR  AZAMGARH

JALAUN  BARELI

FATEHPUR  PRATABGARH  BALLIA

JHANSI  HAMIRPUR  JAUNPUR  GHAZIPUR

BANDA  ALLAHABAD  BENARES

MIRZAPUR

settlement that "Its chivalry was that of Robin Hood, who is said to have robbed the wealthy and to have given to the poor. Robin Hood, however, managed to secure the favour of those to whom he gave his loot. We managed to make them as hostile as those we plundered."[2]

At a loss to explain such apparently irrational behavior, the British concluded that the Indian people were incorrigibly conservative. The pre-Mutiny reformers had believed that human nature was the same everywhere and that all men were educable and rational. On this ground they had built their plans for a regenerated India, with a newly prosperous peasantry as the agents of agrarian progress. The uprising in Oudh rudely shattered this vision. The peasantry, it appeared, clung obstinately to their traditional ways and cared nothing for the benefits Britain offered. Reform was not only pointless but dangerous. As Sir Charles Wood told the House of Commons, "They [the peasants] preferred the former system to that which we had introduced. The mistake we fell into, under the influence of the most benevolent feelings, and according to our notion of what was right and just, was that of introducing a system foreign to the habits and wishes of the people." Henceforth, he said, "we ought to adopt and improve what we find in existence and avail ourselves as far as possible of the existing institutions of the country."[3]

Among those institutions there was one which, after the Mutiny, the British found they could no longer ignore—the taluqdari system of land tenure. During the anarchy in Oudh they saw the taluqdars resume control of their old estates, with the willing acquiescence of the villagers, and then stand forth as the leaders of the insurrection. Consequently the British soon came to the conclusion that, as Robert Montgomery put it, "the superiority and influence of

[2] Undated memo 1858, Ellenborough Papers.

[3] Speech of 13 August 1860, Hansard, CLX, 1196. See also letter of Wood to Canning, 10 October 1859, Wood Papers.

these Talookdars form a necessary element in the social constitution of the Province."[4] More significantly, they realized
that a class with such widely acknowledged influence could,
if properly conciliated, prove a useful instrument in restoring
order and tranquillity. This new policy of conciliation developed slowly, however, for it was so completely at odds
with all the assumptions of pre-Mutiny British land policy.
Ever since they had first ventured into Oudh the British had
looked upon the taluqdars with hostility, and had denounced
them as an incubus pressing down upon the countryside. This
prejudice lingered on into the early days of the Mutiny.
Throughout 1857 the Government remained convinced that
the 1856 settlement was inherently just, and that the taluqdars
deserved to be stripped of the possessions they had extorted
by fraud and violence. In July the Governor-General summarily rejected a proposal put forward by the Commissioner
of Benares that the village settlement be cancelled in order to
obtain aid from the taluqdars in the relief of Lucknow.[5] Yet
from the beginning of the revolt the Government encouraged
overtures on an individual basis to several of the more prominent taluqdars. They were particularly anxious to win over
Raja Man Singh, who exercised immense influence throughout
Faizabad District, and who in July still remained loyal. No
man, Wingfield said, "has more influence or possesses a higher
reputation for courage and ability."[6] He requested, and received, permission to advance him Rs. 50,000. In September
the Government went a step further. Canning authorized Sir
James Outram, the Chief Commissioner of Oudh, to "promise
to any Landed Proprietor who deserves well of the Government and who has suffered by the summary settlement, that
. . . his case shall be heard anew and that he shall certainly

---

[4] Oudh Administration Report 1858-59, P.P. Lords 1859, Session II, VIII, 42.
[5] H. C. Tucker to G.G., 12 July 1857, S.C. 18 December 1857, No. 673.
G.G. to H. C. Tucker, 17 July 1857, *ibid.*, No. 676.
[6] Wingfield to Sec. Govt. India, 4 July 1857 and 14 July 1857, S.C. 25
September 1857, Nos. 519 and 548.

not be worse off than he was before our rule." A general Proclamation to this effect was issued on 20 September, and personal letters were sent to Man Singh and several other taluqdars, promising restoration of their estates if they continued "to give effective proof of fidelity and good will to the British Government." At the same time, however, Canning flatly refused to "promise a general reversal of the settlement as an unjust one," although he admitted that in some instances "it has borne hardly upon the chiefs."[7] The taluqdars were warned that if they took arms against the British they would lose all their possessions.

By the end of the year the British position in Oudh had become, if anything, more desperate than before. Apart from Outram's token force at the Alambagh, no Englishmen remained in Oudh, and the people were universally hostile. The Chief Commissioner was therefore all the more anxious to win over the taluqdars. With their assistance, and utilizing their influence over the people, the province could be quickly pacified; otherwise each town and fort would have to be reduced individually by a large British force. Outram accordingly suggested, in a memorandum of 15 January 1858, that the taluqdars be promised restoration of all their former holdings, despite their rebellion, if they now cooperated with the British Government. "I see no prospect of restoring tranquillity," he said, "except by having recourse for the next few years to the old talookdaree system." The village proprietors, he maintained, "have not influence or weight enough" to make their support of any real value.[8]

Canning did not at once adopt this proposal. Instead in March 1858, on the fall of Lucknow, he issued a Proclamation confiscating to the British Government all proprietary right in the soil in Oudh. Five named landholders, among them the Raja of Balrampur, were excepted and confirmed in their

[7] Canning to Outram, 17 September 1857, S.C. 18 December 1857, No. 613-14.

[8] Memorandum of 15 January 1858, F.C. 5 November 1858, No. 192.

hereditary possessions. For the rest only their lives and honor were guaranteed; further indulgence was at the discretion of the Government. When he received notice of the proclamation, Outram protested vigorously against its apparent harshness. He was convinced that confiscation would render hopeless the attempt "to enlist the landholders on the side of order." As soon as they heard that the Government intended to confiscate their rights, they would betake themselves to their domains and "prepare for a desperate and prolonged resistance." In any case, he said, the landholders "were most unjustly treated under our settlement operations" and should be looked upon as "honourable enemies" rather than as rebels deserving severe punishment. He concluded by putting forward once again his proposal that the taluqdars be given back all their former possessions.[9]

Canning agreed to mitigate the apparent severity of the proclamation by inserting an additional paragraph holding out a large measure of indulgence to those who came forward promptly. Beyond this he authorized the Oudh Government to promise restoration of their estates to men such as Man Singh, who had sided with the rebels, provided they could advance a fair claim to the property, and now lent "hearty support to the British Government in re-establishing order."[10] But Canning stood by the Proclamation as a whole. He insisted that confiscation was the only way to avoid the appearance of rewarding rebellion. To have offered land to men in arms against the Government, he said, would have been "to treat the rebels not only as honourable enemies but as enemies who had won the day." He still denied that justice demanded any reversal of the 1856 settlement. His intention, he told Outram, was to scrutinize the claims of every landholder, and "to give back to each Talookdar just as much as he may be found to

[9] C.C. Oudh to Sec. Govt. India, 8 March 1858, S.C. 30 April 1858, No. 116.
[10] Sec. Govt. India to C.C. Oudh, 10 March 1858, S.C. 30 April 1858, No. 119; Sec. Govt. India to C.C. Oudh, 28 March 1858, S.C. 28 May 1858, No. 394.

deserve, whether his claims rest upon active good service or upon early submission and reconciliation." This could be done only if the land had first been confiscated.[11]

Similar sentiments were voiced by Charles Wingfield, the former Commissioner of Bahraich and later as Chief Commissioner a dedicated protagonist of the taluqdar system. In February 1858 he wrote from Gorakhpur urging that no leniency be shown to those taluqdars who "have taken an active part against us." The taluqdars of Bahraich, he said, had no excuse whatever for rebellion, as they had lost few villages at the settlement and were not subject to the pressure put upon chiefs nearer Lucknow by the rebel court; yet they were "among our most bitter enemies." They had rebelled, he continued, not "in revenge for our treatment of them at settlement" but simply because British rule compelled them to obey the law and pay their taxes regularly. Little encouragement would be held out to loyalty in the future if such men were to be treated with generosity.[12]

The Proclamation had in the end very little tangible effect upon the settlement of the province. As Outram had predicted, it prolonged the rebellion for several months. The taluqdars were convinced that Canning really meant to confiscate their lands, and so remained in arms. Yet the provincial authorities from the outset ignored the confiscation clauses, and made no attempt to judge the merits of individual claims to land. The taluqdars eventually emerged in a far stronger position than Canning had originally intended. Outram initiated this policy by forwarding a covering letter with each copy of the Proclamation. He promised the taluqdars that no land would be confiscated if they submitted, and that claims to land held before annexation would be reheard. This letter implied, as W. H. Russell put it, "Don't mind the Governor General; his

[11] Canning to Outram, 29 March 1858, Canning Papers; Sec. Govt. India to C.C. Oudh, 31 March 1858, S.C. 30 April 1858, No. 120.

[12] Commissioner Gorakhpur to Sec. Govt. India, 6 February 1858, Canning Papers Miscellaneous No. 273.

TABLE 3

OUDH LAND SETTLEMENT SYSTEM[a]

I. SETTLEMENT OF 1856-1857

| Holders | Villages | Revenue Demand |
|---|---|---|
| Taluqdars | 13,640[b] | Rs. 35 lakhs |
| Villagers holding land formerly in taluqas | 9,900 | 32 " |
| Villagers continued in possession | 11,650 | 38 " |
| Rent free villages | 1,670 | (6) " |
| Total | 36,870 | Rs. 105 lakhs |

II. REVISED SETTLEMENT OF 1858-1859

| Holders | Villages | Revenue Demand |
|---|---|---|
| Taluqdars | 22,650[b] | Rs. 62 lakhs |
| Villagers holding land formerly in taluqas | 906 | 4 " |
| Villagers continued in possession | 11,650 | 38 " |
| Rent free villages | 1,670 | (6) " |
| Total | 36,870 | Rs. 104 lakhs |

III. CHANGES IN LAND HOLDING AS A RESULT OF 1858-1859 SETTLEMENT

| Nature of Change | Villages | Revenue Demand |
|---|---|---|
| Settled as before annexation | 27,100 | Rs. 77 lakhs |
| Continued in 1856 status | 3,600[c] | 14½ " |
| Settled with new holders | 4,500[d] | 12½ " |
| (confiscated for rebellion) | | (9½) " |
| Total | 35,200 | Rs. 104 lakhs |

[a] The figures given here have been rounded off and are approximate only. The totals do not always agree, for the sources from which the statistics have been taken are themselves internally inconsistent. The major source of settlement data is Major Barrow's Report on Settlement Operations in Oudh, dated 24 June 1859 (Political Collections to Dispatches, Vol. 17, Dispatch No. 33 of 1860, Part II, Collection 37, India Office Library.)

[b] Out of 23,500 villages included in taluqas upon annexation, 13,640 were settled with taluqdars and 9,900 with other claimants in the 1856 summary settlement. Upon re-settlement during 1858-1859, 9,000 of these villages were restored to the taluqdars, giving them total holdings of 22,650. The 906 villages still settled with small proprietors represent villages redeemed

bark is worse than his bite; come in at once to me and I'll make it all right for you and your lands."[13] However, when Robert Montgomery took over as Chief Commissioner in April few taluqdars had submitted, and pressure was mounting for an early settlement. The military, in particular, were anxious to avoid an extensive campaign for the recovery of Oudh in the autumn. Montgomery therefore opened negotiations with the taluqdars through Major L. Barrow, former Deputy Commissioner of Salone. Barrow was himself very favorably disposed toward the taluqdars as a result of his experiences during the Mutiny, and he looked upon them as the natural leaders of Oudh society. In the ensuing negotiations all pretence of adjudicating claims to land was dropped, and the District Officers were instructed to revert to "the order of things in Oude as regards proprietary right at the time of annexation."[14] As Barrow later pointed out, "a most unreserved settlement" was offered to the taluqdars, for in the absence of military force no other terms could possibly have reduced to submission this powerful body of men.[15] Barrow's efforts

[13] William Howard Russell, My Indian Mutiny Diary (London, 1957), p. 116.

[14] Settlement Circular of 1 May 1858, F.C. 30 December 1859 (Supplement), No. 505.

[15] Letter of 3 January 1866, For. Rev. A., June 1867, No. 30.

---

from mortgage, or resettled as they were in 1856 on account of the rebellion of the old taluqdari proprietor. As a result of the 1858-1859 settlement taluqdars held 63 per cent of the villages, and were responsible for 60 per cent of the revenue, of the province of Oudh.

c Of the 3,600 villages continued in their status as of the 1856 settlement, the majority represent villages which had been mortgaged before annexation and were redeemed during 1856, or which had been improperly taken possession of by government officials or contractors, and were restored to their rightful proprietors in 1856.

d The villages settled with new holders in 1858-1859 comprise primarily those confiscated for rebellion. The majority of those confiscated were resettled with taluqdars as a reward for service during the Mutiny, although some were given as individual villages to other claimants. The most substantial beneficiaries were Man Singh, the Raja of Balrampur, and the Raja of Kapurthala.

achieved rapid success. As word got around of the lenient
treatment being meted out, the taluqdars overcame their
initial distrust of British intentions and flocked into Barrow's
camp. Two-thirds tendered their allegiance before the army
took to the field in October, and the remainder submitted
before the year was out. Only those who remained hostile to
the very end were excluded from settlement. Altogether
some fourteen taluqdars, including the Rajas of Gonda,
Churda, and Tulsipur and the valiant Beni Madho of Shan-

TABLE 4

LANDS CONFISCATED AFTER THE MUTINY[a]

| Province | Total Holdings | Revenue Assessment |
|---|---|---|
| Madras | 0 | 0 |
| Bombay | 12 | Rs. 71,610 |
| Bengal | | |
| (Patna Division) | - | Rs. 1,54,582 |
| Punjab | | |
| (Delhi Division) | - | Rs. 11,916 |
| Oudh | | |
| Lucknow | - | Rs. 2,38,222 |
| Faizabad | - | 65,687 |
| Khyrabad | - | 62,692 |
| Bahraich | - | 5,80,232 |
| Total | | Rs. 9,46,833 |
| North-Western Provinces | | |
| Meerut | 1067 | Rs. 4,34,852 |
| Rohilkhand | 2395 | 5,28,331 |
| Agra | 575 | 2,97,911 |
| Allahabad | 880 | 4,52,128 |
| Benares | 284 | 1,99,370 |
| Jabalpur | 110 | 32,693 |
| Jhansi | 565 | 2,60,989 |
| Total | 5880 | Rs. 22,07,954 |

SOURCES: F.C. 30 Dec. 1859 (Supplement), No. 579-89; and Major Barrow's Report on Settlement Operations in Oudh.

karpur, lost their lands. The others were all reinstated in their former holdings.[16]

When news of the Proclamation reached England, it provoked an immense outcry. The British public, and the Home Government, saw only the harsh confiscation provisions, and not the moderation with which they were carried out. The initial reaction in India had been no less violent. W. H. Russell, the *Times* correspondent, could find no one who approved the policy of confiscation, while John Lawrence was sure that it would "bind all men in one desperate confederation against us."[17] But the most stinging censure of all came from Lord Ellenborough at the Board of Control. Writing to Canning on 19 April 1858, Ellenborough asserted that "this decree, pronouncing the disinherison of a people, will throw difficulties almost insurmountable in the way of the re-establishment of peace," for it "will appear to deprive the great body of the people of all hope upon the subject most dear to them as individuals." In inflated and rhetorical language he went on to point out how the annexation and summary settlement had given just cause for hostility to the people of Oudh. As a result, he said, they "should rather be regarded with indulgent consideration than made the objects of a penalty exceeding in extent and in severity almost any which has been recorded in history as inflicted upon a subdued nation."[18]

Canning refused to be goaded into resignation by Ellenborough's "taunts and sarcasms." In reply he admitted that the 1856 settlement was to some extent impolitic, that many of the taluqdars had legitimate grievances, and that they must therefore "be viewed in a very different light from that in

[16] The total value of land confiscated for rebellion in Oudh was Rs. 9½ lakhs, of which one-half was located in the Bahraich Division. In Bahraich District alone out of 3,000 villages held in taluqdari tenure some 1,850 were confiscated and resettled, mostly with other taluqdars, *Gazetteer of the Province of Oudh*, I, 135. See Tables 3 and 4.

[17] *Indian Mutiny Diary*, p. 115. Lawrence to Mangles 6 May 1858 in Bosworth Smith, *Life of Lord Lawrence*, II, 179.

[18] Secret Committee to G.G., 19 April 1858, Ellenborough Papers.

which rebels in our old provinces are to be regarded."[19] But, he insisted, confiscation and submission must precede mercy and leniency. Throughout Canning justified his Proclamation on the ground that only a positive declaration of confiscation would induce a rebel landholder to submit. "It is in the nature of those to whom the proclamation was addressed," he said, "to care very little for the threats, but to have a great respect for the distinct orders of superior authority."[20] Like so many Englishmen Canning believed that the average Indian was rarely moved by rational argument. Although inherent in much British thinking about India, this belief that the Indians were a different order of people was amply reinforced by the experiences of the Mutiny. A people who could willfully reject the benefits of British rule could hardly be amenable to logical persuasion. They would respond only to peremptory commands and a display of force.

Canning's Proclamation also formed the subject of heated debate in Parliament during May 1858, and almost unseated the Derby Government. The issue owed its appearance in the political arena to the fact that Ellenborough's letter of 19 April, with its censure of Canning, had been made public, in spite of its being a secret letter, almost immediately upon its dispatch. The Opposition charged Ellenborough with undermining the Governor General's authority by publicly proclaiming their censure, a censure which they considered in any case most unjustified. On this ground the Whigs attempted to bring down the Derby Government. A Tory ministry commanding only minority support, the Government owed its existence solely to Whig dissatisfaction with Palmerston's leadership, and was thus extremely vulnerable to attack. The Government made no attempt to defend the publication of the dispatch. That was admitted on all sides to be indiscreet, and was an act for which Ellenborough himself assumed sole responsibility. On 11 May he resigned from the Presidency

---

[19] Canning to Secret Committee, 17 June 1858, P.P. 1859, xviii, 284.
[20] Canning to Court of Directors, 4 July 1858, *ibid.*, p. 293.

of the Board of Control, sacrificing himself to save the Government from almost certain defeat on the issue. Ellenborough's resignation did not silence the critics, however. On 14 May Shaftesbury moved a vote of censure on the Government in the House of Lords. Its defeat by the narrow margin of nine votes emboldened the Opposition to press their attack in the House of Commons, where there was a substantial Whig majority. In the ensuing debate the Whigs closed ranks in defence of Canning's Proclamation. Much like Canning himself, they insisted that "in dealing with Orientals the first step was to show your power." As Sir Charles Wood commented, "the Proclamation is not an undesirable mode of dealing with an Oriental people. First manifest your power, then display your clemency."[21] Wood, and several others, including Viscount Goderich (later Lord Ripon), also defended the Proclamation on the ground that it would enable the Government at last to get rid of the oppressive taluqdar class by confiscating their property. The new appreciation of the taluqdars had not yet made itself felt at home. Beyond this, the Opposition cited Canning's reputation for clemency during the Mutiny, and urged that he was entitled to the confidence of the Government until it was proved that he had embarked on a policy of wholesale confiscation. The tone of Ellenborough's dispatch also came in for criticism. Its aspersions on the validity of the British title to Oudh roused considerable excitement among several members, who felt that such hesitation in asserting British authority would "shake and finally dissolve the magnificent fabric" of the Indian Empire.[22] Derby, and the members of the Government, on their part stood by the principles of Ellenborough's dispatch; they insisted that confiscation would only exasperate the people and protract the war "for months, perhaps years, to come."[23]

[21] Speech of 17 May 1858, Hansard, CL, 779. See also Vernon Smith speech of 14 May 1858, *ibid.*, p. 734.

[22] Speech of Lord John Russell, 14 May 1858, *ibid.*, p. 760.

[23] Derby speech of 14 May 1858, *ibid.*, p. 654.

The debate finally ended inconclusively with withdrawal of the motion of censure on 21 May. When James Outram's opposition to the Proclamation became known, the Whigs retreated hurriedly, Russell voicing the predominant sentiment when he said, "With the conflicting opinions of Outram and Canning, the subject is of the greatest weight and importance, and I must say I am glad to be relieved of the necessity of giving an opinion on it."[24] Behind the sudden collapse of the Opposition, and indeed behind the entire debate, lay, as John Bright noted at the time, "quite as much zeal for what is called 'place' as for the good of India."[25] On this occasion, as so often when Indian questions received sustained Parliamentary attention, considerations of English party politics dictated the course and outcome of the controversy. The Whigs saw in the Oudh Proclamation a handy stick with which to beat the Derby Government. But they soon discovered that they had not, after a bare three months in opposition, sufficiently composed their differences to supplant the Tory ministry with one of their own. So the Derby Government was suffered to exist for another year, and was turned out only in June 1859.

By the time the debate on the Oudh Proclamation had died down, in June 1858, Canning had become a convinced adherent of taluqdari settlement. He now justified the Proclamation on the ground that it facilitated restoration of the taluqdars. Once the land had been confiscated, and thereby cleared of all previous titles, it could more easily be awarded to the taluqdars as a "free and incontestable grant from the paramount power." Canning still had no particular love for the taluqdars as individuals. The majority, he said, were men "distinguished neither by birth, good service, or connexion with the soil" and had risen by usurpation and fraud to positions of power under the Nawabi.[26] But he had now

<hr/>

[24] Russell speech of 21 May 1858, *ibid.*, p. 1,055.
[25] Bright speech of 20 May 1858, *ibid.*, p. 956.
[26] Canning to Secret Committee, 17 June 1858, P.P. 1859, xviii, 287.

decided that the villagers preferred the taluqdari system to their own independence. As he put it in October: "They acted in fact as though they regarded the arrangements made at settlement as valid, and to be maintained, just so long as the British rule lasted and no longer, and as though they wished the talookdar to re-assert his former rights and resume his ancient position over them at the first opportunity. Their conduct amounts almost to the admission that their own rights, whatever these may be, are subordinate to those of the talookdar; that they do not value the recognition of these rights by the ruling authority; and that the Talookdaree system is the ancient, indigenous, and cherished system of the country."[27] There could accordingly be no injustice to them in its restoration. In Canning's eyes, justice and policy alike dictated a return to taluqdari settlement in Oudh.

In fact, however, this alliance with the taluqdars in battle did not necessarily mean that the villagers preferred the taluqdari system of land settlement. To a large extent they simply shared the taluqdars' feelings of loyalty to their deposed sovereign, and the sepoys' fears for their religion. Thus they readily identified themselves with the rebel cause, and were swept up in the current of disaffection. In a common struggle against the hated infidel the villager naturally looked for leadership to the local taluqdar, for with his strong fort and armed retainers he provided the obvious focus for resistance. Moreover as head of the local Rajput lineage he could often lay claim to the allegiance of many village clansmen. Even those who preferred to remain inactive could not avoid at least a nominal submission to the local taluqdar, for they could not otherwise secure themselves from plunder and spoliation.

Nor were the villagers, as it turned out, at all anxious to have the taluqdar back as their landlord. Throughout 1859 and into 1860 the former proprietors hoped that the settle-

[27] Sec. Govt. India to C.C. Oudh, 6 October 1858, F.C. 5 November 1858, No. 193.

ment might be reversed, and they be once again put into possession. Major Barrow noticed that they were only waiting for "the slightest sign of our again relenting in their favor once more to resume the contest warmer than ever."[28] On Man Singh's estates this restive spirit erupted into acts of violence, while the tenants of Hurdeo Baksh "who had been admitted to direct engagements with the Government in 1856 have since proved refractory and have been running about the country to petition Your Lordship." To put a stop to this antagonism Wingfield urged his officers to impress upon the villagers the absolute finality of the revised settlement. He himself took the opportunity of "admonishing and convincing" Hurdeo Baksh's tenants of the "fruitlessness of this opposition."[29]

The taluqdars were themselves surprised at the liberality with which they had been treated. Conscious of the extent of their rebellion, they could not at first believe that the new settlement was really permanent. They thought that their estates had been restored only to purchase their submission, and that they would again be ejected at the next settlement. The very indulgence and generosity of the Government provided a source of suspicion, which Montgomery and Wingfield labored to set at rest throughout 1859. In January Montgomery stated that the land settlement then in progress was to be "final and lasting," and that appeals by disappointed claimants would be discouraged.[30] When he became Chief

[28] Major Barrow, Report on Settlement Operations in Oudh, dated 24 June 1859, in Political Collections to Dispatches, Vol. 17, Dispatch No. 33 of 1860, Part II, Collection 37, India Office Library.

[29] Wingfield to Canning, 24 December 1859, Canning Papers. See also Wingfield to Commissioner Faizabad, 22 August 1860: "C.C. is surprised to find that the zemindars of 1263 still entertain some hopes of being reinstated in their proprietary rights. He was aware that this feeling was generally prevalent in the autumn of last year [but thought it had since disappeared]. You should take every opportunity of dispelling this delusion." File No. 2057, Oudh General Proceedings 1860, U.P. Records, Allahabad.

[30] Circular No. 31 of 28 January 1859, F.C. 30 December 1859 (Supplement), No. 504.

Commissioner, Wingfield argued that the only effective remedy for "this unsettled state of public opinion" would be a formal expression by the Governor-General of the finality and permanence of the settlement. He suggested that this be done by the award of *sanads* to all the principal taluqdars, confirming them in possession of their holdings.[31] Canning agreed that such a measure would be desirable, and authorized Wingfield to prepare the necessary *sanads*. By the terms of the *sanad* each taluqdar received full proprietary title in his estate, subject to the conditions of paying revenue, showing loyalty to the British Government, and preserving "all holding under you . . . in possession of all the subordinate rights they formerly enjoyed."[32]

In October 1859 Canning travelled to Lucknow, where he met the taluqdars in open Durbar, and personally conferred the new *sanads* upon them. Canning also used the occasion to distribute rewards for service during the Mutiny to several of the more prominent taluqdars. Man Singh and Balrampur were each awarded the title of Maharaja Bahadur, and were granted sizable taluqas confiscated from persistent rebels. Man Singh obtained the Gonda estate assessed at Rs. 94,000, and Balrampur the Tulsipur estate valued at Rs. 1,70,000, plus other smaller properties. As a result both came out of the Mutiny very wealthy men, for their estates now comprised some 500 square miles, and provided them with an annual income of up to four lakhs of rupees apiece.[33]

The Durbar and the *sanads* finally dispelled all apprehensions among the taluqdars as to their ultimate fate. In December Wingfield rejoiced in the "unmistakeable signs of satisfaction" which he now saw among them, while Canning noted that, although "many firmly believed to the last moment that some trap was laid for them . . . they were re-assured at

[31] C.C. Oudh to Sec. Govt. India, 4 June 1859, *ibid.*, No. 493.

[32] P.P. 1861, XLVI, 429.

[33] "Memorandum on Talookdars Present at the Durbar of 1861," *ibid.*, p. 480. For taluqdari holdings in Oudh by district see Tables 5 and 6.

last."[34] This re-assurance was, however, obtained only by sacrificing the detailed and thorough investigation of claims to land which customarily accompanied a settlement. No in-

TABLE 5

LAND TENURE IN OUDH BY DISTRICT, 1858-1859

| | | Number of Villages | | |
|---|---|---|---|---|
| Division | District | Taluqdari[a] | Zamindari[b] | Pattidari[c] |
| | Lucknow | 512 | 515 | 458 |
| Lucknow | Rae Bareli | 1,031 | 786 | 15 |
| | Unao | 177 | 635 | 313 |
| | Faizabad | 3,116 | 532 | 1,002 |
| Faizabad | Sultanpur | 2,109 | 324 | 259 |
| | Pratabgarh | 2,904 | 387 | 229 |
| | Gonda | 3,361 | 25 | 772 |
| Bahraich | Bahraich | 3,700 | 91 | — |
| | Mahumdi | 1,702 | 376 | 21 |
| | Durriabad | 1,064 | 626 | 341 |
| Kyrabad | Hardoi | 418 | 1,447 | 680 |
| | Sitapur | 2,564 | 1,069 | 6 |
| | Total | 22,658 | 6,813 | 4,096 |

[a] *Papers Relating to Land Tenures and Revenue Settlements in Oude* (Calcutta, 1865), Appendix E.

[b] *Ibid.*, Appendix H. According to our calculations, approximately 750 villages have been omitted; most of them are probably held on undivided *bhaiacharya* tenure. The term *zamindari* here refers to land held on separate tenure by individual proprietors not entitled to the status of taluqdar. *Pattidari* land is that held on hereditary fractional shares by the members of a co-parcenary village community.

quiry was made into the title on which the taluqdars held their estates, nor were the former village proprietors given any opportunity to put forward claims to land taken from them by the taluqdars. The speed with which the settlement operations were completed, and the harsh treatment meted out to

[34] Canning to Wood, 12 November 1859, Wood Papers; Wingfield to Canning, 24 December 1859, Canning Papers.

the villagers, provoked a good deal of criticism. The strongest opposition came from the District Officers in Oudh. Several openly protested what they considered "simply an act of con-

TABLE 6

REGULAR SETTLEMENT OF THE 1860's

A regular thirty-year settlement was carried out between 1860 and 1878. During the course of this settlement, although no change took place in the pattern of landholding, the number of villages recorded in the settlement records was reduced in number. There is considerable disagreement among the authorities as to the total number of villages and the number held in taluqdari, zamindari, and pattidari tenure. The following is a rough list of the land holdings by district compiled from the *Gazetteer of the Province of Oudh* and the *Memorandum Upon Current Land Revenue Settlements in the Temporarily Settled Parts of India* (Calcutta, 1880), pp. 153-73.

| District | Taluqdari | Zamindari | Pattidari | Total Villages |
|----------|-----------|-----------|-----------|----------------|
| Pratabgarh | 1,779 | 373 | 309 | 2,561 |
| Bara Banki | 850 | 320 | 425 | 1,595 |
| Rae Bareli | 1,037 | 263½ | 190½ | 1,491 |
| Lucknow | 375 | 683 | 421 | 1,479 |
| Sultanpur | 1,022 | 232 | 659 | 1,913 |
| Sitapur | 1,083 | 1,226 | 409 | 2,718 |
| Bahraich | 1,760 | 226 | 275 | 2,261 |
| Kheri | 1,020 | 617 | 69 | 1,706 |
| Gonda | 2,114 | 974 | 448 | 3,536 |
| Unao | 267 | 560 | 364 | 1,194 |
| Hardoi | 392 | 823 | 746 | 1,961 |
| Faizabad | 2,383 | — | — | ca.3,026 |
| Total | 14,022 | 6,297½ | 4,315½ | 25,423 |

The definitive list of taluqdars and their holdings is found in Act I of 1869. Under the provisions of this act taluqdari status was awarded to 276 persons. (For. Pol. A., July 1869, No. 349.) See *List of Talukdars in Oudh* (Lucknow, 1900.)

fiscation of the rights of the many in favour of the few." The small holders ought not to be trampled underfoot, they contended, solely because, as the weaker party, they had been dispossessed during the revolt.[35] Montgomery admitted that

[35] W. Balmain, Deputy Commissioner of Mahumdi, to Barrow, 7 February

"three fourths of the Oude officers are entirely opposed to the Talookdary arrangement," and Wingfield agreed that there was "an intense dislike" of the new revenue system among many civil officers.[36] To a far greater extent than their superiors, the District Officers retained the "levelling leaven" of the pre-Mutiny era. The impetus behind the taluqdar settlement came not from the District level, but from the provincial authorities and the Governor-General.

The new policy at first obtained only a lukewarm reception at home. During the debates on the Oudh Proclamation in May 1858, Sir Charles Wood had expressed the common pre-Mutiny sentiment that the peasantry was the class whose welfare Britain should strive to promote. In defending the Proclamation, he took pains to describe the misdeeds of the taluqdars, and urged that confiscation of their property would be "mercy to the people."[37] When he discovered that Canning's policy was directed to a taluqdar and not a peasant settlement, Wood was shocked. As he wrote to Canning on 10 October 1859: "I cannot get over the confiscation in Oudh having enabled you to upset so completely all that we have been doing in settling the tenures of that country ever since we took it. It is so directly the contrary of what we supposed was the intention or could be the effect of the Proclamation that it takes one aback."[38]

In 1860 when the final settlement reports came home, Wood was disturbed at the cavalier manner in which the village proprietors had been treated. Those deprived of their lands, he said, should have been given an opportunity to put forward claims to restoration before the land was finally awarded to the taluqdars.[39] But Wood's protests accomplished nothing.

---

1859; and W. A. Forbes, Officiating Commissioner of Bahraich, to Barrow, 11 February 1859, File No. 6, Oudh General Proceedings, 1858-1859.

[36] Montgomery to Canning, 9 May 1859, and Wingfield to Canning, 3 July 1859, Canning Papers.

[37] Wood speech of 17 May 1858, Hansard, CL, 778.

[38] Wood to Canning, 10 October 1859, Wood Papers.

[39] Dispatch of 24 April 1860, P.P. 1861, XLVI, 439.

This was partly because from London he was unable to exert much influence upon an already settled policy; but it was also because he had himself become converted to taluqdari settlement. By the autumn of 1859 he was applauding Canning's effort to create "a native gentry playing their part in the social and administrative scale," and he spoke of the "wise policy of elevating rather than depressing the local aristocracy."[40] Voicing these sentiments, Wood was never able to make more than ineffectual protests against the treatment of the peasantry. Swept along with the prevailing current of opinion, he did little to make or to modify policy.

Conciliation of the taluqdars did not stop with the restoration of their estates. In October 1859 the Government invested six of the most prominent with the power to adjudicate revenue disputes and to act as Deputy Magistrates within their estates. In his role as Assistant Collector the taluqdar could hear suits for arrears of rent brought by his agents against his tenants, and execute decrees enforcing collection; his tenants, on their part, could bring claims of exaction or ejectment into the taluqdar's court. As Magistrate the taluqdar could try offenders brought before him by the police in petty criminal cases. He was obliged to conform to the British system of criminal procedure, and to allow the defendant a right of appeal to the Deputy Commissioner. The number of taluqdars possessing these powers increased considerably as time went on. By the end of 1860 there were 17 exercising both magisterial and revenue powers, and 12 more with revenue powers alone; together they disposed of over 1,200 cases. Two years later there were 48 taluqdars handling 3,000 suits annually in the revenue, civil, and criminal departments.

The grant of these powers was a logical extension of the general policy of building up the taluqdar class. As Canning realized, "now that the revival in perpetuity of the Talookdaree system in Oude has been declared it becomes more than ever

[40] Wood to Trevelyan, 25 December 1859, and Wood to Canning, 18 January 1860, Wood Papers.

necessary that the authority of the Talookdars should, within wholesome bounds, be sustained."[41] Nevertheless the decision to confer administrative powers on these men was a radical departure from the usual principles of Indian government. Previously the British had striven to provide efficient administration under Government officials, and to reform obsolete customs through their influence. With taluqdars as magistrates reform would of necessity be discarded, while efficiency and impartiality would at best be imperfectly attained. But this provided no cause for concern. During the Mutiny the British had seen the *tahsildars* and other native subordinates of Government fleeing for their lives, and angry mobs destroying courts and *cutcherries*. Henceforth, they decided, it would be far better—and safer—to work through the indigenous leaders of society, and to maintain the traditional Indian pattern of government. Lasting reform could come only from within Indian society, and when it had the support of the influential classes. To force the pace of change, to insist upon efficient British administration, was to undermine the structure of Indian society and to invite explosive disaffection. Wood, expressing his satisfaction with the appointment of taluqdars as magistrates, defined the new policy in these terms: "It should always be our aim to adopt and improve that system of administration to which the people in any part of India have been accustomed under their own rulers, guarding it from the abuses to which it may have been liable, than to introduce new measures, even though they may be founded on sounder principles, or have been tested by experience in our colonies, or even in other parts of India."[42]

Inasmuch as the scheme was presumably in accord with "the native system," the British were prepared to overlook the fact that the taluqdars, being interested parties, might abuse their powers. Canning urged Wingfield not to allow the taluqdars to shirk the onerous magisterial duties for the

[41] Memorandum of 31 October 1859, F.C. 18 November 1859, No. 130.
[42] Dispatch of 24 April 1860, P.P. 1861, XLVI, 441.

revenue jurisdiction from which they gained personal advantage; and Wood in 1864 even suggested that the taluqdars be confined to the discharge of their magisterial duties. But these suggestions produced no result. Wingfield insisted that as revenue jurisdiction "comes natural to every landholder," it should be widely distributed among them. Beyond this, he said, it was an immense benefit to the people that their disputes with each other were settled, in patriarchal fashion, by their feudal superior rather than in an alien court.[43] This opinion, which Canning and many others shared, reflects once again the disillusioning experience of the Mutiny, and the subsequent belief that the Indian people really preferred their traditional social order. Judged by these standards, the scheme of taluqdar magistrates was quite obviously a success. The taluqdars took up their work with enthusiasm, and few appeals were lodged against their decisions; they had after all ample power to intimidate discontented suitors. Both Canning and Wingfield sent home reports full of praise for the taluqdar magistrates, and Wood, despite the fact that his suggestions were not acted upon, echoed their sentiments.

The grant of revenue power was but the most striking of several measures designed to enhance the status and position of the taluqdar class. They were granted direct access to the District Officers, to free them from the harassments and petty tyrannies inflicted by the native subordinates of Government; and District Officers were directed to show them the utmost consideration and courtesy. In judicial proceedings Montgomery urged that "particular care should be taken to avoid summoning in person respectable talookdars to answer the petty summons of some trifling complainant." He went on to say that: "Much, very much, of the unpopularity of our rule is attributable to that principle of equality, which renders every man liable to be sued and summoned into a public court by any mean man who may choose, or be hired, to offend

[43] Oudh Administration Report for 1859-60, F.C. August 1860, Part A, No. 371.

the dignity of his superior. To English ideas, such fears regarding dignity and station may appear frivolous, but they assume a serious importance in the mind of the Natives of the East, and we must legislate and deal with the people of a country as we find them."[44]

The cherished English ideal of equality before the law was henceforth to be subordinated to the needs of taluqdar goodwill, and to the special requirements of the "Oriental mind." The events of 1857 had convinced the British that the Indian people were somehow different and inherently conservative. Now even the laws must bend to conform to their deeply rooted customs. The taluqdars required special treatment before the law not only because it was politically expedient but because such subservience to rank was traditional in the Orient.

The Government soon discovered that to create a landed aristocracy in India it was not enough simply to restore the taluqdars to their former lands and privileges. Custom might award the landholder a superior status in society, but it provided no guarantee for its continued maintenance. Like landholders throughout India the taluqdar customarily observed the Hindu law of inheritance, by which the estate was divided among all the heirs. He was equally tempted by extravagance to become mired in unproductive debt. It quickly became obvious that if the taluqdars were to be turned into a prosperous landed gentry on the English model, special legislative assistance would be necessary. Without it their property would soon be broken up into fragments, or sold for debt, and the taluqdari system would disappear.

In February 1860 Wingfield, moved by these considerations, suggested that inheritance by primogeniture be inserted in the taluqdars' *sanads* as one of the fundamental conditions on which they held their estates.[45] Both the taluqdars themselves and Sir Charles Wood at the India Office strongly supported

---

[44] Circular No. 46 of 30 December 1858, F.C. 21 January 1859, No. 279.
[45] C.C. Oudh to Sec. Govt. India, 13 February 1860, P.P. 1861, XLVI, 444.

this proposal. Indeed the taluqdars went even further, for they advocated the enactment of a law of entail, which would make it impossible for their estates ever to pass out of the hands of their families.[46] Canning, however, refused to impose any limit on the power of the taluqdar over his property. He insisted that taluqdars should retain the full proprietary title guaranteed by the *sanads*. In March 1862, on his last day in office, he brought forward a bill explicitly confirming the absolute control of the taluqdar over his estate, but making provision for inheritance by primogeniture whenever the owner died intestate. No action was taken on this draft act, and the subject was revived only in 1867, when John Strachey introduced a new bill which applied the rule of primogeniture generally to all taluqas. The enthusiastic reception accorded the bill by Man Singh and Balrampur (the latter sitting on the Legislative Council at the time) overcame all lingering scruples on the question; the measure was finally passed into law in January 1869, on Lawrence's last day in office, as the Oudh Estates Act of 1869.

During the course of this protracted controversy over inheritance, the taluqdars were becoming ever more deeply involved in debt. By 1869 seventy-one estates, paying an annual Government revenue of Rs. 16 lakhs, were encumbered with debts amounting to Rs. 37 lakhs. Prominent among them were those of Man Singh (with debts of Rs. 3 lakhs) and other substantial taluqdars in Faizabad and Gonda.[47] Faced with the imminent prospect that these estates might be sold to meet the demands of their creditors, the Government reluctantly bestirred itself to consider measures of relief. In 1865 several taluqdars petitioned the Commissioner of Faizabad, F. O. Mayne, asking him to take over the management of their estates in order to restore solvency and pay

[46] Memorandum of Man Singh approved by B.I.A., 10 March 1862, For. Gen. B, March 1863, No. 262.

[47] Financial Commissioner to C.C. Oudh, 13 August 1869, For. Rev. A, March 1871, No. 17.

off the hordes of creditors. Mayne listened sympathetically to these petitions and urged the Government to extend the encumbered taluqdars a helping hand. Otherwise, he said, "they would soon collapse and the Talookdaree Settlement be thus imperilled."[48] This request put the Oudh Government in a most awkward dilemma. They were committed to the maintenance of a landed aristocracy, and they naturally wished to see it flourish unhindered. Yet they recoiled from "special nursing measures" to protect this class from the consequences of its extravagance. Such interference was economically unsound, since it prevented the transfer of land from an incompetent to an enterprising and solvent owner; and it involved at the same time a confession that the taluqdar system was too weak to stand upon its own feet. The Financial Commissioner, R. H. Davies, an unreconstructed radical, went even further. He questioned the value of conciliating the landlord class at all, pointing out that "in the next *émeute,* which will probably be popular not military, we may lean on a broken reed if we trust too much to the influence of a hereditary aristocracy." Torn by these conflicting pressures, the Chief Commissioner finally authorized assistance in the form of loans "to old hereditary chiefs of clans, whom, on political grounds, it may be desirable to preserve from extinction."[49]

In 1869 the Oudh Government revived Mayne's original proposal. It submitted to the Government of India the draft of an Encumbered Estates Act, by which any taluqdar on petition could vest the management of his estates in the Government for a period not to exceed twenty years. While under management the estate would be secure from attachment or sale; and all income, beyond the Government revenue demand and a fixed maintenance allowance for the taluqdar,

[48] Mayne to Financial Commissioner, 13 October 1865 and 29 November 1865, For. Rev. A, April 1866, No. 20.

[49] Financial Commissioner to C.C. Oudh, 2 January 1866; and C.C. Oudh to Financial Commissioner, 17 January 1866. *Ibid.*

would be used to liquidate the encumbering debts and liabilities. Upon their discharge the estate would be restored to the possession of the taluqdar. The Viceroy, Lord Mayo, reluctantly agreed that some such measure was necessary, and it was accordingly enacted as Act XXIV of 1870. No one had any fondness for the principle of the act, and there was no attempt to defend it on theoretical grounds. It was, as Strachey pointed out, "a purely political measure" designed to save from destruction "the great experiment being tried in Oudh," on which so much had been staked since the Mutiny.[50] To secure the success of that experiment the Government was willing to forego a good many of its accepted principles.

Solicitude for their interests and privileges was quite naturally reciprocated by loyalty and affection on the part of the taluqdars. They realized that their new position was intimately bound up with continued British rule, and so remained staunch bulwarks of the Empire until its final collapse. In March 1861 they formed the British Indian Association of Oudh, in order better to defend their newly won privileges. This organization, to which all taluqdars subscribed, was their main political organ until the very end of British rule. As a favored and socially superior class, marked off by their *sanads* from other landholders, the taluqdars were able when organized to bring considerable influence to bear upon the Government. Yet few ever took an active part in the proceedings of their association. They were for the most part uneducated men, totally unfamiliar with this kind of modern political activity. Canning described them in 1859 as "a coarse looking lot" and at that time few of them had ever ventured far off their estates.[51] Most taluqdars were acquainted only with their local Hindi dialect, despite the fact that Urdu had for years been the literary and administrative language of

[50] Notes by Mayo of 31 December 1869 and by Strachey of 1 January 1870, For. Rev. A, March 1871, No. 22. Strachey speech in Legislative Council, 28 January 1870, *Proceedings*, IX, 42-43.

[51] Canning to Wood, 12 November 1859, Wood Papers.

the province. Consequently control of the new association fell into the hands of its two most active members: Man Singh, the vice-president; and Babu Dakhinaranjun Mukerji, the secretary. Mukerji, a Kulin Brahmin from Bengal, had been awarded the confiscated estate of Shankarpur after the Mutiny by Lord Canning, and was the only Bengali among the taluqdars. He was largely responsible for the foundation of the Association, and modeled it on the British Indian Association in Calcutta, of which he had been a member. As secretary he conducted the correspondence and managed the newspapers (one in Hindi and one in English) published by the taluqdars. Man Singh was the most prominent taluqdari spokesman and the driving force behind the association.[52] The presidency was held by Digvijai Singh, Maharaja of Balrampur, who served for twenty years until his death in 1882. As owner of the largest taluqa, and a distinguished ally of the British during the Mutiny, Balrampur was automatically made president of the new organization. The presidency in fact was always reserved for the holder of the largest estate with an adult male head, and until 1921 this meant either Balrampur, Ajodhya, or Mahmudabad. The B.I.A. thus reflected in its organization the aristocratic and hierarchical principles to which its members were wedded. The majority always believed that elections were indecent, that status should determine leadership in the society, and that political activity should be left to the few energetic officeholders.

As a propaganda organization for the views and interests of the taluqdar class the B.I.A. was quite effective, but it rarely ventured outside these bounds. Throughout the 1860's it dedicated itself primarily to the defence of the taluqdari land settlement. It issued a steady stream of resolutions and petitions denouncing as incompatible with that settlement all

[52] On foundation of B.I.A. see Yule to Canning, 15 August 1861, in Canning Papers; and reports of B.I.A. meeting of 12-13 November 1862, in *Proceedings of the British Indian Association of Oudh from 1861 to 1865* (Calcutta, 1865), pp. 97-101.

attempts to regulate the power of the taluqdars over their tenants and put forward various measures designed to strengthen their position. Although they took no part in the founding of this association, the British looked on with satisfaction as it took root and flourished. They saw in the association a useful way of gauging taluqdari opinion and an encouraging sign of independent political life among this important class. Indeed Wingfield hoped that "by frequently meeting together, and by the habit of free discussion, the landed gentry of Oudh will learn to divest themselves of old prejudices and jealousies, and to cooperate in schemes of social and material improvement."[53] The Oudh Government invariably consulted the B.I.A. before proceeding with major legislation, and gave their views a sympathetic hearing. In November 1861 Canning gave them the Kaiserbagh Palace in Lucknow, confiscated from the former Oudh King, as a meeting place and town residence. In 1876 the Government extended them further assistance by collecting B.I.A. dues as a regular assessment along with the land revenue. As the taluqdars came to play an ever more important role in government, the British Indian Association, as the instrument of taluqdari politics, likewise grew in power and prestige.

Conciliation of the landlord class was by no means confined to Oudh, although there it achieved its most striking success. In 1860 Canning set out to restore the aristocracy of the entire Bengal Presidency from Calcutta to Lahore. In Bengal itself the zamindars, confirmed in possession of their estates by the Permanent Settlement of 1793, already formed a substantial landed aristocracy, but they had long been excluded from any share in the administration. To Canning this separation between property and official authority was both undesirable and unnatural. He recommended that the zamindars be given a recognized place in local administration by investiture with magisterial powers on the Oudh model. The Lieutenant-

[53] *Oudh Administration Report for 1862-63* (Lucknow, 1863), p. 38.

Governor, J. P. Grant, protested weakly against the creation of "petty autocracies" and pointed to the difficulty of working a system of gentry magistrates in a province which contained so many European planters, and where land was often an object of commercial speculation. But these objections were ignored. Canning remained convinced that "the measure is founded on truth and common sense," while Bartle Frere rejoiced in the arrival of a "new era in Bengal" and the correction at last of "a capital defect" in the whole system of British administration.[54]

In the North-Western Provinces the task was rendered more difficult by the twenty years of village settlement which had elapsed. The original aristocracy had largely disappeared and Canning admitted that "we should be puzzled to hunt out many of them." Still he hoped to restore some at least to the position of "independent Gentlemen of property and influence."[55] The Lieutenant-Governor, G. F. Edmonstone, entirely concurred in these sentiments, as did the District Officers, but they had difficulty finding qualified candidates. The province contained few men of sufficient eminence and ability to warrant such a distinction. The Commissioner of Allahabad recommended only six for his entire division. Eventually in January 1862 fifty-seven men, including thirteen Europeans, were invested with magisterial powers in the pargana of their residence.[56]

In the Punjab, Canning was more confident of success, for many substantial landholders still remained, especially in the

---

[54] Frere to Canning, 10 November 1860, Canning Papers. Canning Minute of 13 November 1860 and Grant Minute of 3 November 1860, Home Judl., 18 December 1860, No. 11-12. The Government was, however, at the same time enacting legislation which curbed the power of the zamindars over their tenants. This legislation (Act X of 1859) will be discussed in the next chapter.

[55] Canning to Wood, 6 November 1859, Wood Papers.

[56] Edmonstone to Canning, 15 July 1860, Canning Papers. Sec. Govt. N.W.P. to Sec. Govt. India, 14 October 1861, Home Judl. 18 November 1861, No. 14. For reports of District Officers see North-West Provinces General Proceedings, 24 May 1862, No. 170-189, Lucknow Secretariat.

Cis-Sutlej territory, despite the peasant settlement policy pursued by John Lawrence before the Mutiny. Henry Lawrence had preserved many Sikh sirdars before he was forced out of the province in 1853, and during the subsequent eight years the processes of subdivision and sale of land for debt, which had ruined so many old landed families in the North-Western Provinces had not had time to take full effect. Still the "deliberate and avowed thrusting aside and lowering of every great family for ten years past," combined with their exclusion from administrative power, had set in motion a process of decline which Canning was determined to reverse. At a Durbar held in Lahore in February 1860 he informed the assembled sirdars that the Government would confer upon them revenue and judicial powers, and would in addition consolidate their estates. Up to that time large compact estates had been consciously broken up, and each man's holdings scattered through several districts in order to diminish his importance. Now, however, as the sirdars were to obtain administrative responsibility, it was necessary to "establish for each who shall be considered worthy of trust a recognized influence in some one part of the Punjab."[57]

The Lieutenant-Governor, Robert Montgomery, fresh from Oudh, took up the new policy with enthusiasm. He viewed a native aristocracy as "a great bulwark for the State" and rejoiced at the repudiation of the policy of "bringing all to a dead level."[58] Among the District Officers of the Punjab the measure generally evoked a favorable response. Even those who had few landholders to recommend hailed the recognition of the upper classes as a step forward in Indian Government. The Commissioner of Amritsar, R. N. Cust, alone stood out against the measure. Many of the landholders in the Central Punjab, he pointed out, were Sikh sirdars of recent

---

[57] Canning to Wood, 27 February 1860, Wood Papers. Canning to Granville, 4 July 1860 in Edmond Fitzmaurice, *Life of the Second Earl Granville* (London, 1905), I, 384.

[58] Montgomery to Canning, 10 July 1861, Canning Papers.

origin, creatures of Ranjit Singh, who had no sympathy with the inferior classes and would inevitably abuse any powers entrusted to them.[59] The Punjab Government made no attempt to deny the truth of this contention. Instead it recited, in a clear and explicit fashion, the political necessities which dictated the new policy—and indeed had dominated British thinking about India since the Mutiny.

"It is well to be careful of the interests of the people, but to be so effectually it behooves us first to look to those of our own government. Dearly bought experience may teach us that political security is not necessarily attained by just laws, equitable taxation, and material progress. . . . If there is a body scattered throughout the country considerable by its property and rank it will for certain exercise great influence whether its position be hereditary or not. If this body is attached to the state by timely concessions . . . and obtains a share of power and importance, it will constitute a strong support to the existing Government. It may be true that such a body may become too powerful or . . . oppress a people not protected by efficient laws. But neither of these evils is more to be feared than that which threatens a foreign rule from the ignorance and indifference of its alien subjects, when unattached through their natural leaders and held in allegiance only by military force."[60]

Even though the Sikh sirdars might possess little traditional influence, they were (or could be made into) "natural leaders" of the people. Hence they deserved support and encouragement.

The strongest opposition to the Punjab sirdar scheme came from the Council of India in London. The Council was largely composed of men who had returned to England before, or immediately after, the Mutiny, and who, far from the scene, retained the reforming enthusiasm of the earlier period. Cherishing the ideal of peasant proprietorship, they

[59] Minute of 18 February 1860, F.C. May 1860, Part A, No. 171.
[60] Sec. Govt. Punjab to Sec. Govt. India, 30 April 1860, *ibid.*, No. 167.

considered the new policy antagonistic to the demands of social justice, and they could see nothing in the events of the Mutiny to justify such a change. John Stuart Mill, who had turned down a seat on the new India Council in 1858, voiced the sentiments of many of its members when he stood up for "the interests of the great mass of the people" and deprecated the "greater fear of the natives, and desire of conciliating the natives, which have existed since the Mutiny (the 'natives' being as usual a mere synonym for the powerful classes)."[61] On the Council John Lawrence became the most outspoken critic of new policy after his return from India in 1859. The peasant settlement in the Punjab had been largely his handiwork, and he viewed with suspicion any attempt to alter it. He considered the sirdars untrustworthy, and the consolidation of their estates a reckless act. In Oudh Lawrence likewise felt Canning was "only breeding up a class of people who will turn against you on the first opportunity."[62] With his great Indian reputation Lawrence easily won the support of the majority of the Council, including the entire Political Committee. Even Wood felt obliged at times to defer to his authority on Punjab questions. But the Council was not able to halt or to reverse Canning's policy. Although Wood often moderated the tone of his dispatches to meet their objections, the Secretary of State possessed ultimate authority (subject to Parliament) on Indian matters, and he insisted upon approval of the course taken by Canning.[63]

Canning was well aware of the opposition his aristocratic policies encountered in the India Council at home. Above all he feared the effect if John Lawrence were appointed as his successor. Subject to the hostile scrutiny of the peasant enthusiasts, he was convinced the new policy would not long survive. Even if the system remained undisturbed on paper,

[61] Mill to Maine, 1 January 1869 in H. S. R. Elliot, ed., *Letters of J. S. Mill* (London, 1910), II, 169.

[62] Wood to Canning, 10 August 1860, Wood Papers.

[63] Wood to Canning, 9 January 1861, Wood Papers.

"a shrug or a sneer from the incoming Governor-General pointed at some unhappy sirdar or talookdar who had blundered in his duties, would be a signal for consigning the whole class once more to snubs and obstructions."[64] So during his last two years in office Canning set out to build up a solid base of support for his policy among the District Officers. Only their enthusiastic backing, he realized, could insure eventual success. He kept a close watch upon their temper, and continually urged the local authorities "to confirm heartiness where it exists, and to induce it where it is wanting." With the Punjab District Officers, John Lawrence's old subordinates, he was remarkably successful; but in Oudh the officials proved less malleable. In February 1861 Canning commented that the only risk the taluqdar system ran was "the unfriendliness of some of our officers. Very few of these are earnestly in favor of it."[65] Canning himself kept this discontent in check. There was no outbreak of open hostility while he remained. Yet an undercurrent of opposition persisted, and Lawrence's arrival as Viceroy in 1864 provided the signal for a renewed attack upon aristocratic land settlement.

Canning's immediate successor, Lord Elgin, carried on the established policy of encouraging a landed aristocracy, and indeed sanctioned its extension into the new Central Provinces. The Central Provinces had come into existence as a separate administration under a Chief Commissioner in November 1861. It comprised the Saugor and Narbada Territories (annexed in 1818 and previously part of the North-Western Provinces), Nagpur Province (annexed in 1854), and several smaller districts (Jabalpur, Sambalpur, and Nimar), all joined together solely for purposes of administrative convenience. Prior to the formation of the new province its component parts had been settled, usually on a summary or short-term basis, with a class of revenue farmers known as malguzars;

---

[64] Canning to Granville, 29 May 1860, in Fitzmaurice, *Life of Granville*, I, 378-79.

[65] Canning to Yule, 24 February 1861, Canning Papers.

and the Government retained the proprietary right in its own hands. In 1862 the Government initiated a regular thirty-year settlement, under which the malguzars were given a full proprietary title in the land they had previously held on lease; and the feudatory or tributary chiefs, who controlled large tracts of wild forest country, were confirmed in their quasi-sovereign powers.

These malguzars formed the superior landholding class throughout most of the Central Provinces. They were not a powerful landed aristocracy like the Oudh taluqdars, for they customarily held only one or a few villages, but by virtue of their position as revenue farmers under the Maratha government they had gained substantial power over the peasantry. In origin some were village headmen or *patels*, others were land speculators and court favorites introduced by the Maratha government; yet all alike, whether they had held the land for generations or for a few years, were recognized as absolute proprietors in the settlement of 1862-1867. As in Bengal so in the Central Provinces, though on a much smaller scale, the British created a class of landlords out of a class of revenue farmers.

At the time of its introduction the malguzari settlement provoked little discussion or controversy. Sir Richard Temple, Chief Commissioner of the Central Provinces, spoke warmly of the benefit to society of fostering "a middle class among the agriculturists," and considered the malguzars politically "a useful link between the Government and the mass of the agricultural population." It was accepted without question that "an estate cannot be managed without a responsible head belonging to it" and that "the occupant cultivators must be dependent for support and guidance on a landlord."[66] Only after the settlement was practically complete did any ryotwari sentiment appear, but by then it was too late to reverse the proceed-

[66] *Central Provinces Administration Report for 1861-62* (Nagpur, 1863), pp. 68-69; and *Central Provinces Administration Report for 1862-63* (Nagpur, 1864), p. 51.

ings. The malguzars could not be deprived of the title they had so recently been awarded. In Sambalpur, where the settlement had been delayed by rebellion, the land was eventually settled on a ryotwari basis.[67] Elsewhere in the province efforts were made to protect the peasantry by the award of occupancy rights under Act X of 1859. Generally speaking, however, the settlement of the Central Provinces reflects the characteristic post-Mutiny determination to seek out and support a landlord class wherever it might be found.

As in North India, the chiefs and landholders of the Central Provinces were invested with judicial powers. Like Wingfield, Temple was convinced the possession of such powers by the upper classes would benefit the mass of the people, for "the interest of the chief is identical with that of his people."[68] In much the same manner the semi-independent tributary zamindars of the more remote regions regained the almost unlimited powers they had traditionally exercised. The steady encroachment of the British courts upon their civil jurisdiction was reversed, and the chiefs awarded the full powers of a judge in civil and revenue suits. They were permitted once again to govern their estates as of right in return for the payment of a fixed tribute.


Much of the appeal of Canning's policy of creating "independent Gentlemen of property and influence" lay in its congeniality to the social ideals of mid-Victorian liberalism. Most Indian officials in mid-century considered themselves Liberals, and the principles of liberalism, as they saw them, provided strong support for the new policy. By 1860 the egalitarian enthusiasm of the Benthamites had given way to a more cautious, conservative, and eclectic liberalism. The prosperous

[67] B. H. Baden-Powell, *The Land-Systems of British India* (Oxford, 1892), II, 463.

[68] *Central Provinces Administration Report for 1861-62.* pp. 48-49. C.C. Central Provinces to Sec. Govt. India, 31 October 1863, For. Pol. A, June 1864, No. 14-16.

mid-Victorian liberal was quite satisfied with his traditional social order, and was convinced that further progress would come naturally through the workings of free trade and laissez faire. He no longer retained the apocalyptic vision of a regenerated India which had sustained Bentinck and James Mill, and he had far less faith in the Government as an instrument of social reform. Bagehot, not Bentham, was his prophet. After the Mutiny, when this brand of liberalism found its way into India, its blend of social conservatism and liberal economics powerfully reinforced the landlord policy.

With Bagehot the English in India sought a stable balanced society, in which government was entrusted to "a select few" and the poorer classes rendered due respect and deference to their social superiors. Like their contemporaries at home, they believed a landed gentry provided the only real source of leadership. It was "against all reason," Canning protested, to obliterate the landed gentry of India, as the Benthamites had done, for this class played a vital role in society. When critics charged that these men might abuse their powers, the Government simply pointed to the English country gentry, who had performed "useful activity in the public service through many generations and centuries of increasing wealth." These English prejudices were enough to convince many Indian officials that, as Wood put it, "the dead level of nothing between our officers and the people is an unnatural state of society."[69] When this assumption was combined with the belief that the Indians really preferred their traditional feudal order and the rule of their local gentry, there no longer remained the least doubt as to the propriety of the new policy. English notions and the lessons of the Mutiny each reinforced the other.

The theories of laissez faire gave a further measure of support to the landlord policy. Although a persistent strand in English liberalism, dating back to Adam Smith and his con-

---

[69] Canning to Wood, 27 February 1860; Frere to Canning, 10 November 1860; and Wood to Frere, 1 August 1862; Canning and Wood Papers.

cept of the "invisible hand," laissez faire had exercised little influence on Indian land policy. Before the Mutiny, apart from Bengal, it was always pushed aside by the Benthamite philosophy of peasant settlement and an active reforming government. In this respect India contrasts sharply with Ireland, where, due largely to the influence of an entrenched landed gentry, the theories of laissez faire had exercised unchallenged sway since 1815. In the 1860's laissez faire at last found receptive soil in India. As in Ireland it strengthened the forces of landlordism, for, according to the political economists, a capitalist landlord class was essential to agricultural prosperity. This class should be freed from all restrictions imposed by the Government, and allowed to exercise unfettered control over their estates. Contract alone should determine the relation of landlord and tenant. As Charles Wingfield, the most thoroughgoing Indian exponent of this theory, asserted: "The relations between the hirer and letter of land should be as unrestricted as between the buyer and seller of merchandise. The owner of land has as much right as the owner of a house to let his property on the best terms, and any limitation of his power over it must tend to deter the application of capital to land, and check the development of its productive powers and consequently of the wealth of the country."[70] Even Sir James Outram asked whether "the universal laws of social progress do not hold as regards India," and put forward his opinion that the happiness of the masses would be promoted as satisfactorily "under a system which recognizes the legitimacy and advantages of capital and of baronial landlordism, as under a system which tends to reduce the entire population to the dreary and ever-sinking level of a demi-pauperised peasant proprietary."[71]

For all its apparent clarity and rigor, the principle of laissez faire was rarely carried out with any consistency. As the in-

[70] C.C. Oudh to Sec. Govt. India, 26 March 1864, P.P. 1865, XL, 212.
[71] Outram Minute of 2 May 1858 in F. J. Goldsmid, *Life of Sir James Outram* (London, 1881), II, 339.

dustrialists in England often found it little more than a convenient slogan, so the adherents of laissez faire in India never hesitated to call upon the Government when it was in their interest to do so. The Government was expected to maintain private property rights in the hands of the aristocracy, and to rescue encumbered landlords from the weight of their debts. In fact in India, where the Government played such a dominant role in society, laissez faire was usually honored more in the breach than in the observance. Yet, in spite of this, laissez faire contributed largely to the success of the landlord revival, for it was a principle to which liberals gave unquestioning allegiance. It made palatable to the mid-Victorian conscience a policy dictated by the interests of political stability.

The policy which Canning inaugurated marked the beginning, as Sir Charles Wood at once realized, of "a new and most important era in our Indian administration." After fifty years the ideal of peasant proprietorship was set aside, and the old landlord classes reinstated in power and prestige. Only in Oudh was the pre-Mutiny pattern of peasant settlement completely upset, for in that province alone did popular rebellion destroy the old tenures and provide "a clear stage upon which to work out anything that might seem fittest." Elsewhere, as Canning admitted, the legacy of peasant settlement "made it a difficult and ticklish matter to hark back," for men in possession could not be ousted without good cause.[72] Nevertheless throughout India the British sought the support and affection, not of the middle and lower classes, but of the gentry and aristocracy. Their aim was "to enlist on our side, and to employ in our service, those natives who have, from their birth or their position, a natural influence in the country."[73] This attitude persisted well into the twentieth century. Harcourt Butler, Governor of the United Provinces in the 1920's,

[72] Canning to Granville, 4 July 1860 in Fitzmaurice, *Life of Granville*, I, 384.

[73] Wood to Canning, 3 January 1860, Wood Papers.

described the Oudh policy as "the policy of sympathy and trust" and the landed aristocracy as the natural mediators between the masses of the people, incapable of politics, and their rulers. Outside the big cities, he said, "the landed aristocracy affords the only possible foundation for the devolution of political power."[74] Few went so far as Butler in their adulation of the aristocracy, but few, on the other hand, were willing to deny the closeness of the ties which had grown up between the British and the Indian gentry since the Mutiny.

[74] Harcourt Butler, *Oudh Policy: The Policy of Sympathy* (Lucknow, 1906), p. 40.

CHAPTER V

# LANDLORD, TENANT, AND MONEYLENDER

With the conclusion of the Oudh taluqdar settlement the process of land settlement in British India came to a close. No further provinces were annexed, and in the older provinces the existing settlements, although revised at regular intervals, of necessity remained in force. Yet the Government continued to make its influence felt upon the structure of rural society through the enactment of tenancy legislation. In South India, where the occupying cultivator was usually the settlement holder, the question of tenant right rarely arose, but in North India the British Government played a decisive role in determining the relationship between the various classes on the land.

Despite certain superficial similarities, the traditional Indian land system bore almost no resemblance to that with which the Englishman was familiar at home. Above all, before the British arrived, land in India was never held in outright ownership as private property. The State, the intermediary classes, and the cultivators themselves shared what the English regarded as the prerogatives of ownership. The State, standing at the apex of society, always claimed a share of the produce and was often considered the ultimate owner of the soil. The taluqdars, zamindars, and other revenue-collecting intermediaries possessed considerable power over the land, and during the anarchy of the eighteenth century had encroached upon the rights of the State. But their power even then fell far short of a true proprietary title, for they had to take account of the customary rights of the cultivators. The peasant, or ryot as he was usually known, although obliged to pay a share of his produce to the superior holder as tax or rent, usually paid over an amount fixed by local custom, and so long as it was paid the cultivator and his heirs were entitled to remain on the soil. Despite this the superior landholder, or even the State itself acting as landlord, did occasionally eject cultivators and enhance rents in an arbitrary manner, since there were no laws to restrain him and the peasantry lacked the power to prevent it. Indeed during the eighteenth century the large landholders, unchecked by any superior authority, were often able to subject their tenantry to extortion and force them to contribute to the support of armed bands of retainers. Still, however, the cultivator was in a strong bargaining position, for the population was relatively small and much land lay uncultivated. A ryot who considered himself oppressed could usually obtain favorable terms from a neighboring landholder. Thus when the British arrived, the cultivator, though bereft of legal protection, had a reasonably secure tenure and the support of strong customary sanctions.

As part of their settlement proceedings the British invariably awarded proprietary rights in the soil to those responsible for the payment of the land revenue, whether the individual zamindar, as in Bengal, or the corporate village community of the North-Western Provinces. In creating these rights the British did not intend to destroy the traditional rights of the tenants. As early as 1769 Verelst had tried to record and define the rights of the cultivators in Bengal, and Cornwallis in 1793 coupled measures of tenant right with his zamindari settlement. Under Regulation VIII of 1793 it was enacted that those who had held land at a fixed rate for twelve years were entitled to hold permanently at that rate, while all others were to pay no more than the customary pargana rates. Yet once the Permanent Settlement was in operation, no further

efforts were made to record or preserve the pargana rates, and
the courts lacking detailed information were unable to enforce
the old assessments. As the Deputy Collector of Champaran
pointed out in 1855: "The curse of this district is the insecure
nature of the ryot's land tenure. The cultivator, though
nominally protected by regulations of all sorts, has, practically,
no rights in the soil. His rent is continually raised; he is
oppressed and worried by every successive teekadar, until he
is actually forced out of his holding."[1]

Depression of the peasantry was further accelerated by the
economic changes which followed the introduction of British
rule. Law and order—the "Pax Britannica"—gave an impetus
to population growth, and triggered a rise in the value of land.
By mid-century the zamindars were in a position to dictate
terms. The same process took place in the North-Western
Provinces during the 1860's. Despite the recognition of
occupancy rights under Thomason's settlement, prosperity and
population growth together enabled the landholders to mount
a successful attack upon the traditional position of the cultivator. Competition was fast displacing custom as the criterion
of rental demand.

Faced with this social upheaval the British had at last to
decide whether they wished to protect the occupancy tenant
by special legislative action. No one denied that the Government had an obligation to preserve established customs and
place them on a secure legal footing. As the Duke of Argyll
put it in 1869, the "basic principle" of all tenancy legislation
should be "to ascertain the relative rights and relations of
the landowners and occupiers as they actually were before we
took the country, to give to these rights and relations a new
sanction, and not to upset or interfere with them."[2] Yet this
ideal was in practice rarely carried out. Indian land tenure

[1] Memorandum cited in Govt. of Bengal to Board of Revenue, 5 March
1855, Papers Relating to Act X, N.A.I.

[2] S. of S. to Govt. of India, 28 October 1869, For. Rev. A, January 1870,
No. 70.

was a highly complex subject, comprising a great many diverse local customs, which the British, accustomed to absolute private property and contractual landlord-tenant relations, at best only vaguely comprehended. Moreover during the anarchy of the eighteenth century, land tenures had become so disorganized that, as Sir George Campbell noted, "We found all the interests in land throughout most of India in a sort of fluid state, to be moulded much as we thought expedient and just."[3] But even if the British had understood Indian land tenures, the act of preserving customary rights by legislative enactment was bound to alter their very nature. A custom ignored under the British legal system was often a custom destroyed (as in Bengal from 1800 to 1850); but a custom defined by law and enforced by the courts was a new legal right which had never existed before. It was ultimately impossible simply to define and preserve traditional customs under the changed conditions of British rule. Preconceived ideas of what tenant right ought to be inevitably intruded into any inquiry as to what such rights actually were; and legislation turned as much upon personal preference as upon ascertained fact.

Most Victorian Englishmen approached India with their basic ideas already formed in the great school of English liberalism. Between them the theories of laissez faire and of Benthamite utilitarianism provided the backdrop against which much of the struggle over tenant right in India was carried on. The laissez faire liberal, convinced that agrarian progress required a capitalist landlord class, looked upon tenancy legislation as harmful and retrograde. By restricting the landlord, he argued, it would stifle capital investment and perpetuate uneconomic small holdings. This faith in the landlord reflected ultimately the success of large-scale capitalist farming in England. As free contract and unfettered proprietorship had made English agriculture the most advanced in the world, so would they shake Indian agriculture out of its centuries-old stagnation. Despite the obvious inability of the Bengal zamindars

[3] Campbell, *Memoirs*, II, 44.

to act like English gentry, and the dismal failure of laissez faire in Ireland, the English liberal of 1860 still maintained, with Charles Wingfield, that "The majority of our Talooqdars do, I think, largely share the feelings of English landlords. . . . The demands of the landlord are fair, and observed with good faith, and innumerable little kindnesses, so dear to the Natives of this country, are shown, which cease when our laws, by creating rights on the part of the peasantry, set the two classes in antagonism. I firmly believe that half the bickering and bad blood that prevails between landlord and tenant . . . have been caused by our ill-judged interference."[4]

The theories of laissez faire gained further reinforcement from aristocratic prejudice. The English landed gentry saw clearly that tenancy legislation, with its restraints upon the landlord, posed by implication a challenge to their own dominant position in society. By interfering with the rights of property, indeed, such legislation was the first step on the road to socialism, and had therefore to be opposed wherever it raised its head. The Duke of Argyll, for instance, as Secretary of State for India in the first Gladstone Government, repeatedly urged the Viceroy to "defend property where it has, fortunately, grown up under our system"; in 1880 as Lord Privy Seal he bitterly denounced Gladstone's Irish Land Act as a "plan to destroy ownership" and resigned from the Cabinet in protest.[5]

The supporters of tenant right in India also drew upon the storehouse of English liberalism. They looked, however, to its authoritarian Benthamite side, and found their justification in Ricardo's theory of rent. By the 1860's, as we have seen, utilitarianism was in the process of decay. As a fixed creed and body of doctrine it no longer exercised the attraction it had in the time of James Mill; while in India the Mutiny

---

[4] Wingfield to Maine, 3 November 1863, enclosure in Maine to Wood, 20 November 1864, Wood Papers.

[5] Argyll to Northbrook, 23 May 1873 in the Duke of Argyll, *Autobiography and Memoirs* (London, 1906), II, 283. Argyll to Gladstone, 3 November 1880 et seq., *ibid.*, p. 355ff.

dealt a severe blow to all hopes of thoroughgoing agrarian reform. Yet the ideal of peasant proprietorship, and the reforming enthusiasm which sustained it, were by no means dead. John Stuart Mill, for instance, retained undiminished the utilitarian ardour of his youth. Much as his restless mind helped smash the rigid framework of philosophical radicalism in other fields, in agrarian questions he remained a true son of his father. He adhered to the Ricardian theory of rent throughout his life, and continued the struggle for tenant right even after his departure from the India Office in 1858. Among the younger generation of Indian officials, perhaps the most outspoken radical was Sir John Strachey, who rose from Collector of Moradabad to Finance Member of the Viceroy's Council. Like Mill, Strachey upheld the discredited Ricardian rent theory, and maintained that "the class of small proprietors cultivating their own land, and the class of tenants with a permanent interest in their holdings, are the classes from which all real improvement of the land in India is derived, and that without security of tenure and some limitation of rent, it is vain to expect agricultural progress."[6]

Once the fledgling British officer had arrived in India, his ideas were further shaped by his choice of service and the nature of his work. From the outset each of the major provincial services developed its own distinctive attitude toward land tenure. In Bengal the aristocratic sentiments of Lord Cornwallis still dominated the civil service seventy-five years after the Permanent Settlement. The Bengal civilian instinctively thought in terms of laissez faire, and left the peasantry in the care of the zamindar. As Wingfield noted, in choosing a successor "I would rather prefer a Bengal man to any other because he must be presumed to be favorable to the existence of a class of large landed proprietors."[7] In the Punjab, on the other hand, the District Officer, armed with far-reaching power, looked upon himself as the father of his

[6] Speech in Legislative Council, 19 October 1868, *Proceedings*, VII, 432.
[7] Wingfield to Canning, 7 March 1861, Canning Papers.

district. Like his hero John Lawrence, the Punjab officer usually combined a rough-and-ready paternalism with the reforming zeal of Bird and Thomason. He considered it his duty above all to aid and encourage the tillers of the soil. In much the same fashion, those who served in the revenue line were more favorably disposed toward the peasantry than those whose duties were exclusively judicial or political. Out in the field settling disputes and making assessments, the young Collector soon developed feelings of sympathy and affection for the sturdy yeomen of the soil. He readily identified himself with their aspirations and stood up for their interests. The Judge, by contrast, saw the peasantry only as litigants, lying and cheating in his court, while the "politicals," who acted as Residents in the Indian States, easily imbibed the aristocratic prejudices of those about them. Consequently the ranks of the tenant party were not materially depleted by the decline of utilitarian theory. There remained, not only the few agrarian reformers, but the much larger number who cherished the vision of a contented peasantry tilling the soil under the benign and watchful guidance of British officers. Even the Mutiny could not completely shatter these ingrained sentiments of paternal affection.

Tenancy legislation in India was therefore the subject of protracted controversy. Landlord and tenant alike had powerful spokesmen in the Government, and neither party, during the 1860's, was strong enough to impose its will completely upon the other. Each act that emerged from the legislative mill bore the scars of battle and the marks of compromise. Since the nature of the controversy varied widely throughout northern India it is necessary to look at the course of events in each province in turn.

### Bengal

The first effective tenancy legislation was enacted in Bengal as Act X of 1859. As originally drafted, the bill provided that every resident ryot was entitled to a right of occupancy in the land cultivated by him, on payment of a rent fixed according to the established pargana rates. To prevent exaction of rent beyond these rates jurisdiction in revenue suits was to be vested in the Collectors, who were not subject to the cumbrous legal procedure of the courts and who were presumably better acquainted with questions of land tenure. According to its author, the bill simply re-enacted in a clear and distinct form what had been the law since the Permanent Settlement, and awarded the power of adjudication to those best able to correct injustice.[8] The proposed legislation met with general sympathy in the Government. The Lieutenant-Governor, F. J. Halliday, echoed widespread opinion when he commented on the award of occupancy rights that "in doing this we shall be discharging a heavy obligation towards the Ryots, long unfulfilled by our legislation."[9] Yet at the same time he, and others, objected to the indiscriminate award of such rights to all cultivators, no matter how long they had been in possession of their land. Further objection was made to the use of pargana rates as a standard of rental demand, for they had long since ceased to have any real meaning. In its final form, therefore, the act stated that "every ryot who has cultivated or held land for a period of twelve years has a right of occupancy in the land so cultivated by him," and that all ryots having rights of occupancy should pay rent at "fair and equitable rates" liable to enhancement only if their rate was below the prevailing rental of the area, or if the value of the land and its produce had increased other than by the effort of the ryot. The twelve-year rule was avowedly artificial, and was drawn from current practice in the North-Western Provinces. In this way the Government hoped to give some legal precision to the vague concept of permanent residency; but in so doing, of course, they placed a new right, hitherto unknown, in the hands of every twelve-year occupier, and

[8] E. Currie speech in Legislative Council, 10 October 1857, *Proceedings*, III, 437-39.

[9] Minute of 27 November 1858, Papers Relating to Act X.

put every man who had held for less than twelve years outside the pale of the law.

Surprisingly, the events of the Mutiny did not provoke extensive opposition to the measure, nor did the implication—alien to English concepts of property—that mere lapse of time could create rights against a landlord. Few District Officers objected to the award of occupancy rights, and in Calcutta the only protests came from the Board of Revenue and from the zamindars themselves in the British Indian Association. Sir Barnes Peacock, the most outspoken critic of the act in the Legislative Council, confined his criticism to the procedural sections of the bill, primarily the transfer of revenue jurisdiction to the Collectors.[10] Although the act came under consideration during the height of the revolt, the Mutiny did not provide occasion for hesitation. Alone among the provinces of North India, Bengal had remained relatively free of disturbance. The zamindars, in particular, were conspicuous for their loyalty. Hence their protests could safely be ignored, and a measure of justice, so long denied, awarded the peasantry.

The act also applied to the North-Western Provinces, where conditions were altogether different. Under Thomason's settlement rights of occupancy had been awarded to all resident ryots, and the rents payable by such cultivators were fixed by the Government on the basis of the customary local rates.[11] Indeed rents were usually fixed at settlement for the duration of the settlement, and could be raised only by the expensive and hazardous process of a regular suit in the civil courts. With the enactment of Act X the landlord obtained for the first time a way of raising his rent apart from an increased government demand, for he had now only to show that there had been a general rise in prices or that the existing rent was below the average of the neighborhood. Prosperity and in-

10 Speech in Legislative Council, 9 April 1859, *Proceedings*, v, 226-29.

11 J. Thomason, "Directions for Settlement Officers," P.P. 1852-53, LXXV, 32-33. The twelve-year rule grew up during the 1840's as a convenient way of deciding who was a resident ryot; it had no legal sanction until 1859.

creasing population in the years after 1860 meant that the final obliteration of the old customary rates was merely a matter of time. As the Collector of Meerut reported in 1871: "We find constant and bitter struggle between the landlord on the one side and the tenants on the other to extinguish and to defend the occupancy rights of tenants, going hand in hand with a persistent determination on the part of most landlords to exercise the harshest measures for the prevention of any occupancy rights being acquired by their tenants-at-will." The rent act, he concluded, was "emphatically a landlord's act"; for the cultivator, though still preserved from laissez faire, had lost his former security of tenure.[12]

TABLE 7

SUITS UNDER THE RENT LAW IN THE NORTH-WESTERN PROVINCES

| | *Average 1865-1866 to 1868-1869* | *1869-1870* | *1870-1871* | *1871-1872* |
|---|---|---|---|---|
| *Brought by Tenant* | | | | |
| Complaints of excessive demand and claims to abatement | 2,468 | 1,964 | 1,950 | 1,214 |
| Suits to recover occupancy by tenant illegally ejected | 3,025 | 2,716 | 1,996 | 1,446 |
| *By Landlords* | | | | |
| Arrears of rent | 34,516 | 35,768 | 41,736 | 41,903 |
| Suits to eject or cancel lease | 4,812 | 5,359 | 6,365 | 2,893 |

The suits for arrears, which form 75 per cent of the whole number of suits brought under the Act, were usually simply a device to force the tenant to accept an enhancement of his rent. *Report on the Revenue Administration of the North-Western Provinces for 1871-2* (Allahabad, 1873), p. 40.

[12] *Report on the Revenue Administration of the North-Western Provinces for 1870-71* (Allahabad, 1872), p. 61. For a detailed account of rent and occupancy tenure in the N.W.P. see A. Colvin, *Memorandum on the Revision*

Even in Bengal the protection afforded by the Act could easily be whittled away. During 1860 and 1861 English planters in the Nadia District enhanced the rents of their ryots as a means of forcing them to grow indigo. The ryots took their case to the Bengal High Court, alleging that they were protected from enhancement by Act X. The Chief Justice, Sir Barnes Peacock, ruled, however, that the "fair and equitable" rent to which the occupancy tenant was entitled by the act was nothing more than a preferential right to occupy the land at a competitive market rate. Any lower rate would not be fair and equitable to the landlord, who as proprietor was entitled to the full rental value of his land. Peacock denied that the ryots ever had enjoyed beneficial rights of occupancy before 1859, and held that for the legislature to confer such rights now would be an unjust interference with the rights over their estates guaranteed to the zamindars by the Permanent Settlement.[13] But Peacock was by no means an organ of the planter class. A theoretical jurist, he rested his case upon the principles of political economy. In his decision he ordered the judge to determine the rent according to the principles laid down by Malthus; and, urging repeal of Act X, he pointed out how "it tends to perpetuate small holdings which must ultimately become injurious to the best interests of the country." He concluded by stating that "it will be far better to leave the parties to make their own terms than to drive them into a court of law to have that done for them which they are much better able to do for themselves."[14]

In the Government Peacock's decision precipitated a storm

---

of Land Revenue Settlements in the North-Western Provinces 1860-1872 (Calcutta, 1872), pp. 110-14; and Walter Neale, Economic Change in Rural India (New Haven, 1962), pp. 64-72 and 82-87.

[13] Case of Ishwar Ghose v. James Hills 24 September 1862 in Decisions Under the Rent Laws of the High Court of Judicature from 1860 to 1863 (Calcutta, 1865), pp. 80-82. The decision was re-affirmed on 2 September 1863.

[14] Minute of 31 March 1864, enclosure in letter from Maine to Wood of 2 April 1864, Wood Papers.

of protest. As Sir Charles Trevelyan noted indignantly, "He has disfranchised and reduced to the state of tenants at will the great body of the Bengal ryots."[15] The English press and the Indian zamindars naturally rallied to Peacock's support, but the Government saw only endless litigation and eventual agrarian unrest. So they set out at once to draw up corrective legislation which would insure that "enhancement of the rent shall only be in proportion to the rise in the value of the produce since the rent was last fixed."[16] Trevelyan indeed would go further. He submitted a scheme for a permanent settlement of rent between ryot and zamindar, along the lines of the settlement between Government and landholder. The proposal received a sympathetic hearing and was taken up by the Bengal Government, who saw in it a way of preventing oppression of their tenants by planters determined to expand indigo cultivation.[17] Most officials, however, were reluctant to see the Government interfere so openly in the relation of landlord and tenant, and they were not at all anxious to face the bitter antagonism such a scheme would provoke among the landholding classes. Henry Maine also pointed out that any such measure would "turn the zemindar into the receiver of a mere rent charge" and hence destroy the incentive to improve.[18] But he refused on that account to abandon Act X; and in this he was supported by the Secretary of State, Sir Charles Wood. Maine and Wood both accepted the theories of political economy, and acknowledged that "they are not good things, these rights of occupancy." Nevertheless they were convinced that long-established custom had given the Bengal ryot a beneficial right of occupancy, and that the ryot who

[15] Trevelyan to Wood, 8 September 1863, Wood Papers. Trevelyan was Finance Member of the Council of India from January 1863 to April 1865.

[16] Wood to Lawrence, 16 August 1864. He also pointed out that in the absence of any proof of increased value the previously existing rent should be deemed fair and equitable, Wood Papers.

[17] Sec. Govt. Bengal to Commissioner Nadia, 4 April 1864, Home Judl., June 1864, No. 36.

[18] Maine to Wood, 12 June 1864, Wood Papers.

possessed a claim to a share of the produce had a right to share in any increase in the value of that produce. Act X had simply placed these rights on a firm legal basis, and should on no account be tampered with.[19]

While the Government was drafting its legislation, its labors were anticipated by the Court itself. The other judges of the High Court had never acquiesced in Peacock's decision, and one, George Campbell, had even handed down a contrary opinion in September 1864.[20] Finally in March 1865 the rent case was brought before the full court. By a vote of 14 to 1 the Court overturned Peacock's decision, and established the rule of proportional enhancement for which the Government was contending. With this decision the necessity for legislation disappeared, and the Bengal tenancy question lapsed into quiescence. The victory of the tenantry was more apparent than real, however, for Act X even in its original form was a flimsy bulwark against a powerful zamindar. The Act could easily be evaded, as the zamindars soon discovered, by the simple expedient of shifting the cultivator from one field to another before the twelve-year period had expired. Even when the cultivator was left physically undisturbed the zamindar was often able to check the growth of occupancy rights through his control of the *patwari's* books; all he had to do was to show that every so often a break in the ryot's possession was recorded in the records. The Act had, moreover, to contend with the traditional laissez faire sentiments of the Bengal civilian, who rarely took up the cause of the peasantry with any enthusiasm. If differences arose between landlord and tenant, he said, they could always be settled in court. As one officer fresh from the Punjab noted with some surprise: "It was held in 1862, and for long after, that the Collector and other public officials had no right and no business to inquire how the zemindar managed his estate, or how he dealt with

---

[19] Wood to Lawrence, 27 February 1865, 27 March 1865, and 3 April 1865; Maine to Wood, 13 August 1865, Wood Papers.

[20] Campbell, *Memoirs*, II, 105.

his immense body of tenants. . . . When I spoke to my Collector about the welfare of the peasant class . . . he laughed at me and told me it was no business of ours; the zemindar had a right to do what he liked with his ryots."[21]

As a result, land tenure continued to be a serious source of agrarian discontent in Bengal. Eventually in 1879 a Rent Commission was appointed, extensive inquiries were carried out, and in 1885 a new tenancy law was put on the books. This complex and lengthy act marked a significant step forward in tenancy legislation. Under it the practice of shifting was stopped by the award of occupancy rights to all ryots who had held any land in the same village or on the same estate continuously for twelve years. In other respects the Act very much resembled the Irish Land Act of 1881; it gave the Bengal tenant the famous 3 F's—fair rent, fixity of tenure, and free sale of his occupancy right—plus compensation for disturbance and for improvement in the case of eviction. The power of the zamindar, however, was by no means broken. The zamindar was still able to intimidate his tenants, and even at times to break down their privileged status, by the threat of legal proceedings. The complexities of the Act afforded ample opportunities for litigation, and the zamindar, once in court, would not admit defeat until he had exhausted every avenue of appeal. Rather than face this prospect, the tenant, with his meagre resources, would usually bow before his landlord's demands. As a rule the mere threat of a suit for arrears was sufficient to induce him to accept a small enhancement of his rent.[22]

## Oudh

In Oudh the question of tenant right provoked a bitter and protracted controversy within the Government. When it was all over, the vast majority of the cultivators found themselves

[21] John Beames, *Memoirs of a Bengal Civilian* (London, 1961), p. 129.

[22] R. Carstairs, *The Little World of an Indian District Officer* (London, 1912), pp. 88-98.

with no protection at all, while the taluqdars were more firmly entrenched in power than ever before. For this result the harsh lessons of the Mutiny, and the determination of one man, Charles Wingfield, are largely responsible. After the Mutiny the Viceroy, Lord Canning, was interested solely in building up the taluqdars and securing their good will. He made a few feeble efforts to secure the position of the cultivators, but he really did not care very much what happened to them. Their hostility during the revolt had convinced him that "these village occupants deserve little consideration from us," and he therefore wasted little time upon them.

From 1859 onward land policy in Oudh was entrusted to its Chief Commissioner, Charles Wingfield; and he set out at once to reduce all occupants to the status of tenants at will. In the Record of Rights circular issued in September 1860 he directed his Settlement Officers to confirm under-proprietors and intermediate holders only in those rights they held as of 1855; rights which had lapsed after that date would not be recognized or recorded. Occupancy rights in the hands of ordinary cultivators were to be disregarded altogether. "The Chief Commissioner has determined," the circular stated, "to make no distinction in the records between cultivators at fixed rates and cultivators at will. Abstractedly viewed, he considers that to give a right of permanent occupancy at an unvarying rate to the tiller of the soil is an invasion of the rights of property and a clog on enterprise and improvement."[23] These instructions were generally approved by the Government of India, and Canning gave them his explicit sanction. They excited no notice until 1862, when the Judicial Commissioner, George Campbell, long an advocate of peasant proprietorship, challenged Wingfield's denial of occupancy rights. Campbell asserted that, though there might be in Oudh no cultivators at fixed rates, "there certainly were cultivators possessing rights of occupancy and liable to regu-

[23] C.C. Oudh to Sec. Govt. India, 7 September 1860, For. Rev. A, March 1862, No. 7-13.

lated rates, by which they were distinguished from tenants at will"; and he went on to criticize the Record of Rights for its evil tendency to "reduce the whole of the cultivators to the dead level of rack rented tenants at will."[24]

The issue was thus fairly joined. But at the time Campbell's protest evoked little response either in Lucknow or Calcutta. Campbell was very much in a minority among the Oudh Secretariat, most of whom, including the Settlement Commissioner, Charles Currie, supported their chief; and Campbell himself left to take up his seat on the Calcutta High Court during 1862. Wingfield was home on leave during much of 1861 and 1862, but his *locum tenens*, G. U. Yule, was a Bengal civilian carefully picked by Canning for his aristocratic sentiments. Canning continually impressed upon him the importance of giving to the taluqdari settlement "a fair, and even a partial and indulgent trial." Yule in return readily admitted that he was "no great believer in the rights of cultivators" and carried on Wingfield's policy of ignoring all claims to occupancy tenure.[25] Canning's successor, Lord Elgin, was considerably disturbed by Wingfield's cavalier treatment of the Oudh peasantry. He detected in Wingfield a disposition to sacrifice undoubted rights to speculative theory "which rather alarms me."[26] But he was reluctant to take strong action, and his death in November 1863 cut short a projected inquiry.

Only with the arrival of Sir John Lawrence as Viceroy in January 1864 was the question prosecuted with vigor. Lawrence's training and background prompted him at once to champion the interests of the peasantry. He made no attempt

[24] Report on Administration of Justice in Oudh 1861, dated 28 April 1862; For. Judl. A, December 1862, No. 11. So far back as 1859 Campbell had advocated rights of occupancy at a fixed rent, holding that "it is by such small tenures . . . that I believe most improvement of the land may be effected." Note on Oudh Settlement and Tenures of 7 February 1859, Oudh General Proceedings 1858-59, No. 305, U.P. Records, Allahabad.

[25] Canning to Yule, 29 August 1861, and Yule to Canning, 20 September 1861, Canning Papers.

[26] Elgin to Wood, 21 May 1863, Wood Papers.

to overthrow the taluqdars and return to the peasant settlement of 1856. Much as he preferred that system, he realized
that Canning's pledges bound the Government to support of
the taluqdars, and that any wholesale revision of settlement
would provoke an immense outcry. But he was determined
to salvage all rights of occupancy that could be proved to
have existed at annexation.[27] He accordingly initiated an
inquiry in October 1864, under the supervision of R. H.
Davies, a Punjab officer specially appointed Financial Commissioner of Oudh for the purpose.

The inquiry revealed quite clearly the nature of occupancy
tenure in Oudh, but it provided no clear-cut victory for either
side in the controversy. The protagonists of the taluqdars and
those of the tenants both found in it ample evidence to substantiate their claims. When questioned, the cultivators almost
invariably admitted that they possessed no legal right to hold
land against the will of their landlord. The taluqdar could
raise rent or evict his tenants at any time. Yet customs had in
fact grown up, in Oudh as elsewhere, which severely restricted
the landlord's power.[28] In the unsettled conditions of Oudh
under the later Nawabs, although the taluqdars had gained
much political power, they needed tenants in order to defend
their interests against the Nawab's *chakladars* and to prosecute
their quarrels with fellow taluqdars. As one District Officer
noted, "Good fighting men and retainers of a superior stamp
were just as necessary to the taluqdar's existence as rent, and
he usually purchased the former by a slight sacrifice of the
latter." Shortage of population further limited the taluqdar's
arbitrary power. "Competition," the same officer pointed out,
"was among landlords for cultivators, not among cultivators
for the possession of land."[29] Despite the lack of legal pro-

[27] Lawrence to Wood, 28 June 1864, Wood Papers.

[28] For results of inquiry see R. H. Davies to C.C. Oudh, 19 June 1865, For.
Rev. A, February 1866, No. 72.

[29] E. Thompson, Deputy Commissioner Sitapur, 22 April 1865, For. Rev.
A, February 1866, No. 73-124.

tection, therefore, most cultivators possessed a fairly secure tenure and freedom from the worst forms of extortion.

With the introduction of British rule, the taluqdar no longer stood in need of the aid and attachment of his tenants. Consequently, as one officer reported, his interest "instead of being principally directed to the conciliation of his tenants, as it was then, will be directed to the increase of his rental to as much as he finds the land can bear."[30] This tendency gained further momentum with the treatment of the taluqdars as a privileged and favored class after 1858. The support of men like Wingfield and Canning emboldened them to press forward their attack on the customary rights of the cultivators. Indeed the award of revenue jurisdiction over their estates gave them a handy instrument for the obliteration of such rights. By 1865 competition was fast displacing custom as the criterion of rental demand. The Government detected a steady rise in rents from 1860 onwards, and an increase of about 25 per cent per year in the number of suits brought for enhanced rent or ouster of recalcitrant tenants.[31]

Davies viewed this process with alarm. As a man bred in the Punjab tradition and a disciple of J. S. Mill, he saw "no hope whatever" for agricultural improvement in Oudh "by the expenditure of capital on the part of large landholders." He was convinced that competition for land would soon reduce the peasantry to impoverishment. So he recommended in his final report that the "existing beneficial customs" be preserved by the introduction of Act X in Oudh. It would, he said, "merely transmute Customs into Rights."[32] In this opinion he found considerable support among the Oudh District Officers, many of whom, only with difficulty reconciled to taluqdari settlement, were deeply disturbed by

[30] P. Simson, Commissioner Faizabad, 10 October 1863, For. Rev. A, February 1865, No. 121.

[31] *Oudh Administration Report for 1861-62*, p. 20; and *Oudh Administration Report for 1862-63*, p. 21.

[32] Letter of 19 June 1865, *loc.cit.*

the plight of the peasantry under Wingfield's arrangements. In their view, the wretched condition of the cultivating community under a class of rack-renting landlords in no way resembling the English gentry justified any action the Government might take for their protection.[33]

Wingfield denied that the results of the inquiry gave the Government any warrant to intervene on behalf of the Oudh peasantry. He disparaged the customs alluded to by Davies as being nothing more than "the will of the landlord restrained in its exercise by a sense of his own interests." Instead he pointed to the fact that the peasantry possessed no legal rights in the land, and asserted that to give them such rights now through the introduction of Act X would be an unjustifiable infringement of the rights guaranteed to the taluqdars.[34] Wingfield's determined, even obstinate, resistance to any recognition of occupancy rights reflects his belief that they were both politically unwise and economically unsound. To a far greater extent than most of his contemporaries, Wingfield pursued the theories of laissez faire to their logical conclusion. At the same time he was convinced that the security of the British Indian Empire depended upon "the attachment of the landed aristocracy." For him, as for so many others, this was one of the chief lessons driven home by the Mutiny. But for Wingfield it was more than an academic argument; it was a fact whose truth he had himself tested. Wingfield's advocacy of the taluqdar cause was in part an expression of gratitude for the shelter he had received when forced to flee his post at Bahraich. As the taluqdars had saved him and his fellow officers, so would they help to preserve the British Empire in India.

[33] H. S. Reid, Commissioner Biaswara (Rae Bareli) Division, 28 June 1865, For. Rev. A, February 1866, No. 9; G. Tucker, Commissioner Khyrabad (Sitapur) Division, 28 October 1863, For. Rev. A, February 1865, No. 123; R. M. King, Deputy Commissioner Pratabgarh, 2 June 1863, For. Rev. A, February 1865, No. 110.

[34] C.C. Oudh to Sec. Govt. India, 14 July 1865, For. Rev. A, February 1866, No. 71.

Despite his attachment to the taluqdars, Wingfield was by no means oblivious to the interests of the peasantry. He simply viewed them according to his own laissez faire philosophy. A rise in rent, for instance, far from being an evil to be combatted, was "a sign of an increase in the value of produce and consequently of progress in wealth and prosperity." As a good Victorian liberal, he was confident that the prosperity of the peasantry "is most likely to be promoted by emancipating them from the idea that they are bound to the soil on which they are born, by teaching them to rely on their own exertion to better their condition . . . and by giving free scope to the ordinary laws of social progress." The solution to the problem of agrarian distress was not occupancy tenure, which only encouraged population growth, but emigration. Tenants who objected to paying the full market rate for land should leave it to others who would, and take their labor to the uncultivated wastelands of Northern Oudh. As with the English workman, so with the Indian peasant, the inculcation of self-reliance and individualism was ultimately "the kinder and wiser policy."[35] This abstract benevolence of course took no account of the strong attachment of the cultivator to his ancestral village, the impossibility of his moving long distances without funds or transport, and the lack of alternative employment in a land of rapidly rising population.

Sir John Lawrence saw no reason to hand over the "weak and friendless" village occupants to the tender mercies of their landlords. Indeed the rapidly growing power of the taluqdars evoked his natural solicitude for "the humbler classes in Oudh" who now, he felt, "require our protection."[36] He was certain that hereditary occupancy rights did exist in Oudh, and he hoped in the inquiry to gain some general recognition of their existence. In the end he had to admit that no clear-cut legal rights had been found. Yet, like Davies,

---

[35] C.C. Oudh to Sec. Govt. India, 26 March 1864, For. Rev. A, February 1865, No. 105.
[36] Minute of 12 September 1864, For. Rev. A, February 1865, No. 160.

he felt there clearly were "prevailing usages" in favor of resident cultivators which deserved legal standing. Accordingly
he recommended the introduction of Act X into Oudh, or at
least the recognition of rights of occupancy at prevailing local
rates.[37]

This proposal, however, encountered strong opposition both
within the Government and without, and had eventually to be
abandoned. Non-official opinion rose up unanimously against
Lawrence. The mercantile community of Calcutta, the Anglo-
Indian press, and the Bengal zamindars and planters, all
united behind the rights of property and the principles of
free contract.[38] The taluqdars themselves, through the British
Indian Association, vociferously defended their right to do as
they pleased with their property. Man Singh appealed to
"religion, morality, law, and social usages" to prove that
rights of occupancy had never existed in Oudh.[39] At home
Lord Stanley, the Conservative press, and many members of
the India Council saw in Lawrence's policy the first step in
the destruction of the taluqdari system. The Secretary of
State, Sir Charles Wood, was himself skeptical of the wisdom
of the inquiry and repeatedly urged Lawrence on no account
to antagonize the taluqdars or give them any "reasonable
cause of complaint." Although Wood formally supported Lawrence and agreed that "the just rights of the subordinate
holders must not be sacrificed," he refused to go beyond the
narrow limits of the inquiry. As no rights had been made out,
none could be awarded. With his laissez faire bent, Wood
had never looked favorably upon the creation of occupancy

[37] Sec. Govt. India to C.C. Oudh, 16 January 1866, For. Rev. A, February
1866, No. 126.

[38] Richard Temple, *Men and Events of My Time in India* (London, 1882),
p. 323. The *Englishman, Indian Daily News, Friend of India*, and *Delhi
Gazette*, among others, denounced Lawrence's "act of spoliation" in Oudh.

[39] Speech of 30 December 1864 before British Indian Association, *Proceedings from 1861 to 1865*, p. 181. As a defender of law and morality Man
Singh cut a rather ludicrous figure, since his estate was of extremely recent
origin and put together with a good deal of force and violence.

rights, but in this case his opposition was determined by practical political considerations. Outbursts of discontent among the taluqdars must be avoided at all costs. Nothing should be done which might in any way undermine "that position of consideration and dignity" conferred upon them by Lord Canning.[40] Lawrence met with no greater encouragement from the members of his Council. Trevelyan alone shared his views. The others, if not opposed to inquiry, refused to sanction the introduction of Act X into Oudh or the creation of occupancy rights.[41]

In March 1866 Lawrence sent John Strachey to Oudh as Chief Commissioner. Despite his own strong peasant sympathies, Strachey at once realized that under the circumstances it was quite impossible to give rights of occupancy to the mass of the cultivators. So he set out to negotiate a compromise settlement, winning from the taluqdars such concessions as they could be induced to make. In particular he wanted to obtain some protection for the ex-proprietary cultivators, who, he felt, possessed especially strong claims to consideration. These were men who during the preceding thirty years had lost all proprietary right in the land but still cultivated their ancestral fields. The taluqdars readily agreed to grant this class a right of occupancy at favorable rates ($12\frac{1}{2}$ per cent below that paid by ordinary tenants), provided all further claims were dropped. This agreement provided the basis of the Oudh Compromise of August 1866, later confirmed in the Oudh Rent Act (No. XIX of 1868).

As they had no doubt calculated, the taluqdars' moderation in this settlement won them a great deal of praise and did much to efface the bitterness of the previous controversy. Strachey even commented that "the talookdars have shown in all the late proceedings a spirit of conciliation and liberality which deserves the acknowledgement of Government"; and he went on to recommend Man Singh, the taluqdari leader,

[40] Dispatch of 10 February 1865, Political Dispatch No. 3 of 1865.
[41] For. Rev. A, February 1865, No. 129-34.

for a K.C.S.I.[42] Yet for all of this effusive good will the Oudh settlement was really a surrender to the taluqdars. Indeed it was a far more complete surrender than was realized at the time, for the extent of protection afforded by the Rent Act had been greatly over-estimated. The ex-proprietary cultivators comprised not 20 per cent of the whole body of cultivators, as Lawrence and Strachey had estimated in 1866, but only 1 per cent. The rest—the overwhelming mass of the peasantry—were left without any rights at all.

The taluqdars were not slow to take advantage of their new position. By 1873 notices of eviction were being issued at the rate of 60,000 annually, with the object not of clearing the land but of forcing the tenant to submit to an enhanced rent.[43] Ten years later extensive inquiries revealed that rent rates had risen an average of at least 25 per cent since settlement, and that rack-renting was widespread. Throughout much of the province, rent rates were regulated solely by the land hunger of an increasing population. "They have now reached a limit so high," one officer reported, "as to press most severely on the tenants," for "the only law guiding the landlord is to get all he can and let the tenant shift for himself."[44] As a result further tenancy legislation was enacted in 1886. By the provisions of this act (No. XXII of 1886), all ordinary tenants were entitled to remain in possession of their land at a fixed rate for seven years. At the end of each seven-year period the landlord could eject the tenant altogether, or enhance his rent not more than 6¼ per cent. The Oudh peasantry thus obtained at last some protection against arbitrary enhancement. But the power of the landlord was in no way curbed. Not only was he free to oust the tenant every seven years; he even managed to defeat the intent of the

[42] C.C. Oudh to Sec. Govt. India, 20 August 1866, For. Rev. A, June 1867, No. 43; Strachey to Lawrence, 7 December 1866, Lawrence Papers.

[43] Oudh Revenue Proceedings, February 1873, No. 8, Lucknow Secretariat Records. See also Campbell, *Memoirs*, II, 60.

[44] Maj. W. E. Forbes, Commissioner Lucknow Division, 29 March 1883 in *The Condition of the Tenantry in Oudh* (Allahabad, 1883), I, 25.

act by extorting large sums of money, known as *nazrana*, from the cultivator before reinstating him in his holding.[45] As nowhere else in India, the landlord class in Oudh emerged almost completely victorious from the tenancy controversies of the post-Mutiny era, and they were able to turn aside or blunt all challenges to their dominant position until well into the twentieth century.

## Punjab

In the Punjab the tenantry fared far better than in Oudh or Bengal. The Punjab was overwhelmingly a country of small proprietors, and their tenants had been largely granted occupancy rights on the North-Western Provinces model at the time of the original settlement. Since there was no appreciable popular uprising in the Punjab during 1857, this settlement survived the Mutiny intact. It provided, however, no obstacle to the growth of landlord sentiment. Canning's attempt in 1860 to restore the landed gentry was followed in 1863 by a concerted attack upon the rights of the occupancy tenants. The opportunity was provided by the expiration of the original settlement in Amritsar Division. Edward A. Prinsep, Settlement Commissioner, during his preliminary inquiries there discovered numerous errors in the settlement record. Many persons awarded occupancy rights under the twelve-year rule had been, in his view, tenants at will before annexation. Indeed, he said, occupancy rights in the Punjab were a creation of the British, for in Sikh times "the landowner had the right to evict any tenant, and could do so at any time."[46] In the revised settlement Prinsep set out to correct these alleged errors. The result was that by 1866 out of 60,000 tenants recorded as hereditary cultivators in Amritsar all but 15,000 had been reduced to tenants at will.

Prinsep justified these wholesale proceedings on the ground that they simply reinstated the traditional local practice in

[45] Baden-Powell, *Land-Systems of British India*, II, 250-51.
[46] Prinsep to Financial Commissioner, 28 April 1863, P.P. 1870, LIII, 454.

place of an alien and arbitrary rule. But behind this argument
lay a sympathy with the class which had felt "the reality of
confiscation" in the previous settlement. At the time of
annexation land was of such little value that the landlords,
anxious to retain cultivators, willingly saw them recorded as
hereditary occupants. With the rise in the value of land under
British rule, they came to regret their earlier generosity, and
pleaded for revision of settlement.[47] Prinsep agreed they had
been unjustly treated. Indeed, rejecting the utilitarian rent
theory of his younger days, he now asserted that a superior
class "exercising an absolute right of property" had always
existed in the Punjab. From this class, once secure in its
traditional rights, would come the future prosperity of the
province.[48] Among the District Officers of the Punjab, Prinsep
found considerable support. Most admitted that the power of
the landholder over his tenants was unlimited, although as
in Oudh several pointed to the growth of customs which had
in practice restricted that power and produced a mutual dependence of landlord and tenant.[49] The Lieutenant-Governor,
D. F. Macleod, gave Prinsep wholehearted support. While admitting that eviction was uncommon in Sikh times, Macleod,
like Prinsep, believed that "the right of the proprietor to
dispose of his lands, however it may have remained in abeyance, has never ceased to be acknowledged and will never
be contentedly surrendered." He opposed recognition of
occupancy rights on the ground that they would produce
"great and permanent dissatisfaction" among the landlord
classes and at the same time prove a "serious obstruction to
progress" by binding the people to the land. Like Wingfield,
he subscribed to the laissez faire view that mobility of labor

[47] Sec. Govt. Punjab to Sec. Govt. India, 3 February 1864, For. Rev. A,
March 1864, No. 9. See also Baden-Powell, *Land-Systems of British India*, II,
707-08.

[48] Settlement Report of 1865-66, dated 12 August 1866, P.P. 1870, LIII,
535-37.

[49] See Reports of District Officers in Appendix II of Proceedings of Punjab
Tenant Right Committee, *ibid.*, pp. 458-64.

was the only remedy for rural poverty and stagnation. Yet his landlord inclinations were somewhat less extreme than Prinsep's, for he proposed, and tenaciously advocated, a scheme of compensation for eviction.[50]

Prinsep's proceedings obtained a much colder reception at the hands of the Government of India. Sir John Lawrence was furious at the thought of a minor Punjab official tampering with his cherished peasant settlement. He at once challenged the contention that the cultivators did not have any beneficial interest in the land under native rule. Lawrence claimed that, whatever the theoretical right of the landlord, in practice he did not evict, for he needed tenants on his fields. This gave to the peasants "an absolute security from eviction" which it would "be unadvisable now to deny them," when rising land values were giving the proprietor an inducement to evict.[51] In Oudh the strong vested interests of the taluqdars, and British reluctance to antagonize them, had prevented the conversion of such customs into effective tenancy legislation; but in the Punjab tenant rights of occupancy were already well established when Prinsep started his settlement operations. On this ground Lawrence was able to rally a good deal of support not available to him in Oudh. Men like Henry Maine who cared little for tenant right as such nevertheless believed that it was "just as much deserving of respect as any other form of property," once it had existed (as in the Punjab) for fifteen years and been vested in specific individuals. For Maine it was not a question of the expediency of tenant right, or of the correction of mistakes made long ago; it was a simple matter of the sanctity of property, which once created ought to be maintained. "I say let us stand even by our mistakes. It is better than perpetual meddling."[52] At the heart of these outspoken remarks lay a conservative lawyer's

[50] Sec. Govt. Punjab to Sec. Govt. India, 15 September 1866, *ibid.*, p. 432; and Minute of 10 February 1868, For. Rev. A, January 1870, No. 48.

[51] Minute of 30 April 1867, P.P. 1870, LIII, 555.

[52] Minute of 26 October 1866, *ibid.*, p. 552; and Speech in Legislative Council, 19 October 1868, *Proceedings*, VII, 414, 423.

veneration for the stability of private property, but his forthright logic impressed itself upon the other members of the
Viceroy's Council. Sir Richard Temple, although admitting
that Britain had gone too far in creating occupancy rights at
settlement, agreed with Maine that "it was now too late to
interfere with such tenures, or to deliberate whether the
settlement was right or not. . . . Men should not now be
required to defend a position so long ago recognized, so
formally guaranteed, so continuously enjoyed."[53]

The Punjab Rent Act (No. XXVIII of 1868) thus saved
for the peasant a much greater residue of right than was the
case in Oudh. Prinsep's proceedings in Amritsar were reversed,
and all tenants hitherto recorded as possessing rights of occupancy were presumed legally to possess such rights until the
contrary was proved by the landlord in a regular suit in court.
In this way, although aggrieved landlords could regain lost
rights, the process was made as difficult and cumbrous as
possible; and few landlords did in fact challenge the presumption of occupancy.[54] The law further provided that the
rent payable by an occupancy tenant could only be enhanced
by decree of court and must be at least 15 per cent below a
rack-rent. Two clauses benefitted the landlord: the first, that
no rights of occupancy could be acquired by mere lapse of
time, as under Act X; and second, eviction even of occupancy
tenants was permitted on payment of compensation.

Passage of the Act, however, did not still the controversy.
Its opponents, heartened by the appointment of a new Viceroy
and new Secretary of State in January 1869, put up a last-
ditch fight to have the Act disallowed at home. Macleod in
India, and Wingfield, Frere, and Montgomery on the India
Council in London, bombarded the Government with protests and petitions. They were at first hopeful of success, for

[53] Speech in Legislative Council, 19 October 1868, *ibid.*, p. 404. See also
speech of 11 April 1868, p. 271.
[54] Memorandum by R. E. Egerton, Financial Commissioner, Punjab, 29
June 1870, For. Rev. A, September 1870, No. 18.

both Argyll and Mayo were members of the landed aristocracy. Indeed, as J. S. Mill noted with some bitterness: "India has now got an Irish landlord to rule over her; and it is quite uncertain whether his official superior, the Duke of Argyll, will be any check upon his landlordism. There has been no more determined defender than the Duke of the evictions, in utter defiance of customary and traditional ideas of rights, which have depopulated the North of Scotland."[55]

Yet Mayo at least was by no means a doctrinaire advocate of laissez faire. Despite his Anglo-Irish family background, he was fully aware of the misery of the Irish cottier tenant, and determined to avoid a repetition of "the Irish difficulty" in India. As Chief Secretary for Ireland in several Tory Governments he had (unsuccessfully) advocated the right of the tenant to compensation for improvement; as Viceroy his sympathies were even more fully enlisted on the side of the peasantry. "We should aim," he said, at giving "to the cultivator and occupier as much security of tenure as is possible, consistent with proprietary right." Such security was not only essential for agricultural prosperity in India, it was "in conformity with ancient custom and the feelings of the people." He therefore refused to accept the argument against the Punjab Act brought forward by Macleod—that "real progress" could come only from large landholders untrammelled by subordinate rights in the soil—and he recommended that the bill not be vetoed.[56] Argyll was far more a typical Whig aristocrat. He was anxious always to defend the rights of property, and his landlord enthusiasm was not dampened by the fact that in India this class rarely undertook agricultural improvement.[57] Prinsep's proceedings thus met with his general approval. But he was reluctant to overrule the Viceroy,

---

[55] J. S. Mill to Henry Maine, 1 January 1869 in Elliot, ed., *Letters of J. S. Mill*, II, 171.

[56] Mayo to Argyll, 21 July 1869 and 29 July 1869, Argyll Papers. Memorandum by Macleod of 18 April 1869, P.P. 1870, LIII, 798.

[57] See, for instance, his letter to Northbrook, 23 May 1873, in Argyll, *Memoirs*, II, 282-83; and Public Works Dispatch No. 51 of 22 May 1873.

and like Mayo he had no desire to see revived the bitter controversy which had surrounded the bill. So the Act came at last into operation in October 1869.[58]

Each of these tenancy controversies indicates, as does Canning's Oudh settlement, the extensive growth of landlord sentiment among the British in India after the Mutiny. In Bengal a single judge was able to nullify the intent of a legislative act, and his decision was reversed only with difficulty. In Oudh the Chief Commissioner consciously, and successfully, set out to destroy what tenant right still remained. In the Punjab, where peasant settlement had reached its finest flower, many officials, including the Lieutenant-Governor, were by 1864 converts to landlordism and settlement revision. At home such sentiment was even stronger. Among the mercantile and landed community, tenant right found almost no supporters; and the Secretary of State, nourished on the theories of laissez faire liberalism, was often drawn to the side of the landlord. Yet, during the same post-Mutiny decade, tenancy legislation was put on the books in each of these three provinces. The protection afforded under this initial legislation was limited— in Oudh, where a strong taluqdar class was deemed essential to the security of the Empire, the peasantry obtained very little—but these acts did recognize the principle that the people "who actually occupy and cultivate the land" deserved a permanent interest in it.[59] This principle was extended and strengthened in all later legislation. The acts of the 1880's, and the subsequent rounds of tenancy legislation in the 1920's and 1930's, further restricted the prerogatives of the landlord and gave the peasantry ever greater protection against extortion and rack-renting.

During the later years of their rule, then, the British in

[58] S. of S. to Govt. India, 28 October 1869, For. Rev. A, January 1870, No. 70.

[59] Strachey speech in Legislative Council, 18 October 1868, *Proceedings*, VII, 431.

India undertook simultaneously to conciliate the landlords and to protect the peasantry. At no time did they ever cease to acknowledge a responsibility for the welfare of the peasantry. This after all was the ultimate justification of British rule: that they could best judge the needs and look after the interests of the Indian people. Indeed with the rise of middle-class nationalism toward the end of the century, the Government asserted that it alone represented the "real people of India," the silent masses who tilled the soil. The opposition of the educated Bengali community to the Tenancy Act of 1885, which in the end was passed only by the weight of the official majority in Council, seemingly confirmed this belief and helped sustain British confidence in their mission in India. Similarly, the Punjab Land Alienation Act of 1900, which the leading Congress politicians all denounced, and R. C. Dutt's defence of the Permanent Settlement, bolstered Britain's claim to speak for the Indian peasantry.[60] Yet, at the same time, the Government was always sensitive to the interests of the Indian aristocracy and responsive to their demands. Tenancy legislation was carefully tailored to avoid any real damage to the position of the landlord community, and was rarely enacted without their consent. Even the Bengal Act of 1885 was considerably diluted to meet the objections of the zamindars (and then further watered down to meet the laissez faire sentiments of the India Office). In an era of rising nationalism the Government simply could not afford to antagonize this influential and conservative class. Indeed the nationalist challenge to British power made the good will of the landed aristocracy all the more essential. The decisive step of zamindari abolition had to await the coming of an independent Government of India.

[60] See for instance Curzon speech of 16 November 1905 in Sir Thomas Raleigh, ed., *Lord Curzon in India* (London, 1906), pp. 584-85. On the opposition of the educated Indian to tenancy legislation see B. B. Misra, *The Indian Middle Classes* (London, 1961), pp. 344-47 and 355-56.

TABLE 8

PATTERNS OF LAND HOLDING: NORTH INDIA

(Figures represent percentage of cultivated land.)

| Type of Holder | North-Western Provinces[a] | Punjab[b] | Oudh[c] |
|---|---|---|---|
| Proprietor | 24.0% | 61% | 7.5% |
| Occupancy tenant | 37.5 | 11 | 4.5 |
| Tenant at will | 38.5 | 28 | 88.0 |

[a] *Report on the Administration of the North-Western Provinces and Oudh for 1882-83* (Allahabad, 1883), p. 41. The Famine Commission of 1880 stated that proprietors held 28%, occupancy tenants 41%, and tenants at will 31%. P.P. 1880, LII, 595.

[b] Baden-Powell, *Land-Systems of British India*, II, 721-22. This data is for 1888.

[c] *The Condition of the Tenantry in Oudh*, II, 240. These figures are for 1882. According to the *Administration Report* for 1882-1883 proprietors held 14%, sub-proprietary tenants 7%, occupancy tenants 1%, and tenants at will 78%.

## The Moneylender and the Mutiny

Even where peasant settlement had survived the Mutiny and the enthusiasms of the landlord party, the cultivators were by no means secure in their holdings. Throughout much of North India and Bombay they were often as tightly bound to the village moneylender as any Oudh tenant at will to his taluqdar. The moneylender was already an established figure on the rural scene when the British arrived. His advances alone enabled a peasantry perennially short of capital to survive during seasons of famine, and his shop could be found throughout the rural areas. But he was then restrained both by the village community and by the state. Land was held jointly by the community as a whole and was never alienated to outsiders. Consequently the moneylender could not obtain possession of the cultivator's holding, nor could he afford to defy the village headmen who stood behind his debtors. Though indispensable to the village, because he alone had access to capital, the moneylender was little more than its humble servant. Often in fact he was a bania or marwari, an outsider, whose closest ties were with his kinfolk in Rajasthan, and who was looked upon with suspicion by the villagers. The State, on its part, gave the moneylender little assistance in the recovery of debt. If not actively hostile, it was apathetic. There were no civil courts, and the creditor was left to collect his due as best he could by intimidation or threats.

The advent of British rule destroyed this system of mutual dependence between cultivator and moneylender, and enabled the latter for the first time to gain real power over the village community. Under the new Government the landholder was awarded a full proprietary title with the power of sale and transfer. Land thus became a marketable commodity, and with rising prices acquired what it had never had before—a mortgageable value. Even when the land revenue demand was settled with the village community as a whole, the shares of each individual member were recorded; and he was permitted to separate his own interest from that of the joint village at any time. Under these circumstances, as land increased in value, the partition of joint estates was only a matter of time.[61] At the same time the village community was itself collapsing under the impact of British rule. The new courts and police slowly but inevitably encroached upon, and undermined, the authority of the local headmen and *panchayat*. By mid-century the village community of the Northwest had ceased to exercise effective political power. The individual peasant proprietor was thus left, whether by choice or necessity, to face his creditor on his own. Furthermore the British legal system made land transfer a matter of extreme, almost fearful, simplicity. Ignoring Indian custom, the civil courts rigorously enforced the English contract law which made a man's entire property liable for the satisfaction of his debts. Upon production of a bond from the moneylender, the courts would

[61] For an illustration of this process in operation see Charles Raikes, *Notes on the North-Western Provinces of India* (London, 1852), pp. 90-107.

automatically decree sale of a defaulting cultivator's land-holding.

Under these circumstances the moneylender naturally extended credit without restraint, for he knew that in case of default he could claim the best possible security—his debtor's land. The peasantry, on their part, soon saw their new security pledged to the hilt. As always they were forced to borrow in years of bad harvest to meet their immediate needs of food, grain, and livestock. Improvident and extravagant, they also borrowed heavily for such unproductive purposes as marriage feasts, social ceremonial, and the purchase of jewelry. Beyond this there was the pressure of the land revenue demand. Pitched high and rigidly collected during the early years of British rule, it drove the peasant to the moneylender to meet its inexorable claims. The initial plunge into debt was usually the result of economic necessity, as in pre-British times; but its greater extent in the nineteenth century reflects the increased value of land under British rule. With a far better security than ever before, the cultivator was now tempted (indeed encouraged) to indulge his more extravagant tastes. Those with the best security to offer were invariably the deepest in debt.[62]

Once in debt a peasant was usually unable to extricate himself. Most debt was incurred for non-productive purposes. Interest rates ranged upwards of 25 per cent, so that even small debts rapidly mounted up to enormous proportions. The moneylender was adept at fraudulent practices in the keeping of accounts, and did not in any case want to be paid off. His aim was to make the peasant into a perpetual bond servant by a mortgage which gave him control of the crop, or by a forced sale in which he would take title to the land while retaining the former proprietor as his tenant. In either case the moneylender had the upper hand, and the courts—

[62] See Report of Deccan Riots Committee (Bombay, 1876), pp. 38ff.; Report of Famine Commission of 1880, P.P. 1880, LII, 610; and Malcolm Darling, *The Punjab Peasant in Prosperity and Debt* (Oxford, 1947), pp. 209-13.

restrained by their belief in freedom of contract and laissez faire—were little more than instruments of his will.

The outbreak of the Mutiny found the transfer of land far advanced in one area only, the North-Western Provinces, where 114,000 acres were sold for debt in 1853 alone and moneylenders held over ten per cent of the agricultural land of the province.[63] In Bombay the pressure of debt was also beginning to be felt, but the sale of land was still relatively rare. Bengal escaped the worst effects of moneylender dominance altogether, for there the cultivators, already dependent upon the zamindar for their land, looked to him for their supply of credit as well. The zamindar, determined to keep a firm grip on his tenants, did his best to exclude the moneylender from his estates.[64] As a general rule, apart from Bengal, the longer a province was under British rule the more involved it was in debt. The first few years of British rule saw relatively little change in the pattern of landholding or the burden of debt. This reflects the slow and gradual introduction into each province of a regular land settlement and courts of justice. Only when the Record of Rights was drawn up and the revenue demand fixed on a long-term basis was it possible for land to acquire a mortgageable value. This process was complete in Bombay and the North-Western Provinces by the 1840's, and the rapid growth of indebtedness in those provinces dates from this period. Land transfer had to await also the opening of the civil courts. For this reason the Punjab did not feel the effects of indebtedness until the 1870's. Although the province was annexed in 1849, normal law courts were not established for two decades. Only in 1866 was the Code of Civil Procedure extended to the Punjab, and a High Court set up; and even then the civil courts had no cognizance over suits for debt until 1874. Until that time law was administered

[63] *Report by the Sudder Board of Revenue on the Revenue Administration of the North-Western Provinces for 1852-53* (Agra, 1854), pp. 46-48. See also H. Trevaskis, *Land of the Five Rivers* (Oxford, 1928), p. 338.

[64] See R. Carstairs, *Little World of an Indian District Officer*, p. 97.

by the District Officers, who decided cases more by broad principles of equity and custom than by rigid adherence to the letter of the law. For many officers the existence of these restraints helped account for the peaceful character of the Punjab during 1857. George Campbell even went so far as to say that, "If the land of the Punjab had been transferred as that of the Northwest Provinces has been, it is quite certain that we should not now be here."[65]

The reforming liberals of the pre-Mutiny decade saw in these extensive sales of land a healthy sign of progress. Far from trying to slow down the process of change, they set out consciously to smash the village communities and to afford the greatest possible facilities for land transfer. In Bombay George Wingate, Superintendent of the Revenue Survey, rigorously enforced the principle of individual responsibility, for he considered joint proprietorship "unjust in itself" and a drag on individual exertion.[66] Economic progress likewise required a free market in land and encouragement to the investment of capital. It was obviously desirable, he said, to get land out of the hands of impoverished cultivators and into the possession of "someone better able to turn it to advantage." Wingate readily admitted that "the customs and native revenue systems of India are adverse to such transfers," but that only made it "all the more necessary to adopt measures for giving them effect."[67] In the North-Western Provinces there was less enthusiasm for the destruction of the village communities. Yet sale of land for debt was still considered a "just and necessary" feature of the whole system of individual property, and no protest was raised against its operation. Inquiries carried out in 1854-1855, which revealed the extent of land transfer, evoked little concern. One officer boldly suggested that sale of land for debt be prohibited, and a few spoke vaguely of encouraging thrift by education.

[65] Campbell, *Memoirs*, I, 279.

[66] Report of 17 October 1840, P.P. 1852-53, LXXV, 367.

[67] Wingate to Townsend, 23 December 1848, *ibid.*, pp. 348-49.

For most, however, the collapse of the village communities was part of the march of progress. John Strachey, for instance, saw no reason to lament the fate of the ancient village institutions, for they "were necessarily doomed to decay with the establishment of good government and the progress of civilization." Nothing the Government could do could possibly "preserve the vitality of a system which natural causes are breaking up." Indeed, he went on, "one of the greatest advantages which the last settlement conferred upon these provinces was this possibility, before almost unknown, of disposing freely of land like any other property."[68]

The Mutiny provided a rude jolt to this complacency. On the outbreak of the revolt the former proprietors almost universally resumed possession of their old estates, driving out the auction purchasers installed by the British. Once back in possession, these men were of necessity committed to the rebel cause and led the countryside in revolt. In this defiance of British authority they readily gained the support and sympathy of the villagers, for the peasantry had never ceased to view the ousted proprietors as the rightful owners and the moneylenders as interlopers in agrarian society.[69] Although their interests were bound up with British rule, the auction purchasers were helpless to stem the tide of disaffection. With no roots in the community and no supporters among their new tenantry, they were swept away without a trace. The action of British laws and courts simply could not efface the attachment of the traditional landed classes to their hereditary estates, nor could they transfer the popular respect accorded these men to a new class of mercantile purchasers.

The British soon realized that compulsory sale of land had done much to alienate the people and to provoke rebellion in the Northwest. George Campbell even claimed that "whatever popular opposition there is in our old districts, beyond

---

[68] Report of 16 July 1855, *Selections from the Records of the Government of the North-Western Provinces* (Agra, 1856), IV, 213.

[69] See above, pp. 63-64.

the mere freebooting of plundering tribes, may be traced almost exclusively to this one great source of hostility which has raised many people against us."[70] Looking back, many officers bitterly criticized the Government for its willingness to incur the hatred of the mass of the people in order to placate "the most cowardly and ungrateful moneyed class on the face of the earth." No men, they pointed out, "have acted with so vindictive a hate against us as the smaller class of landholders whom the bunyahs had dispossessed through the medium of our courts."[71] As early as August 1858 the Court of Directors asked the Government of India to consider the question of restricting future sales of real property for debt, and in January 1859 the Secretary of State, Lord Stanley, recommended the enactment of remedial legislation.[72] Canning, sympathetic to the idea, at once initiated inquiries among the officers of Bengal and the North-Western Provinces. The reports submitted clearly show how the Mutiny forced the British to reconsider many of their accepted ideas about India, yet how tenaciously they clung to the doctrines of Victorian liberalism.

In the North-Western Provinces there was a good deal of sentiment in favor of an outright ban on the sale of land for debt. William Muir on the Board of Revenue pointed out that however indefensible such a measure might appear "to our European notions of political economy, it would be in close accordance with the habits and customs of the country, and as such would be highly popular."[73] The District Officers almost universally agreed that compulsory land sale was far too dangerous to be any longer tolerated. Some officers would allow temporary alienation of land to the creditor for a term of years, or the sale of personal effects, but beyond this few

[70] Campbell, *Memoirs*, I, 278-79.

[71] H. Dundas Robertson, *District Duties During the Revolt*, pp. 135-37.

[72] Dispatch of 4 August 1858, Public Dispatch No. 113 of 1858; and Dispatch of 25 January 1859, Judicial Dispatch No. 4 of 1859.

[73] Memorandum of 20 April 1859, Home Judl., 16 September 1862, No. 43.

were willing to go.[74] For them political expediency seemed now to demand enactment of the restrictive legislation for which there had been so little enthusiasm only four years previously. The Lieutenant-Governor, G. F. Edmonstone, on the other hand, refused to support any restriction on land sale. He acknowledged that "it is for our interest to protect the old hereditary proprietors in the possession of their estates," for they "are better able to support the Government in time of difficulty"; but he stood by the "just principle" that the whole of a man's property should be liable for his debts. The Government could not with propriety violate that principle in order to secure a political end, however desirable.[75]

In Calcutta the proposal to restrict land sale met with an extremely hostile reception. J. P. Grant, Lieutenant-Governor of Bengal, and H. B. Harington, the Legislative Member of the Viceroy's Council, denounced the entire scheme as both economically unjustifiable and politically unnecessary. Taking their stand upon the principles of political economy, they insisted that such sales only replaced a "prodigal owner" with a "thrifty capitalist." Any legislative interference with this process would prove injurious to the general prosperity of the country. The Government should rather afford encouragement to men of capital to invest their money in the purchase of land. They simply ignored the fact that the auction purchasers, usually moneylenders, rarely invested any capital in their new estates or undertook any agricultural improvement. In similar fashion they denied that the experience of the Mutiny afforded any justification for restrictive legislation. Grant argued that the Government would benefit from the existence of "a large number of landed proprietors who know that if the Government is overturned, they will lose their lands." He further questioned the loyalty even of those old proprietors who remained. In a time of anarchy, he said,

[74] For reports of District Officers see Home Judl., 16 September 1862, No. 44-55.

[75] Minute of 26 May 1860, *ibid.*, No. 40.

every man naturally betook himself to arms for the prosecution of his quarrels and the plunder of his wealthier neighbors. No particular blame for these disturbances could be attached to the Government's policy of land sale.[76]

This line of reasoning had a powerful appeal for Englishmen brought up in the principles of liberalism. Even those who did not follow Grant in his enthusiasm for land transfer, and who challenged his reading of the events of the Mutiny, had to admit that legislative interference could not be justified on grounds of economic theory. Contemporary political economy clearly dictated that the problem of indebtedness be tackled along the lines set out by the Irish Encumbered Estates Act of 1849, which facilitated the sale of the estates of an impoverished squirearchy. Those who wished to pursue an opposite policy at once found themselves stranded on unfamiliar ground. As one District Officer admitted, "all the suggested remedies involve the anomaly of declaring that what is the highest wisdom in Ireland (a country in many respects resembling India . . .) is the highest folly in India." Yet, when confronted with the unpopularity of the auction purchasers and their total incapacity during the revolt, he decided that "my political economy must bend before the force of local and national circumstances, and I must give my vote in favour of some remedy."[77]

Apart from the District Officers of the Northwest, however, few Englishmen in the 1860's were willing to sacrifice their principles in order to restrain the moneylender. If they did not accept the pure doctrine of political economy, they still believed, with Edmonstone, that unfettered freedom of contract and the liability of property for debt must be upheld. These principles lay at the heart of Victorian liberalism, and seemed somehow intimately connected with the security of

[76] Minute by H. B. Harington of 22 October 1858, *ibid.*, No. 31; and Minute by J. P. Grant of 6 June 1860, *ibid.*, No. 37.

[77] Minute by J. H. Batten, Commissioner of Rohilkhand, 26 May 1859, *ibid.*, No. 49.

property itself. They could not be challenged without at the same time challenging the whole Victorian social order—a task from which most Englishmen in India drew back. Consequently when the various reports were finally submitted to the Viceroy in 1862, Lord Elgin quietly shelved them.[78] By that time also a measure of partial relief had been provided by Section 244 of the Code of Civil Procedure (Act VIII of 1859). This authorized the Court to make provision for the satisfaction of debt by temporary alienation of land on representation by the Collector that sale would be objectionable. Strangled by a cumbrous procedure, this measure, which was only optional in any case, did nothing but soothe the consciences of British officialdom.

The question of sale of land for debt was occasionally raised in other provinces during the 1860's, but the outcome was almost invariably the same. In Oudh alone was any effective action taken, with the Taluqdar Encumbered Estates Act of 1870. On that occasion the Government reluctantly, and with some hesitation, provided special protection for that valuable class of landholders, the Oudh taluqdars; but beyond that it refused to go. In Bombay Lord Elphinstone tried repeatedly to save the lands of *inam* holders from sale for debt. As part of the general settlement by which claimants of rent-free land were confirmed in their holdings on payment of land tax at ¼ of the ordinary assessment, Elphinstone recommended that such land be exempted from sale for debt by the civil courts.[79] Lord Canning, although willing to admit that the action of the courts had excited discontent, saw no reason to grant such an extraordinary boon to this small group of landholders. Only Sir James Outram stood behind Elphinstone's proposal. In a forthright Minute the old general poured forth his conservative sympathies: "I confess to strong opinions on this subject, in my anxiety to preserve old family possessions as the only means whereby old families, however

[78] Note by Elgin of 29 August 1862, *ibid.*, No. 65.
[79] Minute of 4 April 1859, Home Rev., 5 August 1859, No. 8.

high, or however humble, may yet be retained in existence, the rapid extinction of whom is, I consider, greatly to be deplored, as perhaps the most serious source of discontent with our rule, not merely of the dispossessed families themselves, but of every class of people who witness their degradation. . . . I should be glad indeed were exemption of such lands from liability to sale for debt extended throughout India."[80] In the end, after vigorous protest, Elphinstone won exemption for his inamdars from sale for simple debt, leaving sales of specifically mortgaged property unrestricted. This was not much of a concession, but it was the most he could wring out of a reluctant Viceroy and Council.[81]

By 1870 the pressure of debt was beginning to make itself felt in the Punjab. The extension of the Code of Civil Procedure to the province in 1866 gave the moneylender his opportunity, and falling prices after 1869 set off a rapid rise in land sale and mortgage debt. Official discussion on the subject within the Punjab Government revealed the same wide differences of opinion, and came to the same inconclusive end, as in the North-Western Provinces, even though the Lieutenant-Governor, D. F. Macleod, sided with the advocates of prohibition. The Government of India simply refused to consider any measure which involved an attack upon the sanctity of contract or the security of property. The Legislative Member of the Viceroy's Council, J. F. Stephen, asserted in his confident imperial manner that "if the people of the Punjab do not understand that when they borrow money they must repay it, and that the whole of their property is liable for its repayment, they cannot be taught that lesson too soon or too emphatically. It appears to me to be one of the chief lessons which we are here to teach." He continued, "I do not indeed understand what is the use of a

[80] Minute of 19 July 1859, *ibid.*, No. 19.

[81] Sec. Govt. India to Sec. Govt. Bombay, 24 April 1860, Home Rev., 31 May 1860, No. 2-13.

regular government if it does not compel people to keep their contracts." The Viceroy, Lord Mayo, agreed that Britain's mission in India was to "establish the first Element of Civilization," which he defined as complete security of property and enforcement of contract. The Punjab Government was ordered to rely upon Section 244 of the Code of Civil Procedure as affording an adequate remedy.[82]

The Government was roused to action only by the Deccan riots of 1875, directed specifically against the moneylender. Goaded to desperation, villagers throughout the Poona and Ahmadnagar districts in May of that year set fire to houses and shops, and destroyed the bonds and decrees in the hands of their creditors. Here at last was the spur required to shake the Government from its lethargy, for they saw that these riots might well touch off a general Maratha uprising. A Commission of Inquiry was at once appointed and remedial measures introduced into the Legislative Council. The Deccan Agriculturists' Relief Act, passed in 1879, marked a decisive break with the tradition of laissez faire and freedom of contract. The courts were enabled for the first time to go beyond the letter of the contract in debt cases and to award only reasonable interest according to considerations of equity. The Deccan was the scene of the first violent outburst largely because it presented in an acute form symptoms gradually becoming widespread throughout India. More than elsewhere Maharashtra had suffered from the heady prosperity of the American Civil War years and the prolonged depression which followed in the 1870's. English demand for cotton while the American market was closed vastly enhanced the value of land in the Deccan, the best cotton producing area in India, and gave the Maratha peasantry access to almost unlimited supplies of credit. With the inevitable fall in prices after the war the peasantry found themselves so burdened with debt,

[82] Minute by Stephen of 20 June 1870, and by Mayo of 6 July 1870, Home Judl. A, 24 September 1870, No. 37-41.

and so strapped for funds, that they could not meet their obligations. To make matters worse, the original land revenue settlement in the Deccan expired during this brief period of prosperity, and the land was resettled at enhanced rates of up to 50 per cent—rates the cultivator was soon unable to pay without recourse to the moneylender. Between 1868 and 1874 seven lakh rupees worth of land was sold in satisfaction of debt in Ahmadnagar District alone. The explosion of 1875 followed as a natural consequence.[83]

Yet, though the Relief Act of 1879 was a first step toward control of the moneylender, it went a very little distance. Land could still be sold for debt so long as it had been specifically mortgaged, and sales continued to mount throughout the last twenty years of the century. Effective legislation was not enacted until 1900 in the Punjab. By the provisions of the Punjab Land Alienation Act, the sale of agricultural land by decree of court was forbidden, and—far more significantly —all transfer of land to non-agriculturists was prohibited. Henceforth no person not a member of an agricultural tribe could obtain land in the Punjab for any reason whatever.[84] By this act the British in effect repudiated the contractual and legal view of property which they had introduced into Punjab land tenure fifty years earlier. Status was to replace contract as the criterion of landholding; rural society was to be restored to its traditional form and then guarded by a paternal government free of theoretical scruples. The Act went so far partly because unrest among the martial peasantry of a strategic border province had at all costs to be avoided, but also because the decline of laissez faire removed the major obstacles in its path. By 1900 political economy was no longer a binding orthodoxy in England; hence deviation from it in India had ceased to be heresy. With the rejection of the narrow Victorian

---

[83] See Report of Deccan Riots Commission, *passim*.

[84] A similar act was enacted for Bundelkhand in 1903. Otherwise the North-Western Provinces gained no legislative protection against land transfer.

approach to private property rights, comprehensive treatment of rural indebtedness was at last possible.

Throughout these protracted controversies, remarkably few people ever considered whether such restrictions would effectively meet the root cause of indebtedness—the cultivator's dependence upon the moneylender for a supply of capital. In the discussions following the Mutiny only one man, John Strachey, then Collector of Moradabad, sought a solution of the problem not in restrictions on the sale of land (which in fact he opposed), but in the provision of an alternative source of credit for the cultivator. He pointed out that it was impossible to provide genuine relief by administrative or judicial reform so long as the cultivators were unable to obtain advances of money on fair and reasonable terms. He suggested that the Government instead establish banks in every district for the purpose of making loans to the agricultural community. Only in this way could the moneylender be effectively displaced. As a utilitarian bred in the tradition of Bentham and James Mill, Strachey was quite willing to see the Government undertake a large measure of initiative in agricultural improvement. "It is my conviction," he said, "that there are hardly any duties which in countries more advanced in knowledge and civilization fall on the landlord and capitalist, which may not in this country be undertaken with propriety by the Government."[85] But such ideas were totally unacceptable to most mid-Victorian liberals, who considered such dramatic interference in society outside the legitimate sphere of Government. Even those who advocated legislative restraints upon the sale of land would not allow the Government to step boldly forth as the provider of credit. Strachey's suggestion was quietly ignored. When the question was reopened in 1884 by the Bombay Government, their scheme for agricultural banks in the Deccan received the same treatment. The Secretary of State simply said that the "Government

[85] Minute of 19 May 1859, Home Judl., 16 September 1862, No. 55.

cannot directly do much more for the relief of the agricultural debtor" than provide cheap and equal justice.[86] Only in the twentieth century, with the enactment of the Cooperative Societies Act of 1904, was it possible to inaugurate a successful rural credit movement. As with restrictions upon land transfer, the principles of Victorian liberalism were an insurmountable obstacle so long as they remained in the ascendant.

[86] S. of S. to G.G., 23 October 1884 cited in S. C. Ray, *Agricultural Indebtedness in India and Its Remedies* (Calcutta, 1915), p. 253.

# CHAPTER VI

# THE PRINCES AND THE PEOPLE

FOREMOST among the causes of the revolt was Lord Dalhousie's policy of annexing the princely states of India. The fate which befell so many states during his tenure of office excited widespread apprehension, not least among the remaining princes, and contributed largely to that spirit of unrest from which the revolt gathered strength. Moreover, during 1857 those princes dispossessed by Dalhousie provided what leadership the Mutiny obtained. Perhaps the most prominent was Nana Saheb, who had been refused the pension and titular dignity of Peshwa in 1851. His name still remains indelibly etched upon the British memory as a veritable embodiment of evil. Similarly the aggrieved Rani of Jhansi by her gallant resistance revived the flagging spirit of the mutineers in the later stages of the revolt, while Begam Hazrat Mahal, Queen Regent of Oudh, carried on the struggle in that province until forced across the border into Nepal. By 1858, after these clear indications of Indian feeling, the British were convinced that to persevere in the course of annexation would be foolish and reckless in the extreme. As Lord Stanley, the Secretary of State, told the House of Commons in February 1859, "I think also that the Government, whether in India or in this country, have profited sufficiently by the recent and costly experience, not to feel inclined to pursue that policy of annexation, which, whether well or ill founded, has undoubtedly, in a great degree, been the cause of the present disaster."[1] A good many

[1] Speech of 14 February 1859, Hansard, CLII, 358.

officers insisted that Dalhousie's annexations were not responsible for the subsequent outbreak, or that they were in
any case amply justified by the "countless blessings" thereby
conferred upon the people. The annexation of Oudh in particular found staunch defenders, and any idea of handing it
back to its deposed sovereign was indignantly rejected.[2] Yet
there was little enthusiasm for renewed annexation. Vernon
Smith admitted "a desire to swallow some of the little states
interspersed with our territories which are an immense in-
convenience and very little strong."[3] But few followed him
and he himself soon repudiated the idea. The Mutiny had in
fact completely destroyed that self-confident enthusiasm which
had led Dalhousie down the path of annexation.

More remarkable perhaps than the hatred of the deposed
was the loyalty of the reigning princes. Like the British they
were caught almost entirely unaware by the initial outbreak,
and had suddenly to decide upon a course of action in the
prevailing anarchy. Temptations to join the rebel cause were
not lacking. There was always the hope of shaking off the
British suzerain, avenging their former defeats, and regaining
the independence of their ancestors. At the least they saw
plentiful opportunities for plunder and aggrandizement at the
expense of their neighbors. Yet almost without exception they
cast in their lot with the British. Ellenborough noted that they
"have shown tact and judgment as well as firmness and
fidelity," citing in particular the services of Sindhia at Gwalior,
Holkar at Indore, and the Nawab of Bhopal.[4]

Sindhia's loyalty was conspicuous from the very beginning.
As soon as news of the outbreak reached him, he placed his
troops at the disposal of Colvin in Agra; but, as it turned out,
the Gwalior Contingent, being composed of the same elements
as the Bengal Army, was equally unreliable. In June 1857 it

---

[2] Argyll in House of Commons, 11 August 1859, Hansard, CLV, 1323;
Vernon Smith, 16 February 1858, *ibid.*, CL, 1502; Richard Temple, *Men and
Events of My Time in India*, p. 111.

[3] Vernon Smith to Canning, 5 April 1858, Canning Papers.

[4] Memorandum of 19 November 1857, Ellenborough Papers.

rose up in mutiny. However, by affecting to take the mutineers into his service, Sindhia restrained them from marching upon Agra or Delhi throughout the summer. A formidable body of armed men was thus kept idle and ineffective while British fortunes were at their lowest ebb. Later, in June 1858, when the rebels attacked the fort of Gwalior, Sindhia resisted; and, though forced to retire, he soon returned with the British column under Sir Hugh Rose. Holkar's fidelity has been the subject of some controversy, largely because he was not trusted by the Political Agent, H. M. Durand, and did not act decisively on the first outbreak of mutiny at Indore. He seems nevertheless to have afforded no encouragement to the rebels, even though—like Sindhia—he lost control of his own troops.[5] The assistance rendered by the small Sikh states of the cis-Sutlej territory was, at least in the crucial early months of the revolt, perhaps the most important of all. As Sir John Lawrence told Canning, "It would be difficult to overrate the value of their services in the late crisis. Had the chiefs of Patiala, Jheend, and Nabha fallen away in May and June last, our troops could never have marched to Delhy. Had they deserted our cause any time before the fall of Delhy, the communications with the Punjab would have been cut off. . . . These chiefs not only remained staunch, but acted vigorously on our behalf. They spared neither men nor money."[6]

In each case, though most prominently in that of Sindhia, loyalty rested upon a clear perception of the strength of the British position in India. Sindhia was on terms of close affection with his Resident, Major Charters Macpherson; he had an able minister in the person of Dinkar Rao; and he had visited Calcutta in March 1857. There he had seen the visible magnitude of British power and had received specific assurances from Lord Canning that his territories were safe from annexation. The Punjab princes had been on the best of terms with the British ever since they had voluntarily sub-

---

[5] Sen, *Eighteen Fifty-Seven*, pp. 312-14; Kaye, *Sepoy War*, III, 338-41.

[6] John Lawrence to Canning, 16 February 1858, Canning Papers.

mitted to Sir Charles Metcalfe in order to avoid the armies
of Ranjit Singh. Their very existence depended upon the protection afforded by the British alliance; of all people they
had the least desire to see revived Mughal or Maratha power.

The moral the India Office drew from these demonstrations
of loyalty was obvious. To annex states was a sure method
of courting disaffection, while to respect their independence
was an equally sure way of gaining their friendship and
support. Indeed if the support rendered by these princes during the Mutiny were reciprocated, they could be made into
staunch pillars of the Empire, and British rule more firmly
established in India than ever before. As Lord Stanley pointed
out, "It is only by imparting security to others that we can
permanently establish our own." And he urged Canning to
spare no effort in rewarding "those native allies who have
really stood by us."[7] Even Vernon Smith, for all his dislike
of the Indian states, acknowledged in 1859 that they "had
cordially supported our cause" and that it would be "expedient,
not only from motives of gratitude, but in order to secure
the future well-being and tranquillity of India, that some token
of our approbation—that some reward—should be given to
these men." Hereafter, he said, he hoped that "we were to
govern India by the sympathy of the native princes, carrying
them along with us" in the administration.[8] In the post-
Mutiny era the political value of these men far outweighed
any moral or administrative shortcomings they might possess.

Rewards, both monetary and territorial, were distributed
with a lavish hand at a series of Viceregal durbars held during
1859. Among others, Sindhia received land with an annual
income of three lakhs of rupees, Rampur land worth one
lakh, and Patiala and Jhind *jaghirs* of over two lakhs each.
Canning at one stage even proposed that the Assigned Dis-

[7] Secret Dispatch of 17 December 1858. Also Stanley to Canning, 2 August
1858, Canning Papers.

[8] Vernon Smith speech in House of Commons, 11 February 1859, Hansard,
CLII, 274.

tricts of Berar be returned to the Nizam in recognition of his role in maintaining tranquillity in the Deccan; but despite Stanley's approval the scheme eventually fell through.[9] Those who participated in the reconquest of Oudh were especially well rewarded. Jung Bahadur of Nepal brought down 9,000 troops in December 1857 (in addition to 3,000 Gurkhas sent to Gorakhpur in July) and personally assisted in the final reduction of Lucknow. In return he received those districts of the Terai which had been ceded to Britain, and made over to Oudh, at the close of the Nepal War of 1816. The Sikh Raja of Kapurthala, who at the outbreak of the Mutiny supplied a contingent force used first in the Punjab and then in Oudh, got Rs. 10,000, an honorary title, a salute of eleven guns, and two forfeited estates in Oudh. These estates were valued at a lakh of rupees and were held by him on taluqdari tenure at half the fixed rate of assessment.[10] Apart from these specific territorial rewards, the Government did its best to conciliate the princes by assurances of favorable treatment and the grant of special honors. In the Queen's Proclamation of November 1858 they were told that the British "desire no extension of our present territorial possessions" and would "respect the rights, dignity, and honour of the native princes as our own." In 1859 Canning and Outram recommended the establishment of a special order of knighthood, with the Queen as master. Since titles emanating directly from the Crown were always more highly regarded than traditional Indian honors, Canning saw in the creation of such an order a most effective way of enhancing the loyalty of the princes and rewarding their continued services to the Empire.[11] The order eventually took shape in 1861 as the Star of India. It was at once, and to the very end of British rule continued to be, eagerly sought

[9] Canning to Stanley, 29 January 1859, and Stanley to Canning, 10 March 1859, Canning Papers.

[10] Dispatch of 8 November 1859 to G.G., Political Dispatch No. 54 of 1859.

[11] Dispatch of 24 December 1859 from India, Foreign Department Dispatch No. 27 of 1859.

after, not only by the Indian princes for whom it was originally designed, but by the officers of the I.C.S., who considered the K.C.S.I. the most fitting reward for a successful Indian career.

By far the most valuable boon conferred on the Indian princes was the recognition of the right of adoption; for, by permitting a prince to adopt an heir, it protected his state from lapsing to the British Government, and thus secured its independent existence. Canning had long been disturbed by the lack of any clear and precise rule governing a subject so close to the hearts of the princes as that of succession. Even though the Government might be liberal in recognizing adoptions, he pointed out, there still remained "a haze of doubt and mistrust" in the mind of each chief as to the policy which would be applied to his own state; and this feeling could not but sap his loyalty and contentment. On his tour through Upper India in 1859 Canning granted the right of adoption to those princes he met in durbar, and saw the news received with unrestrained rejoicing in every court. Before the year was out he had reached the conclusion that no act would meet with such universal acclaim among the princes as a general recognition of the right of adoption. Such a measure, he realized, would cut off all possibility of extending British administration in India, with "its surer promise of future benefit to the people." But this was of little importance compared with the powerful adherents the measure would gain for the British Raj. The Indian states had already proved themselves "breakwaters to the storm which would otherwise have swept over us in one great wave." Should British power ever in the future be challenged by a foreign foe, or British resources be drained from India to fight a European war, the support of these princes would be worth more to the Empire than any number of British troops. Even if India remained at peace, loyal feudatories dotted over the country would be "invaluable to us," for they possessed a "sympathy with and a hold over the feelings and hearts of the common herd which they cannot bequeath to us." So long as "we make them fear and respect us, and show them that their interests and honor are really our care, they will be the best anchor we can have."[12] Canning accordingly urged that the right of adoption be promptly and unreservedly conceded, for no other measure could so readily win the confidence of the princes and "give a character of immoveability to the policy which it initiates."[13]

Both at home and on his Council Canning's proposal evoked a favorable response. Bartle Frere described the effects of the measure in glowing terms and told Canning that it would "do more for tranquillity and good government in India than years of legislation and successful campaigns." Never an ardent reformer, he felt no pangs of conscience at the thought of millions left under Indian rule. "Every real advantage to the people which can be expected from our rule," he said, "can be secured through a Native ruler, with the aid of an English Political Agent of average ability, more surely, easily, and cheaply than by any form of direct administration with which I am acquainted."[14] The Secretary of State, Sir Charles Wood, was unwilling to go quite so far in commending the princes, but he recognized the value of attaching these "influential classes" to the British standard; and in a dispatch of 26 July 1860 he authorized the issue of adoption *sanads* to all sovereign chiefs under British protection.[15] The measure was equally well received by the Indian people, though for different reasons. To the educated Indian the states were islands of self-government in a sea of alien rule. They provided an outlet for political ambition denied in British India, and a standing affirmation of the ability of Indians to rule themselves. Thus

[12] Dispatch of 30 April 1860 from India, Foreign Department Dispatch No. 43A of 1860. See also Canning to Edmonstone, 23 November 1859, Canning Papers.

[13] Canning to Wood, 13 June 1860, Wood Papers.

[14] Minute of 19 June 1860, Canning Papers.

[15] Dispatch of 26 July 1860, Political Dispatch No. 57 of 1860. One hundred and sixty of the more important chiefs ruling their own states were granted *sanads*.

any measure designed to strengthen these states or confirm them in their independence automatically won applause. As early as August 1858, the *Hindoo Patriot*, under Harish Chandra Mukherjee, had advocated recognition of the right of adoption, and it went on to recommend that the princes be freed from the surveillance of British Residents. India, the paper suggested, should be organized on a federal basis, with the various states and provinces left free to manage their own internal affairs.[16] With considerably more vehemence the vernacular Bengali press deplored British interference in the princely states. One paper even asserted in 1863 that despite adoption "there is no independence allowed to Native Rajahs," and concluded: "Not only history but the conduct of all people proves that every nation desires to be subject to its own Rulers."[17] In the absence of anything more hopeful, nationalist sentiment in the 1860's attached itself to the Indian states, despite their patently illiberal and despotic form of government. The princes themselves naturally welcomed these concessions with open arms, and responded precisely as Canning had hoped they would. Without exception they put their influence at the service of the Empire and identified themselves with its fortunes. Like the taluqdars and other landed aristocrats who had gained so much from the Mutiny settlement, the princes remained loyal to the very end of British rule.

The recognition of adoption by no means disabled the British Government from stepping in to set aright abuses in the administration of a state, or even, if occasion demanded, assuming temporary control of the administration. Canning in fact expressly reserved this power to the Government on the ground that, with annexation repudiated, such intervention was a necessary deterrent to the opportunities otherwise presented for gross misrule. As the paramount power Britain was of course sole judge of the extent and occasion of its intervention. Con-

[16] *Hindoo Patriot*, 26 August 1858, vi, 267.
[17] *Soma Prakash* of 21 September 1863 in Home Public, 22 October 1863, No. 23.

sequently the effective power of the ruler was often closely circumscribed. British standards of morality and administrative efficiency were continually pressed upon him by the Resident, while the Government of India claimed the right to maintain ministers in office (most notably Salar Jung) against the will of the sovereign, to regulate succession, and to depose recalcitrant or oppressive rulers altogether (such as the Gaekwar of Baroda in 1875). Yet the British usually kept their interference to a minimum, and their power in the background, until a state was on the verge of anarchy. So far as possible they tried to avoid lecturing a ruler "as if he were a minor of whom we are the guardians."[18] As Sir Charles Wood put it, "I should let any ruler do nearly what he liked within his own state. If the condition of his territory affects that of his neighbors, he becomes a public nuisance and we should interfere. So perhaps if a long state of anarchy and bloodshed prevails, but I would not interfere for mere family quarrels."[19] Even when they were forced to take over a state, the British retained the traditional system of administration, improving it where necessary, but avoiding undue innovation or anglicization. Their ideal was to associate the leading elements of the court in reform, and to disturb customary ways as little as possible. The impact of change was minimized, and the state invariably returned to princely rule.

## The Case of Mysore

Despite this general aversion to annexation, the idea was not without its attractions. For most Englishmen, direct British rule was so far superior to Indian administration that they were willing even after the Mutiny to consider taking over a state if a legitimate opportunity presented itself. No states were in fact annexed, but one, the large and populous South Indian state of Mysore, escaped by only the narrowest of margins. After the defeat of Tipu Sultan in 1799 the British Gov-

[18] Northcote to Lawrence, 1 November 1867, Lawrence Papers.
[19] Wood to Lawrence, 9 November 1864, Wood Papers.

ernment set up an independent Hindu state in Mysore, and
placed Kristna Raj Wodyar, at the time a boy of five, upon
the throne as Maharaja. In 1810 he assumed the direct government of the country, although the British retained by treaty
the right to intervene if necessary to safeguard the welfare of
the people. Twenty years later, in 1831, after a long period of
maladministration culminating in insurrection, the British took
over the government of Mysore and set aside the Maharaja.
Under the efficient and enlightened rule of Sir Mark Gubbon,
Commissioner from 1834 to 1861, order was soon restored and
Mysore became a model province of British India. With Gubbon's departure in 1861, the Maharaja petitioned the Government for the restoration of his kingdom. But as the province
was now firmly within the British orbit, Canning was reluctant
to let it go, and the Maharaja's request was refused. Britain's
duty toward the people of Mysore, he told the Maharaja, demanded the retention of British administration; without it
the peace and prosperity of the province would soon be at an
end.[20] The Maharaja renewed his pleas the following year,
and met with the same response from the new Viceroy, Lord
Elgin. In England, however, he obtained a more sympathetic
hearing. Several members of the India Council maintained
that, having brought Mysore into a state of order, the British
were now bound to restore it to its ruler. Sir Frederick Currie,
for one, denied that Britain's duty to the people of Mysore in
any way compelled it to retain possession of the country. Like
Frere a conservative, he insisted that "a native administration,
efficiently superintended and controlled" was far better adapted
to Indian conditions than one in which the European element,
and European modes of procedure, pervaded all the departments.[21] Swayed by his Councillors, Wood at first leaned
toward the view that Mysore must be handed back, subject
to the condition that it revert to Britain on the death of the
Maharaja. But, indecisive as usual, he abandoned this position

---

[20] Canning to Maharaja, 11 March 1862, P.P. 1866, LII, 493.
[21] Dissent of 17 July 1863, *ibid.*, p. 510.

in March 1863, under pressure from the Viceroy, and adopted Elgin's point of view. In a dispatch of 17 July 1863 the Maharaja's claim to restoration was conclusively negatived. Three members of the India Council dissented from the dispatch, but the more radical officials, such as Charles Trevelyan, welcomed its decisive tone.[22]

This decision did not, however, finally settle the Mysore controversy, for the Maharaja was an old man with no heir, and the question of succession was still unresolved. Canning, Wood, and Elgin were determined to retain possession of Mysore, and incorporate it into British India on the death of the Maharaja. Their unanimous rejection of the Maharaja's claim to restoration was in fact largely prompted by this consideration. On no account did they want to do anything which might prolong the sovereignty of this dynasty over Mysore. But at the same time they were anxious to avoid drastic measures or the use of force. They hoped the Maharaja could be induced to bequeath the state to the Crown of his own free will. As Wood put it, "We ought to have the country, but we cannot well *take it*. It would be in too flagrant opposition to all that you [Canning] have been so wisely and so successfully doing of late." And he later told Elgin that "I do not wish to take it as Dalhousie took Oudh, but I should like to have it."[23] There was little assurance, however, that the Maharaja would act in this accommodating fashion. On one occasion in 1860 he had told Canning's wife that he intended on his death to give everything he possessed to the British Government. Upon these chance remarks Canning placed an almost pathetic reliance; but they had no binding character, and were in any case made before the Maharaja's claim to restoration was disallowed. After that event the Maharaja was little inclined to be conciliatory. Nevertheless Wood hoped that,

[22] Dissents were submitted by Sir H. Montgomery, Sir F. Currie, and J. P. Willoughby. On Trevelyan see his letter to Wood of 8 September 1863 in Wood Papers.

[23] Wood to Canning, 25 December 1861, and Wood to Elgin, 10 July 1862, Wood Papers.

by keeping him in good humor, and soothing his vanity on small points, he might still be induced to make over the country on his death. "I am willing to agree to almost anything which will only be for his life," he told Lawrence, "provided you secure the consent to our succession after his death."[24] In pursuit of this fantasy, the Government paid off the Maharaja's debts to the extent of 33 lakhs of rupees and gave *jaghirs* to his illegitimate sons. In 1864 Lawrence even agreed to "let the Raja have a lakh of rupees with which to make merry on his birthday."[25]

But it was all in vain. In June 1865 the Maharaja adopted an heir, a boy two and one half years old, and placed the Government in precisely the awkward situation it had hoped to avoid. Legally an adopted heir had no right to succeed to the throne of Mysore, for the Maharaja was not a ruling prince in 1860 and had not received a *sanad* of adoption. The adoption could therefore be set aside, and the state made to lapse upon the death of the incumbent Maharaja. This was not a pleasant prospect, but by this time Wood had reconciled himself to it, and had screwed up his courage sufficiently to face the consequences. In Lawrence, moreover, he had a Viceroy far less interested in conciliating Indian princes than either Canning or Elgin. From the beginning of his Viceroyalty Lawrence adamantly opposed any recognition of a right of adoption on the part of the Mysore Maharaja. The reversion of Mysore to princely rule, he wrote, would be "synonymous with the withdrawal of the European officers, and the abandonment of a system of upwards of thirty years growth. It is tantamount to the collapse of order, and a rapid return to the state of confusion and of insecurity of life, honor, and property, from which, in 1831, the people of Mysore were rescued."[26] Long before the adoption was carried out, therefore, Lawrence officially disallowed it so far as the Raj of

24 Wood to Lawrence, 18 April 1864, Wood Papers.

25 Lawrence to Wood, 16 June 1864, Wood Papers.

26 G.G. in Council to Wood, 5 May 1865, P.P. 1866, LII, 545.

Mysore was concerned. (There was of course no objection
to the Maharaja's adopting an heir for his private property.)
This action received the sanction of the Secretary of State
in a dispatch of 17 July 1865, although as before Wood had to
face a large body of opposition in his Council.[27]

Again, however, the question was not finally resolved. In
February 1866 Wood retired from the India Office, and in
June of that year the Whig-Liberal Government of which he
had been a member fell from power. In February 1867 the new
Tory Secretary of State, Lord Cranborne, reversed Wood's
decision. Without consulting the Indian Government or his
own Council, he suddenly announced to the House of Commons that Mysore would not be annexed on the death of the
Maharaja. Not as of right, he said, but as a favor "to calm the
minds of those influential feudatories who are in alliance with
us," the state would be restored, in whole or in part, to
Indian rule when the adopted heir came of age. The exact
amount of power to be given to the young ruler would be
decided only when his character and ability could be clearly
determined.[28] Having tossed his bombshell, Cranborne retired,
and left his successor Sir Stafford Northcote to wrestle with
the problems it created. The members of the India Council
were furious at having been bypassed, and this blow to their
pride was made worse by the fact that a majority still adhered
to the views of Sir Charles Wood. But as the decision had
been publicly announced, it could not be reversed; the Council
could only bow before the inevitable. Northcote himself agreed
with his predecessor that Mysore ought not to be annexed,
but he saw no point in leaving the final settlement in a state
of uncertainty for twenty years. Accordingly, in a dispatch
of 16 April 1867, passed over the opposition of ten members
of his Council, Northcote ruled that the adopted son, when
he came of age, would succeed to the Raj of Mysore, subject

[27] Dissents were submitted by Currie, Willoughby, Sir George Clerk, East-
wick, and Montgomery, *ibid.*, pp. 557-69.

[28] Speech of 22 February 1867, Hansard, CLXXXV, 838-41.

only to the negotiation of a new treaty clearly defining his obligation to provide good government for his subjects.

Mysore therefore came within a hair's breath of being annexed to British India. Indeed had it not been for the change of administration in England, its independent existence almost certainly would have ended in March 1868 with the death of the Maharaja. This eagerness to get hold of Mysore, remarkable though it may seem, reflects to a large extent the imperfect conversion of such men as Wood and Canning to the support of princely rule. As liberals they were always torn between the demands of political expediency and of moral duty. Wood saw clearly that the annexation of Mysore would be severely criticized at home, would deeply disturb all the Indian princes, and would be widely regarded as a breach of faith, in view of the promises and declarations of good will made to the princes in the years just after the Mutiny. Yet he shrank from the prospect of consigning a people who had experienced the benefits of British rule to the vagaries and uncertainties of a native government. As he told Northcote in 1867: "Now it is a very serious matter to hand over to a native ruler people who have long been used to our rule. We may commit plenty of blunders and do some injustice but upon the whole our worst governed districts are infinitely better governed than any native state. . . . I admit that native rule is improving and I am against annexing native states where they go on decently, but I have grave misgivings about restoring to native rule districts which we have long administered."[29]

Much as they recognized the political utility of the princely class, and sought its friendship, the liberals of the post-Mutiny generation never abandoned the conviction that Britain had a duty to bring good government to the people of India. Although princely conciliation usually claimed first priority, the liberals' support of this class was always qualified, always

[29] Halifax to Northcote, 24 April 1867, Wood Papers.

somewhat reluctantly given. The retention of Mysore was to have been a mark of their good intentions.

By no means all English officials viewed Mysore from this vantage point. Those who retained the reforming enthusiasm of the pre-Mutiny era had no hesitation in calling for the immediate annexation of the province. For them the conciliation of Indian princes was of small importance compared with the paramount duty laid upon Britain of protecting the Indian people from oppression. J. S. Mill commented in 1866 that he considered Canning's universal recognition of adoption "most ill-advised," for it lumped together ancient states, such as those of Rajasthan, with modern ones created by conquest or by grant from the British Government. Only the former, he said, should be exempt from annexation on failure of heirs; the others should be at the disposal of the British Government.[30] Sir John Lawrence likewise had little love for the Indian princes, whom he regarded in much the same light as the taluqdars of Oudh. Men controlled by no legal restraints, they were, in his view, often vicious and corrupt, and usually surrounded by ministers who encouraged them in indulgence while preying upon the resources of the state. Together with such erstwhile radicals as Ross Mangles and Sir Charles Trevelyan, he lamented the sacrifice of the "real and permanent interests of the millions of Mysore" which took place in 1867.[31] But the radicals now exercised far less influence in the counsels of Government than in the days of Dalhousie. Even though they could count the Viceroy among their numbers, they were unable to do very much. The pledges Canning had given the princes, like the *sanads* awarded to the Oudh taluqdars, barred the way to comprehensive reform, while the willingness of the more moderate liberals, such as Sir Charles Wood, to conciliate the princes

[30] Mill to John Morley, 26 September 1866, Elliot, ed., *Letters of J. S. Mill*, II, 65.

[31] Lawrence to Northcote, 25 June 1867, Lawrence Papers; Mangles Dissent of 24 April 1867, P.P. 1867, L, 581; C. Trevelyan Evidence to House of Commons Committee on Indian Finance, 21 February 1873, P.P. 1873, XII, 61.

deprived them of the bulk of their support. They had to contend as well with a vigorous conservative reaction, which
challenged the basic assumption that British rule was necessarily better than Indian.

The decision of Cranborne and Northcote to return Mysore
to Indian rule was not simply the result of short-term political
calculations, although these of course played a part. Cranborne
was anxious "to do anything consistent with our duty to
India which may be pleasant and agreeable" to the princes;
and he pointed out that the states provided "an outlet for
statesman-like capacity" which, bottled up in British India,
might well become explosive.[32] But beyond this lay a consistent conservative philosophy. Much as Indian rule might
be violent, inefficient, even corrupt, it was peculiarly adapted
to the society out of which it had grown. It expressed the
desires, and served the needs, of the Indian people better
than any alternative system of government. As Lord Cranborne
put it: "I do not deny that our mission in India is to reduce
to order, to civilize and develop the Native governments we
find there. But I demur to that wholesale condemnation of
a system of government which would be utterly intolerable
on our own soil, but which has grown up amongst the people
subjected to it. It has a fitness and congeniality for them
impossible for us adequately to realize, but which compensates
them to an enormous degree for the material evils which its
rudeness in a great many cases produces."

Princely government, moreover, was usually cheaper than
British administration, more efficient in emergencies, and more
responsive to the wishes and feelings of the people. The Indian
ruler possessed, what the British administrator notoriously
lacked, "a knowledge of and sympathy with" his subjects.
The people would be far happier if traditional forms of government were retained and improved, rather than pushed
aside. "If you intend to develop their moral nature only after
an Anglo-Saxon type," Cranborne warned the House of Com-

[32] Speech of 22 February 1867, Hansard, CLXXXV, 838-39.

mons, "you will make a conspicuous and disastrous defeat."[33] Such sentiments were echoed by the conservative members of the I.C.S., such as Sir George Clerk and Sir Bartle Frere. Both acknowledged the merits of Indian rule and urged the Government to give the princes the largest possible amount of support and encouragement.[34] Cranborne's remarks, on the other hand, only stung Sir John Lawrence into an empassioned defence of British administration. Although the native state might well, he said, offer an attractive prospect to the politically ambitious Indian, repelled by the "monotonous machinelike" quality of the British system, "the masses of the people are incontestably more prosperous and far more happy in British territory than they are under Native rulers."[35] He went on to substantiate his claim by submitting reports from many local officers. But by that time, at least so far as Mysore was concerned, the battle was already over.

Confronted with these conflicting pressures, the Government of India throughout the rest of the century tried to avoid the extremes of both annexation and complete non-interference. In Mysore, although the continued existence of the state had been guaranteed, the Government did its best to insure that the system it had introduced would not be abandoned. The young ruler was brought up under the guardianship of an English tutor and educated along the best European lines. When he was finally installed by Lord Ripon in 1881, he was tightly bound by a detailed Instrument of Transfer, defining the conditions on which he was to hold power and reserving ample powers of intervention to the British Government. Northcote, in authorizing the restoration of princely rule, had specifically recommended the negotiation of such an agreement, and, as drawn up by Ripon, it was extremely comprehensive. The Maharaja promised to pay a subsidy of

[33] Speeches of Northcote and Cranborne in House of Commons, 24 May 1867, Hansard, CLXXXVII, 1,069.74.

[34] Sir G. Clerk, Dissent of 24 July 1865, P.P. 1866, LII, 559; Frere to Wood, 27 January 1865, Wood Papers.

[35] Circular of 1 July 1867, P.P. 1867-68, LI, 434.

35 lakhs, to afford all facilities for cantonments, railways, and telegraphs, to adopt the coinage of British India, to maintain his military force at the level fixed by the Governor-General, and to comply with the wishes of the Governor-General in regard to the manufacture of salt and opium. Beyond this he agreed to refrain from making any changes in the laws, the revenue settlements or the system of administration without the consent of the British Government. He promised at all times to conform to the advice of the Governor-General on all matters relating to the management of his kingdom, the happiness of his subjects, and his relations with the British Government. Any breach of these conditions could lead to the resumption of his state or any other arrangements the Government might think fit to take "for the good government of the people of Mysore."[36]

Yet the last decades of the nineteenth century must still be considered a golden age for the Indian princes. Anxious not only to control the princes but to gain their support, the Government carefully refrained from antagonizing them or incurring their hostility. The lesson of the Mutiny was never forgotten. Even Ripon, the Gladstonian liberal, saw in the princes an element of strength for the British Raj, and he urged the Government to respect "their customs and susceptibilities." If we succeed, he said, in securing their loyalty and confidence, "we may contemplate without fear the intrigues of foreign foes or the efforts of internal opponents."[37] In this endeavor the British were completely successful. The states soon became an integral part of the imperial structure, and their loyalty provided a strong defensive position from which to combat the nationalist challenge. Indeed ultimately they proved less amenable to liberal and nationalist pressure than the British Government itself. They remained bastions of conservatism well into the twentieth century, and as the

[36] "Instrument of Transfer," P.P. 1881, LXX, 581-83.
[37] Speech of 20 October 1885, published as *The Native States of India* (Leeds, 1886), p. 14.

devolution of power progressed, became something of an embarrassment. After rejecting the Government of India Act of 1935, the princes were left to fend for themselves. In independent India there was clearly no place for them.

In many ways the system of subordinate alliance with local rulers developed in India after the Mutiny achieved its most striking successes elsewhere. An India largely under direct district administration afforded little scope for its expansion. In Southeast Asia and tropical Africa, by contrast, as British influence expanded into those areas after 1875, imperial administrators were faced with the task of controlling vast territories with extremely limited amounts of men and money. Here Indian experience with the princely states provided a model and a precedent. By the end of the century these principles of government had taken shape from Malaya to Nigeria as the famed system of "indirect rule." But the basic aims were still the same in the Africa of Lugard as they had been in the India of Canning: the maintenance of indigenous authorities, the preservation of traditional customs, and a vigorous assertion of British paramountcy.

## Inams, Redemption, and Permanent Settlement

Conciliation of the Indian people did not stop with aristocratic taluqdars and princely rulers. In the years immediately after the Mutiny, the Government set out to win the affection, and alleviate the grievances, of all the influential groups in Indian society. "If we are wise," Canning said, "we shall lose no time in binding to ourselves the Chiefs, the Landholders, great and small, and the wealthy classes . . . by stronger and more substantial ties. We must impress them all with this plain conviction that, come what may, the fall of our power will be no gain to them."[38] Among the most discontented were the claimants to rent-free land. Anxious to recover all revenue lost by their predecessors, the various local governments during the 1840's and 1850's empowered certain officers to scru-

[38] Canning to Wood, 13 June 1860, Wood Papers.

tinize claims to rent-free tenure, known as *inam* or *lakhiraj* land, and to resume those holdings which were not grounded upon a secure title. In Bombay the task was entrusted to a special Inam Commission set up in 1852. As few landholders possessed the written title which alone would satisfy the Government, an enormous number of rent-free holdings, some of considerable antiquity, were confiscated or subjected to taxation. During the first five years of its existence the Inam Commission in Bombay confiscated some 21,000 estates. These investigations contributed to the spirit of agrarian unrest which accompanied the Mutiny and kept alive continual apprehension among those whose titles were still to be examined. After 1857, however, the Government was little inclined to pursue the matter, even though claims to 75 lakhs of alienated revenue remained to be adjudicated in Bombay alone. As the Governor of Bombay, Lord Elphinstone, pointed out, "Nothing would tend more to tranquillize this part of India than a speedy and final settlement of all claims to alienated revenue." In 1859 he ordered the investigation brought to a close as soon as possible. But he was reluctant to sacrifice the entire sum to which these *inamdars* laid claim, for much of it was income to which the Government considered itself justly entitled. Hence a compromise settlement was drawn up, under which all *inam* land would be assessed at one-fourth of the ordinary revenue demand, and no further inquiries into individual land holdings would be carried out.[39] This "large measure of healing and pacification," as it was called in the Legislative Council, met with no opposition and was finally enacted in 1861.[40] Meanwhile Sir Charles Trevelyan in Madras had gone ahead with a compromise plan of his own for the settlement of *inam* claims in that Presidency. His scheme was far more lenient than that adopted in Bombay, for it recognized fifty years' possession as conferring a valid title, and it was therefore subjected to severe criticism in Calcutta. H. B. Harington pro-

[39] Minute of 4 April 1859, Home Rev., 5 August 1859, No. 8.
[40] Speech by Erskine of 8 June 1861, *Proceedings*, VII, 590.

tested that, by these proceedings, "income of upwards of half a million will be jeopardized, if not altogether sacrificed." But it was practically impossible to reverse such a measure once underway, and in any case it received support from the more conservative members of Council. Bartle Frere was pleased to have settled so easily and so quickly a "question which threatened to become one of the cancers of our system."[41]

The *inam* proceedings affected relatively few people. In 1861 a far more comprehensive measure of conciliation came under discussion—a permanent settlement of the land revenue throughout India. But as this involved a far greater potential sacrifice of revenue, the Government was obliged to move more cautiously. Permanent settlement had so far been conceded only to the zamindars of Bengal and Bihar. Elsewhere the land revenue demand was fixed for a period never exceeding thirty years, and was liable to enhancement at the end of the term. The Government quite naturally claimed the right to share in the increase in the value of land which took place under its rule, and Ricardian rent theory, with its concept of land revenue as an "unearned increment," insured that assessments would be pitched at the highest possible level. Pressure for a substantial change in this system first came from the English mercantile community, who had long chafed under the restraints of the Indian land system. In their view, English capital, enterprise, and energy were "effectually kept back" from productive investment in India because of the insecurity of land tenure. If only the Government of India would grant land in fee simple, free of all revenue demand, they said, European merchants and planters would flock to the country.[42] They wanted in India essentially what they had in England—landed property unfettered by obligations either to the state or the tenantry—and they saw in the dissolution

[41] Minute by Harington of 14 December 1859, and by Frere of 9 January 1860, Home Rev., 27 January 1860, No. 1-5.

[42] Memorial of Landholders and Commercial Association, Calcutta, 31 May 1861, Home Rev., 6 June 1861, No. 6.

of the East India Company an excellent opportunity to renew their demands.

The Government of India had no objection to the sale of waste lands in the hills to an intending settler; indeed it had a rather exaggerated idea of the role European settlers could play in "the material and moral improvement" of the "half-civilized tribes" inhabiting the hill regions.[43] In the plains, however, the mercantile objective of freehold tenure could be met only by redemption of the land revenue: that is, by the payment of a single lump sum, usually set at twenty years' assessment, to extinguish all future liabilities. This posed serious financial problems for the Government, for its Exchequer would first be glutted with funds and then deprived of a steady and stable source of income. On the other hand, the Government realized, the scheme had distinct political advantages if it were extended generally to all Indian landholders. A zamindar who had redeemed his land tax would obviously be tightly bound to the British Government upon whose continued existence his exemption depended. For many Englishmen, including Lord Canning, this was the chief recommendation of the scheme, and it was sanctioned by the Government of India in October 1861.[44] Yet, as many officers pointed out, few Indians had sufficient capital to undertake redemption, and those who possessed the money found more profitable employment for it elsewhere, largely in agricultural moneylending. Several officers in the North-Western Provinces even went so far as to state that the people of India did not "have sufficient confidence in the perpetuity of our rule" to invest their money in it.[45] Consequently in 1862 the Secretary

[43] Resolution of Govt. of India, 17 October 1861, Home Rev., 17 October 1861, No. 98.

[44] Resolution of 17 October 1861, *ibid*. To relieve the strain on the Exchequer the Government limited the amount of permissible redemption in any one district to 10% of the total land tax.

[45] Notes by W. Muir of 5 November 1859 and H. B. Harington of 5 September 1861; and letter of R. M. Edwards, Collector of Muzaffarnagar, 11 November 1859, Home Rev., 17 October 1861, Nos. 28 and 41.

of State ruled that the right of redeeming the land revenue should be confined to plantations and similar areas liable to benefit from European investment. But the Indian landholder was not ignored. In place of this complicated and expensive scheme of redemption, he was to have the more tangible benefit of a permanent settlement.[46]

The idea of permanent settlement was first revived and promoted by Colonel Baird Smith in 1861. In February of that year Baird Smith was sent by Lord Canning to inquire into the causes and extent of the famine which had afflicted much of the Northwest during 1860, and to suggest measures which might guard against the recurrence of such calamities. Baird Smith had been appointed because of his reputation as an engineer in the construction of irrigation works, and it was expected that his report would be confined to such measures.[47] Instead, however, he claimed that the best protection against famine would be a permanent limitation of the Government revenue demand. The certainty that his revenue assessment would never be raised, he pointed out, would encourage the proprietor to improve his land and to invest capital in it; as prosperity took root, the community would "grow stronger and stronger, and the risk of its collapsing under any such calamities as that we are now considering would gradually become less and less."[48]

Canning joined wholeheartedly in Baird Smith's recommendations. Permanent settlement, in his view, possessed not only economic but political advantages. As he wrote to Wood in October 1861: "I should like much to launch the measure in my time. I am certain that it would do for all holders of tax-paying lands all that the adoption measure has done for independent Chiefs in the way of binding them to our Government, and more than Lord Cornwallis's permanent settlement

[46] Dispatch of 9 July 1862, Revenue Dispatch No. 14 of 1862.

[47] Govt. of India to Baird Smith, 2 February 1861, Home Public, 8 February 1861, No. 13-20.

[48] Report of 14 August 1861, cited in Romesh C. Dutt, *The Economic History of India* (Delhi, 1960), II, 205-06.

has done for Bengal. . . . It would be worth an army of European troops."[49] The response on his Council and among many of the provincial authorities was equally enthusiastic. Frere and Beadon urged that the measure be introduced at once, while Edmonstone, the Lieutenant-Governor of the North-Western Provinces, and William Muir on the Board of Revenue at Allahabad gave a ready assent to the proposal. Although they admitted that permanent settlement provided no guarantee against rebellion, nevertheless "the absolute limitation of demand upon their land will be received by an agricultural people with the highest satisfaction, and will produce, if anything can, feelings of attachment to the Government, and of confidence in its desire to promote the best interests of the country." Nor were the economic considerations, which had originally prompted the measure, overlooked in the subsequent discussions. Its proponents invariably cited the "increased incentive to improvement and expenditure of capital" which the security of a permanently fixed demand would provide, and looked forward to a new era of Indian prosperity.[50]

Despite this overwhelming body of favorable opinion in India, Sir Charles Wood at first hesitated. Although he saw "all the advantages to the people," the financial implications of the scheme rather frightened him. With the land revenue—the Government's major source of income—permanently fixed, and the expenses of Government liable to "increase rapidly with increasing civilization," he could not see "whence any additional income is to come."[51] This awkward fact always remained the basic stumbling block in the way of permanent settlement. In 1862, however, it was brushed aside, and Wood's fears assuaged, by two counter-arguments: that "the proba-

[49] Canning to Wood, 8 October 1861, Wood Papers.

[50] Minutes of Cecil Beadon, 13 March 1862; and S. Laing, 7 April 1862, Home Rev., 5 September 1862, No. 28-29. Frere to Canning, 25 September 1861, Canning Papers. Minutes of Muir, 16 December 1861; and Edmonstone, 27 May 1862, Home Rev., 5 September 1862, No. 37-38.

[51] Wood to Canning, 18 November 1861, Wood Papers.

bility of any considerable increase in the land revenue appears to be but slight"; and that in any case permanent settlement would so accelerate the prosperity of the country that other branches of the revenue (such as customs and excise) would make good the deficiency. Neither of these confident assumptions was based on any real knowledge of the Indian economy; in fact, as events soon proved, they were completely invalid. Yet permanent settlement remained attractive, because it embodied the ideals of laissez faire liberalism. The English liberal always maintained that progress and prosperity were best promoted when the Government held its hand and left capital to fructify in the possession of enterprising men. Whatever its apparent financial drawbacks, permanent settlement would encourage the virtues of thrift and individual initiative, which alone could stimulate rapid economic growth. As Sir John Lawrence noted, "what is really wanted is to give the intelligent, the thrifty, and the enterprising among them, the opportunity of improving their own condition, by the exercise of such qualities, and this can be best done by limiting the public demand on the land."[52] In a more grandiose fashion the Duke of Argyll, after pointing out that "under permanent settlement the cultivator is sure that he will reap all the fruits of his own industry," went on to state that: "There are some principles which are of universal application, because they rest on the nature of man, and can never cease to operate on the Wealth of Nations. One of these is the close connection which obtains between the progress of industry and the certainty of enjoying its results. . . . Nothing is lost, but much is gained, when a Government yields to its people that which will stimulate their industry, and tend to the accumulation of their wealth."[53] Permanent settlement thus found its ultimate theoretical justification not in India at all, but in the laissez faire theories of English liberalism.

[52] Minute of 5 July 1862, P.P. 1862, XL, 866-67.
[53] Duke of Argyll, *India Under Dalhousie and Canning* (London, 1865), pp. 141-42.

The opponents of the measure often approached it from an equally theoretical point of view. For men trained in the doctrines of Ricardo and Mill the State was owner of the soil and received the land revenue as rent, in the increase of which it was justly entitled to share. To alienate these rents to individuals would be a serious error. As John Strachey, the radical Collector of Moradabad, put it, "It is clear gain to the public that a large portion of the rent of land should remain the property of the public, instead of going into the pockets of private landholders." Ross Mangles on the India Council in London similarly tried to educate his colleagues in the principles of Ricardian rent theory, and even quoted James Mill for their benefit.[54] But it was all in vain. After the Mutiny the forces of laissez faire were too strong and the demands of political security too insistent. By July 1862 the Government of India was committed to permanent settlement.

It still remained, however, to carry the measure into effect, and here the Government soon found itself mired in a sea of difficulties. The Governments of Madras and Bombay rejected the proposal outright. They claimed that their thirty-year ryotwari settlements afforded adequate security for an improving tenant without debarring the Government from future increase of revenue. The Punjab Government on their part stated that, since the province had only recently been brought under British rule and was still largely in "a backward state of cultivation," they did not consider it wise to give up at that time the Government's right to an increased revenue from agricultural improvement.[55] In the Central Provinces, on the other hand, permanent settlement found a devoted enthusiast in the Chief Commissioner, Richard Temple, who urged that it be introduced at once in all or part of some eight districts. But the Central Provinces were in an even more backward

[54] Strachey letter of 30 September 1859, Home Rev., 17 October 1861, No. 42. Mangles Dissent of 3 July 1862, P.P. 1862, XL, 856-61.

[55] Sec. Govt. Madras to Sec. Govt. India, 8 February 1862; Minute by Sir G. Clerk, Governor of Bombay, 3 March 1862; Sec. Govt. Punjab to Sec. Govt. India, 25 April 1862, Home Rev., 5 September 1862, Nos. 22, 30, 33.

state than the Punjab. Vast tracts of land were waste, with the revenue demand pitched correspondingly low; and in many districts the revenue data were rudimentary or defective. The Viceroy, Lord Elgin, therefore considered Temple's proposal "precipitate" and ordered that all settlements be concluded for the usual thirty-year period.[56] In Oudh the Officiating Chief Commissioner during 1861-1862, George Yule, a Bengal civilian, recommended that the seven densely populated districts west of the Gogra be granted a permanent settlement as soon as the revenue survey could be completed. His Bengal experience had convinced him, he said, that such a settlement was "beyond all comparison the best both as regards the people and ourselves."[57] Canning, for whom the pacification of Oudh and the firm establishment of its taluqdar system had always been a matter of anxious concern, agreed that "the time for giving to Oude ... a permanent settlement is *now*; without going through a transition stage of temporary settlement, long or short." He continued, "It is this that more than anything that could be devised will consolidate the new condition of Native Society there, and secure expenditure of capital, Native and English. . . . The sooner a measure is taken which will confirm for ever the present warm intelligent loyalty of its population, secure the future peace of the province against all disturbance, and justify a still further reduction of its expensive garrison, the better."[58] However, Canning's departure from India in March 1862 removed the main spur to action; for Elgin was far more cautious, and Wingfield, on his return to duty in 1863, came out in opposition to the measure. So it was put aside pending completion of the revenue survey until events in the North-Western Provinces prompted a complete reconsideration of the question.

[56] Sec. C.C. Central Provinces to Sec. Govt. India, 22 July 1862; and note by Elgin, 3 September 1862, For. Rev. A, October 1862; Nos. 3-4. Sec. Govt. India to C.C. Central Provinces, 21 March 1863, For. Rev. A, March 1863, No. 76.

[57] Yule to Canning, 15 August 1861, Canning Papers.

[58] Memorandum of 1 March 1862, For. Rev. A, March 1862, No. 7-11.

The North-Western Provinces were generally regarded as
the area most suited for permanent settlement. They had been
under British rule for sixty years; ample revenue experience
had been gained during the course of the previous settlements;
and the current thirty-year settlements all expired during the
1860's. But in concluding a permanent settlement in the North-
Western Provinces, the Government was determined to avoid
Lord Cornwallis's mistakes in Bengal. Before declaring any
settlement permanent, the local authorities were ordered to
undertake a careful and thorough revision of the assessment
levels and to record all rights in the hands of subordinate
holders. Even the most meticulous revision, however, could
not take into account the expansion of cultivation or the
growth of irrigation facilities. In either case the Government
stood to lose a good deal of revenue under a permanent settlement, for newly cultivated or irrigated tracts would be far
more productive than before, while the land tax remained at
its original level. Hence, while the revision of settlement was
in progress, the Government set out to devise some way of
minimizing the loss of revenue from these causes. With regard to waste lands, the Secretary of State ruled in 1865 that
permanent settlement would be restricted to those estates in
which at least 80 per cent of the total arable land was under
cultivation. Where the proportion of waste exceeded one-
fifth, the estate was to be settled for thirty years in the normal
manner.[59] Irrigation posed a more complex problem. If all
land liable to benefit from irrigation in the future were excluded from settlement, little land would ever be settled
permanently, for irrigation was susceptible of almost indefinite
extension in the Doab and Upper Ganges. If, on the other
hand, the Government reserved the right to raise assessments
on irrigated land, it would introduce an element of uncertainty
into the settlement, arouse suspicion, and so neutralize the
benefits of the measure. Faced with this prospect, the Lieutenant-Governor, E. Drummond, recommended that the

[59] Dispatch of 24 March 1865, Revenue Dispatch No. 11 of 1865.

Government give up its claim to a share of the profits from canal irrigation altogether. It would be better, he said, to suffer some loss of revenue, rather than hamper the "promised boon" with further conditions.[60] The Viceroy, Sir John Lawrence, entirely agreed. Reciting once again the "great social and political benefits" of permanent settlement, he urged that no conditions be imposed which would "shackle this great work or mar its success."[61] The Home Government, however, was far more concerned with the effect of the measure on Indian finances, already depleted by the expiration of the income tax. By 1865 Wood's earlier enthusiasm had evaporated, and he continually implored Lawrence to move with caution. His successors, deGrey, Cranborne, and Northcote, shared these misgivings. Consequently, although acknowledging the "great importance of connecting the interests of the proprietors of land with the stability of the British Government," Northcote refused to sacrifice the revenue irrigation would make available. In March 1867 he ruled that permanent settlement should be withheld whenever canal irrigation was likely to raise the value of an estate 20 per cent within the next twenty years.[62]

So far the opposition was confined to the India Office in London. In 1868, however, during the final review of assessments in the Meerut Division, the local Government itself began to draw back from permanent settlement. On a visit to Meerut soon after taking office as Lieutenant-Governor, Sir William Muir discovered that both agricultural prices and the rental value of land were rapidly increasing; he concluded that the assessments were pitched too low. Reversing his former opinion, he recommended that permanent settlement be deferred until land had reached its full economic value. To grant a permanent settlement on an "imperfectly developed rental" would involve a gratuitous and indefensible

[60] Minute of 24 September 1866, Home Rev., 20 November 1866, No. 1.

[61] Note of 27 October 1866 incorporated in Rev. Letter No. 29 of 20 November 1866 to S. of S., Home Rev., 20 November 1866, No. 4.

[62] Dispatch of 23 March 1867, Revenue Dispatch No. 15 of 1867.

sacrifice of revenue.[63] This recommendation was accepted by
the Government of India in 1871. They were now fully aware
of the "economical revolution" wrought by a decade of in-
flation and railroad construction, and determined to obtain
their share of the increased wealth.[64] Permanent settlement
was first postponed and then abandoned as inappropriate for
an era of depreciating currency and rising prices. A few voices
were raised in protest, most notably those of Sir John Lawrence
and Sir Charles Trevelyan, but in retirement they exercised no
influence, and the measure was never revived.[65]

The permanent settlement scheme thus had a short life-
span of some ten years, and came to absolutely nothing. Still,
its rise and fall provide an illuminating commentary on the
influence of the Mutiny on British attitudes toward India.
Immediately after 1857 all considerations were subordinated
to the requirements of political security and pacification. For
this purpose there were few measures better suited than
permanent settlement of the land revenue. It could effectively
conciliate all the landholding classes and remove one of the
major causes of agrarian discontent. The measure gained
strength, and found ample theoretical justification, in the
assumptions of laissez faire liberalism. But in 1868, when the
time came to declare permanent the first revised settlements,
the political climate had changed. Peace and security had
now been secured, and the fears of the Mutiny era were little
more than a memory. Fiscal considerations took on a new
importance. What had appeared a political necessity in 1862
was, a decade later, an expensive luxury the Government
could not afford.

[63] Minute of 14 December 1869, cited in Auckland Colvin, *Memorandum
on the Revision of Land Revenue Settlements in the North-Western Provinces
1860-72*, p. 71.

[64] Resolution of 26 May 1871, *ibid.*, p. 72.

[65] Evidence of C. Trevelyan to House of Commons Committee on Indian
Finance, 28 February 1873, P.P. 1873, XII, 112; and 7 March 1873, *ibid.*, p.
163; and of J. Lawrence, 10 June 1873, *ibid.*, pp. 368-69. The measure was
finally officially abandoned by the Secretary of State in March 1883.

## CHAPTER VII

# COURTS, COUNCILS AND CIVIL
# SERVANTS

ONE of the most widely detested of all British institutions in
India was the system of judicial procedure. If not among the
major causes of the Mutiny, the complexity and corruption
of the courts certainly helped pave the way for rebellion. As
Canning himself acknowledged, "the complicated, vexatious,
and costly proceedings in our courts have caused great discontent."[1] Few District Officers disagreed. Charles Raikes, Judge
of the Sadr Court at Agra, stated flatly that the people of the
Northwest Provinces "disliked, for very sufficient reason, our
system of civil procedure."[2] Despite considerable reform in
Bentinck's time, notably the award of magisterial authority to
the Collector, the administrative system of the North-Western
Provinces in 1857 was still based upon the Bengal Regulations
and embodied a good deal of the Cornwallis tradition. As in
Bengal the judiciary was tightly bound by its own rules of
procedure and clearly marked off from the executive. The
courts stood as a perpetual reminder to the executive branch
that their actions were subject to the restraints of law. Only
under the rule of law, Cornwallis and his successors maintained, would property be secure and individual initiative find
ample scope. This Regulation system, however, never obtained
much popularity outside Bengal. It appealed neither to the

[1] Canning to Vernon Smith, 24 September 1857, Canning Papers.
[2] Raikes, *Notes on the Revolt*, p. 7.

conservative paternalist nor to the radical reformer. The one sought a simple patriarchal system, the other a powerful authoritarian government. Hence the administrative system of the Northwest had long been subjected to severe criticism, and the Punjab, after its annexation, was governed on entirely different principles. All governmental power, both executive and judicial, was there concentrated in the hands of one officer, the Deputy Commissioner, who was responsible only to his Divisional Commissioner and through him to the Chief Commissioner. There was no separate judiciary and no attempt to enforce the Bengal Regulations. A remarkable mixture of unbounded power and tight discipline thus permeated the whole structure.

The Mutiny vastly enhanced the prestige of the Punjab system. In the minds of many Englishmen, the hostility shown by the people toward the courts seemed clearly to indicate that they preferred a simple unitary form of government. The Punjab system, Raikes claimed, "is so simple, so powerful, so entirely adapted to the genius of the people, that it must, like truth, prevail, and sooner or later extend over the entire peninsula." We cannot, he continued, any longer try to rule Asia on the constitutional principles of Europe. "However much philosophers may sneer, a 'paternal despotism' is not only the happiest, but the only regime for India." He recommended accordingly that the District Officers in the Northwest be given full power over all functions of Government and that a simple summary method of judicial procedure take the place of the Bengal Regulations.[3] In this Raikes spoke for many of his fellow officers. The other Judges of the Agra Sadr Court might argue that "the civil law has nothing to do with the present disturbances" and that its abrogation would in no way benefit society;[4] but most officers urged the Government to build a new and streamlined structure upon the ruins of the

[3] *Ibid.*, pp. 171-73.
[4] Minutes by H. Unwin and R. B. Morgan of 4 August 1857, Home Judl., 1 July 1859, No. 10.

old judicial system. As Bartle Frere pointed out, "We have enveloped ourselves in rules and regulations till we have left ourselves no power of individual action. We have guarded ourselves against doing evil till we have left no power of doing good. . . . The remedy is very simple, though not easy, for it is opposed, not only to existing habits and prejudices, but to all our English ideas of government. . . . Throughout your whole machinery of government . . . let every official be a real ruler in all things to those below him, and let him be really ruled by the functionary above him."[5]

Even at the highest levels of Government the Mutiny brought into sharp relief the merits of paternal rule. The Court of Directors suggested that the suppression of the revolt in the Northwest ought to be followed by the introduction of a code of procedure "more expeditious and simple, and more in accordance with native feeling and habits, than the complicated procedure of the regulations."[6] Canning agreed that such a change, though it might be called a retrograde step, would be a wise one "if there is wisdom in removing first causes of discontent." In September 1857 he offered the post of Lieutenant-Governor of the North-Western Provinces to John Lawrence, with a special mandate to simplify the administrative system and to assimilate it to the Punjab model.[7] Lawrence preferred to stay in Lahore, but the man selected, G. F. Edmonstone, was no less an advocate of the Punjab system. In July 1859 he recommended that the unwieldy district of Gorakhpur be divided into three separate districts, and that they be administered on the principles in force in the Punjab. He defended the proposal from the hostile criticism of H. B. Harington and other Bengal civilians by pointing out that it was in part simply a return to the traditional Indian

[5] Frere to Goderich, 15 June 1858 in Martineau, *Life of Frere*, I, 267. See also Outram Memorandum of 15 January 1858, F.C. 5 November 1858, No. 192; Commissioner of Meerut to Govt. N.W.P., 12 October 1857, Home Judl., 1 July 1859, No. 11; and Gubbins, *The Mutinies in Oudh*, pp. 491-93.

[6] Dispatch of 1 September 1858, Public Dispatch No. 139 of 1858.

[7] Canning to Vernon Smith, 24 September 1857, Canning Papers.

system of government, under which authority was always centered in some one individual. As such, he insisted there was a "strong presumption" that it would meet with the approval of a people "proverbially attached to their ancient customs."[8]

In fact, however, nothing ever came of these various proposals for a return to patriarchal rule. In the settled complex society of British India it was simply impossible. Much as a system of simple laws and unfettered executive discretion might be suited to newly conquered territory, it was, as several officers pointed out, "totally unadapted for the various and complicated wants of an old society, which has been under British jurisdiction for more than eighty years."[9] Nor were the Indian people necessarily attached to the patriarchal system. They would doubtless have preferred a cheaper, more efficient system of procedure than was possible under the Bengal Regulations, but this by no means implied any affection for arbitrary despotism. Among the educated classes at least the Punjab system met with universal condemnation. They detested the assumption, implicit in the paternal ideal, that the Indian people were like children, in need of guidance by wise and benevolent superiors. What India needed, Harish Chandra Mukherjee insisted, was not the arbitrary rule of inexperienced youths, but good laws administered by a competent judiciary. Through the pages of the *Hindoo Patriot* he continually pressed for the complete separation of judicial and executive functions, and the whittling down of executive discretion wherever it was still to be found.[10] Sayyid Ahmad Khan at Moradabad put forward much the same opinion. The system of civil administration in the North-Western Provinces,

[8] Sec. Govt. N.W.P. to Sec. Govt. India, 8 July 1859, Home Public, 19 December 1860, No. 19; and Minute by Edmonstone, 24 October 1860, *ibid.*, No. 23.

[9] Edwards, *Facts and Reflections*, p. 22

[10] See his essays on "The Patriarchal System," "Collector-Magistrates," and "Constitutionalism in India," in Sen-Gupta, ed., *Selections from the Writings of Hurrish Chunder Mookerji*, pp. 235-44.

he said, was "highly commendable" and had nothing to do with the rebellion. So far as the courts had borne the brunt of popular hostility it was simply the result of their connection with land transfer and peasant indebtedness. In the Punjab, on the other hand, where so much was left to individual discretion, and judicial questions received only the most summary consideration, the action of the courts would in time, he said, provoke "much disgust and vexation."[11] Men like Sayyid Ahmad had of course a vested interest in the maintenance of the judicial system, for it provided one of the few respectable careers open to the educated Indian. Only as a pleader before the courts, or a *sadr amin* in government service, was the young Indian at all likely to find remuneration commensurate with his abilities. The great merit of an independent judiciary, however, was the support it gave to constitutional government. The courts, in Indian eyes, were above all a check on arbitrary rule and a guarantee of civil liberty. The Cornwallis system won Indian approval for the same reason that it was so heartily disliked by many British officers: because it was modelled on British institutions and reflected the ideals of English liberalism.

Although the idea of restoring paternal rule eventually had to be dropped, the Mutiny did leave its mark on the statute book. It finally prompted the Legislature, after years of delay and hesitation, to enact the codes prepared by Macaulay and the two Law Commissions which had sat under Bentinck and Dalhousie. Between them the Penal Code, the Code of Civil Procedure, and the Code of Criminal Procedure, all enacted between 1859 and 1861, substantially improved and simplified the system of law in India. If they did not satisfy the devoted paternalist, the new codes did at least remove many of the more objectionable features of the Bengal Regulations. The Code of Civil Procedure (Act VIII of 1859) abandoned the elaborate and time-consuming series of written pleadings which had hitherto preceded trial. Instead parties were to be

[11] Sayyid Ahmad Khan, *Causes of the Revolt*, pp. 29-31.

confronted and examined orally, with written statements confined to a simple narrative of facts. In similar fashion the
Code of Criminal Procedure (Act XXV of 1861), though
poorly drafted, did away with the use of written depositions,
and enforced upon the Judge the duty of recording the
evidence of witnesses with his own hand. Dependence upon
low-paid subordinates, with its inevitable corruption, was
thereby avoided, and a fairer trial assured to the defendant.
Macaulay's Penal Code likewise reached the statute book substantially unaltered as part of the same spurt of legislative
activity, despite criticism by those frightened at its Benthamite
inspiration. Once these codes were in force, the movement
to extend the Punjab system to the North-Western Provinces
immediately lost much of its support. Indeed the controversy
ceased to have much significance, for the new codes applied
to the Punjab as well as to the rest of India. Henceforth the
only distinctive feature of the Punjab administration was the
union of executive and judicial authority in the hands of the
District Officer, and for this few were willing to fight.

The first major casualty of these altered circumstances
was Edmonstone's proposal to place the district of Gorakhpur
under the non-Regulation system. Canning pointed out
that as the new codes would of necessity be enforced in
Gorakhpur, the change would be of doubtful value, while Edmonstone himself acknowledged that the Civil Procedure
Code "has removed many of the objections to which the actions
of the Civil Courts in these Provinces were formerly obnoxious."[12] The scheme was abandoned by the Government
of India in 1863 and never revived.[13] In the end, therefore,
despite the revival of paternalist sentiment, the scope of executive action underwent continuous and steady restriction during
the last half of the nineteenth century. In a developing com-

[12] Canning to Edmonstone, 19 September 1861, Edmonstone to Canning,
30 September 1861, Canning Papers.

[13] Sec. Govt. India to Sec. Govt. N.W.P., 4 February 1863, Home Judl., 4
February 1863, No. 20. The district was however split in two in 1864, in
order to relieve its overworked staff.

mercial society it could not be otherwise. The new codes subjected the whole of India to a comprehensive and uniform legal structure; High Courts soon were established in all the provincial capitals, including Lahore; and in 1884 the Punjab District Officers were at last divested of their judicial functions and placed upon the same footing as the Collector-Magistrates in the Northwest Provinces. The District Officer remained the embodiment of British authority on the local level—the *hakim* in the eyes of the villager—but, viewed from above, he was far more a cog in a vast bureaucratic machine than a paternal despot.

The same controversy was also being fought out at the national level, for Calcutta in 1860 wielded over the inferior governments an autocratic power no less marked than that exercised by the Punjab District Officer over his subordinates. The local governments had always chafed under this close supervision, but until the 1860's their protests evoked little response. The governmental machinery at the time of the Mutiny still reflected the authoritarian sentiments of the early reformers, who held that a centralized administration, tightly controlling its inferior members, was far better adapted to the efficient conduct of business than a collection of semi-independent Presidencies. Indeed under the Charter Act of 1853 Madras and Bombay only with difficulty retained some semblance of their former independence, while the new Lieutenant-Governor of Bengal was placed completely under the authority of the Viceroy. After the Mutiny, however, as government grew more complex, and the requirements of the individual provinces more varied, the question of decentralization became at last a live political issue. Bartle Frere at Bombay and Henry Maine on the Viceroy's Council, with the encouragement of the India Office, undertook to secure for the local governments more freedom of action, particularly with regard to finance, and at the same time to emancipate the Lieutenant-Governor of Bengal from his dependence upon the Viceroy. But they had to contend with a powerful band

of opponents, for whom the supremacy of the central government was the only security against confusion and chaos, and
whose most dedicated champion was the powerful Sir John
Lawrence. As Viceroy, Lawrence carried on a running battle
with the Bombay Government over finance, tried unsuccessfully to abolish the newly created Bengal Legislative Council,
and torpedoed a proposal, supported by Maine and by Stafford
Northcote at home, to make the Lieutenant-Governor of Bengal a full-fledged Governor with an Executive Council.

Finances formed the first, and most enduring, subject of
controversy. Under the Charter Act of 1833 all revenue from
all the provinces of British India was treated as part of a
single fund, and was disbursed only on the orders of the
Governor-General in Council. This system, which forced the
local governments to obtain prior sanction from Calcutta before spending any money, naturally aroused a good deal of discontent. In particular the Governors of Madras and Bombay,
who were not dependent on the Viceroy for their appointment,
resented this subordination to the central secretariat in matters
of financial detail. By 1860 the process of centralization had
reached its furthest point. The construction of railways and
telegraphs at last made it possible to exercise really effective
control over the local governments, while the Mutiny, for a
time at least, made such control a necessity. The suppression
of the revolt cost the Government some £40,000,000 and
saddled its finances with an annual charge of £1,900,000 in
interest payments.[14] In the face of this alarming increase in
the public debt, the Government embarked upon a policy of
strict economy and financial control. Under the guidance of
James Wilson, the whole system of Indian finance was
reorganized, an income tax was introduced, and all expenditure
carefully scrutinized. Wilson's successor, Samuel Laing, recommended that the provincial governments be charged with

[14] Speech of James Wilson in Legislative Council, 18 February 1860, *Proceedings*, VI, 94. The Indian debt rose from £59 million in 1857 to £97
million in 1860.

responsibility over certain heads of expenditure, and that they be empowered to raise revenue by local taxation.[15] But nothing came of this proposal, and so the local governments found themselves more tightly reined in than ever before. To a proud Bombay or Madras civil servant this subservience to Calcutta was intolerable. Lord Elphinstone, Governor of Bombay, burst out in 1860 that, so far as he could see, the central government was bent upon assimilating everything, in every part of India, to the practice in Bengal. It was, he said, "a sort of Procrustean bed to which men of the most different statures must be made to conform." The outcome of this process could only be "to weaken the authority of the subordinate Governments, and to deaden the energies of all who are employed under them."[16] Sir Bartle Frere, when he became Governor, protested repeatedly to the Secretary of State against the petty and vexatious interference to which his expenditures on public works were subjected. The Public Works Department, he said, not only laid down the general principles along which work should proceed, and set limits to total expenditure, but insisted upon scrutinizing "the minutest detail of plan and estimate."[17] Moreover, he continued, the slightest variation from the budgeted estimates or any expenditure, however necessary, made without prior sanction, brought down the wrath of a suspicious secretariat. A Government unwilling to trust its own subordinates, he concluded, would eventually paralyze all sense of responsibility and initiative.[18] Both from Wood and from Northcote, Frere gained a sympathetic hearing. But they could make little headway against the obstinate opposition of Sir John Lawrence, who insisted that only bringing the subordinate authorities to book by making them prepare a clear exposition of what they required, and obliging them to submit their requirements to the scrutiny

[15] Temple, *Men and Events of My Time in India*, pp. 216-17.

[16] Minute of 5 January 1860, Home Public, 8 September 1860, No. 13.

[17] Frere to Col Strachey, 12 October 1863 in Martineau, *Life of Frere*, I, 423.

[18] Frere to Lawrence, 11 May 1864, *ibid*., pp. 434-38.

of a superior authority, would secure habits of economy and foresight in the management of public finances.[19]

By 1867, however, even the members of Lawrence's own Council had become convinced that efficient government demanded some form of provincial responsibility for finance. The result was the adoption, after Lawrence's departure, of a comprehensive scheme of financial decentralization, prepared by John Strachey and Lord Mayo. By a Resolution of 14 December 1870 fixed yearly grants were awarded to the local governments, out of which they were to defray the costs of jails, police, education, medical services, roads, and public works. The apportionment of the imperial allotment among these various heads was left to the discretion of the provincial authorities, and they were permitted where necessary to raise additional funds by local taxation. The local governments were of course still dependent upon the Supreme Government for the bulk of their income, and they were subject to general budgetary controls, but at least they now possessed genuine responsibility, both financial and administrative, over certain areas of government, and were free within limits to spend their money as they pleased. For most British officers decentralization was simply a way of rejuvenating the structure of the Empire by imparting to it increased efficiency and economy of operation. Lord Mayo alone had a broader vision. It would, he pointed out, "afford opportunities for the development of self-government, for strengthening municipal institutions, and for the association of Natives and Europeans to a greater extent than heretofore in the administration of affairs."[20] Although little was done at the time, Mayo's Resolution of 1870 can be viewed as the first step toward local self-government in India. Ripon's Resolution of 1882, and the subsequent Municipalities Act, only embodied in legislative form the suggestions Mayo had put forward twelve years earlier.

Meanwhile the Orissa famine of 1866 had touched off a

[19] Lawrence to Northcote, 13 March 1868, Lawrence Papers.
[20] Hunter, *Life of Mayo*, II, 59.

general discussion of the efficiency of the Lieutenant-Governor system as practiced in Bengal. Had the Lieutenant-Governor, Sir Cecil Beadon, been surrounded by an Executive Council, as were the Governors of Madras and Bombay, his error of judgment in denying the likelihood of serious famine might, it was felt, have been corrected. The Secretary of State, Sir Stafford Northcote, suggested accordingly that Bengal be placed on the same footing as Madras and Bombay, with a Governor and Council. The proposal was taken up with enthusiasm by Bartle Frere and Henry Maine. Frere, now on the India Council in London, argued that a civilized and settled province like Bengal could not be subjected indefinitely to the autocratic rule of a Lieutenant-Governor. Such a form of government could be successful only as a temporary expedient in a newly conquered province, where it was the natural successor to a military occupation. Once society had become settled, and the tasks of government more complex, personal despotism inevitably fell by the wayside. By himself one man simply could not efficiently rule "so large and so complicated a community as that of Bengal." In the end, he insisted, "perpetual infancy of civil government is just as impossible as perpetual reconquest."[21]

Henry Maine, and several other members of the Viceroy's Council, agreed that the autocratic Lieutenant-Governor system was hopelessly out of place in a modern commercial society. They were convinced as well that the Imperial Government would be far stronger if it were relieved of intimate supervision over Bengal, while the presence of a Council would provide the latter government with an effective safeguard against error or mediocrity on the part of its chief. Such arguments made no mark at all upon Sir John Lawrence. He retained undiminished the idyllic paternalism of his Punjab years. So far as he was concerned, the only form of government for India was "personal administration by a single head, without a Council." It alone "secured the momentum of improve-

21 Memorandum of 2 December 1867, P.P. 1867-68, XLIX, 207, 210.

ment, the exaction of responsibility, the exercise of vigilance in the highest degree ordinarily obtainable." That the world might be changing, that Bengal was not the Punjab, never crossed his mind. Moreover, as a radical, with something of the old Benthamite tradition behind him, Lawrence was extremely reluctant to weaken the authority of the central government. With James Mill he believed that only a strong central government could secure that uniformity of action and concentration of power upon which all real progress depended. As he wrote to Northcote in 1868, "I am more and more convinced every day that if we are to have a strong government in India, more power must be given to the Governor General, and more authority to the Government of India over the local Governments than we are now able to exercise." The experience of the Mutiny, as Lawrence saw it, only reinforced this conviction. That particular crisis might not recur, but should an emergency of any sort arise, if the Viceroy were only the head of a loose confederation of local governments, the whole British position in the East might be placed in jeopardy.[22]

Frere, on the other hand, for all his paternalism, had never had much faith in centralized government. Like most Bombay officers, he was too much a conservative to appreciate the merits of uniformity. He preferred instead to preserve local customs through a system of provincial autonomy. With Maine he was far more impressed by the diversity of India than by its homogeneity. Consequently, when Lawrence went on to propose that the newly created Bengal Legislative Council be abolished, both men rallied to its defence. Lawrence could see no point in having local legislative councils. By encouraging fruitless discussion over petty matters, they distracted the local governments from the weightier business of administration, and badly impaired the vigor and efficiency of their operation. The Lieutenant-Governor, he suggested, should be

[22] Minute of 20 January 1868, Home Public, 28 March 1868, No. 151. Lawrence to Northcote, 28 March 1868, Lawrence Papers.

given powers of summary legislation for limited purposes, while all major questions should be reserved for the Imperial Legislative Council.[23] In this opinion Lawrence found himself quite alone. Almost none of his advisers, even those opposed to the creation of a Presidency government in Bengal, were prepared to abolish the Bengal Legislative Council. Maine heatedly denied that there would be any gain in efficiency if legislation were confined to the central council. That body, he asserted, was already overloaded with business; the addition of Bengali legislation would break it down altogether. Besides, he pointed out, Bengal was an advanced society with its own distinctive character. Its progress should not be impeded "by the doubts of gentlemen intimately acquainted only with the less intellectual and less supple population of Upper India." Similarly the Foreign Secretary, Sir William Muir, although an advocate of the Lieutenant-Governor system, contended that legislation of a purely local character could best be handled in a local body; and he urged that the North-Western Prov-inces and Punjab also be awarded Legislative Councils of their own. But efficiency was not the only consideration. Ever since its foundation in 1862 the Bengal Legislative Council had con-tained representatives of the European business community and a sprinkling of educated Bengalis. There was no question, Maine pointed out, of giving this latter class representative institutions; but it was "a very serious matter to withdraw from them a formal legislature when they have once had it, and to subject them to that concrete form of despotism which consists in the complete blending of executive and legislative power."[24] Since voices were already beginning to be raised on behalf of "an Indian Parliament," Lawrence realized that his scheme would provoke an immense outcry, and so reluctantly abandoned it.[25] But he kept up his opposition to the principle

[23] Minute of 19 February 1868, Home Public, 28 March 1868, No. 150.

[24] Minute of H. S. Maine, 27 February 1868, *ibid.*, No. 155; and Sir W. Muir, 25 February 1868, *ibid.*, No. 153.

[25] Minute of 23 March 1868, *ibid.*, No. 160. See "An Indian Parliament,"

of local legislation, and effectively thwarted all attempts at founding such councils in the North-Western Provinces or Punjab.[26]

As Maine and Frere, if not Lawrence, had perceived, the question of council reform could no longer be separated from that of Indian representation. Henceforth the two of necessity went hand in hand, for educated Indians were now too numerous to be ignored. As originally constituted under the Charter Act of 1853, the Imperial Legislative Council was purely a body of officials, the Viceroy's Executive Council enlarged for the purpose of legislation by the addition of two judges and four civil servants, one each from Bengal, Madras, Bombay, and the North-Western Provinces. The British Indian Association had recommended that native members be placed on the new Council, and a few radical M.P.'s took up the cry.[27] But neither Charles Wood at the Board of Control nor Ross Mangles on the Company Directorate were willing to consider such a step; and even John Stuart Mill, for all his theoretical radicalism, came out in opposition to the proposal. The country was too vast, they said, and the people divided into too many antagonistic sects, for any system of representation to be effective. In the absence of national sentiment the introduction of a few Indians into the Legislative Council would only excite the jealousy of those who were left unrepresented. And in any case, Mangles insisted, "there were hundreds of European servants of the Company who knew far more of India and of its inhabitants than any of the Natives themselves."[28] Dalhousie did not share this opinion. He had hoped to put a "Native gentleman" on the Council as an aid

---

in Sen-Gupta, *Selections from the Writings of Hurrish Chunder Mookerji*, pp. 213-15.

[26] The North-Western Provinces obtained a Legislative Council only in 1886, and the Punjab in 1898.

[27] See speech of Joseph Hume, 18 July 1853, Hansard, cxxix, 428.

[28] Mangles speech of 18 July 1853, *ibid*., p. 425. Mill evidence to House of Lords Committee, 22 June 1852, P.P. 1852-53, xxx, 325.

to efficient legislation, and when deprived of this opportunity he appointed Prasanna Kumar Tagore to the post of Clerk of the Council.[29] Despite its purely official composition, Dalhousie went on to provide the Council with a Parliamentary form of procedure, and encouraged it to assert its independence as a separate organ of government. Debates were conducted orally, bills passed through the usual three stages, and a miniature Hansard was published. This was not what Wood had had in mind. The Council, he told Dalhousie, was simply a machine for lightening the labor of the Governor-General and giving him the use of a wider range of expert advice. It was not meant to be an independent body, and it was certainly not intended as the beginning of a constitutional Parliament in India. "I do not want to see a debating society but a working body of committee men."[30] But as Wood had no control over the operation of the Council, and Canning acquiesced in Dalhousie's arrangements, the Legislative Council was left to parade its independence unchallenged.

The Mutiny brought home to the Government the futility of trying to govern India with the aid of official opinion alone. Sir Bartle Frere saw clearly that only by admitting Indians to the Legislative Council could the Government hope to rule in peace and security. Much like Sayyid Ahmad Khan, whose pamphlet he had just finished reading, Frere pointed out in a Minute of 16 March 1860 that the great evil of the present system was that the Government rarely knew how its measures would be received or whether they suited the people, until criticism took the form of bitter hostility and rebellion. Any respectable native gentleman or merchant, he said, "would give us the most valuable aid by looking at questions from a Native point of view, and this is aid of a kind for which I know no substitute and it certainly could not be obtained from any European."[31] But there were other reasons why the Legis-

[29] Lee-Warner, *Life of Dalhousie*, II, 232.
[30] Wood to Dalhousie, June 1854, *ibid.*, p. 237.
[31] Minute of 16 March 1860, Home Public, 31 January 1861, No. 76.

lative Council required reform. With the growth of education and commerce, Frere pointed out, society itself was changing; a Legislative Council of officials was as much an anachronism as a simple paternal form of administration. The days are gone, he said, "when you could govern India without much caring what the Europeans and Europeanized community say or think of your measures, and unless you have some barometer and safety-valve combined in the shape of a deliberative Council, I believe you will be always liable to very unlooked-for and dangerous explosions." He recommended therefore that Indians and non-official Europeans be admitted in equal numbers to the Legislative Council, and that local legislative bodies be set up on the same principle in all the divisions of the Indian Empire.[32]

Sir Charles Wood, now the Secretary of State for India, was not reconciled by these arguments to the notion of an independent Legislative Council. He still very much regretted that the Council had been set up on a parliamentary basis by Dalhousie, and he could see no point in encouraging such pretensions by the addition of non-official members. "It may satisfy the English at Calcutta to have an English merchant or English planter in the Council, but I am by no means sure that it would improve the legislation; and you cannot put natives in who are in any sense the exponents of native opinion, or who could take part in the deliberations."[33] He wanted instead to reduce the Legislative Council to its original position as an advisory body, and to divest it of its "spouting character" by prohibiting speech-making and excluding the public from its sessions.[34] In this he obtained a good deal of support from Lord Canning, who as Viceroy had been left to deal with Dalhousie's intractable and self-willed creation. Canning, like Wood, soon regretted that the Legislative Council had ever been invested with parliamentary forms and

[32] Frere to Wood, 10 April 1861, and 6 July 1861, Wood Papers.
[33] Wood to Frere, 18 February 1861, Wood Papers.
[34] Wood to Canning, 24 November 1860, Wood Papers.

allowed to assume a quasi-independent status, for the judges and provincial representatives, under the leadership of Sir Barnes Peacock, lost no time in setting themselves up as a kind of spurious Opposition, ready to challenge the Government upon any convenient pretext. Peacock in particular could not resist the opportunity of making speeches, and as he had no executive responsibility and no knowledge of India outside Calcutta, he set out to gain the applause of the European community. Skillfully exploiting the parliamentary procedures of the Council, he bombarded the Government with petitions, fought for the exclusion of his countrymen from the Arms Act, and generally did his best to appear as a "Patriot Judge," defending the liberties of Englishmen from executive tyranny.

The most successful of Peacock's little essays into parliamentary government was the debate on the Mysore grants of December 1860. On that occasion Peacock succeeded in winning a favorable vote in the Council on a petition presented by the European residents of Calcutta protesting against a grant of £34,000 to the princes of the Mysore family, and demanded the production of papers on the subject. Frere, representing the Government, refused to hand over the papers on the ground that the subject was outside the competence of the Legislative Council; but the affair won for Peacock an immense popularity among his chosen "constituents," and showed only too clearly the capabilities for obstruction inherent in the Legislative Council as it was then constituted.[35] It was apparent to everyone in the Government that the judges had now to be curbed, and the Legislative Council confined to its proper sphere. A small white settler class could not be permitted to dominate the Indian Legislature under the guise of colonial self-government.[36] Yet, as Frere had pointed out, it was impossible to go back to the ideas of 1853. Publicity once

[35] Frere to Canning, 15 December 1860, Canning Papers; and Frere to Wood, 18 December 1860, Wood Papers.

[36] Wood to Canning, 26 March 1861, and Wood to Frere, 17 August 1861, Wood Papers.

conceded could not be withdrawn, nor could the Europeans
be deprived of their spokesmen in the Council without provoking an enormous outcry. Hence the legislation which
emerged—the Indian Councils Act of 1861—was something of
a compromise. The Legislative Council was stripped of its
complex procedure, the judges were removed, and oratory
was discouraged by the requirement that members speak from
their seats; but the public was admitted as before, and half the
additional seats were reserved for non-officials, both European
and Indian. The Act also created local legislative bodies on
the same pattern in Bombay, Madras, and Bengal, and gave
the Governor-General authority to establish councils in the
North-Western Provinces and Punjab if he saw fit.

Although it could no longer ape the House of Commons,
the Imperial Legislative Council gained from its enlarged
membership a greater measure of respect and a more substantial base. Three Indians—the Maharaja of Patiala, Dinkar
Rao, and Deo Narain Singh—sat upon the Council in its
first session under the new Act, and Canning wrote home
with enthusiasm of their performance.[37] But the addition of
these Indian members carried with it no commitment to
political advance in the direction of representative government.
The British found room on the reformed Council for Indian
members partly because they had no choice—when non-official
Europeans were admitted, the natives, who had "a far greater
stake in the country," could scarcely be excluded—and partly
because they had no wish to repeat the experience of the
Mutiny. Like Frere, Canning was forced to acknowledge that
the views of the Indian people on British legislation were often
"very shrewd and just," and that their participation in the
legislative process would be "a help to us."[38] But the Indians
selected for this honor were always carefully hand-picked for

[37] Canning to Wood, 3 February 1862, Wood Papers.
[38] Frere to Wood, 10 April 1861, Wood Papers; Canning to Wood, 15
January 1861, P.P. 1861, XLIII, 295.

their loyalty and their conservative sentiments. Any idea of forming electoral constituencies was rejected out of hand, and the claims to representation of "Young Bengal" were conveniently ignored.[39] As Maine commented: "There would be no more dangerous element in the Council than a large number of educated Bengalee Natives. Nobody charged with the conduct of the Legislative Department will ever fail to be inundated with their proposals for legislative innovation; and if these proposals are serious, all I can say is that there are many of them which Bentham himself would have thought premature."[40]

Canning in fact looked upon the admission of natives to the Legislative Council in much the same fashion as he did the award of magisterial powers to the Oudh taluqdars. It was a way to secure the good-will of the influential aristocratic and princely classes. Once in the Legislative Council, as Wood put it, "they will no longer feel, as they have hitherto done, that they are excluded from the management of affairs in their own country." Representative government was in no way a part of the scheme. Wood assured the House of Commons that "you cannot possibly assemble at any one place in India persons who shall be the real representatives of the various classes of the Native population of that empire."[41] And when Stanley suggested that the Council might some day form a nucleus for representative institutions, Canning quickly replied that such institutions were so remote that "there is no object in forming a nucleus for them now."[42] The reformed Legislative Council in many ways simply embodied the lessons of the Mutiny: that Indian opinion was worth listening to, but that power must be kept firmly in British hands.

[39] See Table 9, "List of Indian Members of Legislative Council 1862-73."
[40] Minute of 27 February 1868, Home Public, 28 March 1868, No. 155.
[41] Wood speech of 6 June 1861, Hansard, CLXIII, 641-43.
[42] Stanley to Canning, 16 May 1859; and Canning to Stanley, 24 June 1859, Canning Papers.

TABLE 9

INDIAN MEMBERS OF THE LEGISLATIVE COUNCIL, 1862-1873[a]

| | Occupation | Date of Membership |
|---|---|---|
| *Hindus* | | |
| Maharaja of Patiala | ruling prince | January 1862-1864 |
| Deo Narain Singh | landholder of Benares | January 1862-1864 |
| Dinkar Rao | late Dewan of Gwalior; landholder of Agra | January 1862-1864 |
| Maharaja of Vizianagram | zamindar of Madras | January 1864-1866 April 1872-1876 |
| Raja of Kishankot | jagirdar of Amritsar, Punjab | January 1864-1866 |
| Maharaja of Burdwan | zamindar of Bengal | November 1864-1866 |
| Prasanna Kumar Tagore | landholder of Bengal member Bengal Legis. Council | December 1867-August 1 |
| Dheoraj Singh | jaghirdar of Kashipur, North-western Provinces | January 1868-1870 |
| Maharaja of Balrampur | taluqdar of Oudh | October 1868-1870 |
| Maharaja of Jaipur | ruling prince | August 1868-1870 August 1871-1875 |
| Ramnath Tagore | landholder of Bengal | February 1873-1875 |
| *Muslims* | | |
| Nawab of Rampur | ruling prince | September 1863-1864 October 1866-1867 |
| Nawab of Dacca | zamindar of Bengal | December 1867-1869 |

[a] SOURCE: P.P. 1890, LIV, 104-05. Out of a total of 36 Indian members during the years 1862 to 1888, 23 were landholders, 6 ruling princes, 3 lawyers, 1 editor of the *Hindoo Patriot*, 1 officiating magistrate, 1 Parsi merchant, and 1 Burmese.

## Indians and the Indian Civil Service

Ever since the days of Warren Hastings, Indians had found service with the British Government. It was as impossible to run the administrative machinery without them as to wage war in India without sepoy troops. But they were rigorously excluded from all responsible positions. Convinced that Indians were neither trustworthy nor honest, Cornwallis in 1790 had placed Europeans in charge of the criminal courts, ousting the old Muslim judges, and had restricted Indian magistrates to cases of less than Rs. 50. At the same time, with the establishment of the Board of Revenue and the reorganization of the central secretariat, Indians found themselves displaced not only from the higher posts they had occupied in the nawab's *Khalsa* but from such subordinate positions as *serishtadar*, accountant, and registrar. By the time Cornwallis had completed his overhaul of the governmental machinery, it operated with a smoothness and efficiency inconceivable a decade earlier—but there was only a very small place in it for Indians.

During the nineteenth century the civil service was divided into two distinct branches, one of which, the covenanted (so-called because its members had to sign a bond of loyalty and integrity before employment) was recruited in England and guaranteed employment in India. The members of this service, nominated by the Directors of the East India Company until 1853 and then chosen by competitive examination, always regarded themselves as a superior governing class, and filled the bulk of the higher executive posts in the Government of India. From 1830 to 1900 their numbers remained stable at between 800 and 900. The other branch of the service, the uncovenanted, was selected in India by the various local governments, and its members were relegated either to clerical duties at headquarters or to subordinate positions within the district administration. These men had no security of employment and usually very poor prospects of advancement. Although their numbers continually increased with the growth of government employment, the opportunities available in this branch of the service for Indian candidates were at first severely limited due to Cornwallis's Europeanization policy.

The exclusion of the Indian people from the government of their own country first came in for sustained criticism during the debates in Parliament on the 1833 Charter Act. To liberal members like Macaulay such a policy was totally incompatible with Britain's mission in India, which was based upon equality and justice and which had as its aim the training of the Indian people in self-government. The new Charter Act consequently stated that no native of the British territories in India should "by reason only of his religion, place of birth, descent, or colour, or any of them, be disabled from holding any place, office, or employment under the said Company."[43] Fitness alone was henceforth to be the criterion of eligibility. But so far as the superior covenanted service was concerned, this clause, "that wise, that benevolent, that noble clause," as Macaulay described it, was a dead letter. The Directors had no intention of distributing their valuable patronage among native Indians, few of whom were in any case well enough versed in English to warrant the honor, nor did they believe that the admission of Indians would at all improve the government of the country. As they pointed out, in a dispatch drawn up by James Mill: "Facilities of official advancement can little affect the bulk of the people under any Government, and perhaps least under a good Government. It is not by holding out incentives to official ambition, but by repressing crime, by securing and guarding property, by creating confidence, by ensuring to industry the fruit of its labour, by protecting men in the undisturbed enjoyment of their rights, and in the unfettered exercise of their faculties, that Governments best minister to the public wealth and happiness."[44]

In the uncovenanted service, however, the scope of Indian employment was continually widened from Bentinck's time onward. Exclusive reliance upon European agency was if nothing else too expensive when Indian labor could be obtained for a fraction of the cost. The Indian judicial officers of *sadr amin* and *munsif* were given greater powers of jurisdiction, a new and higher post of principal *sadr amin* was created, and the salaries of all officers were raised to a more attractive

[43] Courtenay Ilbert, *The Government of India* (Oxford, 1898), p. 237.
[44] Public Dispatch of 10 December 1834, *ibid.*, p. 530.

level. The principal *sadr amin*, for instance, was authorized to try suits of any value and was paid up to Rs. 600 a month. Bentinck also placed Indians in the executive branch as Deputy Collectors, and in 1843 they were made eligible for the post of Deputy Magistrate, where they obtained limited criminal jurisdiction for the first time. By 1849, twenty years after Bentinck's arrival, the number of Indians employed in the civil service had more than doubled, rising from 1,197 to 2,813.[45]

But this was only a beginning. When the East India charter came up for renewal in 1853, the Company was subjected to severe criticism for its continued exclusion of Indians from the covenanted civil service. The 1853 Act abolished the system of nomination by the Directors and threw open the service to competition among all natural-born subjects of the Queen. But the examinations were held only in London, a fact which posed a formidable obstacle to prospective Indian candidates. Few could afford the expense of a journey to London, while overseas travel of any kind was repugnant to most orthodox Hindus, for it was difficult, if not impossible, to keep up caste restrictions in a strange environment. Returned travellers were often outcasted by their family and friends. Several members of Parliament therefore urged the Government to hold examinations in India as well as in England. Otherwise, Lord Stanley asserted, the Government would be "negativing that which they declared to be one of the principal objects of their Bill, and confining the Civil Service, as heretofore, to Englishmen," a result which he considered unjust and highly pernicious.[46] John Bright even went so far as to recommend that all districts be split in two, and Indian Collectors be appointed to fill the new posts.[47] But the Government steadfastly refused to accede to any such arrangement. Intellectual attainment, no matter how great, they maintained, could never be a sub-

---

[45] Cited in B. B. Misra, *The Indian Middle Classes*, p. 178. The number of Indian employees remained stable during the 1850's. In 1857 there were 2,846, of whom 74 earned over £600 per annum. P.P. 1857-58, XLII, 153.

[46] Speech of 22 July 1853, Hansard, CXXIX, 684.

[47] Speech of 25 July 1853, *ibid.*, p. 781.

stitute for that moral training which came from prolonged residence in England. Indeed, Sir Charles Wood insisted "the only place where an education could be acquired that would fit a person for employment in India was at Haileybury. . . . It could not be gained in India."[48] The closing of Haileybury in 1857 in no way affected this argument; its justification lay in the fact that, as George Campbell pointed out, Indian government business was conducted by "English gentlemen dealing with English gentlemen." An Indian could be admitted to the Civil Service only if he had "become so completely Europeanized as to be really and practically on the footing and imbued with the character of an English highly educated gentleman."[49] The House of Commons nevertheless gave 47 votes in 1853 to a proposed amendment of the Charter Act empowering the Government to hold examinations in India, and on several occasions during the last half of the nineteenth century gave a sympathetic hearing to proposals for simultaneous examination. In 1893 they even passed a resolution in favor of the measure, which the Government politely ignored. The House was in fact far more susceptible to sentimental liberalism than the hard-headed officials of the India Office.

In 1858, as part of the general policy of conciliation which followed the Mutiny, the British Government re-affirmed the principle of equality and non-discrimination in employment. The Queen's Proclamation solemnly promised that "so far as may be, our subjects, of whatever race or creed, [shall] be freely and impartially admitted to offices in our service, the duties of which they may be qualified by their education, ability, and integrity duly to discharge."[50] The immediate beneficiaries of this clause were, however, not so much those qualified by education as those "of station and character" who still exercised power and influence over the people. As Sir

---

[48] Speech of 22 July 1853, *ibid.*, p. 685.
[49] George Campbell, *India As It May Be*, p. 229.
[50] Ilbert, *The Government of India*, pp. 572-73.

Charles Wood told Trevelyan in 1860: "I am very anxious to introduce into our system the employment, in some way or another, of the *better class* of Natives. I do not mean the mere creatures of *competitive*, or other, examination, but members of the classes possessing property or station or influence in the country. It seems to me most desirable to attach to our rule what remains of the upper and middle classes in India. . . . What we want in Natives is moral character, which no examination can test;—and taking people from the better classes in such a way as to attach those classes to us."[51]

The most successful attempt at drawing the aristocracy into the administrative system was of course the employment of taluqdars and zamindars as honorary magistrates, but it was not the only one. Efforts were also made to find regular employment in the uncovenanted service for such men as the ex-Amirs of Sind and their families. In this way, it was hoped, a "better class of native servants" could be obtained, and "an idle, dangerous, and discontented class of public pensioners" turned into a useful aristocracy.[52] But the members of these old aristocratic families generally had no education and no interest in the day-to-day work of administration, except where they saw the opportunity of personal gain. They found neither the salary nor the social prestige of government work at all attractive, and so had to be dragooned into accepting posts which they soon resigned. Even when Lord Lytton in 1879 established the Statutory Civil Service with the express aim of drawing young men of good family into the Government the response was no more enthusiastic. Pride and lethargy combined to keep the aristocratic classes on their estates.

The real pressure for the extension of civil service opportunities came not from the aristocracy but from the English

[51] Wood to Trevelyan, 9 April 1860, Wood Papers.

[52] Commissioner of Sind to Governor of Bombay, 2 November 1860; and Note by Bartle Frere of 16 January 1861, Home Public, 30 January 1861, No. 69-71. See also Resolution of Bombay Government of 16 May 1861, Home Public, 29 July 1861, No. 24.

educated class. By 1860 they were too numerous to be ignored, and too well educated to be content with those petty posts which alone were open to them. The Government was well aware of the frustration and resentment which this exclusion produced in the heart of the educated Indian, and the experience of the Mutiny had taught the British, if nothing else, that discontented and unhappy men were a fertile breeding ground for sedition. Wood realized that British rule, so long as it remained British, was unlikely ever to be really popular with the educated classes; but it was no less necessary, he said, to find "a more important, dignified, and lucrative sphere of employment" for them, and to win their support so far as it was possible.[53] It was only in 1867, however, under the prodding of Sir Stafford Northcote, that the Government came to grips with the question of opening specific posts to Indian candidates. Northcote himself felt that the simplest, and most effective, solution would be to open a certain number of positions in the covenanted service to competition in India. The successful candidates, he said, could then be sent to England for a few years of additional training at government expense before taking up their appointments.[54] The educated Indian community was of course unanimously in favor of simultaneous examination, and sent several petitions on the subject to Northcote during 1867 and 1868. Even though one Indian, Satyendranath Tagore, had by this time successfully negotiated the examinations, his countrymen still looked upon the enforced journey to London as a serious obstacle in the way of an "honorable career," and urged the Government to do away with "the objectionable regulations."[55] But the Government of India was, as before, unyieldingly hostile to all schemes of simultaneous examination; and so Northcote, despite his

[53] Wood to Maine, 30 October 1863, Wood Papers.

[54] Dispatch of 31 May 1867, Foreign (Rev.) Dispatch No. 33 of 1867. Northcote to Lawrence, 24 June 1867 and 15 August 1867, Lawrence Papers.

[55] Memorials of B.I.A. and of Bombay Association, 5 March 1868, Home Public B, 12 December 1868, No. 2.

sympathy with the Indian petitions, had no option but to reject them.[56]

Attention was therefore directed to the uncovenanted service, and the local governments were asked to see what could be done within those limits to enlarge the sphere of Indian employment. In the decade since the Mutiny the number of Indians in government service had risen by forty per cent, and now stood at 4,039. But of these only 81 earned over Rs. 600 a month, and only one, as a Judge of the Bengal High Court, held a position of real responsibility. The overwhelming majority were still confined to subordinate posts in the revenue and judicial departments.[57] A wide variety of suggestions for improvement were put forward, but two alone received serious consideration: the promotion of Indians in the non-Regulation provinces to the rank of Assistant Commissioner, the lowest grade in the regular civil service; and the wider use of Indians as district and High Court Judges. Although sanctioned by the Government at Calcutta, the first proposal evoked no enthusiasm among the provincial authorities. Bengal and Punjab rejected it out of hand as inappropriate, and confined their suggestions to the post of Extra Assistant Commissioner, already held by Indians, which they wished to see strengthened and made more attractive.[58] The Governments of Oudh and of the Central Provinces each agreed to open two Assistant Commissionerships (out of a total in Oudh of 28, and in the Central Provinces of 16), but they would go no further. This provision, the Chief Commissioner of the Central Provinces replied, "would for the present give ample incentive to our native officials."[59] The appointment of

[56] S. of S. to Governor of Bombay, 14 October 1868, Public Dispatch No. 36 of 1868.

[57] Home Public, 26 December 1868, No. 16.

[58] Sec. Govt. Bengal to Sec. Govt. India, 30 September 1867, For. Gen. A, October 1867, No. 42; Sec. Govt. Punjab to Sec. Govt. India, 23 April 1868, For. Gen. A, May 1868, No. 1-2. The post of Extra Assistant Commissioner was the highest uncovenanted executive position, and was roughly comparable to that of Deputy Magistrate in the Regulation Districts.

[59] Sec. C.C. Central Provinces to Sec. Govt. India, 6 September 1867, For.

Indians as judges met with less resistance. Canning had already placed one Indian, Ramapersand Roy, on the Bengal High Court, in order, as J. P. Grant put it, "to show that the provision in the Act is not intended to be inoperative, and to withstand that growing spirit of contempt with which Europeans now treat all native officials."[60] Lawrence suggested that such appointments be increased in number, and that Indians be made eligible as well for the post of Small Cause Court Judge.[61]

Viewed as a whole, however, the Government's recommendations were disappointingly timid and hesitant. They fell far short, not only of the Indian community's demands, but of the Home Government's expectations. Northcote chastised Calcutta for unduly restricting the scope of the discussion, while Frere on the India Council denounced "the self-satisfied supercilious spirit" he detected in many of the reports. Much more might be done, he said, even under the present law, to employ Indians in responsible positions "if those who have the distribution and control of patronage were really in earnest in their professions of anxiety to see native agency more extensively used." The Indian Government, he continued, has made "a rather pompous parade of a few crumbs of patronage which can now be thrown to the natives"; but it had made no effort to raise the character of its Indian employees so that they might someday be fit for the positions now held by Europeans. I believe, he concluded, "it is very possible to do much to Anglicize our native servants, not in manner or costume, nor even necessarily in language, but in feeling; to make them feel towards our Government, as being *their* Government, *the* Government to which they

---

Gen. A, September 1867, No. 39; Sec. C.C. Oudh to Sec. Govt. India, 22 October 1867, For. Gen. A, November 1867, No. 4.

[60] Canning to Grant, 25 September 1861; and Grant to Canning, 5 November 1861, Canning Papers.

[61] Lawrence to deGrey, 4 May 1866, Lawrence Papers. Resolution of Govt. of India, 19 August 1867, For. Gen. A, August 1867, No. 35.

belong . . . the best possible Government for India. The feeling may never rise to exactly the same kind of loyalty which is felt for a sovereign of the same race and religion . . . ; but it might be an identification of interest and feeling, which is rare now, and is daily, I fear, becoming rarer."[62]

Behind this extraordinary reluctance to advance Indians even one small step on the official ladder lay a variety of reasons, both rational and emotional. Much as it might deplore it, the Government could not ignore the racial feeling of the non-official Europeans, who despised all Indians, no matter how eminent, and who refused, as Strachey pointed out, "to be placed in any way under the authority of natives." Wood doubted that Indian judges or district officers would be able to hold their own when confronted with insolent European planters, and the Government had no desire to antagonize the settler community by attempting such an experiment.[63] But outside the few large Presidency towns, and parts of Bengal and Assam, non-official Englishmen were almost non-existent; there was consequently no need in most of the country to avoid the employment of Indians on this ground. Yet even there no greater progress was made. To some extent it was simply a matter of job security. The members of the Indian Civil Service, like the members of any close corporation with a vested interest in the status quo, had no desire to see jobs they had filled handed over to outsiders, and the prestige and importance of the Service diminished accordingly. The Home Government, on the other hand, with much less to lose by change, could afford to take a more liberal stance. In fact resistance to the employment of Indians mounted steadily the closer one came to the provincial and district levels of the administration. Only the most exceptional

---

[62] S. of S. to Govt. of India, 8 February 1868, For. Gen. A, March 1868, No. 123. Frere Minute of 18 February 1868, P.P. 1867-68, L, 293-94.

[63] Wood to Maine, 17 October 1863 and 30 October 1863, Wood Papers. Strachey Minute of 17 December 1868 in Printed Notes of Govt. of India No. C114-427.

official, such as Bartle Frere, could so far rise above the prejudices of the Service as to sympathize with the Indian point of view.

But there were greater issues at stake. Only one class of their Indian subjects, the British realized, was at all likely to benefit substantially from increased employment opportunities: the English-educated Bengalis. In no other province had the people been subjected to English education for such a long period of time, or taken to it with such enthusiasm. Yet educated Bengalis were by 1860 precisely the class of people whom the British wished to keep out of high government positions. The Bengali, though intellectually acute and mentally alert, simply did not have in him, so the British insisted, the moral fibre and strength of character required for a first-rate administrator. His physique, Lawrence noted, "is poor and weak, and his heart is feeble and timid."[64] Excellence in competitive examination might be a true test of ability among Englishmen, but in India it was completely meaningless. As Strachey pointed out, "Not the least important part of the competitive examination of the young Englishman was passed for him by his forefathers, who, as we have a right to assume, have transmitted to him not only their physical courage, but the powers of independent judgment, the decision of character, the habits of thought, and generally those qualities that are necessary for the government of men . . . and which have given us our empire."[65] Such qualities were also, to be sure, found in India, but not in Bengal. The "vigorous races of India" were those of the Northwest—the Punjabis, Pathans, and Sikhs—and they were no more willing to be ruled by Bengalis than by Englishmen. Indeed they preferred British rule to government by "the feeble and effeminate foreigners of another Indian country, however intellectually acute those foreigners may be." It was as impossible to place Bengalis over "the hardy races on the

64 Lawrence to Cranborne, 8 November 1866, Lawrence Papers.
65 John Strachey, India (London, 1888), p. 358.

frontiers" as over the independent English settlers and merchants.[66]

This prejudice against the Bengali was of long standing,
and was found at home as well as in India. G. O. Trevelyan,
for instance, told the House of Commons in 1868 that the
natives of Bengal, while remarkable for quickness and clever-
ness, as compared with Europeans "are singularly deficient in
the bolder and hardier virtues—in pluck, self-reliance, and
veracity—the three great national attributes by which we
gained, and by which we retain our hold upon British India."[67]
After the Mutiny, however, these sentiments gained new
strength, for British opinion was now moulded far more by
conservative paternalism than by the optimistic liberalism of
Macaulay. The Englishman of the 1860's, bred in the tradition of the Punjab school and no longer an enthusiast for
reform, saw little that was attractive in "the highly crammed
Calcutta Baboo," always spouting sedition and demanding
representative government. He preferred the company of the
rough tribesmen of Upper India, as yet untutored in politics
and ready to join him in the chase or on the sporting field.
The paternal vision was ultimately one, not of representative
assemblies, but of enlightened despotism, of justice meted out
from horseback: and to this ideal the Bengali intellectual could
never conform.

This prejudice against the Bengali, however, only partially
concealed a far more basic objection to increased Indian employment: that it posed a threat to British supremacy in
India. If Indians were admitted indiscriminately to the civil
service, they would as a matter of course rise through the
ranks until in time they commanded the heights of power
and the Empire ceased to exist. This prospect had been fore-
seen and accepted by those who in the 1830's had set India
upon the path of Western education. As liberals they had con-

[66] *Ibid.*, p. 361. See also Lawrence to Northcote, 17 August 1867, Lawrence Papers.
[67] Speech of 5 May 1868, Hansard, cxci, 1845.

templated with equanimity the eventual dissolution of the Empire, and they were quite prepared, as education spread through the country, to advance Indians step by step to the highest posts in the Government.[68] To some extent of course they were willing to concede so much because the question was not one of practical significance. When educated Indians did not exist, talk of eventual self-government for India was a gratuitous form of liberalism. By 1860, with Indians clamoring for admission to the Civil Service, liberal sentiments could no longer be indulged so lightly, or their consequences so freely ignored.

The unyielding opposition of the Indian Government to increased Indian employment was not simply a matter of frightened liberals running for cover. It also reflected that new imperial spirit which had arisen from the struggles of 1857. After the Mutiny it was no longer possible to assume that the Indian people would follow their foreign rulers down the path of reform. They had, or so it appeared, repaid British trust by rebellion, and willfully rejected the benefits of British rule. Dismayed and disillusioned, the British now acted on the assumption that the Indians were a different breed of people, moved by sentiments altogether different from their own. They neither thought like Englishmen, nor could they be made over into Englishmen. As "Orientals" they were ultimately incapable of ruling themselves. India did not contain the clay out of which self-government could be modelled. In these circumstances the British Empire took on a new validity, for it provided the only possible framework for a successful Government of India. To bow to the demands of a small educated class would be irresponsible and unjustifiable. Not only in our own interests, Strachey commented, "but because it is our highest duty towards India itself, we intend to maintain our dominion. We cannot foresee the time in which the cessation of our rule would not be the signal for universal anarchy and ruin, and it is clear that the only

[68] See above, pp. 11-12.

hope for India is the long continuance of the benevolent but strong government of Englishmen." Hence, Strachey continued, the admission of Indians to responsible government positions had to be carefully regulated and controlled. He acknowledged that they were entitled to a share in the administration of their own country. Indeed they deserved a larger share than they had hitherto obtained. But there was a line which could not be crossed and there were certain posts which must remain forever outside their grasp. Let there be no hypocrisy, he said, "about our intention to keep in the hands of our own people those executive posts—and there are not very many of them—on which, and on our military and political power, our actual hold of the country depends. Our Governors of provinces, the chief officers of our army, our magistrates of districts and their principal executive subordinates ought to be Englishmen under all circumstances that we can now foresee."[69] Although few Government officials were as outspoken as Strachey, most found themselves in agreement with him. Lawrence, for instance, defended his Government's action in much the same terms: "We conquered India mainly by force of arms. . . . In like manner we must hold it. The Englishman must always be in the front rank, holding the post of honour and of power. . . . The District Officer is the unit of the whole civil system of administration. He is the official to whom, in the first instance, the Government looks for information as to all which may be going on. . . . This post must be held by the English official."[70]

These political considerations account for the relative ease with which educated Indians rose to high positions in the judicial service, while they were at the same time excluded from such comparatively minor executive posts as Assistant Commissioner. As judge the Indian posed no threat to the British Raj. "I am not afraid," as Wood put it, "of being

[69] Strachey, *India*, p. 360.
[70] Lawrence to Northcote, 17 August 1867, Lawrence Papers.

turned out of India by the ermine of the Judgement seat."[71]
The Government hoped in fact, by throwing the judicial
service wide open, to satisfy the growing Indian demand for
greater employment opportunities. Once Indians were admitted to "every grade of the judicial service without exception," and were as well paid as their European counterparts,
they would, Strachey insisted, "have no reasonable grounds
for complaint left." The educated Indian was, moreover, extremely well qualified for judicial duty. The exclusively intellectual upbringing which disqualified him from the more
strenuous executive posts was a distinct advantage when he
was faced with the sedentary life of a judge.[72] As Assistant
Commissioner, on the other hand, the young Indian had his
foot on the ladder which led up into the higher reaches of the
district administration. If he rose no further, it might be
unobjectionable to place him in that particular post, where
he was under constant supervision by European superiors;
but to subject him to the "periodical mortification" of super-
session by his juniors was hardly a step calculated to produce
contentment, and he certainly could not be permitted to rise
to the charge of a district. In his usual blunt fashion Strachey
denied that it was at all possible, as Frere had hoped, so to
Anglicize the Indian servants of Government that they might
be entrusted with real responsibility. The educated Indian
was at heart no more loyal than the sepoy, and could be
trusted no further:

"There is hardly any class of the population which hates
us more thoroughly than the highly educated gentlemen of
Lower Bengal. Physical peculiarities of race render the political
opinions of Bengalees of comparatively little importance, but
when the time arrives, as it certainly will arrive, in which the
brave and high-spirited gentlemen of Northern India are as

71 Wood to Denison, Governor of Madras, 10 March 1863, Wood Papers.
72 Strachey Minute of 17 December 1868 in Printed Notes No. C114-427.
See also Campbell, *India As It May Be*, p. 232; and Evidence of J. Lawrence
to House of Commons Committee on Indian Finance, 1 July 1873, P.P.
1873, XII, 487.

well educated as the gentlemen of Bengal, the matter will be one of very different political import. I hope I need not say that I am far from thinking that the increase of knowledge can lead to any but good results and I am satisfied that the most serious of all the dangers to which our supremacy in India is exposed, are the dangers that arise from the ignorance of the people. All I mean is that it would be unwise to suppose that the progress of education will enable us to give with safety great political power to our native subjects."[73]

Hence it was only fair to the ambitious Indian to draw a sharp line of demarcation between European and Indian spheres of employment, and to exclude him from the covenanted Civil Service. Even the more liberal British officials, such as J. S. Mill and Charles Trevelyan, agreed that so long as Indians were not considered fit for the highest appointments, they should not be admitted to the regular covenanted Service. It would be wiser, Mill suggested, to appoint Indians directly to the positions for which they were qualified, without making them go through the ranks of the Service or binding the Government to promote them to any given position.[74]

Such ultimately was the policy enunciated by the British Government in 1870. Under the India Act of that year, the Government of India was given the power to appoint natives of India to all offices at its disposal, including those hitherto reserved for members of the covenanted Civil Service. The Act further empowered the Indian Government, subject to the sanction of the Secretary of State, to draw up the rules under which Indians were to be selected for these posts. In this way the scope of Indian employment could be considerably widened, yet the structure of British rule could remain intact. On the latter point Argyll, the Secretary of State, laid special

[73] Minute of 17 December 1868 in Printed Notes No. C114-427.

[74] Evidence of J. S. Mill to House of Lords Committee on Indian Affairs, 22 June 1852, P.P. 1852-1853, xxx, 324. See also Evidence of W. W. Bird, 18 May 1852, *ibid.*, pp. 120-21; and Evidence of C. Trevelyan to House of Commons Committee on Indian Finance, 11 March 1873, P.P. 1873, xii, 180.

emphasis. Above all, he told the Government of India, "it is one of our first duties towards the people of India to guard the safety of our own dominion" by retaining "large proportions of British functionaries in the more important posts."[75] Even within these limits, however, protracted controversy over the framing of the rules rendered the Act for years little more than a statement of good intentions. Both Argyll and the Government of India were determined to exclude educated Bengalis from whatever appointments might be made, and so unhesitatingly threw out all schemes based upon competitive examination. Argyll suggested in 1873 that previous service in subordinate positions be made the criterion for selection, on the ground that, as he put it, "nothing but acute trial in official work can be worth anything as indicating the value of a native."[76] But the rules drawn up by the Government of India on this assumption were in their turn disallowed as unduly limiting the field of selection. In the end the controverted regulations took shape only as part of Lytton's Statutory Civil Service in 1879. Under the rules as then laid down up to 20 per cent of the total number of civilians appointed each year were to be Indians nominated by the local governments, preferably from among those not in Government service who combined good family and social position with fair abilities and education.[77] The creation of this service did not of course satisfy the educated classes, nor was it intended to do so. Lytton's objective was entirely political. He hoped, by bringing the aristocracy into the administrative service, to evoke an active loyalty among them, and to offset the growing radicalism of the "Babu" class. Rather like Canning, Lytton saw in the conservative landed and princely

[75] Dispatch of 8 April 1869, Educational Dispatch No. 3 of 1869; and Dispatch of 22 October 1872, Public Dispatch No. 113 of 1872, P.P. 1878-1879, LV, 307, 310.

[76] Argyll to Northbrook, 7 January 1873, Northbrook Papers. See also B. B. Misra, *The Indian Middle Classes*, pp. 372-73.

[77] Lady Betty Balfour, *Lord Lytton's Indian Administration* (London, 1899), pp. 533-34.

classes the strongest bulwark of the British Raj. "The most important problem before us," he told Lord Salisbury on one occasion, is "to secure completely, and efficiently utilise" these men.[78] But unlike Canning, Lytton was a Tory, a follower of Disraeli, and a man of considerable romantic imagination. He believed that the Indian aristocracy could easily be swayed by appeals to sentiment and emotion. Hence he pursued a policy at times flamboyant and insubstantial, as in the Delhi Durbar of 1877, but marked as well by such imaginative, if abortive, proposals as the creation of an Indian peerage and Privy Council. He had even hoped to make the new Statutory Civil Service a close service with a hierarchy of its own and a large number of reserved appointments. As finally constituted, however, the new Service had no real prestige or status, attracted few men of "good family," and had soon to be terminated. It was replaced in 1892 by a system of provincial services separately recruited in each province.

The new imperial spirit did not go altogether unchallenged. Although the old liberalism of Macaulay and Bentinck had been badly battered by the tidal wave of the Mutiny, it could still claim adherents both within the Indian Government and, to a much greater extent, at home. By far the most fearless and influential advocate was Sir Charles Trevelyan. In 1873 he came out of retirement to restate before a House of Commons Committee the ideals of his youth. The Indian Civil Service, he pointed out, although it embodied much that was admirable in the English character, was "a provisional temporary arrangement," a sort of scaffolding which should be taken down as "the edifice of the Indian Empire is completed." He urged the Government to establish an uncovenanted service chosen by local competitive examination, to employ Indians widely in all branches of the administration, and to promote them according to their qualifications through the Collectorships and judiciary even to the highest posts. As a man bred in the liberal tradition he did not hesitate to proclaim that the

[78] Lytton to Salisbury, 11 May 1877, *ibid*., pp. 109-10.

"ultimate end of all our proceedings" in India was "to train
the natives to self-government." Indeed he criticized the Government severely for its refusal to take even the first step in
this direction. The time of promising was past, he said; "the
time of acting has come."[79] But Trevelyan, though a distinguished public servant and a man who commanded wide
respect, was by 1870 at the end of his long career. Effective
reform required a band of dedicated enthusiasts in the lower
ranks of the service, young men who could prod the Government as Trevelyan himself had done in the 1830's; and such
men were rarely to be found in the years after the Mutiny.
Only a few mavericks, among them A. O. Hume, William
Wedderburn, and Henry Beveridge, kept alive the ideals of
liberalism in the Civil Service. All three threw themselves
wholeheartedly into the cause of education, and warmly encouraged Indian political aspirations. As District Officer in
Etawah from 1857 to 1867 Hume established by his own
efforts a network of local schools and a vernacular newspaper,
"The People's Friend," which soon obtained the largest cir-
culation of any paper in the North-Western Provinces.[80] His
later efforts on behalf of the Congress are of course well
known. Similarly Beveridge, writing the history of his district
in Bengal in 1876, urged that "we should look forward to
the time when India can be left to herself." He suggested
that the Government "hasten its coming" by stopping re-
cruitment for the Indian Civil Service and putting "the internal administration more and more into the hands of
natives."[81] But without support from the Government none
of these men were able to accomplish very much.

[79] Evidence to House of Commons Committee on Indian Finance, 25
February 1873, P.P. 1873, XII, 96-97; and 11 March 1873, *ibid.*, pp. 180-81.
[80] Sec. Govt. N.W.P. to Sec. Govt. India, 25 January 1861, North-West
Provinces General Proceedings, 26 January 1861, No. 56, Lucknow Secretariat. M. Kempson, Director of Public Instruction, to Sec. Govt. N.W.P., 1
September 1862, Home Public, 4 March 1864, No. 15. See also W. Wedderburn, *Allan Octavian Hume* (London, 1913), pp. 15-22.
[81] H. Beveridge, *The District of Bakarganj* (London, 1876), p. 396.

Liberalism made itself felt at the highest levels of the Government on one occasion alone: during the Viceroyalty of Lord Ripon (1880-1884). A liberal imbued with the spirit of Midlothian, Ripon came out to India on the crest of Gladstone's victory in 1880 determined to further the political education of the people and to win the friendship of the educated classes. With Gladstone he denied that benevolent authoritarianism could ever be a permanent form of government for a country like India. We ought, he said, "to endeavour to govern more and more by means of, and in accordance with, that growing public opinion, which is beginning to show itself throughout the country."[82] His most successful efforts in this direction were in the field of local government, where he set up elected local boards free of official domination, and gave them control over all local rates and cesses. But in civil service reform he made little headway against the prevailing current of official hostility. He was unable either to secure a higher age limit for the London examination or to institute a system of simultaneous examination in India. All his liberal measures in fact were bitterly opposed by the official class, and several, most notably the Ilbert Bill, had to be abandoned. The Civil Service, as Northbrook pointed out, "with all their magnificent qualities have strongly ingrained in their minds . . . that no one but an Englishman can do anything."[83] Despite his good intentions, therefore, Ripon succeeded in producing little more than a stormy interlude in the era of paternalism which had swept over India since the Mutiny. By the time he sailed for England it was apparent that the Government would not willingly give any substantial degree of power to the Indian people.

[82] Ripon to Hartington, 31 December 1881, cited in S. Gopal, *The Viceroyalty of Lord Ripon 1880-1884* (London, 1953), p. 84. See also Memorandum of 25 December 1882, cited in Lucien Wolf, *Life of the First Marquess of Ripon* (London, 1921), II, 92-95.

[83] Northbrook to Dufferin, 8 September 1884, cited in Bernard Mallet, *The Earl of Northbrook* (London, 1908), p. 133. For discussion of the Ilbert Bill controversy see *infra*, pp. 308-09.

No matter how far Indian employment might be extended, the ultimate controlling power had always to remain in British hands. The maintenance of the Empire was the *sina qua non* of Indian progress.[84] Yet even this apparent failure had at least one salutary result. It taught the Indian people the futility of expecting freedom as a gift from the British Government. As Ripon's compatriots had forced him to acknowledge defeat, so might they, united, challenge the imposing structure of the British Raj. English liberalism, weak and divided, could not, it was clear, do more than afford encouragement from the sidelines. As Surendranath Bannerjee wrote in 1883 in the annual report of the Indian Association: "The triumph of the Anglo-Indian agitation has taught us a memorable lesson. It has shown how even, in this country, discipline and organized union have triumphed in an unholy cause. The time has come when we must sink our petty and personal differences and learn to make common cause for the advancement of our country's interests."[85] The fruit of this resolve was the Indian National Congress.

[84] See, for instance, S. of S. to Govt. of India, 22 June 1893, P.P. 1893-94, LXIV, 861; and Curzon speech in Indian Legislative Council, 30 March 1904, cited in Thomas Raleigh, *Lord Curzon in India* (London, 1906), pp. 143-44. The Civil Service examination was not held in India until 1923.

[85] *Indian Association Annual Report* (Calcutta, 1883), p. 13.

CHAPTER VIII

# THE LEGACY OF THE MUTINY

THE most pervasive legacy of the Mutiny can be found perhaps in the intangible sphere of human relations, in the attitude of the British and Indian peoples toward each other. On the surface all went on as before, but a year of bitter racial warfare left an abiding mark. The British, suspicious and alert, were now far more clearly an occupying power, garrisoning a hostile land, while the Indians sought sustenance and self-respect increasingly within the bounds of their traditional culture. The British had formed a separate community in India from the beginning. To a large extent this was inevitable, given their position as a small ruling class, set off by religion and culture from those about them. Evangelical religion, with its stern disapproval of Indian ways, and the arrival of European women in the early nineteenth century only reinforced this social estrangement. As the British abandoned the *zenana*, set up homes in India, and regulated their conduct by European standards, they naturally drifted into insular little communities. Rarely did they have much contact with Indians except as servants or in the course of official business. But this exclusiveness, and the patronizing superiority that often went with it, did not necessarily involve any belief in inherent racial difference. Sunk though he might be in idolatry and debauchery, the Indian could still be endowed with the elements of civilized existence; and to that task the early reformers, full of hope and enthusiasm, had set their hand. From 1830 onwards, as we have seen, British policy was built upon the assumption that

Indian society could be regenerated, and reformed on a British model. "At the commencement of 1857 humanity and philanthropy were the order of the day."[1]

Across this scene the Mutiny cut a violent swath. Stunned and shocked, the British saw the complaisant sepoy suddenly revealed as a rapacious murderer, the faithful bearer a treacherous villain. Safety, they discovered, could be found only among their own countrymen. Once betrayed by those whom they had trusted, the British could no longer bring themselves to trust anyone with a brown face: all alike were tainted. Hence the bonds of race were quickly tightened, for survival itself was seen to depend upon it; and the British from their entrenchments looked out upon the Indian people with increasing bitterness and hatred. This growing racial antagonism was exacerbated beyond measure by the reports of massacres and atrocities, in which English women and children were murdered in cold blood. Nothing could arouse such a frenzy of hatred in the Victorian Englishman as to see his womenfolk, so long safe from foreign invaders and hedged round by sentiment and chivalry, hacked to pieces by barbarous ruffians. The Kanpur massacre in particular roused the most intense and passionate desire for vengeance. All too often it was satisfied at the expense of the nearest Indian. G. O. Trevelyan tells of a corporal fresh from England who reported a mutiny among the bullock drivers. His story was simple: "I seed two Moors talking in a cart. Presently I heard one of 'em say 'Cawnpore.' I knowed what that meant; so I fetched Tom Walker, and he heard 'em say 'Cawnpore,' and he knowed what that meant. So we polished 'em both off."[2] Even at home, Trevelyan noted, a favorite amusement on a wet afternoon for a party in a country house was to sit on and about the billiard table devising tortures for the Nana.[3]

Yet the Kanpur massacre alone does not account for the

---

[1] G. O. Trevelyan, *The Competition Wallah* (London, 1864), p. 281.
[2] *Ibid.*, p. 294.
[3] *Ibid.*, p. 283.

wild and unprincipled spirit of vengeance which overtook the
English during the summer of 1857. It burst forth in fact even
before the Kanpur garrison had surrendered, when Neill in
June let loose his soldiers on the countryside round Allahabad.
His official orders at that time exude a note of ferocity rarely
found in British military documents. All sepoys from mutinous
regiments who could not give a good account of themselves,
he told Major Renaud, were to be hanged, while rebellious
villages along the line of march were to be destroyed and all
male inhabitants killed.[4] When he actually reached Kanpur and
set eyes on the scene of the massacre, Neill ordered that "every
stain of that innocent blood shall be cleared up and wiped
out, previous to their execution, by such of the miscreants as
may hereafter be apprehended, who took an active part in the
mutiny . . . ; the task will be made as revolting to his feelings
as possible, and the Provost-Marshal shall use the lash in
forcing anyone objecting to complete his task. After properly
cleaning up his portion, the culprit is to be immediately
hanged."[5] In a similar vein John Nicholson in the Punjab at
the end of May proposed a bill for "the flaying alive, impale-
ment, or burning of the murderers of the women and children
at Delhi. The idea of simply hanging the perpetrators of such
atrocities is maddening."[6] The British in Calcutta were no less
deeply stirred. Colonel Malleson, writing his famous "Red
Pamphlet" in early July, urged the Government mercilessly
to hunt down every mutineer. "India will not be secure so
long as a single man remains alive."[7] Even in the remote
hill station of Simla the District Officer reported that it was
at one time impossible "to persuade Europeans that every
Native did not desire or was not encompassing his immediate
destruction. Dread of treachery and an ardent desire for re-

[4] Cited in Kaye, *Sepoy War*, II, 274-75.

[5] *Ibid.*, p. 399.

[6] *Ibid.*, p. 401.

[7] G. Malleson, *The Mutiny of the Bengal Army* [The Red Pamphlet] (London, 1857), p. 46.

venge filled their breasts to the exclusion of every other feeling."[8]

This extraordinary outburst, though aggravated by tales of atrocities, was at heart simply a reflection of the precarious nature of the British position in India. So few in numbers were they, and so uncertain their hold over the people, that as their familiar world collapsed about them they responded by striking out madly and wildly in all directions. They hoped by unremitting terror to regain some sense of security in an alien land, and by brute force to subdue that which they no longer understood. As a result the struggle soon became, as John Lawrence realized, "a war of races" in which every Indian was looked upon as fair game.[9] There is, Canning reported to the Queen, "a rabid and indiscriminating vindictiveness abroad, even amongst many who ought to set a better example, which it is impossible to contemplate without something like a feeling of shame for one's fellow countrymen." The vast majority of the European community, he continued, "would hear with pleasure and approval that every Hindoo and Mahomedan had been proscribed, and that none would be admitted to serve the Government except in a menial capacity. That which they desire to see is a broad line of separation, and of declared distrust drawn between us Englishmen and every subject of your Majesty who is not a Christian, and who has a dark skin."[10] In the first impulse of terror and panic the same feelings swept through England itself. As the distant tragedy unfolded during the summer of 1857, "intense compassion, intense wrath, the injured pride of a great nation . . . surged in upon the agitated community."[11] Victorian restraint was abandoned in

[8] Lord William Hay, Deputy Commissioner of Simla, to G. C. Barnes, Commissioner of Trans-Sutlej States, 6 February 1858, *Punjab Government Records*, VIII, Part I, 73.

[9] John Lawrence to Dalhousie, 16 June 1858, in Bosworth Smith, *Life of Lord Lawrence*, II, 196.

[10] Canning to the Queen, 25 September 1857, in Arthur C. Benson, ed., *The Letters of Queen Victoria* (New York, 1907), III, 319.

[11] Trevelyan, *The Competition Wallah*, p. 283.

a bloodthirsty cry for revenge. Even the liberal and fair-minded Macaulay was swept along by the current. He found himself admitting that "I, who could not bear to see a beast or bird in pain, could look on without winking while Nana Sahib underwent all the tortures of Ravaillac."[12] With the returning tide of victory, however, these passions soon subsided. In November Charles Trevelyan published his "Indophilus" letters in the *Times*, reminding the British public of their obligations to the people of India; and when Parliament reconvened in December the dominant tone was one of moderation. Throughout 1858 press and Parliament alike urged the Indian Government to deal out justice mixed with mercy and forbearance.

The Viceroy, Lord Canning, though deeply stirred by the events of the Mutiny, never succumbed to the passions which issued in indiscriminate vengeance. From the beginning he remained calm and acted with deliberation. His policy was on no occasion marked by softness or leniency. Indeed in May he severely reprimanded Colvin at Agra for issuing a proclamation which allowed the Meerut mutineers to return unpunished to their homes, and in the autumn he lamented the "unauthorized act at Delhi" which enabled the King to escape with his life.[13] But he refused, despite the excitement which eddied about him, to "govern in anger" or to treat the Indian people as a subject race. He realized that British rule could not long survive if a dark skin was to be considered the mark of a murderer.[14] Hence he took care in enacting emergency legislation to avoid any appearance of racial discrimination. The Press Act of June 1857 subjected all newspapers, English as well as Indian, to the same censorship; and the Arms Act, restricting the carrying of weapons to those holding licenses, was made applicable to all classes of the popula-

[12] Letter of 19 September 1857, in G. O. Trevelyan, *The Life and Letters of Lord Macaulay* (London, 1876), II, 435-36.

[13] Canning to Colvin, 28 May and 31 May 1857, and Canning to Vernon Smith, 25 November 1857, Canning Papers.

[14] Canning to Granville, 11 December 1857, in Fitzmaurice, *Life of Granville*, I, 274-75.

tion. Similarly Canning did his best to check the cry for blood by putting restraints upon the activities of the sanguinary Special Commissions established under Acts XI and XIV of 1857. Under these acts civil and military officers in the Upper Provinces were empowered to try mutineers and other suspected rebels and to mete out punishment, including the death penalty, without appeal. From the outset these powers were badly abused, for few officers ever went through more than the barest formalities of a trial before summarily executing all those who fell into their hands. In the so-called "Clemency Resolution" of 31 July 1857, therefore, Canning cautioned these commissioners against undue severity, and withdrew from them the power of punishing mutineers other than those charged with specific acts of rebellion or belonging to regiments which had murdered their officers. Continued severity after order had been restored, Canning pointed out, would only exasperate the people and stir up feelings of bitterness and animosity.[15] This resolution did not put an end to summary executions or effectively check the activities of the Special Commissioners, who retained large powers well into 1858. But, coming as it did upon the heels of the Press Act, it at once brought Canning into universal contempt among his countrymen in India. They quickly awarded him in derision the title of "Clemency Canning" and petitioned the Queen for his recall. British rule in India, the European settlers insisted, could be secured only by a policy of "vigorous repression and punishment." In no other way could the Indian people be taught the hopelessness of rebellion.[16] The Clemency Resolution met with widespread disapprobation in England as well. Even Vernon Smith, President of the India Board, told Canning that he considered it ill-timed and unfortunate.[17] But

[15] P.P. 1857-58, XLIV, Part I, 10. Mutineers not charged with heinous crimes were to be handed over to the military for regular court martial.

[16] Petition of the Inhabitants of Calcutta for the Recall of the Governor General, P.P. 1857-58, XLIII, 102.

[17] Vernon Smith to Canning, 26 October 1857, Canning Papers.

Canning refused to be swayed by such criticism, and as English opinion swung round to the side of moderation he was soon vindicated. In the years that followed, his clemency was held up as a badge of honor.

When victory was at last in hand, the pent-up emotions of the British burst forth in an orgy of plunder and spoliation. At the fall of Lucknow W. H. Russell stood by aghast as the victorious British soldiers, "literally drunk with plunder," ransacked the palaces of the Nawab.[18] A month later the life of spoliation continued for over four months, and were effectually pleaded with the Commander-in-Chief to call off the prize agents. No one, he said, dared return for fear of losing their property.[19] In Delhi summary executions and systematic spoliation continued for over four months, and were effectively checked only when Sir John Lawrence took the city under his charge in February 1858. Not content with the opportunities for revenge afforded by this protracted reign of terror, many Englishmen wished also to raze Delhi to the ground, or at least to destroy the Jama Masjid. Such an act, Outram pointed out, would be "a beacon and a warning to the whole of India and a heavy blow to the Mahomedan religion."[20] Canning refused to sanction any such wholesale destruction. He suggested that the walls be torn down, and the palace demolished, but he saw no point in penalizing the innocent inhabitants of Delhi or the adherents of the Muslim faith for the atrocities perpetrated by the mutineers. Lawrence similarly set his face from the beginning against indiscriminate revenge, for he saw that it would only "exasperate the natives" and widen the breach "which has taken place between them and us." Consequently the city was spared, the palace was only

[18] W. H. Russell, *My Indian Mutiny Diary*, p. 101.

[19] Sec. C.C. Oudh to C.-in-C., 6 April 1858, Oudh Political Proceedings, 10 April 1858, No. 1, Lucknow Secretariat.

[20] Sec. C.C. Oudh to Sec. Govt. India, 18 January 1858, S.C. 29 January 1858, No. 361. When Delhi was spared, Outram urged that Lucknow be levelled instead.

partially demolished, and the Jama Masjid was eventually handed back to the Muslim community.[21]

In the end, however, neither Canning's clemency nor the preservation of Delhi could alter the fact that a year of racial warfare had permanently changed the position of the British in India. No amount of clemency could undo the distrust and disillusionment which the Mutiny had produced. Nor could it restore the vanished atmosphere of hope and confidence in which the pre-Mutiny reformers had lived. The British did not abandon their responsibilities to the people of India. Once the initial outburst of terror had spent itself, the civil servants generally "harkened to the voice of equity and humanity." They refused to adopt the blatant racial sentiments of the European settlers or to treat the Indian people as a subject race fit only for exploitation. But a line had been drawn across the slate. The Mutiny left its mark, even on the most dedicated English official. As H. M. Durand wrote to his wife from Lucknow in 1861, while he was Foreign Secretary of the Indian Government: "I may keep down, and on principle overrule the boiling wrath which eat [sic] so deep into one's heart in 1857; but I can no more get rid of it than I can of . . . the rage with which I learnt our military disasters in 1841. Time seems only to go on deepening such feelings. . . . The brain can't forget; and the heart neither. . . . In places not marked by the events of 1857 I might come to regard natives with the same feelings, practically, as animated me before the mutiny, but here it would be a hard discipline to walk unmoved, Cawnpore the same, Indore and Mhow the same."[22] Much as the civilian might try to do his duty, it was no longer "a labour of love." The new order of things was simply not as the old. Trevelyan perhaps caught the essence of the change when he said: "The children of the soil are no

[21] Canning to Vernon Smith, 25 November 1857; and Lawrence to Canning, 4 December 1857, Canning Papers. For the aftermath of the Mutiny in Delhi see Percival Spear, *Twilight of the Mughuls*, pp. 218-22.

[22] H. M. Durand, *The Life of Major-General Sir Henry Marion Durand* (London, 1883), I, 291.

longer regarded with the lively interest, the credulous partiality of yore. . . . Men cannot at will cast aside the recollection of those times when all was doubt and confusion and dismay; when a great fear was their companion, day and night; . . . The distrust and dislike engendered by such an experience are too deeply rooted to be plucked up by an act of volition."[23]

The clearest indicator of this new atmosphere was the value placed upon military power. It was no longer possible to assume that the Indian people would automatically stand by the Government in its hour of need. That struggle "irresistibly reminded us that we were an imperial race, holding our own on a conquered soil by dint of valour and foresight."[24] British bayonets were now the only real foundation of the Indian Empire and its preservation was dependent upon those military precautions which political security dictated in a conquered and unfriendly land. Hence the Indian element in the army was drastically reduced (from 238,000 in 1857 to 140,000 by 1863), and the European force increased (from 45,000 to 65,000). At the same time the new recruits were drawn largely from those martial races of the Punjab and Nepal who had proved their loyalty during the campaigns of the Mutiny. The division of the Indian army into three separate Presidency armies was retained, despite its anomalous character in a centralized state, for it seemed well contrived to dampen the spirit of rebellion. Indeed, in keeping with the old Roman policy of "divide and rule," the new recruits were often formed into separate units on the basis of caste or community. As Wood told Canning, "I never wish to see again a great Army, very much the same in its feelings and prejudices and connections, confident in its strength, and so disposed to unite in rebellion *together*. If one regiment mutinies, I should like to have the next regiment so alien that it would be ready

[23] Trevelyan, *The Competition Wallah*, p. 304.
[24] *Ibid.*, p. 302.

to fire into it."[25] The spirit of caution and distrust was further shown by the disbandment of the Indian artillery, which had proved so formidable in the hands of the mutineers. Henceforth, except for a few mountain batteries, all artillery was retained in English hands; and in similar fashion all important stations were garrisoned with British as well as Indian troops.

The most bitter and widespread hostility was reserved for the Muslim community. Almost universally they were regarded as the fomentors of the revolt and its chief beneficiaries. The first sparks of disaffection, it was generally agreed, were kindled among the Hindu sepoys who feared an attack upon their caste. But the Muslims then fanned the flames of discontent, and placed themselves at the head of the movement, for they saw in these religious grievances the steppingstone to political power. In the British view, it was Muslim intrigue and Muslim leadership that converted a sepoy mutiny into a political conspiracy aimed at the extinction of the British Raj.[26] The British were also convinced that the Muslim community, though fewer in numbers, was far more hostile throughout the course of the uprising. In Rohilkhand, in Agra, in Aligarh, the local authorities reported that the Muslims were "for the most part against us," while the Hindus remained "almost universally friendly." Raikes at Agra even claimed that the Muslims had behaved so badly that "if the rest of the population had sympathised with them, instead of antagonised, I should despair of governing India for the future." All over the North-Western Provinces, he said, "a Mahomedan was another word for a rebel."[27] Canning alone stood out against this condemnation of the Muslims. Although

[25] Wood to Canning, 8 April 1861, Wood Papers.

[26] Sec. C.C. Punjab to Sec. Govt. India, 29 April 1858, *Punjab Government Records*, VII, Part 2, 398. Temple, *Men and Events*, p. 113.

[27] Raikes, *Notes on the Revolt*, p. 175. W. J. Bramley, Collector of Aligarh to Govt. N.W.P., 17 November 1858, *Narratives of Mutiny in the Northwest Provinces*, p. 116. Colvin to Canning, 21 June 1857, and Canning to Ellenborough, 2 April 1858, Canning Papers.

admitting that the revolt for a time took the shape of a caricature revival of the Mughal Empire, he insisted that it was no more Muslim than Hindu and he refused to sanction any special measures of retribution directed against the Muslim community.[28] But he could no more stem the tide of anti-Muslim sentiment than stop the cry for vengeance.

Despite its firm hold over the British mind, this prejudice had remarkably little basis in fact. The Mutiny cannot be viewed as the fruit of Muslim conspiracy, nor is it possible to detect any significant difference in the behavior of the two communities. In those areas such as Rohilkhand where there was a cohesive militant Muslim aristocracy, the revolt naturally took on a Muslim character. But even there the Hindus were no less hostile. Outram for instance was convinced the Hindu population of Bareilly were at heart favorably disposed to the British cause, and in September 1857 he received permission to spend Rs. 50,000 in an effort to raise them against the rebel Muslim government of Khan Bahadur Khan. The attempt was a dismal failure. In December, unable to raise any force whatever, he had to return the money unspent to the Government treasury.[29] Throughout Oudh, Bihar, and Central India, on the other hand, the revolt was if anything predominantly Hindu in character. Rajput taluqdars provided the bulk of the leadership in Oudh; Kunwar Singh, a Rajput zamindar, was the moving spirit of the uprising in Bihar; while the three most commanding figures on the rebel side—the Rani of Jhansi, Tantia Tope, and Nana Saheb—were all Marathas. By contrast the Wahabis, the most fanatical of all Muslim sects in India, remained aloof, and the Punjab Muslims joined

[28] Canning to Vernon Smith, 5 June 1857 and 25 November 1857, Canning Papers. Canning was supported by G. Campbell, at the time a District Officer in the Punjab, who endeavored to show in a series of letters to the *Times* that "the accusation against the Mahomedans in general is unjust." Campbell, *Memoirs*, II, 393-97.

[29] Outram to Canning, 13 September 1857, Canning Papers. Sec. C.C. Oudh to Sec. Govt. India, 1 December 1857, Rizvi, *Freedom Struggle in Uttar Pradesh*, I, 472-73.

the British forces as readily as the Sikhs. In Bengal likewise the Muslims were as loyal as any other community. The *Hindoo Patriot* indeed rose to the defence of their Muslim countrymen, and did its best to clear them from the imputation of disloyalty by pointing out the wide difference between the Bengali, of whatever community, and the rebel of the Upper Provinces.[30]

The Muslims did of course have substantial grievances. As the British were well aware, the Muslim aristocracy could not but resent the complete revolution in their fortunes brought about by the imposition of British rule. Once an imperial race, they were now ordinary subjects, on a par with the despised Hindu, and excluded from all higher posts in the Government. They saw those posts which were open to Indians increasingly filled by Hindus, who did not scruple to learn English and to serve their new masters. But the extent of this exclusion, and its political significance, must not be overemphasized. In Bengal, to be sure, the fall from power was complete and catastrophic. Cornwallis and his successors swept away the whole structure of Muslim ad-ministration which they had inherited from the Mughal rulers of the province. The Muslim *faujdars* and judges were dis-charged, the Islamic code was set aside in favor of the British Regulations, and under Bentinck Persian was abandoned as the court language. By mid-century, although one-third of the population of Bengal was Muslim, only a few minor posts remained in their hands. In the North-Western Provinces, on the other hand, the Muslims long retained their dominant position. The overhaul of the governmental machinery there was less drastic and the progress of English education less rapid.[31] Urdu kept its position as the language of administra-

---

[30] *Hindoo Patriot*, 1 October 1857, v, 316.

[31] In 1845, for instance, there were 2,104 students attending Government-supported institutions of higher education in the North-Western Provinces. Of these 507, or 24%, were Muslim. In Bengal, on the other hand, there were 5,093 students, of whom 4,186 were Hindu and only 907 Muslim. P.P. 1847-48, XLVIII, 173-74.

tion throughout the nineteenth century. Hence a traditional Islamic education was no bar to Government employment. Sayyid Ahmad Khan, for instance, rose to the post of principal *sadr amin* with no education other than that which he had received at the court of Delhi. In 1850, although Muslims comprised only 12 per cent of the population of the North-Western Provinces, they held 72 per cent of the judicial positions open to Indians, including almost all the senior posts of principal *sadr amin*.[32] As compared with their co-religionists in Bengal, the Muslims of the Northwest could certainly not complain that they were discriminated against in civil employment. The sources of their discontent must be sought elsewhere.

To a large extent, therefore, the strong British hostility toward the Muslim community appears to have been based upon *a priori* deductive reasoning. As the former rulers of Hindustan, the Muslims had, in British eyes, necessarily to place themselves at the head of a movement for the overthrow of the British Government. And as devotees of a religion which inculcated "fanaticism and ferocity," they were bound to be more actively hostile than the followers of the mild and tolerant Hindu faith.[33] Whether firmly grounded or not, however, this anti-Muslim sentiment left its mark upon British policy for several decades. Raikes spoke for the majority of his countrymen when he insisted that the Muslims "have been too much trusted, and must be watched carefully hereafter." A certain portion of public appointments, he said, should be continued in their hands, proportionate to their numbers, but they should not be allowed to enjoy too large a share of the Government patronage.[34] The statistics of Government employment show how thoroughly this recommendation was carried out. In Bengal the earlier discrimination against the

[32] These figures are based upon returns from 20 of the 32 districts in the North-Western Provinces. P.P. 1852, x, 597-617. Population statistics are given in P.P. 1875, LIV, 394.

[33] Sec. C.C. Punjab to Sec. Govt. India, 29 April 1858, *Punjab Government Records*, VII, Part 2, 398. See also Thornhill, *Personal Adventures*, p. 333.

[34] Raikes, *Notes on the Revolt*, p. 176.

Muslim community was intensified, especially in the judicial service, where by 1886 they could lay claim to only 9 posts out of a total of 284. In the North-Western Provinces, although still disproportionately represented in the public service, the Muslims by 1880 no longer monopolized the higher posts as they had done thirty years before.[35] Much of this discrimination doubtless arose naturally and inevitably from the reluctance of the Muslim community to take up English education. No doubt also the revival of Wahabi activity during the 1860's, culminating in the murder of Lord Mayo in 1872, helped to harden British antagonism toward the Muslim community. But the continuing bitterness and suspicion owed much to the legacy of distrust left by the events of 1857.

The Muslims eventually managed to efface this hostility and to regain the favor they had enjoyed in the early days of British rule. Much of the credit for this rehabilitation must go to Sayyid Ahmad Khan. From 1860, when he published a pamphlet on *The Loyal Mohammedans of India*, until his death in 1898 he did his best to show the British that the Indian Muslims were loyal subjects of the Queen. At the same time he set out to educate his Muslim compatriots in Western knowledge so that they might be able to compete with the Hindus on equal terms. In 1864 he organized the Translation Society, later called the Scientific Society of Aligarh, and in 1875 he founded the Mohammedan Anglo-Oriental College, which taught both European knowledge and Islamic learning. Only with growth of the Indian nationalist movement, however, did Sayyid Ahmad's efforts bear fruit, for only then did British and Muslim interests coincide. The Muslims, when faced with the specter of representative government, found that they preferred British to Hindu rule. The British on their side found the conservative politics of Sayyid Ahmad far more attractive than the subversive radicalism of the Bengali Hindus. By the early twentieth century their ties

[35] See list of Hindu and Muslim appointments in Tables 10 and 11, and W. W. Hunter, *The Indian Musalmans* (London, 1871), pp. 164-66.

with the Muslims closely resembled those with the landlords and the princes.

The Muslims were not the only sufferers from the tragic events of 1857, for the racial animosities roused by that event-

TABLE 10

HINDU AND MUSLIM APPOINTMENTS TO EXECUTIVE AND
JUDICIAL SERVICE, 1886-1887[a]

|  | Hindus | Muslims | Sikhs |
|---|---|---|---|
| *Bengal* | | | |
| Executive Service | | | |
| Deputy Magistrates and Deputy Collectors | 171 | 26 | |
| Sub Deputy Collectors and Tahsildars | 78 | 18 | |
| Total | 249 | 44 | |
| Judicial Service | | | |
| Subordinate Judges | 46 | 1 | |
| Munsifs | 227 | 8 | |
| Total | 273 | 9 | |
| Total of both | 522 | 53 | |
| *North-Western Provinces and Oudh* | | | |
| Executive Service | | | |
| Deputy Collectors | 90 | 51 | 1 |
| Tahsildars | 101 | 122 | 1 |
| Total | 191 | 173 | 2 |
| Judicial Service | | | |
| Subordinate Judges | 20 | 15 | |
| Munsifs | 51 | 47 | |
| Total | 71 | 62 | |
| Total of both | 262 | 235 | |

[a] P.P. 1888, xlviii, 54-56.

ful year long poisoned the relations between the British and all the Indian peoples. Indeed for decades, if not until the end of British rule, fear and suspicion comprised the glass through which ruler and ruled viewed each other. Henceforth, as one District Officer pointed out, "although kind and indulgent to the Hindustani, we must always continue on our guard,

TABLE 11

Proportion of Appointments Held by Hindus and Muslims as Compared with the Proportion of Those Classes to the Total Population of Each Province, 1886-1887[a]

|  | HINDUS | | MUSLIMS | |
|---|---|---|---|---|
|  | *Percentage of Total Population* | *Percentage of Total Number of Persons Employed in the Executive and Judicial Services* | *Percentage of Total Population* | *Percentage of Total Number of Persons Employed in the Executive and Judicial Service* |
| Bengal | 65.3 | Executive 73.4<br>Judicial 96.1 } 83.7 | 31.2 | Executive 12.9<br>Judicial 3.1 } 8. |
| North-Western Provinces and Oudh | 86.2 | Executive 49.4<br>Judicial 52.5 } 50.2 | 13.4 | Executive 44.8<br>Judicial 45.9 } 45. |
| Punjab | 40.7 | Executive 48.1<br>Judicial 53.4 } 51.3 | 51.3 | Executive 41.8<br>Judicial 33.6 } 39. |

[a] P.P. 1888, XLVIII, 57.

however calm the surface."[36] With the loss of trust and affection went the loss of hope. The earlier reformers, with perhaps too much shallow optimism, had set out to remold the Indian character on an English pattern. Now, driven by fear and distrust, they recoiled in the opposite direction. Almost without realizing it, the British threw over the whole notion of Indian regeneration and consigned the Indian people to the status of permanent racial inferiority. From the Mutiny they drew

[36] Robertson, *District Duties*, p. 191.

the lesson that the Indians were not simply backward and inept, in need of guidance, but irredeemably mired in Oriental stagnation. A people who had rejected the benefits of European civilization, they were clearly incapable of appreciating them, and so could never be lifted to the heights of Victorian liberalism. Their only hope lay in the long-continued rule of a beneficent British Government. Outside the small settler community such sentiments were rarely openly expressed. The concept of permanent racial inferiority was not after all a doctrine likely to appeal to the educated Indian. Nevertheless it underlay much of post-Mutiny British thought about India, and found a home in all ranks of the civil service. Its presence can be detected most readily in the debates over the renewal of the Arms Act in 1859-1860.

On the expiration in 1859 of the emergency disarming act passed at the height of the Mutiny (Act XXVIII of 1857), the Government decided to re-enact it on a permanent basis as a general police measure. It anticipated little opposition, as the measure had passed through the Legislative Council without difficulty in 1857, and contained ample provision for the exemption of Europeans and other loyal subjects. In its revised form, moreover, the Act was even milder than before. No licenses were to be required and no one found in possession of arms was to be disarmed unless in the opinion of a Magistrate he constituted a danger to the public peace. But the Act still made no provision for the exclusion of Europeans as a class from its operation. On this ground it was subjected to severe criticism both within the Government and without. The planters and their spokesmen on the Legislative Council, Sir Charles Jackson, Sir Mordaunt Wells, and Sir Barnes Peacock, approached the question from a straightforward racial position. The European community, they said, as a class which had remained loyal during the trials of 1857 and which had fought for its life "against hordes of natives," deserved special treatment. It was insulting to place the Europeans on the same level, and subject them to the same regulations, as those tainted with the spirit of rebellion. Between Indians and Europeans there could be no equality.[37] This opposition by the planters and their allies on the Bench, if disconcerting, was not wholly unexpected, since these men had never made any attempt to hide their racist sentiments. Far more significant, and more ominous, was the stand taken by the Government of the North-Western Provinces. Much like Wells and Peacock, they advocated the exemption of Europeans from the measure. Such men, they insisted, should not be placed under the same restrictions "as those who have taught us by bitter experience how treacherous and truculent they can be, and how unworthy consequently they are to be again entrusted with arms of any description." They then went on to propose stringent new legislation designed to insure the complete disarmament of the Indian people.

Under Act XXVIII of 1857, disarming operations had already begun in the North-Western Provinces, and some thirty-five lakhs worth of arms had been confiscated. The provincial Government now urged that the search for weapons be intensified, and the penalties for concealment stiffened. Those found in possession of arms without a license, they said, should be liable to a fine of Rs. 500, imprisonment for seven years, or corporal punishment at the discretion of the Magistrate. They further recommended that Magistrates be given the power to enter homes in search of arms, and if the presence of hidden weapons was suspected in any village to confiscate all proprietary rights until such time as the arms were handed over.[38] These proposals met with the full support of the majority of the District Officers in the province. Several in fact went well beyond the authorities at Allahabad in their demands for stringent legislation and in the expression of racial bitter-

[37] Speech of Wells in the Legislative Council 23 June 1860, *Proceedings*, VI, 608-10. See also speech of 30 June 1860, pp. 701-07. Wells was a Judge of the Calcutta High Court.

[38] Sec. Govt. N.W.P. to Clerk of Legislative Council, 15 December 1859, Papers Relating to Act XXXI of 1860.

ness. Mayne at Banda urged the enactment of a simple concise act empowering Magistrates to seize all arms under penalty of seven years' imprisonment, a fine of Rs. 5,000, or 100 lashes. "If we ever wish to govern the Natives of India effectively," he said, "we must treat them as they are and not as civilized and intellectual beings. The laws which we make for them should be adapted to their understanding and contain rules of the most simple kind and easiest to be obeyed."[39] Similarly Vans Agnew at Saharanpur, after pointing out that "we can never again trust" the Hindus and Muslims of India, suggested that in future they be prohibited from possessing or bearing arms, either privately or for the state: "In their place we might import foreigners, white and black . . . and we might raise regiments in India from the tribes who possess neither of the proscribed creeds. . . . The effect upon India, and upon its incubus, caste, would undoubtedly be very great. Respect for the European would increase, and the absurd pretensions of the high caste Hindoo, and bigotted Musalman would be lowered." With such a force of foreign mercenaries, he concluded, "we should be rid forever of the bugbear of mutiny or rebellion . . . and be in a position to pass whatever laws, and impose what taxes we choose, without the slightest misgiving or regard for the opinion of the whole native world."[40]

When these papers reached his desk, Canning was shocked beyond measure. The sentiments expressed in them, he told Edmonstone, were more revolting than anything he had heard during the Mutiny, and could be compared only with "the savagery of an American Slave-State newspaper."[41] He absolutely refused to exempt Europeans from the provisions of the new Act or to permit the continuance of a general search for arms in the North-Western Provinces. The bill

[39] F. O. Mayne, Magistrate of Banda, to C. B. Thornhill, Commissioner of Allahabad, 5 October 1859, *ibid.*

[40] J. Vans Agnew, Magistrate of Saharanpur, to F. Williams, Commissioner of Meerut, 8 November 1859, *ibid.*

[41] Canning to Edmonstone, 6 July 1860, Canning Papers.

accordingly passed into law in its original form (as Act XXXI of 1860), and the search parties which had terrorized the rural population of the North-Western Provinces since the Mutiny were called off. But the passage of this Act did not in any way halt the spread of racist sentiment. The psychological gulf between the British and the Indian people continued to widen, and racial bitterness to harden, throughout the 1860's. Succeeding Viceroys saw and deplored the "increased ill-feeling between the two races" which had grown up since the Mutiny, while many Indians, only too conscious of the hostility with which they were regarded, labored in vain to remove its causes.[42] In the press and on the platform the educated classes constantly proclaimed their unshakeable loyalty and denounced the discrimination to which they were subjected. They never hesitated to bring instances of arrogance and oppression to the notice of the Government or to protest the racist sentiments of such men as Sir Mordaunt Wells.[43] From the Viceroy they usually gained a sympathetic response. The Supreme Government generally tried to mete out strict and equal justice between the races and to hold in check the passions of the lower class of Europeans. In 1862 Elgin even brought down upon himself a storm of abuse by refusing to pardon a European charged with the wanton and unprovoked murder of an Indian. But few Englishmen, despite their attempt to balance the scales of justice, ever questioned the assumption that the natives of India were an inferior race, unfit for posts of responsibility.

Indeed the one serious attempt to enforce the principle of racial equality in government employment, the Ilbert Bill

[42] Canning to Wood, 8 October 1860, Wood Papers. Lawrence to Cranborne, 19 December 1866, Lawrence Papers. Lawrence Evidence to House of Commons Committee on Indian Finance, 1 July 1873, P.P. 1873, XII, 487-88.

[43] See for instance the petition criticizing Wells's behavior on the Bench which was signed by 5,000 Indians, including Debendranath Tagore, and sent to the Secretary of State in August 1861. Home Public B, 24 September 1861, No. 137.

of 1883, only revealed the depth of British racial feeling. This bill arose from the fact that under the Criminal Procedure Code Indian Magistrates were debarred from trying European British subjects in the *Mofussil*. To many Englishmen, among them Sir Charles Wood, it seemed only reasonable that the "ruling race" should be exempt from the criminal jurisdiction of the ruled.[44] Ripon, on the other hand, considered this exclusion an "invidious distinction" which had no place on the statute book, and which he accordingly set out to remove.[45] But the measure roused an immense storm of protest among the British in India. Not only were the Calcutta Europeans up in arms, but the civil service was itself almost universally hostile. When the proposed bill was circulated among the local governments, none accepted it as it stood, and Bengal urged its complete withdrawal. The District Officers, apart from such liberals as Henry Beveridge, ranked themselves solidly with the opposition. Even the members of Ripon's Council were divided in their sympathies. Hence Ripon, unwilling to face a long and lonely struggle with the Anglo-Indian community, eventually accepted a compromise settlement under which a European British subject could be brought before an Indian Magistrate but was allowed to claim a trial by jury, with at least half the jurors being Europeans or Americans.[46] The principles of imperialism and racism had emerged triumphant from their severest challenge.

This racial feeling, and the imperial ideology which accompanied it, were not built upon Indian experience alone. They found support and confirmation at home in contemporary scientific and political thought. In fact the pseudo-scientific racism of the late nineteenth century and the authoritarian liberalism of J. F. Stephen together gave the new India policy just the theoretical backing which it needed to be respectable

[44] Wood to Maine, 9 September 1864, Wood Papers.

[45] Ripon to Hartington, 8 September 1882, cited in Wolf, *Life of Ripon*, II, 122.

[46] See S. Gopal, *Viceroyalty of Lord Ripon*, ch. ix.

in English eyes. No longer was the racial inferiority of the Indian an emotional sentiment, it was scientific fact; and the British Empire was not something to be ashamed of, but a positive instrument of morality and order throughout the world. The ideas forged in the crucible of 1857 were hammered into shape on the anvil of racial and political theory.

The instinctive revulsion against something strange and different which lies at the base of racial prejudice has doubtless existed since men of different customs and color first came in contact with each other. Among the self-confident Europeans of the early nineteenth century it naturally took on a distinct moral tone. Their expanding industrial civilization was obviously superior to that of the darker-skinned Negro and Oriental races. But only in the mid-nineteenth century, with the development of anthropology, was racial prejudice placed on a scientific foundation, and the differences between the races adjudged permanent and ineradicable. The most famous and influential of the new racial theorists was the French nobleman, Count Arthur de Gobineau, whose *Essai sur l'Inegalite des Races Humaines*, built upon the earlier pioneering studies of Cuvier, was published in 1853. Despite his stress on racial difference, Gobineau still clung to the traditional Christian view that all men had ultimately derived from a single ancestor. Other, bolder ethnologists followed the theory of race to its logical conclusion and declared that the various races of mankind represented separate and distinct acts of creation. Some even maintained that they were different species of the genus *homo*. As one American writer put it, "There are no greater differences between the lion, tiger, and panther, or the dog, fox, wolf, and jackal than between the White Man, Negro, and Mongol."[47] All agreed, however, that the various races had come down from remote

47 J. C. Nott, "Acclimation; Or, the Comparative Influence of Climate . . . on the Races of Man," in Nott and G. R. Gliddon, *Indigenous Races of the Earth* (Philadelphia, 1857), p. 361.

antiquity with their basic characteristics virtually unchanged. As evidence they cited the portrayal in the art of ancient Egypt of racial types identical with those of the nineteenth century. "So far from there being a stronger similarity among the most ancient races, the dissimilarity actually augments as we ascend the stream of time."[48] Racial characteristics, moreover, were not simply matters of outward appearance, but anatomical features susceptible of precise measurement. The size of the brain, the facial angle, the shape of the head, varied from race to race, and within broad limits were fixed for each race. Cranial structure thus provided "an enduring, natural, and reliable basis upon which to establish a true classification of the races of men."[49]

These racial theorists further argued that intellectual capability was intimately related to physical structure. Each "physical type" had its own "moral and intellectual peculiarities." One could not be separated from the other. As one writer boldly stated, "In the size of the head and face, and their mutual relations, we find the best indications of those mental and animal differences which, under all circumstances and from ante-historic times, have manifested themselves as the dividing line between the Races of Men."[50] Hence, they concluded, it was possible to rank the races of mankind on the scale of civilization with scientific precision. At the top (not unnaturally) stood the white races, particularly the Saxons of Northern Europe. They had the largest cranial capacity, the most advanced anatomical structure, and the greatest appreciation of liberty. The Negro stood at the opposite end of the spectrum. In structure he occupied a place intermediate between the Saxon and the chimpanzee, while his intellectual

[48] Nott and Gliddon, *Types of Mankind* (Philadelphia, 1855), p. 84; and R. Knox, *The Races of Men* (London, 1862), pp. 94-95.

[49] J. Aitken Meigs, "The Cranial Characteristics of the Races of Men," in Nott and Gliddon, *Indigenous Races of the Earth*, p. 364.

[50] *Ibid.*, p. 221.

inferiority was clearly established by the fact that since earliest times the dark races had been "the slaves of their fairer brethren."[51] Nor could the Negro appreciably alter his status, for the size and shape of his brain set rigid limits to his advance in civilization. Barring a miraculous transformation of his cranium, he was irredeemably mired in that "benighted state" to which nature had consigned him. In similar fashion the native races of India, after decades of exposure to European civilization, were "unaltered and seemingly unalterable."[52]

As the races of the world were demarcated by anatomy and intellect, so also were they kept apart by climate. Each had "its prescribed salubrious limits," within which alone it could flourish. Whenever the white races ventured into the tropics, or the Negro into temperate climes, they rapidly deteriorated: "Place an Englishman in the most healthful part of Bengal or Jamaica, where malarial fevers are unknown, and although he may . . . live with a tolerable degree of health his three score years and ten; yet, he soon ceases to be the same individual, and his descendants degenerate. He complains bitterly of the heat, becomes tanned; his plump, plethoric frame is attenuated; his blood loses fibrine and red globules; both body and mind become sluggish; gray hair and other marks of premature age appear . . . the average duration of life is shortened . . . and the race in time would be exterminated, if cut off from fresh supplies of immigrants."[53] Thus, although the white races were destined by virtue of their superior energy and intelligence to dominate the earth, they could neither settle in the tropics nor marry the native races. Such liaisons would only adulterate the superior white blood and produce a weak, short-lived stock. The mission of the white

[51] Knox, *Races of Men*, p. 224; Nott and Gliddon, *Types of Mankind*, pp. 457-65.

[52] Knox, *Races of Men*, pp. 247-48; Nott and Gliddon, *Types of Mankind*, pp. 189-91.

[53] Nott, "Acclimation . . . ," in Nott and Gliddon, *Indigenous Races of the Earth*, p. 364.

man in India and Africa was not to displace the indigenous races, but to rule over them as conqueror and guardian.[54]

Fantastic though these racial theories may appear today, with their easy assumption of European superiority, at the time they marked the first significant attempt to place anthropology on a scientific basis, and met with widespread approval. Even the rise of Darwinism, with its emphasis on evolution, did not shake the hold of this pseudo-scientific racism. If evolution destroyed the ideas of multiple creation and the fixity of racial types, it provided, in the struggle for survival, a mechanism by which racial differentiation and conflict could take place. The white race was dominant because it was more advanced and adaptable, and had emerged victorious in the struggle for existence. Whether based on Darwin or Cuvier, however, these racial theories vastly enhanced the appeal of that new racial feeling which grew up among the British in India after the Mutiny. When the embittered Anglo-Indian proclaimed the inherent superiority of the British race and the futility of trying to civilize the people of India, he found the way already prepared. By 1860 the British people were conditioned to think in racial terms. They saw nothing immoral or unjust in a policy which merely followed the dictates of science. Indeed the Mutiny, with its inexplicable uprising of a pampered army and contented peasantry, seemingly confirmed the views of these "scientific" anthropologists. After the events of 1857 no one could easily deny that the races of man were cut off from each other by enormous differences in behavior and attitude, or that the darker races were permanently consigned to an inferior position on the scale of civilization. Together the new racial thought and the lessons of 1857 reinforced and gave credibility to each other. Cranial measurement and the Kanpur massacre taught much the same thing.

[54] Knox, *Races of Men*, pp. 244-46; Nott and Gliddon, *Types of Mankind*, pp. 77-79.

Similarly the new imperial spirit which barred the path of India's political advance after 1857 was more than just an instinctive response to the lessons of that year. It found justification and support at home in the authoritarian liberalism which grew up among the intellectual community during the Gladstonian era. As democracy took root in the English political system, and the Liberal Party under Gladstone made itself the vehicle of popular sentiment, the intellectuals found themselves increasingly estranged from the party leaders. Nothing could be further removed from true liberalism, they felt, than the rule of a tyrannical majority, manipulated by wire-pullers and party caucuses, and with no object in view other than the satisfaction of its own baser instincts. As Robert Lowe, the leader of the small band of liberal "Adullamites" contesting the 1867 Reform Bill, put it in the House of Commons: "Because I am a Liberal and know that by pure and clear intelligence alone can the cause of true progress be promoted, I regard as one of the greatest dangers with which this country can be threatened a proposal to subvert the existing order of things, and to transfer power from the hands of property and intelligence . . . to the hands of men whose whole life is necessarily occupied in daily struggles for existence."[55]

Much of this opposition to the spread of democracy was a natural response on the part of the educated middle classes to the loss of those privileges they had held since the 1832 Reform Bill. But it rested as well upon a well-developed intellectual foundation, derived in part from the philosophy of Hobbes and Bentham, and in part from an idealization of the practice of the British Indian Government. The most forthright exponent of this authoritarian liberalism was James Fitzjames Stephen, an English lawyer who served two and a half years as Legal Member of the Viceroy's Council (1869-1872) and who published on his return the political manifesto of the new school, *Liberty, Equality, Fraternity*. At the

[55] Speech of 3 May 1865, Hansard, CLXXVIII, 1,439-40.

heart of Stephen's philosophy lay the Benthamite, and ultimately Hobbesian, conception of government as a positive instrument for the propagation of morality and civilization. The aim of government was to secure, not liberty, as J. S. Mill so often proclaimed, but the greatest happiness of the greatest number. Stephen further maintained, with Bentham, that there was no natural propensity for men to treat each other with justice. Most men cared only for their own immediate interests and sought happiness at the expense of their neighbors. The state of nature was one of perpetual conflict and warfare. Only the judicious application of force, wielded by a powerful legislator, could resolve these conflicting interests and suppress the selfish desires of mankind. As expressed in the coercive sanctions of law, force was not an evil, but a necessary element in the creation of a civilized social order. Even in the modern parliamentary state, he insisted, where compulsion was mild and disguised, the power of the sword still underlay the whole social fabric.

So far Stephen was a good Benthamite. But he parted company with the utilitarian reformers over the question of popular education. Bentham had assumed, with the optimism born of the Enlightenment, that the people could in time be trained by good government and education to see their own true interests, and to act spontaneously, without coercion, according to the greatest happiness principle. J. S. Mill had an even greater faith in the potentialities of human nature. He had spoken eloquently in his *Liberty* of the need for the unhampered development of individuality, and he believed that everyone, the English workman and the Indian peasant alike, was capable ultimately of understanding the principles of morality and living in peace with his neighbor. Stephen would have none of this. Human nature was such, he insisted, that the bulk of the people would remain forever under the sway of passion, beyond the reach of rational discussion or improvement.[56] The utmost conceivable liberty could in no

[56] J. F. Stephen, *Liberty, Equality, Fraternity* (New York, 1873), p. 31.

way improve this vast indifferent multitude. They required not universal suffrage but the rule of a gifted minority, able to command their obedience and impose upon them its own ideal of happiness. Society could progress only when men recognized this fact, which Mill and Bentham had obscured, acknowledged that men were "fundamentally unequal," and abandoned the disastrous attempt to introduce democracy.[57]

This pessimistic view of human nature was shared by many of Stephen's contemporaries, among them Sir Henry Maine, the eminent legal scholar who was Stephen's predecessor as Legal Member of the Viceroy's Council. Maine looked with equal suspicion on the growth of democracy. Bentham, he felt, had vastly overestimated the intelligence of the average man. The truths Bentham had seen, he said, were visible only to the few; the multitudes "include too much ignorance to be capable of understanding their interests."[58] If power were placed in the hands of ignorant masses it would inevitably be misused. The upper classes alone were able to advance the cause of progress, and to maintain law and order in society. Maine was in some ways more conservative than Stephen. He was willing, for instance, to entrust the powers of government to an hereditary aristocracy, whereas Stephen's ideal ruler was the trained bureaucrat of the Indian Civil Service. In similar fashion Maine refused to admit that any institution was of universal validity, or that any abstract theory, such as Benthamism, was more than the product of a certain pattern of historical evolution. But Maine's historical jurisprudence did not significantly alter the shape of intellectual liberalism. Indeed his conservatism only reinforced its basic tenets: the glorification of force, the fear of democracy, and the belief in a fixed social hierarchy.

This dislike of democracy did not drive the intellectual community into the Tory Party, for they were not apologists defending the old social order. Their ideal always remained

---

[57] *Ibid.*, p. 235.

[58] H. S. Maine, *Popular Government* (London, 1885), p. 86.

the old liberal one of efficient economical government by an educated and propertied elite. In the British Indian Government they found this ideal realized. In fact Stephen and Maine both derived much of their enthusiasm for autocratic government from their experiences in India, and explicitly acknowledged the debt which their political theory owed to the years they had spent in Indian administration. Stephen even spoke of his book *Liberty, Equality, Fraternity* as "little more than the turning of an Indian lantern on European problems."[59] They saw in the caste system "a social hierarchy corresponding as nearly as possible to the real distinctions between men," and the Indian Civil Service excited their highest admiration. The Indian Government, Stephen told Lytton, was "the best corrective in existence to the fundamental fallacies of liberalism . . . the only government under English control still worth caring about."[60]

By expounding the virtues of autocratic government in a rigorous and consistent fashion, and yet remaining within the tradition of English liberalism, Stephen and his followers greatly enhanced the cause of empire. Taken together, their arguments provided the best possible intellectual justification for the continuance of British rule in India. They made morally respectable that which the events of the Mutiny had made politically expedient: the maintenance of a strong paternal government which brooked no challenge to its authority. Stephen himself never hesitated to draw out from his political theory its practical implications for Indian policy. In 1878, incensed by John Bright's "sentimental" liberalism, he exalted in a letter to *The Times* the positive values of ambition and conquest. "I say that ambition is the great incentive

[59] Stephen to Lytton, 2 May 1876, cited in J. Roach, "Liberalism and the Victorian Intelligentsia," *Cambridge Historical Journal*, XIII, No. 1 (1957), p. 64.

[60] Stephen, *Liberty, Equality, Fraternity*, p. 235; Leslie Stephen, *Life of J. F. Stephen* (London, 1895), p. 243; Stephen to Lytton, 15 March 1878, 10 May 1876, cited in Roach, "Liberalism and the Victorian Intelligentsia," p. 64.

to every manly virtue, and that conquest is the process by which every great state in the world (the United States not excepted) has been built up."[61] Five years later, sensing in the Ilbert Bill a determination to shift "the foundations on which the British Government of India rests," he proclaimed once again in a letter to *The Times* his view of the nature of that Empire:

"It is essentially an absolute Government, founded, not on consent, but on conquest. It does not represent the native principles of life or of government, and it can never do so until it represents heathenism and barbarism. It represents a belligerent civilization, and no anomaly can be so striking or so dangerous as its administration by men who, being at the head of a Government founded on conquest, implying at every point the superiority of the conquering race . . . and having no justification for its existence except that superiority, shrink from the open, uncompromising, straightforward assertion of it, seek to apologize for their own position, and refuse, from whatever cause, to uphold and support it."[62]

Stephen's plea for an "open, uncompromising assertion of superiority" was no mere rhetorical gesture. It flowed directly from his pessimistic Hobbesian view of human nature, that men in general are "extremely ignorant" and likely to abuse power unless they submit to "the guidance of people who know better than themselves." The Indian people, he pointed out, far more than any Europeans, were "ignorant to the last degree" and "steeped in idolatrous superstition," while their rulers were men dedicated to their welfare and imbued with the highest principles of European civilization. Nor was Britain under any obligation to fit the Indian people for representative institutions. If, as was the case in India, an autocratic government was successfully administered and suited the circumstances of those among whom it existed, there was no reason why those who administered it should

[61] Letter of Stephen to *The Times*, 4 January 1878.
[62] Letter of Stephen to *The Times*, 1 March 1883.

seek to substitute for it a representative system, or should feel in any respect ashamed of their position. So long as the British people carried out their responsibilities toward the people of India, Stephen assured his countrymen, they need never hesitate to proclaim their superiority.[63] In thus describing the Indians as an inferior people, incapable of understanding their own true interest or of acting upon the principles of European civilization, Stephen was not putting forward a new or original idea. He simply provided additional confirmation, from the vantage point of political theory, of much that was already implicit in the assumptions of post-Mutiny India policy, and that had found expression in the theories of contemporary racial anthropology. But Stephen was nonetheless important, for his lucid imperial ideology gave the Indian official and the imperially-minded at home first-rate ammunition with which to fight the "sentimental" liberals and the upstart Bengali Babus. Indeed in the Ilbert controversy, when powerful journals like *The Times* echoed Stephen's opinions throughout, they provided a basic ingredient in the formulation of British public opinion.

The British Government of India, Stephen went on, did not exist simply for the exploitation of a subject country. It represented "a belligerent civilization" and was engaged in the noble task of redeeming a people sunk in darkness and superstition. As Stephen saw it, the British power in India was "a vast bridge" over which an enormous multitude of human beings were passing "from a dreary land . . . of cruel wars, ghastly superstitions, and wasting plagues and famine" on their way to a peaceful, orderly, and industrious land which might be the cradle of changes comparable to those of the Roman Empire.[64] In this Stephen stood squarely in the center of the nineteenth century liberal tradition. Everyone from the earliest reformers onward had described Britain's

[63] J. F. Stephen, "Foundations of the Government of India," *Nineteenth Century*, LXXX (October 1883), 544, 551-54.
[64] Letter to *The Times*, 4 January 1878.

mission in India in moral terms, and had justified British imperial rule on the ground that it alone could lead the Indian people toward the light of European civilization. But Stephen's conception of Britain's civilizing mission was sharply and narrowly defined. It involved little more than the establishment of law and order and the enforcement of contracts. The legal codes and elaborate judicial organization of British India were, he acknowledged, "somewhat grim presents for one people to make to another" and were little calculated to excite affection. But they were the base upon which civilization rested, the source from which all other benefits flowed. With an almost evangelical fervor he insisted that: "The establishment of a system of law which regulates the most important part of the daily life of the people, constitutes in itself a moral conquest more striking, more durable, and far more solid, than the physical conquest which rendered it possible. It exercises an influence over the minds of the people in many ways comparable to that of a new religion. . . . Our law is in fact the sum and substance of what we have to teach them. It is, so to speak, the gospel of the English, and it is a compulsory gospel which admits of no dissent and no disobedience."[65]

Many of the early reformers, following Bentham, had also placed great emphasis upon the civilizing power of law. For Stephen, however, law was quite literally the "sum and substance" of the English gospel. Once the governmental apparatus was established, and the courts in operation, nothing remained to be done except to work the machinery efficiently. This exclusive preoccupation with the blessings of law reflects in part of course Stephen's Benthamite heritage, but it also reflects the conservative climate of post-Mutiny British opinion in India. As has already been pointed out, few Englishmen, after the disillusioning experiences of the Mutiny, were prepared to embark upon extensive programs of social and politi-

[65] Stephen, "Legislation under Lord Mayo" in Hunter, *Life of Mayo*, ii, 168-69.

cal reconstruction. The security of the Empire itself demanded a policy of caution and conciliation. Stephen, despite his belligerent tone, was as affected by this atmosphere as any of his more avowedly laissez faire contemporaries. In *Liberty, Equality, Fraternity*, he had pointed out that governments "ought to take the responsibility of acting upon such principles, religious, political, and moral, as they may from time to time regard as most likely to be true."[66] Yet he carefully refrained from advocating State support of Christianity or extensive social reform in India. It would indeed, he said, be "madness" to interfere with the social habits or religious opinions of the people. "I would not touch a single one of them except in cases of extreme necessity." To be sure, he spoke enthusiastically of those reforms which were already on the statute book, such as the prohibition of *sati* and the act which permitted Christian converts to inherit their ancestral property. But he proposed no new legislation and looked forward only to the slow decay of the traditional social order under the influence of peace, law, order and education.[67] An exception might be made for the Civil Marriage Act of 1872, which Stephen himself drafted, but it was carefully drawn so as not to affect any of the major religious groups in India and it had little real significance.

The ideal representative of this conservative temper was Sir Henry Maine. His historical and legal studies led him to emphasize the elements of continuity and complexity in human institutions and to distrust rapid social change. Laws and institutions grow, he said, they are not made by the arbitrary will of a legislator. The society of the present was simply the result of the slow growth of custom in the past. Most people, he continued, were intensely conservative and clung tenaciously to their traditional ways. The Indians, the Chinese, and many others "detest that which in the language of the West would be called reform." Only among the people

[66] Stephen, *Liberty, Equality, Fraternity*, pp. 53, 58.
[67] Hunter, *Life of Mayo*, p. 174.

of Western Europe was there any enthusiasm for change, and even they modified their habits and manners slowly and reluctantly.[68] At the same time Maine accepted the theories of Aryan philology, which through Sanskrit linked the Indian and European peoples in a common racial origin. This conception of a shared racial and institutional heritage helped blunt the racist attack and provided a platform from which the notion of European racial superiority could be combatted. But Maine regarded India as a backward section of the Indo-European community, where the institutions of antiquity had survived almost unchanged. The Indian village community, he said, with its patriarchal family structure and its joint ownership of land, was the counterpart of the old Teutonic township and threw considerable light on the social institutions of Europe in that remote period. India was in fact a "great repository of verifiable phenomena of ancient usage and ancient juridical thought," connected by Roman law with the legal ideas and customs of the present.[69] In Maine's view therefore, although a part of the Aryan world, India had not progressed, like Western Europe, along the path "from status to contract." It was a stagnant society, a "barbarism," which contained "a great part of our own civilization with its elements as yet inseparate and not yet unfolded."[70] Hence, he concluded, social and legal reforms could be introduced only with extreme caution. A society where the old customary bonds had not yet dissolved into contractual relationships simply could not be remodeled overnight. Nor could Benthamite ideas be adopted wholesale. As Maine reminded the members of the Indian Legislative Council in 1866: "The people of this country were not only wedded by custom and religious feeling to complex systems of law, but prided themselves on their usages in proportion to the complexity of those usages.

[68] Maine, *Popular Government*, pp. 132-34.

[69] H. S. Maine, *Village Communities in the East and West* (New York, 1876), pp. 12-13, 22.

[70] *Ibid.*, p. 215.

If this were so, the foundation of Bentham's doctrine collapsed, and the doctrine itself had no application in India. The Legislature was estopped, by the conditions of our tenure of the country, from so simplifying the law."[71] Eventually the spirit of progress could be injected into the Indian body politic, and the people freed from the restraints of custom; but the process would be a lengthy one and would require firm English guidance throughout.[72]

## Conclusion

The character of the Indian Empire in the last decades of the nineteenth century was shaped to a very large extent by the events of 1857. The widespread support which the uprising obtained, and the threat it posed to the very existence of British rule in India during the long summer of 1857, forced the British to examine afresh the whole nature of their connection with that land. Above all else the Mutiny brought home to them the strength and tenacity of the traditional institutions of India. The British still remained convinced of their own moral superiority, and looked upon their presence in India as a tangible manifestation of this supremacy. But their self-confident optimism, and their plans for the rapid Westernization of India, were irreparably shattered. The introduction of Western ideas into a traditional Asian society, they had discovered, was a dangerous and explosive business. The consequences of well-intentioned meddling were at best uncertain, and at worst catastrophic. It was far safer and more sensible, they decided, to take Indian society as it was, and to concentrate upon the provision of sound efficient administration. This new attitude of caution and conservatism can be detected in almost every sphere of British activity in India after the Mutiny. The abandonment of social legislation, the introduction of taluqdari settlement in Oudh, Canning's

[71] Speech of 14 December 1866, in Grant Duff, *Life and Speeches of Henry Maine* (New York, 1892), pp. 251-52.
[72] Maine, *Village Communities*, pp. 238-39.

gentry-magistrate system, the conciliation of the princes, the reform of the Legislative Council—all bear witness to its influence. Even such abortive proposals as the universal introduction of permanent settlement, the restraint of the money-lender, or the return to a patriarchal form of government were motivated by the same objective. The British wished to buttress the traditional institutions of India, to minimize social change, and to soften the impact of Western rule. Though the state of government finances or the principles of Victorian liberalism might ultimately forbid the enactment of some of the more far-reaching proposals, their serious consideration by the Government indicates how anxious the British were after the Mutiny to avoid a recurrence of that catastrophe.

Nor was this policy of conservatism simply a device to dampen the sparks of popular discontent. It went hand in hand with a new and more avowedly imperial sentiment which glorified the British Raj and consigned the Indian people to a position of permanent racial inferiority. By the late nineteenth century the bulk of the British people, conditioned by the theories of "scientific" ethnology and the authoritarian liberalism of J. F. Stephen, were prepared to acknowledge without question that India required, for its own good, the permanent paternal rule of the superior British nation. The Indian people might be intellectually agile, they might individually possess great talents and abilities, but as a community they were morally unfit for self-government. A different order of beings, incapable of assimilating the principles of Western civilization, they had perforce to remain in the status to which God had assigned them. Hence the British quite naturally took their stand alongside traditional India and set out to strengthen the position of its "natural" leaders: the landed gentry and aristocracy. These men alone could command the allegiance of the masses and speak to them on their own terms. Indeed, when confronted with the demands of the early nationalists in the last decades of the

nineteenth century, the British considered themselves the pro-
tectors of an indigenous and cherished way of life against
a small band of upstart agitators. They found of course staunch
allies in the Indian aristocracy, whose dominant position was
similarly challenged by the middle-class nationalists. Tied
together, as Harcourt Butler put it, by "mutual sympathy and
trust," the Englishman and the taluqdar would stand "as
brothers before the altar of the Empire."[73]

Much of the traditionalism which the British saw in the
Indian people was genuine. They clearly preferred their old
patterns of land tenure to the British revenue system, and
their established social customs to mid-Victorian British
morality. The widespread character of the revolt in the
countryside was in fact in many ways simply a reflection of
the deep-seated hatred which the peasants cherished toward
the whole imperial structure, with its alien officials, capricious
courts, and oppressive police. Yet the people were never so
completely devoted to their old ways as the British imagined.
The Oudh villagers, for instance, though willing to follow
their taluqdar into battle in 1857, had little desire to see him
reinstated as an all-powerful landlord. The Western-educated
classes almost universally repudiated the whole patriarchal
and paternal ideal. They had no desire whatever to see the
ancient institutions of India perpetuated unchanged, or the
British established forever in the seat of power. Indeed they
remained loyal during the Mutiny largely because they hoped
that the British would continue the great work of social
and political transformation to which they had set their hand.
Their sympathies with the rebel cause were always tempered
by a deep commitment to the ideals of British liberalism as
expressed by Bentinck and Trevelyan.

It can be said, therefore, that the British built upon their
knowledge of the behavior of the Indian people during the
revolt an exaggerated and stereotyped image of Indian conservatism. This image, generalized into a kind of imperial

[73] Butler, *Oudh Policy*, p. 51.

folklore, was then used as evidence to support the theory of Oriental stagnation. The reasons why the British interpreted the experiences of the Mutiny in this preconceived fashion cannot easily be explained. They seem to arise at least in part, however, from a deep psychological need on the part of the imperial Briton. In India he was faced with a state of society which he found pleasureable and profitable, but which, based as it was on the rule of one people over another, he knew in his heart to be unjust. In this situation his almost automatic response was to emphasize the inferiority of the Indian, and to refuse to mix with him on equal terms, for in no other way could he justify his own elevated position. Indeed the more the Indian, educated in Western ways, came to demand equality, the more the European withdrew into an aloof and distant life, and accentuated the differences which separated him from the "native." The concept of "Oriental stagnation" was in large measure a convenient myth created by the white man to ease his own conscience as he enjoyed the perquisites of power.[74]

But the British position in India cannot be defined so simply. Despite the strength of the conservative reaction after the Mutiny, elements of the earlier reforming sentiment, and of the liberal ideology in which it was embedded, persisted throughout the later nineteenth century. Such feelings were of course most marked in such outspoken reformers as Trevelyan, Ripon, and John Lawrence, but they can be found in a muted form in many Indian officials. Often indeed the two strands of conservatism and of reform existed simultaneously in the same person. Sir Charles Wood and Lord Canning, for instance, torn by the demands of what they considered to be their moral duty, tried to protect the peasantry and the inhabitants of the native states while at the same time courting the favor of the landlords and princes. The measures

---

[74] For further discussion of the psychological implications of racism see the suggestive study by Philip Mason, *Prospero's Magic: Some Thoughts on Class and Race* (London, 1962).

which emerged from this endeavor were usually rather feeble and ineffective, such as the tenancy legislation of the 1860's or the abortive attempt to prevent the retrocession of Mysore. But they do show that among a wide circle of Indian officials the ideals of the earlier era still remained alive. Similarly the continued support given to Western education after the Mutiny was not motivated exclusively by a desire to create a class of competent clerks. Although reluctant to give education much financial assistance, the British still looked forward to the spread of Western knowledge in India and to the eventual reformation of Indian society upon a European model through its influence. This patronage of education is perhaps the strongest testimony to the continued strength of the liberal ideal of Empire in the post-Mutiny years. But after the unsettling events of 1857 the path of moral duty was no longer so straight or so self-evident as it once had been. Troubled with doubts and uncertainties, the British now confined themselves almost exclusively to the maintenance of law and order and the construction of public works. Beyond this all was hazy. In September 1857, at the height of the revolt, *The Economist* told the British people that they had now to decide "whether in future India is to be governed *as a Colony or as a Conquest*; whether we are to rule our Asiatic subjects with strict and generous justice, wisely and beneficently, as their natural and indefeasible superiors, by virtue of our higher civilization, our purer religion, our sterner energies . . . ; or whether . . . we are to regard the Hindoos and Mahomedans as our equal fellow citizens, fit to be entrusted with the functions of self-government, ripe (or to be ripened) for British institutions, likely to appreciate the blessings of our rule, and, therefore, to be gradually prepared, as our own working classes are preparing, for a full participation in the privileges of representative assemblies, trial by jury, and all the other palladia of English liberty."[75] The decision was never made.

[75] *Economist*, 26 September 1857, xv, 1062.

# BIBLIOGRAPHY

## Manuscript Sources

1. Records of the Government of India, National Archives of India, New Delhi:

FOREIGN DEPARTMENT PROCEEDINGS

Foreign Consultations, 1856-60     Judicial, 1860-70
Secret Consultations, 1856-60     Political, 1860-70
General, 1860-70     Revenue, 1860-70

HOME DEPARTMENT PROCEEDINGS

Educational, 1857-70     Public, 1857-70
Judicial, 1857-70     Revenue, 1857-70

PAPERS RELATING TO ACTS OF THE INDIAN LEGISLATIVE COUNCIL:

Act X of 1859     Act XXVIII of 1868
Act XXXI of 1860     Act I of 1869
Act XIX of 1868     Act XXIV of 1870

2. Records of the Government of Uttar Pradesh:

UNITED PROVINCES RECORD OFFICE, ALLAHABAD

Oudh General Proceedings, 1858-60

SECRETARIAT RECORD ROOM, LUCKNOW

North-Western Provinces General Proceedings, 1860-70
Oudh Revenue Proceedings, 1870-73

3. Dispatches to and from India, India Office Library, London:
Educational Dispatches     Political Dispatches
Foreign Department Dispatches     Public Dispatches
Judicial Dispatches     Public Works Dispatches
    Revenue Dispatches

4. Private Papers, India Office Library, London, except as noted:
Argyll Papers, Film No. 311
Canning Papers [Harewood Estate Record Office, Leeds]
Ellenborough Papers [Public Record Office, 30/12, Box 22]
Kaye Mutiny Papers, Home Miscellaneous No. 724a-27.
Lawrence Papers, MSS Eur. F. 90.
Northbrook Papers, MSS Eur. C. 144.
Wood Papers, MSS Eur. F. 78.

## Newspapers and Periodicals

| | |
|---|---|
| *Calcutta Review*, Calcutta | *Hindoo Patriot*, Calcutta |
| *The Economist*, London | *Nineteenth Century*, London |
| *Edinburgh Review*, London | *Quarterly Review*, London |
| *Friend of India*, Calcutta | *The Times*, London |

## Printed Official Sources

*Administration Report of the Central Provinces for 1861-62, 1862-63, and 1863-64.*

*Administration Report of the North-Western Provinces for 1860-61 et seq.* to 1869-70 and for 1882-83.

*Administration Report of Oudh for 1861-62 et seq.* to 1869-70.

*The Condition of the Tenantry in Oudh,* 2 v., Allahabad, 1883.

*Decisions under the Rent Laws of the High Court of Judicature from 1860 to 1863,* Calcutta, 1865.

*Gazetteer of the Province of Oudh,* 3 v., Lucknow, 1877.

Hansard, *Parliamentary Debates,* Third Series.

*Land Revenue Policy of the Indian Government,* Calcutta, 1902.

*Memorandum upon the Current Land Revenue Settlements in the Temporarily Settled Parts of India,* Calcutta, 1880.

*Narratives of the Mutiny in the North-Western Provinces,* Allahabad, 1859.

*Papers Relating to Land Tenures and Revenue Settlements in Oude,* Calcutta, 1865.

*Parliamentary Papers.*

*Proceedings of the Governor-General of India in Council for the Purpose of Making Laws and Regulations* [Indian Legislative Council].

First Series, vols. i-vii, 1855-61.

Second Series, vols. i-x, 1862-71.

*Punjab Government Records*, 8 v., Lahore, 1911.

Mutiny Correspondence, vol. vii, Parts i and ii.

Mutiny Reports, vol. viii, Parts i and ii.

*Report of the Committee on the Riots in Poona and Ahmednagar, 1875* [Deccan Riots Committee], Bombay, 1876.

*Report by the Sudder Board of Revenue on the Revenue Administration of the North-Western Provinces for 1852-53*, Agra, 1854.

*Report on the Revenue Administration of the North-Western Provinces for 1870-71*, Allahabad, 1872; and for 1871-72, Allahabad, 1873.

*Selections from the Records of the Government of the North-Western Provinces*, vol. iv, Agra, 1856.

*Selections from the Records of the Government of India*, vol. liv, Calcutta, 1867.

*Selections from the Records of the Government of India*, vol. lxxvi, Calcutta, 1870.

Sharp, H., and R. A. Richey, *Selections from Educational Records*, 2 v., Calcutta, 1920-22.

## Other Works

Adam, William, *Third Report on the State of Education in Bengal*, Calcutta, 1838.

Argyll, George Douglas Campbell, Eighth Duke of, *George Douglas Campbell, Eighth Duke of Argyll, Autobiography and Memoirs*, London, 1906.

Argyll, Duke of, *India Under Dalhousie and Canning*, London, 1865.

Baden-Powell, Baden Henry, *The Land-Systems of British India*, 3 v., Oxford, 1892.

Baird, G. A., *The Private Letters of the Marquis of Dalhousie*, London, 1911.

Balfour, Betty, *The History of Lord Lytton's Indian Administration 1876 to 1880: compiled from Letters and Official Papers*, London, 1899.

Ball, Charles, *The History of the Indian Mutiny*, London, n.d.

Ballhatchet, Kenneth, *Social Policy and Social Change in Western India, 1817-30*, London, 1957.

Beames, John, *Memoirs of a Bengal Civilian*, London, 1961.

Bearce, George D., *British Attitudes Towards India, 1784-1858*, Oxford, 1961.

Beveridge, H., *The District of Baḳarganj: Its History and Statistics*, London, 1876.

Boman-Behram, B. K., *Educational Controversies in India*, Bombay, 1943.

Buckland, C. E., *Bengal Under the Lieutenant-Governors*, 2 v., Calcutta, 1902.

Butler, Harcourt, *Oudh Policy: The Policy of Sympathy*, Lucknow, 1906.

Campbell, George, *India As It May Be: An Outline of Proposed Government and Policy*, London, 1853.

Campbell, Sir George, *Memoirs of My Indian Career*, London, 1893.

Carstairs, R., *The Little World of an Indian District Officer*, London, 1912.

Chaudhuri, S. B., *Civil Rebellion in the Indian Mutinies 1857-1859*, Calcutta, 1957.

Chunder, Bholanauth, *Raja Digambar Mitra His Life and Career*, Calcutta, 1893.

Colvin, Auckland, *Memorandum on the Revision of Land Revenue Settlements in the North-Western Provinces 1860-72*, Calcutta, 1872.

Cotton, Sophia Anne, *Memoir of George Edward Lynch Cotton*, London, 1871.

Cunningham, Sir H. S., *Earl Canning*, Oxford, 1891.

Danvers, F. C., M. Monier-Williams, et al., *Memorials of Old Haileybury College*, London, 1894.

Darling, Sir Malcolm, *The Punjab Peasant in Prosperity and Debt*, Bombay, 4th edn., 1947.

Duff, Alexander, *The Indian Rebellion*, London, 1858.

Duff, M. E. Grant, *Life and Speeches of Henry Maine*, New York, 1892.

Durand, H. M., *The Life of Major-General Sir Henry Marion Durand*, 2 v., London, 1883.

Dutt, Romesh, *The Economic History of India*, 2 v., New Delhi, 1960.

Edwardes, Sir H. B., *Memorial of the Life and Letters of Major General Sir Herbert B. Edwardes*, Emma Edwardes, ed., London, 1886.

Edwardes, Sir H. B. and H. Merivale, *Life of Sir Henry Lawrence*, 2 v., London, 1872.

Edwards, William, *Facts and Reflections Connected with the Indian Rebellion*, Liverpool, 1859.

Edwards, William, *Reminiscences of a Bengal Civilian*, London, 1866.

Firminger, Walter Kelley, *The Fifth Report from the Select Committee of the House of Commons on the Affairs of the East India Company*, 3 v., Calcutta, 1917-18.

Fitzmaurice, Edmond, *Life of the Second Earl Granville*, London, 1905.

Ghosh, Manmathanath, ed., *The Life of Grish Chunder Ghose*, Calcutta, 1911.

Ghosh, Manmathanath, ed., *Selections From the Writings of Grish Chunder Ghose*, Calcutta, 1912.

Goldsmid, F. J., *Life of Sir James Outram*, London, 1881.

Gopal, S., *The Viceroyalty of Lord Ripon 1880-1884*, London, 1953.

Graham, G. F. I., *The Life and Work of Syed Ahmed Khan*, Edinburgh, 1885.

Gubbins, Martin Richard, *An Account of the Mutinies in Oudh and of the Siege of the Lucknow Residency*, London, 3rd edn., 1858.

Holmes, T. Rice, *A History of the Indian Mutiny*, London, 4th edn., 1891.

Hunter, W. W., *The Indian Musalmans: Are They Bound in Conscience to Rebel Against the Queen?* London, 1871.

Hunter, W. W., *A Life of the Earl of Mayo, Fourth Viceroy of India*, 2 v., London, 1875.

Ilbert, Courtenay, *The Government of India*, Oxford, 1898.

Imlah, Albert H., *Lord Ellenborough*, Cambridge, Mass., 1939.

Ingham, Kenneth, *Reformers in India 1793-1833: An Account of the Work of Christian Missionaries on Behalf of Social Reform*, Cambridge, 1956.

Innes, McLeod, *Lucknow & Oude in the Mutiny*, London, 1895.

Irwin, H. C., *The Garden of India or Chapters on Oudh History and Affairs*, London, 1880.

Joshi, P. C., ed., *Rebellion 1857: A Symposium*, New Delhi, 1957.

Kaye, John William, *Christianity in India*, London, 1859.

Kaye, John William, *A History of the Sepoy War in India 1857-1858*, 3 v., London, 7th edn., 1875.

Kaye, John William, *Selections from the Papers of Lord Metcalfe*, London, 1855.

Khan, Sayyid Ahmad, *An Essay on the Causes of the Indian Revolt*, Calcutta, 1860.

Knox, R., *The Races of Men*, London, 2nd edn., 1862.

Lee-Warner, Sir William, *The Life of The Marquis of Dalhousie*, 2 v., London, 1904.

Lee-Warner, Sir William, *The Native States of India*, London, 1910.

Lovett, Richard, *The History of the London Missionary Society 1795-1895*, 2 v., London, 1899.

Macaulay, Thomas B., *Prose and Poetry*, G. M. Young, ed., London, 1952.

Maclagan, Michael, *"Clemency" Canning*, London, 1962.

Maine, H. S., *Popular Government*, London, 1885.

Maine, H. S., *Village Communities in the East and West*, New York, 1876.

Majumdar, J. K., *Indian Speeches and Documents on British Rule 1821-1918*, Calcutta, 1937.

Majumdar, R. C., *Glimpses of Bengal in the Nineteenth Century*, Calcutta, 1960.

Majumdar, R. C., *The Sepoy Mutiny and the Revolt of 1857*, Calcutta, 1957.

Malleson, G. B., *History of the Indian Mutiny*, 3 v., London, 1896.

Malleson, G. B., *The Mutiny of the Bengal Army* [The Red Pamphlet], London, 1857.

Martineau, John, *The Life and Correspondence of Sir Bartle Frere*, 2 v., London, 1895.

Marx, Karl, and F. Engels, *The First Indian War of Independence 1857-1859*, Moscow, n.d.

Mayhew, Arthur, *Christianity and the Government of India*, London, 1929.

Mehta, Asoka, *1857 The Great Rebellion*, Bombay, 1946.

Metcalfe, C. T., *Two Native Narratives of the Mutiny at Delhi*, London, 1898.

Mill, James, *The History of British India*, 6 v., London, 2nd edn., 1820.

Mill, John Stuart, *Autobiography*, The World's Classics, London, 1955.

Mill, John Stuart, *Dissertations and Discussions*, 3 v., Boston, 1864.

Mill, John Stuart, *Letters of J. S. Mill*, H. S. R. Elliot, ed., London, 1910.

Mill, John Stuart, *Utilitarianism, Liberty, and Representative Government*, Everymans Library, London, 1957.

Misra, B. B., *The Central Administration of the East India Company 1773-1834*, Manchester, 1959.

Misra, B. R., *Land Revenue Policy in the United Provinces Under British Rule*, Benares, 1942.

Moneypenny, W. F. and G. E. Buckle, *Life of Benjamin Disraeli*, 6 v., New York, 1910-20.

Muir, Sir William, *Records of the Intelligence Department of the Government of the North-West Provinces of India during the Mutiny of 1857*, William Coldstream, ed., Edinburgh, 1902.

Neale, Walter C., *Economic Change in Rural India: Land Tenure and Reform in Uttar Pradesh, 1800-1955*, New Haven, 1962.

Nehru, Jawaharlal, *The Discovery of India*, Meridian Books, London, 4th edn., 1956.

Nott, J. C. and G. R. Glidden, *Indigenous Races of the Earth*, Philadelphia, 1857.

Nott, J. C. and G. R. Glidden, *Types of Mankind: or Ethnological Researches*, Philadelphia, 7th edn., 1855.

Nurullah, Syed and J. P. Naik, *A History of Education in India (During the British Period)*, Bombay, 2nd edn., 1951.

O'Malley, L. S. S., *The Indian Civil Service 1601-1930*, London, 1931.

Pascoe, C. F., *Two Hundred Years of the S.P.G.: an Historical Account of the Society for the Propagation of the Gospel in Foreign Parts*, London, 1901.

*Proceedings of the Meetings of the British Indian Association of Oudh 1861-1865*, Calcutta, 1865.

Raikes, Charles, *Notes on the North-Western Provinces of India*, London, 1852.

Raikes, Charles, *Notes on the Revolt in the North-Western Provinces of India*, London, 1858.

Raleigh, Sir Thomas, ed., *Lord Curzon in India*, London, 1906.

Ray, S. C., *Agricultural Indebtedness in India and Its Remedies*, Calcutta, 1915.

Richter, Julius, *A History of Missions in India*, S. H. Moore, tr., New York, 1908.

Ripon, Lord, *The Native States of India*, Leeds, 1886.

Rizvi, S. A. A. and M. L. Bhargava, eds., *Freedom Struggle in Uttar Pradesh*, 5 v., Lucknow, 1957-58.

Robertson, H. Dundas, *District Duties During the Revolt in the North-West Provinces of India in 1857*, London, 1859.

Ross, Charles, ed., *Correspondence of Charles, First Marquis Cornwallis*, 3 v., London, 1859.

Russell, W. H., *My Indian Mutiny Diary*, London, 1957.

Savarkar, V. D., *The Indian War of Independence*, London, 1909.

Sen, Surendra Nath, *Eighteen Fifty-Seven*, Delhi, 1957.

Sen-Gupta, Nares Chandra, ed., *Selections from the Writings of Hurrish Chunder Mookerjii*, Calcutta, 1910.

Sherring, M. A., *The History of Protestant Missions in India, From Their Commencement in 1706 to 1871*, London, 1875.

Sherring, M. A., *The Indian Church During the Great Rebellion*, London, 1859.

Sleeman, Sir W. H., *A Journey Through the Kingdom of Oude in 1849-1850*, 2 v., London, 1858.

Smith, George, *Life of John Wilson*, London, 1878.

Smith, R. Bosworth, *Life of Lord Lawrence*, 2 v., London, 7th edn., 1901.

Spear, Percival, *Twilight of the Mughuls*, Cambridge, 1951.

Stephen, James Fitzjames, *Liberty, Equality, Fraternity*, New York, 1873.

Stock, Eugene, *History of the Church Missionary Society*, 4 v., London, 1899-1916.

Stokes, Eric, *The English Utilitarians and India*, Oxford, 1959.

Strachey, Sir John, *India*, London, 1888.

Temple, Sir Richard, *James Thomason*, Oxford, 1893.

Temple, Sir Richard, *Men and Events of My Time in India*, London, 1882.

Thorburn, S. S., *Musalmans and Money-Lenders in the Punjab*, Edinburgh, 1886.

Thornhill, Mark, *The Personal Adventures and Experiences of A Magistrate During the Rise, Progress, and Suppression of the Indian Mutiny*, London, 1884.

Trevaskis, H., *Land of the Five Rivers*, Oxford, 1928.

Trevelyan, Charles E., *On the Education of the People of India*, London, 1838.

Trevelyan, George Otto, *The Competition Wallah*, London, 1864.

Trevelyan, George Otto, *The Life and Letters of Lord Macaulay*, 2 v., London, 1876.

Victoria, Queen, *The Letters of Queen Victoria*, Arthur C. Benson, ed., New York, 1907.

Wedderburn, William, *Allan Octavian Hume, C. B., "Father of the Indian National Congress" 1829 to 1912*, London, 1913.

Wingfield, Charles, *Observations on Land Tenures and Tenant Right in India*, London, 1869.

Wolf, Lucien, *Life of the First Marquess of Ripon*, London, 1921.

# BIOGRAPHICAL NOTES

BENTINCK, Lord William Cavendish (1774-1839). Governor of Madras 1803-07, recalled as result of the Mutiny at Vellore. British Governor of Sicily during Napoleonic Wars. Governor-General of India 1828-35.

CAMPBELL, Sir George (1824-92). Entered East India Company's service 1842. Served in Budaon and Moradabad 1843-46, and in Punjab 1846-50. Collector of Azamgarh 1854. Commissioner of Cis-Sutlej States 1855-57. Judicial Commissioner of Oudh 1858-62. Judge of Bengal High Court 1862-67. Chief Commissioner of the Central Provinces 1867-68. In England 1869-71, where he worked on behalf of Irish land reform and published *The Irish Land* (1869). Lieutenant-Governor of Bengal 1871-74. Member of Council of India, London, 1874-75. K.C.S.I. 1873.

CANNING, Charles John; Earl Canning (1812-62). Son of George Canning. Peelite. Under Secretary of State for Foreign Affairs 1841-46. Postmaster General 1853-55. Governor-General of India 1856-62.

DALHOUSIE, Marquis of (1812-60). Privy Councillor 1843-45. President of the Board of Trade 1845-47. Governor-General of India 1848-56.

ELLENBOROUGH, Earl of (1790-1871). Lord Privy Seal 1828. President of the Board of Control 1828-30, 1834-35, 1841, 1858. Governor-General of India 1842-44. First Lord of the Admiralty 1846.

ELPHINSTONE, Mountstuart (1779-1859). Entered Company's service 1795. Resident at Nagpur 1804-08. Ambassador to Shah Shuja at Kabul 1808. Resident at Poona 1810-16. Governor of Bombay 1819-27. Author of *The History of India*, 1841, *The Rise of British Power in the East*, 1887, edited by E. Colebrooke.

FRERE, Sir Henry Bartle Edward (1815-84). Entered Company's service 1834. Private Secretary to Governor of Bombay 1842-45. Resident at Satara 1847-49. Commissioner of Satara 1849-50. Chief Commissioner of Sind 1850-59. Member of the Governor-General's Council 1859-62. Governor of Bombay 1862-67. Member of Council of India, London, 1867-77. Governor of the Cape and High Commissioner in South Africa 1877-80. K.C.B. 1859.

LAWRENCE, Sir Henry (1806-57). Entered Bengal Army 1823. Revenue Surveyor, North-Western Provinces 1833-35. Resident at Court of Nepal 1843-46. Resident at Lahore 1847. President of Punjab Board 1849-53. Governor-General's Agent in Rajputana 1853-57. Chief Commissioner of Oudh 1857. Killed in Mutiny 4 July 1857. K.C.B. 1848.

LAWRENCE, Sir John (1811-79). Served at Delhi, Paniput, Gurgaon, and Etawah 1830-40. Magistrate and Collector of Delhi 1843-46. Commissioner of Trans-Sutlej States 1846-49. Member of Punjab Board 1849-53. Chief Commissioner of the Punjab 1853-58. Lieutenant-Governor of Punjab 1859. Member of Council of India, London, 1859-62. Governor-General of India 1864-69. Created Baron Lawrence of the Punjab 1869. K.C.B. 1856.

MACAULAY, Thomas Babington (1800-59). Secretary of Board of Control 1832-34. Member of Governor-General's Council 1834-38. President of the Commission for Composing a Criminal Code for India, 1835. Secretary of War 1839-41. Created Baron Macaulay 1857.

MAINE, Sir Henry (1822-88). Author of *Ancient Law* 1861. Legal Member of the Governor-General's Council 1862-69. Member of India Council, London, 1871.

MACLEOD, Sir Donald Friell (1810-72). Entered Company's service 1828. Collector and Magistrate of Benares 1843-49. Commissioner of Trans-Sutlej States 1849-54. Financial Commissioner of Punjab 1854. President of the Famine Relief Commission 1861. Lieutenant-Governor of Punjab 1865-70. K.C.S.I. 1866.

MAN SINGH, Maharaja, Sir Bahadur (1820-70). On the annexation of Oudh he was deprived of his estates and jailed as a revenue defaulter. When the Mutiny broke out he was released from prison in order to aid the British. After the Mutiny he regained his old estates and also those of the Raja of Gonda. K.C.S.I. 1869.

METCALFE, Charles Theophilus; Baron Metcalfe (1785-1846). Entered Company's service 1801. Resident at Delhi 1811-19. Private Secretary to the Governor-General 1819-20. Resident at Hyderabad 1820-25. Resident at Delhi 1825-27. Member of Governor-General's Council 1827-34. Governor of Agra 1834-35. Provisional Governor-General of India 1835-36. Lieutenant-Governor of the North-Western Provinces 1836-38. Governor of Jamaica 1839-42. Governor-General of Canada 1843-45. Created Baron Metcalfe 1845.

MILL, James (1773-1836). Author of *History of India*, 1818. Assistant to the Examiner of India Correspondence 1819-30. Examiner of India Correspondence 1830-36.

MILL, John Stuart (1806-73). Assistant to the Examiner of Correspondence in the Political Department of India House 1823-56. Examiner of India Correspondence 1856-58. Retired on dissolution of East India Company 1858.

MONTGOMERY, Sir Robert (1809-87). Entered Company's service 1828. Magistrate and Collector of Allahabad 1839-49. Commissioner of Lahore 1849-51. Member of the Punjab Board of Administration 1851-53. Judicial Commissioner of Punjab 1853. Chief Commissioner of Oudh 1858-59. Lieutenant-Governor of Punjab 1859-65. Member of Council of India, London, 1868-87. K.C.B. 1859. G.C.S.I. 1866.

MUIR, Sir William (1819-1905). Entered Company's service 1837. Secretary to the Government of the N.W.P. 1852-55. Member of the N.W.P. Board of Revenue 1856-57 and 1859-64. Head of Intelligence Department, Agra, 1857. Secretary to Lord Canning's Government in the N.W.P. 1858. Member of Legislative Council 1864. Foreign Secretary to the Government of India 1865-68. Member of the Governor-General's Council 1868. Lieutenant-Governor of the North-Western Provinces 1868-74. Finance Member of the Governor-General's Council 1874-76. Member of the Council of India, London, 1876-85. K.C.S.I. 1867.

MUNRO, Sir Thomas (1761-1827). Commissioned Indian Army 1780. Administrative charge of Canara 1792-99. Principal Collector of the Hyderabad Ceded Districts 1800-07. On furlough in England 1807-14. Governor of Madras 1820-27.

OUTRAM, Sir James (1803-63). Commissioned Indian Army 1819. Political Agent in Lower Sind 1839-41, and in Upper Sind 1841-43. Resident at Satara 1845-47. Resident at Baroda 1847. Resident at Lucknow 1854-56. Chief Commissioner of Oudh 1856, 1857-58. Military Member of the Governor-General's Council 1858-60. Author of *Conquest of Scinde*, 1846. K.C.B. 1856. G.C.B. 1857.

RIPON, Marquis of (1827-1909). Secretary of State for War 1863-66. Secretary of State for India 1866. Lord President of the Council 1868-73. Governor-General of India 1880-84. Supported Gladstone's Home Rule policy in Ireland 1885-86. Secretary of State for the Colonies 1892-94. Lord Privy Seal 1906-08. Known as Viscount Goderich until 1859, Earl de Gray and Ripon 1859-71, and the Marquis of Ripon from 1871.

STEPHEN, James Fitzjames (1829-94). Legal Member of the Governor-General's Council 1869-72. Judge of High Court, London, 1879-91. Author of *Liberty, Equality, Fraternity*, 1873, *History of the Criminal Law of England*, 1883, and *Nuncomar and Impey*, 1885.

STRACHEY, Sir John (1823-1907). Entered Company's service 1842. Held various administrative posts in the North-Western Provinces. Chief Commissioner of Oudh 1866-68. Member of Governor-General's Council 1868-72. Acting Governor-General 1872. Lieutenant-Governor of the North-Western Provinces 1874-76. Finance Member of Governor-General's Council 1876-80. Member of Council of India, London, 1885-95. Close friend of James Fitzjames Stephen. Author of *Hastings and the Rohilla War*, 1892, and *India its Administration and Progress*, 1888. K.C.S.I. 1873. G.C.S.I. 1878.

TEMPLE, Sir Richard (1826-1902). Entered Company's service 1847. Secretary to the Chief Commissioner of the Punjab 1854. Commissioner of Lahore 1859. Assistant to the Finance Ministers James Wilson and Samuel Laing 1860-62. Chief Commissioner of the Central Provinces 1862-66. Resident at Hyderabad 1867. Foreign Secretary to the Government of India 1868. Finance Member of the Governor-General's Council 1868-74.

Lieutenant-Governor of Bengal 1874-77. Governor of Bombay 1877-80. K.C.S.I. 1867. G.C.S.I. 1878.

TREVELYAN, Sir Charles Edward (1807-86). Assistant Commissioner at Delhi 1826-31. Secretary to Government at Calcutta 1831-37. Married Macaulay's sister 1834. Assistant Secretary to the Treasury, London, 1840-59. Governor of Madras 1859-60, recalled for publicly opposing the financial policy of Calcutta. Finance Member of Governor-General's Council 1862-65. K.C.B. 1848.

WINGFIELD, Sir Charles John (1820-92). Entered Company's service 1839. Commissioner of Bahraich Division in Oudh 1856-57. Chief Commissioner of Oudh 1859-66. K.C.S.I. 1866.

WOOD, Sir Charles; Viscount Halifax (1800-85). Chancellor of the Exchequer 1846-52. President of Board of Control 1853-55. First Lord of the Admiralty 1855-58. Secretary of State for India 1859-66. Lord Privy Seal 1870-74.

# TERMS OF OFFICE OF INDIAN ADMINISTRATORS,
## 1850-1870

*Governor-General of India* (Viceroy)

| | | |
|---|---|---|
| Marquess of Dalhousie | 12 January 1848 | |
| Earl Canning | 29 February 1856 | |
| Earl of Elgin | 12 March 1862 | (died 20 November 1863) |
| Sir John Lawrence | 12 January 1864 | |
| Earl of Mayo | 12 January 1869 | (died 8 February 1872) |

*President of the Board of Control; from September 1858 Secretary of State for India*

| | | |
|---|---|---|
| Sir Charles Wood | January 1853 | (Aberdeen Government) |
| Robert Vernon Smith | February 1855 | (Palmerston Government) |
| Earl of Ellenborough | February 1858 | (Derby Government) |
| Lord Stanley | May 1858 | (Derby Government) |
| Sir Charles Wood | June 1859 | (Palmerston Government) |
| Earl de Grey and Ripon | February 1866 | (Russell Government) |
| Viscount Cranborne | June 1866 | (Derby Government) |
| Sir Stafford Northcote | March 1867 | (Derby Government) |
| Duke of Argyll | December 1868 | (Gladstone Government) |

*Lieutenant-Governor of the North-Western Provinces*

| | | |
|---|---|---|
| J. R. Colvin | November 1853 | (died September 1857) |
| Earl Canning (the Governor-General in the N.W.P.) | January 1858 | (temporary charge) |

| G. F. Edmonstone | January 1859 |
| E. Drummond | March 1863 |
| Sir William Muir | March 1868 |

*Chief Commissioner of the Punjab;* from January 1859 *Lieutenant-Governor*

| Sir John Lawrence | January 1853 | |
| Sir Robert Montgomery | February 1859 | |
| D. F. Macleod | January 1865 | |
| Maj. Gen. Sir H. M. Durand | June 1870 | (died 1 January 1871) |

*Chief Commissioner of Oudh*

| Sir James Outram | February 1856 | |
| Coverly Jackson | May 1856 | (officiating) |
| Sir Henry Lawrence | March 1857 | (died 4 July 1857) |
| Sir James Outram | September 1857 | |
| Robert Montgomery | April 1858 | |
| Charles Wingfield | February 1859 | |
| George U. Yule | April 1861 | (officiating) |
| Charles Wingfield | December 1862 | |
| John Strachey | March 1866 | |
| R. H. Davies | May 1868 | |

# INDEX